D0797034

The future of the United Nations system

International Peace Research Association

This volume is a project of Research Commissions of the International Peace Research Association (IPRA). The inaugural conference of IPRA was held in July 1965 in Groningen, the Netherlands, the site of its first headquarters. The headquarters has subsequently been located in Norway, Finland, Japan, Brazil, the United Kingdom, Germany, Denmark, and the United States.

The goals of IPRA are to advance interdisciplinary research into the conditions of peace and the causes of war and other forms of violence. To this end IPRA shall encourage worldwide cooperation designed to assist the advancement of peace research and, in particular:

(1) to promote national and international studies and teaching related to the pursuit of world peace;
(2) to facilitate contacts and cooperation between scholars and educators throughout the world;
(3) to encourage the worldwide dissemination of results of peace research.

Since 1994 IPRA has had a President, as well as a Secretary General:

President: Kevin P. Clements, Institute for Conflict Analysis and Resolution, George Mason University, Fairfax, Virginia, 22030-4444. E-mail: kclements@gmu.edu

Secretary General: Bjørn Møller, Copenhagen Peace Research Institute (COPRI), Fredericagade 18, DK-1310 Copenhagen K, Denmark. E-mail: bmoeller@copri.dk

The future of the United Nations system: Potential for the twenty-first century

Edited by Chadwick F. Alger

United Nations
University Press

TOKYO · NEW YORK · PARIS

United Nations University Press
The United Nations University, 53-70, Jingumae 5-chome, Shibuya-ku, Tokyo 150, Japan
Tel: (03) 3499-2811   Fax: (03) 3406-7345
E-mail: mbox@hq.unu.edu

UNU Office in North America
2 United Nations Plaza, Room DC2-1462-70, New York, NY 10017
Tel: (212) 963-6387   Fax: (212) 371-9454   Telex: 422311 UN UI

United Nations University Press is the publishing division of the United Nations University.

Cover design by Kerkhoven Associates

Printed in the United States of America

UNUP-973
ISBN 92-808-0973-3

Library of Congress Cataloging-in-Publication Data

The future of the United Nations system : potential for the twenty-first century / edited by Chadwick F. Alger.
    p.   cm.
  Includes bibliographical references and index.
  ISBN 9280809733 (pbk.)
  1. United Nations.   2. International relations.   3. Peace.
I. Alger, Chadwick F., 1924–
  JZ4984.5 .F88 1998
  341.23′1—ddc21
                                                    98-8997
                                                      CIP

Contents

Preface

Editing a volume linking peace research and the United Nations system has been a special pleasure because it has involved cooperation between two organizations that have had special significance for me: the International Peace Research Association (IPRA) and the United Nations University Press. I have been a member of IPRA since June 1966, and have had my research and teaching agenda continually enriched by the diversity of perspectives encountered in IPRA meetings and publications. Through participation in IPRA I have achieved a growing understanding of a variety of definitions of peace, each emerging out of the different life circumstances of its advocate. I have also learned that the quest for peace requires thoughtful dialogue among those advocating different definitions. Then, between 1977 and 1983, I received my introduction to the United Nations University as a member of the Goals, Processes and Indicators of Development Project. Organized by Johan Galtung, it involved scholars from all continents representing a great diversity of scholarly traditions. In seminars in Bucharest, Dakar, Dubrovnik, Bariloche, Colombo, Tokyo, Geneva, Rome, and other places, I learned that scholarship that will serve the needs of global governance requires contributions from a diversity of perspectives.

The intellectual life of the International Peace Research Association is focused on a number of peace themes that are organized into Commissions. Work on this volume began more than five years ago when all Commissions were asked to propose chapters for a volume that would indicate the contributions that peace research could make in illuminating the future potential of the UN system in the quest for peace. This effort had the involved support of Paul Smoker, then the Secretary General of IPRA. The first project meeting was held at the Fourteenth General Conference of IPRA at Ritsumeikan University in Kyoto in July 1992. At this time we were confident that our volume would be IPRA's contribution to the celebration of the 50th anniversary of the founding of the United Nations in 1995. Clearly we underestimated the time required for producing a volume that would have 12 chapters, each on a specific aspect of activity in the United Nations system, whose writing would involve 22 scholars with roots in 12 countries in Africa, Asia, Europe, and North America.

When this project was launched, Paul Smoker and I shared the goal of placing the UN system more prominently on the agendas of the IPRA Commissions. It is encouraging that contributors to this volume have been most explicitly identified with the work of nine Commissions: Communications, Ecological Security, Global Political Economy, Internal Conflicts, International Human Rights, Peace Education, Refugees, Security and Disarmament, and Women and Peace. I know that all contributors share my hope that these Commissions will sustain their interest in the future of the UN system, and that other Commissions will join the effort.

I am most grateful to all contributors for the cooperative spirit that they have demonstrated throughout the life of this project, by responding to requests for further development of certain topics, for accepting necessary limitations on length, and for bringing their chapters up to date in time for publication. All readers would wish to join the contributors in thanking Ms. Liz Paton, the United Nations University Press copy-editor, for creatively editing a diversity of writing, organizing, and citation styles into a consistent volume. Also appreciated are the effective support of this project by Dr. Manfred F. Boemeke, Head of Publications, and Ms. Yoko Kojima, Senior Publications Coordinator, of the United Nations University Press. Finally, I am grateful to the Mershon Center of The Ohio State University for the support that it has provided for my work on this volume.

Chadwick F. Alger
November 1997

The six other references employ almost identical language and are to be found in the context of the Purposes and Principles of the United Nations (Article 1), the functions and powers of the General Assembly (Article 13), enumeration of the principles for International Economic and Social Cooperation (Article 55), the functions and powers of the Economic and Social Council (Article 62), the provision that ECOSOC shall set up a commission for the promotion of human rights (Article 68), and a statement of objectives of the International Trusteeship System (Article 76).

In retrospect, we might say that the League of Nations, the first general-purpose international governmental organization with universal aspirations, was a laboratory in which "experimenters" gained feedback about the interdependence of "negative peace" and "positive peace." Following World War II, this laboratory was rebuilt and incorporated this experience. The new lab was given a new name, and was built in a different city, in a different continent. Here the universality dreams of League founders were eventually fulfilled. And here "experiments" with the six "peace tools" now available rather quickly led to the development of a number of additional tools (Alger 1996).

Much of the conflict in the United Nations today can be viewed as conflict over the definition of self-determination, of standards for economic and social cooperation, and of human rights. To a considerable degree, although not entirely, the conflict is over differences in definition of these values between the "North" and the "South." Ironically, the existence of this conflict is a result of the successful fulfilment of Chapter XI. The growth in UN membership to 184 has largely come from the creation of new states in Africa, Asia, and the Caribbean.

There is no doubt that the breakup of overseas empires has contributed to the emergence of a new generation of self-determination problems – nations and ethnic groups that are dissatisfied units within territorial states. Readers will find that conflicts in this new generation of self-determination struggles permeate virtually every chapter of this volume. Ironically, just as the United Nations seemed to have achieved universality, new aspirants began the struggle for independence. Each success has led inevitably to a new claim for UN membership.

At the same time, growth in membership has dramatically complicated efforts to fulfil "functional" cooperation on economic and social issues in a manner not foreseen by the Charter. Such cooperation is very difficult between the rich and the poor. This spurred the move toward an emphasis on the "development" of third world countries, essentially the invention of an additional peace "tool." This led to great extension of the field activities of many UN agencies and to the formation of new agencies such as the UN Development Programme (UNDP) and the UN Industrial Development Organization (UNIDO). But the increasing gap between the rich and the poor of the world spurred the insight that much of the gap was caused by the nature of the international economic structure, hence the creation of the UN Conference on Trade and Development (UNCTAD) and the demand for a New International Economic Order. Defining the nature of this order is the basis for much conflict throughout the UN system today.

The General Assembly moved rapidly to build on Charter provisions for human rights by drafting and proclaiming the UN Universal Declaration on Human Rights in 1948. Its 30 articles offer an interesting reflection of the values of its primary drafters, in that civil and political rights are listed first, followed by economic, social, and cultural rights. This priority foretold a conflict over human rights priorities when the former colonies were permitted to participate directly in human rights debates and activity. Although struggles over defining values for human relations have many facets, certainly differences over the priorities to be given to these two categories of rights have been the most prominent.

These three extensions of the functions of global organizations since 1920 offer a useful perspective on what we have learned about overcoming peacelessness in this century. The breakup of overseas empires underlines the fact that we have had some dramatic successes. At the same time, the new generation of self-determination questions and the struggles over the meaning of human rights and the appropriate standards for economic and social cooperation underline the fact that each victory seems to bring with it a new generation of problems. Or would it be more appropriate to say that each success has been accompanied by higher levels of aspiration?

Of course, change in the inter-state system through decolonization has not been the only fundamental transformation that has challenged the UN system. Also propelling change has been the development, and widespread adoption, of new technologies for transportation, communication, production, and the extraction and utilization of resources. In responding, the United Nations has established the UN Environment Programme (UNEP) and environmental programmes in many agencies. Again, the meaning of "development" is being redefined as many call for "sustainable development." At the same time, the Northern-centred communications giants, facilitated by satellites and computers, are penetrating ever more deeply into cultures everywhere. This has led to a strenuous challenge to the notion that "free flow of communication" necessarily contributes to peace. This challenge has been dramatized by the demand for a New World Information and Communications Order, with UNESCO as the main locus of strife, but the dispute naturally challenges traditional modes of operation in the International Telecommunication Union (ITU). Responding to the penetration of new technologies into the waters, continental shelves, and deep seabed of the oceans, the United Nations is now in the process of establishing an International Sea-Bed Authority. As it establishes systems for governance of two-thirds of the surface of the earth, it will inevitably become involved in issues covered in every chapter of this volume.

Meanwhile, procedures for directly attaining "negative peace" have not remained stagnant. In an effort to cope with Covenant shortcomings, procedures for implementing collective security in the Charter (Chapter VII) were made much more specific by requiring that members "as soon as possible" make agreements for making forces available, that a Military Staff Committee lay plans for their "combined action," and that the Military Staff Committee be responsible for their "strategic direction." Of course, these procedures have never been implemented. Instead, the Security Council has twice authorized coalitions led by the United States to repel aggression (Korea and the Persian Gulf). And it has invented peace-keeping forces, acting only in self-defence, to patrol cease-fire lines with the permission of involved states. More recently, challenged by self-determination struggles within states and gross violations of human rights, an effort has been made to invent a new kind of force that can *enforce* peace with arms. But the results of an effort to devise some kind of a force that falls between peace-keeping and collective security, without being swept onto the slippery slope on the way to large-scale violence, have not yet been very promising.

The United Nations has been responsive to transformations in its environment in another way: there has been an escalating involvement of a variety of citizens' groups (non-governmental organizations, or NGOs, in UN terminology) in UN activities. The 1,200 representatives of NGOs present at the San Francisco conference in April 1945 were instrumental in placing Article 71 in the Charter, "inviting ECOSOC to make suitable arrangements for consultation with non-governmental organizations concerned with matters within its competence." Building on this innovation, there are now over 90 offices throughout the UN system dealing with relations with NGOs (Alger 1994: 304–311). In addition, NGOs have well-established procedures for participation in UN global conferences. And agencies such as the World Bank and UNDP have made special efforts to involve grass-roots NGOs in UN-supported development projects. For these reasons readers will encounter the activities of NGOs throughout this volume. These include unarmed peace-keeping forces.

This brief overview of UN experience in coping with peace problems reveals that practice is offering deeper understanding of the meaning of peace.[3] Or we could say that it reveals that peace comprises an interconnected array of facets. In response, the number of approaches to peace has grown. This volume focuses on UN experience with, and the future potential of, 12 approaches to peace. To facilitate initial reader comprehension, the 12 chapters have been divided into four groups. This simple portrayal tends to begin with "negative peace" approaches (the role for weapons in the quest for peace; enforcement and humanitarian intervention; peace-keeping; UN peace-keeping and NGO peace-building; internal conflict resolution), then moves on to "positive peace" approaches (human rights; economic equity; women's rights; refugees). The third group extends the positive peace approaches into the global commons (ecological security; communications), and the fourth group concerns education about all of the approaches.

To a considerable degree, this order of presentation also replicates the historical pattern of invention of approaches to peace. This "logic of discovery" offers insight into the relationship between different stategies. On the other hand, it could be said that this order reverses the order that is most useful for practitioners aspiring to build peace. In practice, it would seem to be most prudent to begin with education strategies (both classroom and participatory), to build the foundations for peace with "positive peace" strategies, and thereby greatly to diminish the need for "negative peace" strategies. Thus, the builder of long-term peace might find it necessary to reverse the order.

Of course, practical responses to the challenges presented by peacelessness in the present world require a more mixed strategy. Practitioners are obligated to employ "negative peace" strategies in order to diminish the shooting already occurring. At the same time, they should employ "positive peace" strategies with the aim of diminishing the need for "negative peace" strategies over the long run. This requires creative mixes of *all* approaches at the same time. In support of this approach, it would be most useful if we presented our 12 approaches as spokes in a wheel, with peace as the hub of the wheel. The practitioner who simultaneously attempts to stop the shooting and build long-term peace must select from a different array of spokes in confronting challenges to peace in different geographic areas and in different time-periods.

It was not easy to decide in what order our 12 topics should be presented to the reader, because different readers have different backgrounds and interests. In the light of the likelihood that most readers have the least knowledge about the items in groups 2–4, largely because the media are imprisoned in present responses to shooting, we were inclined to take the reverse order. On the other hand, there is some advantage in starting with the "known world" of most readers (i.e. group 1) and then taking up other topics.

But, as we do this, we must make it very clear to readers that we do not start with "negative peace" strategies because we believe them to be more important. On the contrary, we believe that creative long-term peace-building based on groups 2 and 3, with a strong foundation of peace education (group 4), could eventually make strategies focused on stopping the shooting unnecessary! Indeed, the reader will soon find that the future recommendations of all authors in part I include elements from parts II, III, and IV. One example: eliminating weapons through the conversion of plants involved in arms production (chap. 1) to the production of consumer goods links arms control with economic peace-building (chap. 7). Another example: implementation of human rights standards (chap. 6) now requires widespread knowledge about these standards such that people everywhere become participants in their implementation, thus linking human rights and education (chap. 12).

Notes

1. The reader will find Alger, Lyons, and Trent (1995), which focuses on the policies of eight member states of the United Nations (Algeria, Canada, France, Japan, the Netherlands, Nigeria, the United Kingdom, and the United States), to be a useful companion to this volume.
2. A very useful brief overview of the development of peace research can be found in Galtung (1988).
3. For a fuller account see Alger (1995).

References

Alger, Chadwick F. 1994. "Citizens and the UN System in a Changing World." In Yoshikazu Sakomoto, ed., *Global Transformation: Challenges to the State System*. Tokyo: United Nations University Press, pp. 301–329.

———— 1995. "The United Nations in Historical Perspective." In Alger et al., eds., *The United Nations System: The Policies of Member States*. Tokyo: United Nations University Press, pp. 3–40.

———— 1996. "The Emerging Tool Chest for Peacebuilders." *International Journal of Peace Studies*, vol. 1, no. 2, pp. 21–45.

Alger, Chadwick F., Gene M. Lyons, and John E. Trent, eds. 1995. *The United Nations System: The Policies of Member States*. Tokyo: United Nations University Press.

Boulding, Elise. 1988. *Building a Global Civic Culture: Education for an Interdependent World*. New York: Teachers College, Columbia University.

Galtung, Johan. 1988. "Twenty-five Years of Peace Research: Ten Challenges." In Johan Galtung, *Essays in Peace Research*, vol. 6. Copenhagen: Christian Ejlers, pp. 213–236.

UNITED NATIONS system

PRINCIPAL ORGANS OF THE UNITED NATIONS

INTERNATIONAL COURT OF JUSTICE | GENERAL ASSEMBLY | ECONOMIC AND SOCIAL COUNCIL | SECURITY COUNCIL | TRUSTEESHIP COUNCIL | SECRETARIAT

- Military Staff Committee
- Standing committees and ad hoc bodies
- International Tribunal for the former Yugoslavia
- International Criminal Tribunal for Rwanda

- Main and other sessional committees
- Standing committees and ad hoc bodies
- Other subsidiary organs and related bodies

▷ **UNRWA**
United Nations Relief and Works Agency for Palestine Refugees in the Near East

■ **IAEA**
International Atomic Energy Agency

▷ **INSTRAW**
International Research and Training Institute for the Advancement of Women

▷ **UNCHS**
United Nations Centre for Human Settlements (Habitat)

▷ **UNCTAD**
United Nations Conference on Trade and Development

▷ **UNDCP**
United Nations International Drug Control Programme

▷ **UNDP**
United Nations Development Programme

▷ **UNEP**
United Nations Environment Programme

▷ **UNFPA**
United Nations Population Fund

▷ **UNHCR**
Office of the United Nations High Commissioner for Refugees

▷ **UNICEF**
United Nations Children's Fund

▷ **UNIFEM**
United Nations Development Fund for Women

▷ **UNITAR**
United Nations Institute for Training and Research

▷ **UNU**
United Nations University

▷ **WFP**
World Food Programme

▷ **ITC**
International Trade Centre UNCTAD/WTO

● **FUNCTIONAL COMMISSIONS**
Commission for Social Development
Commission on Crime Prevention and Criminal Justice
Commission on Human Rights
Commission on Narcotic Drugs
Commission on Science and Technology for Development
Commission on Sustainable Development
Commission on the Status of Women
Commission on Population and Development
Statistical Commission

● **REGIONAL COMMISSIONS**
Economic Commission for Africa (ECA)
Economic Commission for Europe (ECE)
Economic Commission for Latin America and the Caribbean (ECLAC)
Economic and Social Commission for Asia and the Pacific (ESCAP)
Economic and Social Commission for Western Asia (ESCWA)

● **SESSIONAL AND STANDING COMMITTEES**

● **EXPERT, AD HOC AND RELATED BODIES**

■ **ILO**
International Labour Organization

■ **FAO**
Food and Agriculture Organization of the United Nations

■ **UNESCO**
United Nations Educational, Scientific and Cultural Organization

■ **WHO**
World Health Organization

WORLD BANK GROUP

■ **IBRD**
International Bank for Reconstruction and Development

■ **IDA**
International Development Association

■ **IFC**
International Finance Corporation

■ **MIGA**
Multilateral Investment Guarantee Agency

■ **IMF**
International Monetary Fund

■ **ICAO**
International Civil Aviation Organization

■ **UPU**
Universal Postal Union

■ **ITU**
International Telecommunication Union

■ **WMO**
World Meteorological Organization

■ **IMO**
International Maritime Organization

■ **WIPO**
World Intellectual Property Organization

■ **IFAD**
International Fund for Agricultural Development

■ **UNIDO**
United Nations Industrial Development Organization

* **WTO**
World Trade Organization

PEACE-KEEPING OPERATIONS

UNTSO
United Nations Truce Supervision Organization (HQ: Jerusalem)
June 1948 to date

UNMOGIP
United Nations Military Observer Group in India and Pakistan
January 1949 to date

UNFICYP
United Nations Peace-keeping Force in Cyprus
March 1964 to date

UNDOF
United Nations Disengagement Observer Force (Golan Heights)
June 1974 to date

UNIFIL
United Nations Interim Force in Lebanon
March 1978 to date

UNIKOM
United Nations Iraq-Kuwait Observation Mission
April 1991 to date

MINURSO
United Nations Mission for the Referendum in Western Sahara
April 1991 to date

UNOMIG
United Nations Observer Mission in Georgia
August 1993 to date

UNOMIL
United Nations Observer Mission in Liberia
September 1993 to date

UNMOT
United Nations Mission of Observers in Tajikistan
December 1994 to date

UNAVEM III
United Nations Angola Verification Mission III
February 1995 to date

UNPREDEP
United Nations Preventive Deployment Force (The former Yugoslav Republic of Macedonia)
March 1995 to date

UNMIBH
United Nations Mission in Bosnia and Herzegovina
December 1995 to date

UNTAES
United Nations Transitional Administration for Eastern Slavonia, Baranja and Western Sirmium
January 1996 to date

UNMOP
United Nations Mission of Observers in Prevlaka
January 1996 to date

UNSMIH
United Nations Support Mission in Haiti
July 1996 to date

▶ United Nations programmes and organs (representative list only)
■ Specialized agencies and other autonomous organizations within the system
● Other commissions, committees and ad hoc and related bodies

* Cooperative arrangements between the UN and WTO are under discussion.

Published by the United Nations Department of Public Information—DPI/1857—October 1996

UNITED NATIONS

The United Nations system (Source: United Nations Department of Public Information, DPI/1857, New York, October 1996)

Part I
Overcoming and preventing violence

1

Controlling weapons in the quest for peace: Non-offensive defence, arms control, disarmament, and conversion

Hans Günter Brauch, Czeslaw Mesjasz, and Björn Möller

1. Introduction

In the twentieth century we have witnessed the production of ever more destructive weapons that now can reach beyond battlefields and totally destroy human settlements. Efforts throughout the century to control the development and employment of these weapons have had very limited success. Nevertheless, this experience – failures as well as successes – offers valuable lessons for future planning. Some have strived for *disarmament* – often the elimination of all arms except for those needed for internal security. Others would take a more gradual approach, beginning by limiting the use and development of certain kinds of weapons – *arms control*. A specific form of arms control would permit only defensive arms – *non-offensive defence*. Another approach attempts to offer substitutes for the dependence of national economies on arms production – *conversion*. For some, these four approaches are seen not as alternative approaches but as tactics that can be combined in the formulation of comprehensive strategies for diminishing the availability and use of weapons of mass destruction.

In this chapter we will first briefly review how approaches to war prevention evolved from the League Covenant to the UN Charter, and then point out the new opportunities available to the members of the United Nations in the late 1990s. After discussing the expanded concept of security, we will assess achievements and failures in efforts to apply our four approaches, and assess the impact of peace movements on these efforts. We will conclude with proposals for research and policy in the "new environment" of the late 1990s.

The Order of Paris and the League of Nations Covenant

The system of the League of Nations was to pursue war prevention and the maintenance of peace and security: (a) by "a cooling off" period aiming at peaceful settlement of disputes (Arts. 12–15), and (b) if a breach of peace occurred (Art. 16), by its members implementing sanctions against the aggressor. According to Art. 1, Sec. 2 of the Covenant, membership of the League was dependent on the condition that "any self-governing State ... shall give effective guarantees of its sincere intention to observe its international obligations, and shall accept such regulations as may be prescribed by the League in regard to its military, naval and air forces and armaments." In the League's Charter, Art. 8 was specifically devoted to disarmament:

The members of the League recognize that the maintenance of peace requires the reduction of national armaments to the lowest point consistent with national safety and the enforcement by common action of international obligations.

The Council was to formulate such disarmament plans for the consideration of the respective governments. After their adoption, the agreed limits were not to be exceeded without the concurrence of the Council. Given the grave objections to the "manufacture by private enterprise of munitions and implements of war," the Covenant stated:

The Council shall advise how the evil effects attendant upon such manufacture can be prevented, due regard being had to the necessities of those Members of the League which are not able to manufacture the munitions and implements of war necessary for their safety. (FRUS 1947: 82–83)

Furthermore, the Members of the League promised to exchange "full and frank information as to the scale of their armaments, their military, naval and air programs and the condition of such of their industries as are adaptable to war-like purposes." In addition, Art. 9 called for the establishment of a permanent Commission "to advise the Council on the execution of the provisions of Articles 1 and 8 and on military, naval and air questions generally" (FRUS 1947: 83).

However, when the three new autocracies (Japan and Germany in 1933, Italy in 1937) left the League and challenged the new political order, its remaining key members (Britain, France, and, from 1934, the Stalinist Soviet Union) lacked the political will and the means to block their unilateral rearmament and to stop the aggression of these authoritarian revisionist powers. After only two decades, the second international order had collapsed. The Wilsonian or Kantian perspective was discredited both in practice and in theory. "Realist" critics denounced the adherents of Wilsonianism as idealists.

The security system of the United Nations Charter

The UN Charter, as approved on 26 June 1945, distinguished among three supplementary security systems:

(1) A universal security system, contained in Chapter VI on the pacific settlement of disputes (Arts. 33–38) and Chapter VII on "Action with respect to threats to the peace, breaches to the peace and acts of aggression" (Arts. 39–50). Later, through practice, peace-keeping was added.

(2) Regional arrangements or agencies for dealing with regional security issues, in Chapter VIII (Arts. 52–54).

(3) A provision referring to the "inherent right of individual or collective self-defense," contained in Art. 51 appended to Chapter VII.

Before the Dumbarton Oaks meeting in 1944, in American thinking arms regulation was considered as an integral part of the proposed system for maintaining peace and security. At this meeting the Soviets accepted the wording "armament regulation" as opposed to "disarmament," but at their insistence the Assembly was granted the right to consider "principles governing disarmament and the regulation of armaments" (Russell 1958: 476–477). Arms regulation (specifically demilitarization of the enemy) was thus downgraded from a primary goal to a tool for the "maintenance of international peace and security."

The UN Charter (in contrast to that of the League) did not specifically mention "disarmament," arms regulation, or arms reduction, either in its preamble or in its purposes (Art. 1) and principles (Art. 2). Rather it refers to this issue as an agenda item:

[the General Assembly may] consider the general principles of cooperation in the maintenance of international peace and security, including the principles governing disarmament and the regulation of armaments, and may make recommendations with regard to such principles to the members or to the Security Council or to both. (Art. 11, Sec. 1)

17

According to Art. 26, the Security Council shall be responsible "for formulating, with the assistance of the Military Staff Committee ... plans ... for the establishment of a system for the regulation of armaments" with the specific goal "to promote the establishment and maintenance of international peace and security with the least diversion for armaments of the world's human and economic resources."

As a consequence of the emerging fundamental systemic and power conflict of the two new superpowers, especially in its two Cold War phases (1946–1963 and 1980–1986), a new collective security system with teeth was blocked from the outset and the exception became the rule: security by collective self-defence guaranteed by rival military alliances. Even Roosevelt's subdued Wilsonianism once again succumbed to Hobbesian pessimism in the foreign and defence policy of the United States itself.

The second opportunity for the United Nations security system

With the end of the bipolar East–West conflict, the United Nations and its machinery have moved to the "center of international efforts to deal with unresolved problems of the past decades as well as an emerging array of present and future issues" (Boutros-Ghali 1992/1993: 89–102). In his report *Agenda for Peace* (Boutros-Ghali 1992a), the Secretary-General distinguished between preventive diplomacy, peace-making, peace-keeping, and peace-building to develop structures that will strengthen peace. Two of these concepts are of specific relevance for a reconceptualization of disarmament. On preventive diplomacy the Secretary-General recommended measures to build confidence: fact-finding missions, early warning activities, preventive deployment of forces, and demilitarized zones. With respect to post-conflict peace-building, he called for e.g. the removal of land mines, the repatriation of refugees, the reconstruction of water and electricity facilities, and support for the buildup of government facilities. As the global context changes, the three concepts of "defence, disarmament, and conversion" and the historical experience must be reconsidered. With the increasing importance of security organizations, both the analytical contributions of peace research and the activities of non-governmental organizations (NGOs) must be reassessed before conceptual conclusions and recommendations can be made.

2. Defence and security: The conceptual contribution of peace research

The expanded concept of security

The notion of an "expanded" concept of security originated in peace research (Boulding 1962; Galtung 1975; Krell 1981). Proposals were made that included economic, human rights, and environmental issues in the security concept, thus enlarging the referent object and the dimension of security. It was not only states that could be secure or insecure, but also individuals and societal groups, indeed the entire human race, or perhaps the planet Earth itself (Thomas 1992; Renner 1989; for an even more radical approach see Eckersley 1992). Indeed, in many cases the state itself constituted a major threat to the other referent objects of security, with gross violations of basic human rights (e.g. Buzan 1991: 34–56 passim). Whereas state security was a matter of sovereignty (territorially defined), for other referent objects (such as societal groups) "identity" was at stake (Waever et al. 1993). Security could also be endangered by environmental degradation, economic underdevelopment, and other non-military threats.

From concept to policy: Non-offensive defence

The idea of non-offensive defense (NOD), i.e. a defence posture enabling states to defend themselves yet not attack others, became prominent in the 1970s and 1980s. It originated in the peace research community (Afheldt 1976, 1983, 1992, 1993), even though early contributions may be found in strategic studies, such as those of Liddell Hart and von Bonin. In the 1980s, the concept was adopted by students of international relations, was discussed widely in peace research and peace movement circles, and entered party platforms, especially of the social democratic parties of Northern and Central Europe.

It was also carefully studied by Soviet civilian analysts and, more surprisingly, after 1987 and 1988 it was publicly endorsed by the Soviet leadership under Mikhail Gorbachev as one element of "new thinking." As a result, it was on the agenda for East–West negotiations, with the negotiations on conventional forces in Europe (CFE) as the main achievement (Möller 1991, 1992, 1994). In 1990, the NOD concept was also endorsed by the UN General Assembly in a resolution on defensive security. It stipulated that "security concepts and policies should be aimed at enhancing security and stability at progressively lower and balanced levels of armed forces and armaments," and that defence capabilities should reflect "true defensive requirements" (UN GA RE. 45/58 O, 4 December 1990).

Peace research has all along underlined that war prevention through conflict resolution is preferable to deterrence (Sandole and van der Merwe 1993; Kriesberg 1992; Fischer 1990), even the benign variety implied by collective security: stable peace is not obtainable by coercive means, but presupposes a resolution of outstanding issues of contention – ideally prophylactic conflict prevention, which may, in turn, call for non-military measures such as economic support (Boulding 1978). The same philosophy is clearly visible in the Secretary-General's *Agenda for Peace*, where he refers in detail to "preventive diplomacy" and "post-conflict peace-building" (see Roberts and Kingsbury 1993: 476, 488–489), two concepts on which a reconceptualization of disarmament may be based.

3. Disarmament and arms control

Two competing programmes: Disarmament vs. arms control

During the East–West conflict (1946–1989), any comprehensive disarmament strategy comprised at least four conceptual components: disarmament, arms control, crisis management, and confidence-building measures (CBMs). The terms "disarmament" and "arms control" have often been used interchangeably. Whereas the United Nations and the peace research community preferred "disarmament," the Western strategic studies community used "arms control." "Disarmament" or "regulation of armaments" has been used extensively since the Hague Conferences (1899 and 1907) and the end of World War I, whereas the arms control concept was developed in the United States in the late 1950s as a tool to contain "wars by accident, miscalculation and surprise attacks." For Bull (1961: ix), "[d]isarmament is the reduction or abolition of armaments. It may be unilateral or multilateral; general or local, comprehensive or partial, controlled or uncontrolled."

Disarmament has been discussed in relationship to the three related concepts of arms control, crisis management, and confidence- and security-building measures (CSBMs). Prior to 1989, disarmament measures were referred to as "necessary means toward establishing a global collective security system. However, to become effective they have to be supplemented by measures to achieve strategic stability (arms control) between the major military rivals and political stability (conflict resolution, crisis prevention, and crisis control) in those areas of the world where the Cold War has been fought with military means and caused its greatest death tolls" (Brauch 1990: 107).

Originally, arms control denoted rules for limiting arms competition with three major goals: enhancing stability, limiting damage, and reducing costs (Schelling and Halperin 1961; Bull 1961). Arms control included measures intended to "(a) freeze, limit, reduce or abolish certain categories of weapons; (b) prevent certain military activities; (c) regulate the deployment of armed forces; (d) proscribe transfers of some militarily important items; (e) reduce the risk of accidental war; (f) constrain or prohibit the use of certain weapons or methods of war; and (g) build up confidence among states through greater openness in military matters" (Goldblat 1994: 3).

During the East–West conflict, confidence- (and security-) building measures were a political tool both in bilateral US–Soviet relations and in the multilateral context of the Conference on Security and Cooperation in Europe (CSCE) to reduce the likelihood of a nuclear war by accident or misperception or of a conventional surprise attack in Europe. Since the end of the East–West conflict, CBMs have been considered as tools of preventive diplomacy for conflict avoidance and post-conflict peace-building.

Table 1.1 distinguishes these four pillars of a comprehensive disarmament strategy with respect to policy, systemic, and action *goals*, *objects* to be achieved, their regional *scope*, their *substance*, the prevailing *procedures*, and *achievements* during the major phases of the East–West conflict (1946–1989) and in the post–Cold War period.

No global disarmament agreement was reached during the first (1946–1962) and second (1980–1987) Cold War. Disarmament required a relaxation of tensions and contributed towards détente. With the end of the East–West conflict, major bilateral, regional, and global confidence-building, arms control, and disarmament agreements became possible (see below). Disarmament benefited from the global transformation but it was not its cause.

Achievements and failures of the League of Nations

Whereas the proposals by Tsar Alexander I for negotiated disarmament agreements were rejected at the Congress of Vienna (1815),

Table 1.1 **Overview of four related concepts of a broader disarmament strategy**

| | Concepts | | | |
	Disarmament (UN involvement)	Arms control (UN involvement)	Crisis management and preventive diplomacy	Confidence-building measures
Goals				
Policy goals	Peace and international collective security	Prevent war	Prevent escalation into conflict/war	Positive climate for détente, disarmament, peace-building
Systemic goals	Rule of international law	Enhance strategic stability	Code of conduct cooperation	Cooperation to prevent a surprise attack
Action goals	Limitation, regulation, reduction, elimination, destruction	Damage limitation if deterrence has failed Cost reduction	Improvement of communication (societal and political) Non-intervention regime	Openness, transparency, predictability
Objects	Armaments, military industry manpower, bases	Armaments, manpower, budgets, arms transfers	Prevent crises, spillover into war	Information, verification, communication, constraints
Regional scope	Global (UN), regional, subregional, bilateral, and trilateral	Global (UN), regional, subregional, bilateral, and trilateral	Bilateral among nuclear powers Regional among conventional weapons states	Global UN study on CBMs Regional and bilateral agreements on CBMs
Substance	Weapons industry, manpower, base closure	Nuclear and conventional weapons industry	Crisis communication, accident prevention	Counter surprise attack and horizontal escalation

Procedures / Achievements (treaties)[a]	Unilateral, by treaty	Unilateral, gradualist, by treaty	Unilateral and mutual compromise	Unilateral and gradualist, political agreement (treaty)
Cold War (1946–1962)	None	Antarctic (1959)	None	None
Limited détente (1963–1968)	None	B: Limited Test Ban (1963); G: Outer Space, Non-proliferation; R: Tlatelolco	USA–USSR Hot Line Agreement	None
Détente (1969–1979)	G: Biological Weapons Convention	B: SALT I (1972); ABM Treaty; G: ENMOD (1977); Moon Treaty (1979)	Improved Hot Line Agreement; several agreements to prevent nuclear accidents and nuclear war	R: CSCE Final Act of Helsinki (1975)
Cold War 2 (1980–1986)	None	R: Rarotonga (1985)	Risk Reduction Centres (1987)	R: Stockholm Agreement (1986)
Détente 2 (1987–1989)	B: INF Treaty (1987)	B: INF Treaty (1987)		
Post-Cold War period (1990–)	G: Chemical Weapons Convention; R:CFE 1, CFE 1A; B: START I (1991); START II (1993)	B: START I & II; R: Open Skies Treaty (1992), CFE 1 Treaty, CFE 1A Treaty; B: Peaceful Nuclear Explosives Treaty; Threshold Test Ban Treaty	Protocol on Blinding Laser Weapons; Protocol on Anti-Personnel Mines	R: Vienna Documents (1990, 1992, 1994); Lisbon Declaration (1996)

a. G = global; R = regional; B = bilateral.

similar proposals by Tsar Nicholas II resulted in two international peace conferences in The Hague in 1899 and 1907 that restricted the use of certain weapons (e.g. chemical weapons). Major disarmament provisions were also contained in the post–World War I peace treaties (of Versailles, St. Germain-en-Laye, Neuilly, Trianon, and Sèvres). The Covenant of the League of Nations required all states to reduce their armaments "to the lowest point consistent with national safety and the enforcement by common action of international obligations." The Secretariat of the League published an Armaments Yearbook on the strength and equipment of the armed forces and a Statistical Yearbook on international arms transfers. Major efforts within the framework of the League focused on attempts to regulate arms trade and production (e.g. the St. Germain convention of 1919 and the Geneva Conventions on Arms Trade of 1925), to prohibit the first use of chemical and biological weapons, and to organize the peace (e.g. Kellogg–Briand pact). The First Disarmament Conference in Geneva (1932–1936) examined in detail:

(a) establishment of a system of collective security; (b) limitation of the strength of the armed forces; (c) limitation of land, naval and air armaments; (d) limitation of national defense expenditures; (e) prohibition of chemical, incendiary and bacteriological warfare; (f) control of arms manufacture and trade; (g) supervision and guarantees of implementation of the obligations contracted by the parties; and (h) "moral disarmament" intended to create an atmosphere favorable to the peaceful solution of international problems. (Goldblat 1994: 16)

The first major arms control agreement was the Washington Naval Treaty of 1922, which set limits on the size of battleships and aircraft-carriers and a ratio of ship tonnage among the United States, Great Britain, Japan, France, and Italy (5:5:3:1.75:1.75). In the London Treaty of 1930 the United States, the United Kingdom, and Japan for the first time accepted quantitative and qualitative limits on all warship categories. The London Treaty of 1936 regulated certain qualitative aspects of naval competition. When Japan unilaterally abrogated the 1922 Treaty in 1934, three other major naval powers did not join in: the Soviet Union, Italy, and Germany.

Achievements and failures of the United Nations

Since 1945, the United Nations has provided the institutional machinery to perform major disarmament functions: communication (with governments, NGOs, and experts); initiation and conduct of negotiations; and verification and implementation of agreements by specialized agencies, e.g. the International Atomic Energy Agency (in Vienna) and the Organization for the Prohibition of Chemical Weapons (in The Hague), and – since the second Gulf war – also enforcement against violators by the Security Council.

Two major global disarmament treaties have been achieved within the United Nations framework: the Biological Weapons Convention (BWC) of 1972 and the Chemical Weapons Convention (CWC) of 1993. The most significant global arms control agreement has been the Non-Proliferation Treaty (NPT) of 1968, which acquired indefinite extension in 1995. Less significant has been the Environmental Modification Convention (ENMOD) of 1977 and the Moon Treaty of 1979. A Comprehensive Nuclear Test Ban Treaty was approved by the UN General Assembly on 10 September 1996.

The institutional machinery for dealing with disarmament issues was set up by the Charter and subsequent decisions of the General Assembly and the Security Council. Since the 1950s the Assembly, together with its subsidiary bodies (First Committee, Disarmament Commission), has exercised the main initiative and has been the main deliberative organ to facilitate both ongoing negotiations and the implementation of agreements. The Assembly has also set up various ad hoc committees, e.g. on the World Disarmament Campaign (1973) and on the Indian Ocean (1980). In 1978 the Assembly created an Advisory Board on Disarmament Studies, and on 1 October 1980 the United Nations Institute for Disarmament Research was established in Geneva to undertake independent research on disarmament in close cooperation with the UN Secretariat in New York. Furthermore, three UN regional centres for peace and disarmament were set up in Africa (in Lomé in 1986), in Latin America and the Caribbean (in Lima in 1987), and in Asia and the Pacific (in Kathmandu in 1988).

During the East–West conflict, the General Assembly was primarily limited to declamatory politics. Most of its over 1,000 resolutions in 48 years:

have had little effect on national policies or on the course of arms control negotiations. There are several reasons for this failure. In the first place, the accelerated proliferation of resolutions, especially in the 1980s, considerably reduced their value.... Such documents cannot play the role originally assigned to UN resolutions, that of serving as a sounding board for governmental proposals. ... As a result, the other important role of the General Assembly, that of providing guidance for arms control talks, has been weakened. (Goldblat 1994: 26)

Since the 1950s, the role of the Security Council on disarmament issues has been limited. In 1968, the Council adopted a resolution offering immediate assistance to non-nuclear members of the Non-Proliferation Treaty if they became victim to nuclear threats or aggression. In several treaties, the Council was given a role in responding to complaints on treaty violations. Since the end of the East–West conflict, its role in implementing specifically the NPT was strengthened, e.g. in the so-called cease-fire resolution (Resolution 687 of 3 April 1991) in which the Council entrusted the UN Special Commission on Iraq with the implementation of the destruction of Iraq's weapons of mass destruction. In their Declaration of January 1992, the Security Council members "committed themselves to working to prevent the spread of technology related to the research for or production of weapons of mass destruction" (Goldblat 1994: 28).

Within the United Nations Secretariat, on 1 January 1983, the Centre for Disarmament was upgraded into the Department for Disarmament Affairs and in 1992 it was again downgraded to an Office for Disarmament Affairs. This Office has been analysing disarmament-related developments within the UN system, formulating policies, offering administrative assistance to ongoing negotiations (Geneva) and deliberations (New York), and preparing UN disarmament publications: the *UN Disarmament Yearbook*, the *Disarmament Journal* and *Newsletter* (discontinued in 1996), fact-sheets, conference reports of the World Disarmament Campaign, regional symposia, NGO activities, the Disarmament Study Series, and Topical Papers.

While the World Disarmament Campaign was the main contact for NGOs, the Information and Studies Branch was in close contact with both the scientific and peace research community. Many studies were initiated by the General Assembly, and since 1978 by the Advisory Board on Disarmament Studies (since 1989 on disarmament matters). Although some studies succeeded in promoting specific measures (e.g. the NPT, 1967, the BWC, 1969, measures on napalm, 1971, on standardized military budgets, since 1974, on CBMs, 1981, on verification, 1990, and on conventional arms transfers, 1991), others, primarily by governmental experts, contained well-known official positions without overcoming political and ideological differences (Goldblat 1994: 29–30).

During the first Special Session of the General Assembly devoted to disarmament in 1978, French President Giscard d'Estaing proposed the creation of an international institute for disarmament research. Since 1980, the United Nations Institute for Disarmament

Research (UNIDIR) has become the major interface between the United Nations and the academic community with the goal of assisting "ongoing negotiations on disarmament" and stimulating "new initiatives for new negotiations." Between 1981 and 1993, UNIDIR held 20 major scientific conferences and several meetings with directors of research institutes in Africa, Latin America, and the Middle East. UNIDIR has published numerous research reports and books on issues of disarmament (NPT, chemical warfare, conventional disarmament in Europe, verification and aerial reconnaissance, outer space, bilateral and multilateral negotiations, nuclear test ban, unilateral measures), confidence-building measures, arms transfers, satellite warfare, national security concepts of states, security in third world countries, non-military aspects of security, non-offensive defence, economic aspects of disarmament, and economic adjustment after the Cold War.

UNESCO's Division on Human Rights and Peace has been the other major partner of the peace research community, organizing conferences on peace and disarmament education, facilitating communication among researchers, and, since 1980, publishing the *UNESCO Yearbook on Peace and Conflict Studies*.[1] What has been the major contribution of peace research to disarmament research and disarmament negotiations as well as to the global transformation of 1989?

Contributions from peace research

The primary contribution of peace researchers to disarmament and arms control has been conceptual. They challenged the dominant "neo-realist" national security doctrines with the concept of common or mutual security; they offered alternative explanations of arms competition (the theory of armaments dynamics); they called for an assessment of critical military technologies and of their impact on stability and economic competitiveness; they offered both conceptual and practical suggestions for confidence-building and crisis prevention; they suggested alternative modes for treaty negotiations (unilateral restraint and gradualist approaches); and they considered the impact of arms spending and of disarmament on the economy, calling for specific and prospective plans for economic adjustment (conversion). Policy-oriented peace researchers offered alternative concepts for non-governmental organizations (NGOs), opposition parties, and a few concerned politicians, but until the mid-1980s they had little impact on arms control negotiations.

27

In the 1960s and 1970s, a few peace researchers challenged prevailing theories that the East–West (and in particular US–Soviet) arms competition could be explained as an action–reaction process (Richardson 1960a, 1960b). Instead, peace researchers focused on the manifold domestic factors (military service as well as industrial and labour interests, institutional bureaucratic as well as the interests of research laboratories in follow-on contracts, often referred to as the military industrial complex) that nurtured the process of armaments dynamics (Senghaas 1972; Brauch 1990, 1993; Gleditsch and Njölstad 1990). Their conceptual conclusions were that arms control treaties would be necessary but not sufficient as long as the domestic causes of armament dynamics were not overcome. For these very reasons they called for prospective disarmament and conversion planning (Rittberger 1979; Albrecht 1978).

Peace researchers also challenged the "realist" security philosophy, which interpreted the security dilemma as a global zero-sum game. This often led to domino theories, which were used to legitimate the prolongation of military interventions (e.g. in South-East Asia in the 1960s and 1970s). They criticized the process of legitimizing new arms build-ups in the framework of arms control agreements by exploiting arms (im)balances (levelling up). Since the 1960s, social scientists and peace researchers (e.g. Osgood 1962; Etzioni 1962) have called for unilateral arms restraint and gradualist processes of arms reductions, either to initiate negotiations or to overcome obstacles.

Since the 1970s, peace researchers have contributed to the development of the concept of confidence-building measures (IPRA 1980) and have tabled many policy-oriented proposals on the global, regional, and subregional level to supplement different arms control negotiations (Baudissin 1983; Brauch 1986, 1994a). Since the end of the East–West conflict, some of these proposals have become of interest for many crisis regions of the globe (Krepon et al. 1993).

Although there was no discernible direct impact of peace research on policy in Western Europe, success occurred in the mid-1980s when the civilian advisers of Mikhail Gorbachev incorporated many proposals from the peace research community in his "new thinking" on foreign and security policy: mutual security doctrine, defensive military doctrines, non-offensive defence concepts, unilateral force reductions, and conversion. Garthoff (1994: 751–778) disputes the contention that the military build-up by the United States in the 1980s brought about drastic changes in Soviet policy. Rather, it was Gorbachev's "new thinking" that was decisive in ending the Cold War.

From 1985 to early 1987, Gorbachev unsuccessfully invited the United States to join the Soviet Union in a mutual nuclear test ban moratorium. In December 1988, in his speech to the United Nations announcing a unilateral reduction of Soviet armed forces by 500,000 men, Gorbachev sent a clear political signal to a reluctant NATO alliance. However, when President Bush announced a unilateral withdrawal of all American short-range nuclear forces on 27 September 1991, President Gorbachev supported this initiative within a week. By July 1992, this major case of gradualism was successfully implemented by both sides.

Nevertheless a major question remains: the lack of readiness of democratic societies and their governments in the West seriously to consider and to evaluate – detached from their prevailing mindsets – the alternative concepts that have been developed by peace researchers since the mid-1960s. Their contributions took an indirect route, via the anti-nuclear peace movements and transnational NGOs interested in disarmament, human rights, development, and the environment, to reach a receptive new political leadership in the former Soviet Union that was ready both to overcome its own Marxist–Leninist orthodoxy on international affairs and to learn (Gross Stein 1994). At this time many policy makers in the West interpreted power as not having to learn (Deutsch 1963). The relationship between Hobbesian pessimism, neo-realist theories, the dominance of strategic and military thinking on foreign policies and of conservative mindsets in intelligence agencies and planning staffs, and the pathological learning in Western defence institutions still requires detailed study. This official orthodoxy in the West was often challenged by national and increasingly transnationally operating anti-war, peace, human rights, development, and environmental societal movements.

The impact of the peace movement

The peace movements of the late nineteenth century and early twentieth century had an impact on the search for a new international order and security system to overcome and contain the anarchy in the international system. After the concert system based on a complex balance of power had collapsed in World War I, President Woodrow Wilson, in his vision of a new world order, incorporated both major components of Kant's normative prescription (Kant [1795] 1968). With his "four policemen," Franklin D. Roosevelt added teeth to Wilson's idealist concept. However, owing to the East–West conflict, the UN collective security system was blocked from the outset until the autumn of 1989.

During the East–West conflict, two types of non-governmental organization (NGO) have to be distinguished in the world of societies (*Gesellschaftswelt*): (a) independent societal and professional groups, which were often critical of their own governments; and (b) societal groups that propagated the strategies of their respective governments or parties. With respect to the first type of NGO, four waves of critical activities dealing with disarmament can be noted in the OECD countries:

(1) After 1945, nuclear physicists in the United States (many of them founded the Federation of American Scientists) and in the United Kingdom opposed the employment of the bomb against Hiroshima and the nuclear build-up (Wittner 1984, 1993). In 1957, several leading natural scientists heeded the Einstein–Russell appeal and later cooperated in framing the Pugwash Movement (Rotblat 1977).

(2) During the 1950s, many physicians and natural scientists in the United States protested against the negative effects of nuclear testing in the atmosphere, while in Western Europe a broad coalition fought against the deployment of medium-range nuclear missiles and the threat of a nuclear death. This protest resulted in proposals by the US Presidential candidate Adlai Stevenson calling for a nuclear test ban, in more than 100 disengagement proposals (Hinterhoff 1959), and in the arms control concept developed in 1960 by the strategic community in the United States and the United Kingdom (*Daedalus* 1960; Bull 1961; Schelling and Halperin 1961).

(3) The movement against US involvement in the war in Viet Nam and the international student movement (1965 to the early 1970s) contributed to a fundamental challenge to the Cold War assumptions of Western policy. This criticism was instrumental in the emergence of the peace research school in North America, Scandinavia, and Central Europe and in a dispute between scientistic and policy-oriented researchers. It was the latter who developed many of the critical concepts mentioned above.

(4) NATO's decision on intermediate-range nuclear forces (INF) of December 1979, the Soviet invasion of Afghanistan two weeks later, the military build-up of the Reagan administration, and increased public concern about the likelihood of a nuclear holocaust

during the second Cold War fostered the emergence of a broad anti-nuclear peace movement. This called for a nuclear freeze in the United States, for nuclear disarmament (Cortright 1993), for non-offensive defence, and also for human rights in Eastern Europe. In Europe, this public protest movement involved many professional groups (natural scientists, physicians, writers, artists). As "alternative experts," peace researchers offered policy alternatives and thus contributed to a truly democratic and often sophisticated debate on security policy.

Whereas most Western governmental experts and NATO officials rejected these alternatives, Gorbachev's civilian advisers did not. As already indicated, it was the incorporation of many proposals from peace research into the "new thinking" and Gorbachev's efforts to translate them successfully into policies that brought about the global transformation, and not the military build-up of the Reagan administration and of NATO (Garthoff 1994; Gross Stein 1994).

Trends, expectations, and new tasks after the Cold War

The contextual change after 1989 was instrumental in the signing of several significant arms control and real disarmament agreements, but it also put new issues on the arms control agenda: containing horizontal and vertical proliferation and new sources of political instability. Since 1990, several major nuclear arms control and disarmament agreements have been reached between the United States and the Soviet Union: the START I Treaty of 31 July 1991 and the START II Treaty of 3 January 1993 (between the United States and Russia). In May 1991, the INF Treaty was fully implemented. At the multilateral level in Europe, the following disarmament and confidence- and security-building agreements were signed:

- the Conventional Forces in Europe (CFE) Treaty of November 1990 among the then 22 members of NATO and the Warsaw Treaty Organization (WTO), which was supplemented by a Final Protocol of the now 29 parties to the treaty on 5 June 1992;
- the Vienna Document of November 1990 on Confidence and Security Building Measures of the then 34 CSCE states;
- the Open Skies Treaty of 24 March 1992 of 25 CSCE states;
- the Vienna Document of March 1992 on Confidence and Security Building Measures of the then 48 CSCE states;
- the Final Act on the Negotiations on Manpower Strength of the

Conventional Forces in Europe (CFE 1A) Treaty of 10 July 1992 of 29 CSCE states;
• the Vienna Document of 1994 on Confidence and Security Building Measures.

In addition, the reciprocal unilateral announcements by President Bush on 27 September 1991 and Gorbachev's speech of 4 October 1991 to withdraw all land-based short-range nuclear missiles and artillery were implemented by mid-1992. Thus, elements of a gradualist strategy complemented traditional arms control by negotiation. Without a treaty, all American chemical weapons were withdrawn from Germany by September 1990. By the end of June 1992, all Soviet tactical nuclear weapons had also been transferred to Russia from the other members of the Confederation of Independent States. Thus, nuclear disengagement, or a zone free of weapons, has been achieved in Europe from the Baltic through Central Europe to the Balkans. Nevertheless, the weapons innovation process – at least in the West – continues unabated (Brauch et al. 1992).

In October 1992, Secretary-General Boutros-Ghali highlighted three new concepts: "integration of disarmament and arms regulation issues into the broader structure of the international peace and security agenda; globalization through practical engagement of all States in the disarmament process; and revitalization through efforts to build upon past achievements" (1992b: 1). Boutros-Ghali departed from the traditional view that disarmament "as a relatively distinct subject required its own separate organizational framework" by pointing out that "problems in this field can be resolved only in conjunction with other political and economic issues, while solutions to political and economic issues are often found in conjunction with disarmament measures" (1992b: 4). He considered that disarmament, "the structuring of a new system of international relations and improving economic conditions" were complementary measures that should be implemented in a coordinated manner. Especially in peace-keeping and peace-building, "the role of arms limitation can be significant."

The Secretary-General called for the replication in other regions of the model of US–Russian accommodation for "disarmament by mutual example or reciprocated unilateral measures" as first important steps "in the globalization of the disarmament process." He encouraged the development of regional and subregional approaches to arms limitation and confidence-building – especially on arms transfers – that could in turn enhance the process of global arms reduction.

Boutros-Ghali pointed to four major future disarmament tasks: further reductions in weapons of mass destruction (implementation of START I and II, agreement on a comprehensive test ban, complete elimination of nuclear weapons, implementation of the CWC); proliferation control (indefinite extension of the NPT in 1995); limitation on arms transfers; and enhancement of transparency in arms and other confidence-building measures (e.g. an extension of the UN Register of Conventional Arms). Furthermore, openness and transparency measures could make military behaviour more predictable, reassuring potential rivals of non-threatening intentions. He also referred to two new challenges: conversion to alleviate the painful transition to a post-disarmament world, and the creation of new machinery leading to a coordinated system "to address major disarmament problems promptly, flexibly and efficiently." The Secretary-General supported greater involvement of the Security Council in the enforcement of non-proliferation. In his view, the Conference on Disarmament "could also be considered as a permanent review and supervisory body for some existing multilateral arms regulation and disarmament agreements" (1992b: 22).

He pointed specifically to the non-aggression treaty of 11 Central African states as a model of a regional confidence-building measure. As part of the effort to counter nuclear proliferation, Boutros-Ghali called for "international inspections of nuclear facilities in all Member States." With respect to the existing regimes on dual-purpose technologies he called for "the eventual replacement of existing export control regimes by arrangements more satisfactory to the importers" (1994a: 8). On 25 January 1994, in a message to the Conference on Disarmament, Boutros-Ghali welcomed its efforts to complete a comprehensive test ban treaty by 1995. He hoped that the UN Register of Conventional Arms could be further extended into a "far-reaching international confidence-building tool" that could "culminate in the establishment of an early-warning system which would pave the way for the reduction of conventional armaments to the lowest possible level consistent with the principle of the legitimate security needs of States" (1994a: 13). In late 1994, in a position paper on peace-keeping, he also proposed "micro disarmament" on the regional level dealing with light weapons, including the approximately 110 million land mines, and an extension of the Register of Conventional Weapons into a global and non-discriminatory mechanism (1995: 23–25).

4. Conversion

Peace research and conversion

The term "conversion" is used here in its classical meaning, as a shift from military to civilian production, and/or from military to civilian use of resources (Albrecht 1978; Köllner and Huck 1990). It is regarded as a specific form for changes in the military industry, an element of "diversification, restructuring and transformation" (Möller 1991; Hilton 1992; Renner 1992). Conversion studies constitute only a part of the economics of armament and disarmament, which focus on two major issues (Brauer and Chatterji 1993): the impact of military expenditure on economic growth, and the "peace dividend," or, in other words, the benefits and burdens of disarmament and a reduction in military spending. Conversion studies, dealing with the latter, have focused on two problems: the macroeconomic implications of reduced defence spending, and the microeconomic and technical problems of finding alternative uses for the manpower and machinery of the arms industries.

In the 1950s and 1960s, economic peace research studies concentrated on the macroeconomic consequences of arms races and disarmament for developed and developing economies (Boulding 1960, 1970; Boulding and Benoit 1963). Since the 1970s, both before and after the first arms control treaties, research interests shifted to the microeconomic consequences of arms reduction as well (Melman 1970, 1988; DiFilippo 1986; Hartley and Hopper 1990).

Until the late 1980s, before changes in the East, peace researchers addressed their conversion studies primarily to politicians in the West, in the East, and in the developing countries. These "conversion programmes" were based on the following economic and managerial assumptions:

- resources diverted from military spending can be used for the acceleration of economic growth and protection of the environment (e.g. United Nations 1991b, 1991c);
- rich nations should transfer to the developing countries a part of the resources saved by reducing military spending;[2]
- successful conversion programmes could be conducted both in

free market and in centrally planned economies based on relevant, tailor-made programmes;
- the costs of conversion will not undermine the programme;
- international cooperation will be necessary for conversion.

The main aim of these assumptions was to convince politicians and societies that disarmament would be economically feasible as well as (from most points of view) economically advantageous. It was also necessary to show that it would be possible to compensate the losers – trade unions, industrial sectors, geographical regions, and developing countries producing raw materials with important military markets – from the savings in military spending.

This optimistic picture of the macro- and microeconomic advantages of conversion began a trial period at the end of the 1980s. Conversion research is no longer a matter of trying to demonstrate how it would be possible to overcome obstacles to disarmament but a matter of trying to use in the most rational way a disarmament that is already in full swing. It is also possible to show *ex post* the first successes and failures of conversion and to produce recommendations for future actions.

The experiences of all Cold War participants, as well as of developing countries, show that the disarmament process is much more costly than expected. Instead of providing a short-term "peace dividend" it can be treated as a specific kind of investment process that can bring only long-term benefits (Hartley et al. 1993). Conversion of the military industry is especially difficult in the former Soviet Union, mainly in Russia, in the former member states of the Warsaw Treaty, especially in Czechoslovakia, and, since 1 January 1993, in Slovakia. Lack of domestic resources, inadequate foreign involvement (assistance, investment), as well as economic, managerial, and political obstacles make conversion in the former Soviet Union completely unresponsive to earlier needs and expectations. Similarly, although accomplished in much more stable circumstances, conversion in the West does not correspond to earlier expectations.

It is difficult to determine the reasons for such a great discrepancy between the initial vision of post–Cold War conversion and the harsh reality. Awareness of the weaknesses and mistakes of global and local conversion should be helpful in creating new programmes that are more relevant to reality. Economists, peace researchers, and/or specialists from other areas (conversion is a multidisciplinary effort) need to re-evaluate their research programmes and recommendations addressed to governments, industry, and local populations. The changes should be based on more realistic assumptions: limited resources, a limited will for international cooperation, the costs of reforms, managerial and marketing barriers, and, last but not least, the short-sightedness of policy makers.

The existing conversion-oriented institutional infrastructure of peace research should be helpful in preparing for the second stage of the conversion of the military industry on a global and local scale. International organizations such as the International Peace Research Association and its regional affiliates, the Peace Science Society (International), Economists Allied for Arms Reduction, the International Defense Economists Association, and others, constitute an institutional framework for the activities of various institutes and their networks as well as networks of individual researchers.

Conversion-oriented research and activities can be done both inside and outside of governments. Experience gained hitherto shows that not all of the possibilities for improving global conversion programmes have been employed. Much attention is paid to bilateral relations: assistance, investment, and transfers of "know-how." Similarly, countries of the former Warsaw Pact put their hopes in cooperation with NATO within the North Atlantic Cooperation Council and the "Partnership for Peace." However, it is often forgotten that such cooperation can be too much influenced by political interests. The time has come to revise international and national governmental and non-governmental conversion plans and to strengthen the conversion-oriented activities of the United Nations and its specialized agencies and institutions.

Achievements and failures of the United Nations

In all activities undertaken by the United Nations since the 1960s, the question of conversion has been associated with the relationship between disarmament and development. In 1962, the General Assembly adopted Resolution 1837 (XVII), entitled "Declaration on the conversion to peaceful needs of the resources released by disarmament." In the 1970s, conversion of resources was the topic of two studies (United Nations 1970, 1976). Interest in these questions led the United Nations to convene the International Conference on the Relationship between Disarmament and Development in New York (24 August to 11 September 1987).

In the action programme of the Final Document of the conference, the participating states requested the Secretary-General to intensify his efforts to foster and coordinate the incorporation of a disarmament–development perspective in the activities of the United Nations. It was also recommended, *inter alia*, that more studies should be devoted to analyses of the impact of global military expenditures on the world economy. And the United Nations was urged to facilitate an international exchange of views and experience on conversion from military to civilian production (United Nations 1987, 1988). At the forty-fourth session of the General Assembly in 1989, a draft resolution on conversion of military resources was submitted for the first time and adopted as Resolution 44/116 J (United Nations 1991a: 75).

The end of the Cold War created new challenges for UN conversion research and activities. The transformation and subsequent collapse of the Warsaw Treaty made it necessary to elaborate new ideas helpful in dismantling the military complex in the Soviet Union and in other member states of the WTO. In August 1990 an international conference on "Conversion: Economic Adjustments in an Era of Arms Reduction" was held in Moscow. Participants from all over the world discussed the very concept of conversion, the prerequisites for and obstacles to an effective process of adjustment, the use of advanced technology to facilitate conversion, and concerns that arms reductions could result in the dumping of surplus weapons onto the international arms market (United Nations 1991b, 1991c).

Discussion begun in Moscow was continued at the international conference on "International Cooperation in Peaceful Use of Military Industrial Technology" held in Beijing, China, from 22 to 26 October 1991. The conference was organized jointly by a non-governmental organization from China and by the UN Centre for Science and Technology Development. It was pointed out that, as more countries began to deal with conversion, some parts of the UN system, including the International Labour Organization (ILO) and the United Nations Industrial Development Organization (UNIDO), were dealing with specific aspects of the problem. Other views presented in the discussions can be summarized as follows. First, conversion to civilian production is only one among many possible courses of action that major military producers might take. Second, national policies of converting from military to civilian production do not guarantee that programmes of military modernization will not be pursued. Third, successful conversion involves not only re-engineering and cost effectiveness, but also economies of scale, import dependence, and time factors. Fourth, national attempts at conversion are difficult to sustain in isolation from other important features of the world economy, such as access to global markets and transfer of technology (United Nations 1991a: 76–77).

In Beijing, the United Nations drew attention to new opportunities stemming from a reduction in the military burden. An expert study entitled "Study on charting potential uses of resources allocated to military activities for civilian endeavors to protect the environment" was completed in 1991 and submitted by the Secretary-General to the Assembly at its forty-sixth session (UN 1991a: 80). UN support for action on conversion – the area where disarmament and development meet – continued throughout 1992 and 1993. At a conference organized in Hong Kong from 7 to 10 July 1993 (by the organizers of the Beijing conference in 1991), a special declaration was adopted. It was declared that international cooperation, exchanges, and research in support of conversion should be expanded. Multilateral and private financial institutions should address the funding requirements of conversion on a priority basis. It was also stated that training plays an important role in conversion and that information is a crucial resource in the conversion process.

In studies and actions supporting conversion the following parts of the UN system have been involved: the Secretary-General, the General Assembly, UNESCO, the Economic and Social Council, the UN Disarmament Commission, the UN Department of Economic and Social Development, the UN Conference on Trade and Development, UNIDO, the World Bank, and UNIDIR. A special role was assigned to UNIDIR. In response to Resolution 45/62 G of the General Assembly of 4 December 1990, the Institute prepared a report on "Economic Aspects of Disarmament" (*UNIDIR Newsletter*, no. 19, 1992: Hartley et al. 1993). In addition the Institute organized several conferences that resulted in research papers, reports, and publications in books and newsletters in the period 1990–1993 (Sur 1991; Renner 1992; Väyrynen 1992).

Although these meetings and documents have initiated discussions among politicians and academics, efforts to implement their recommendations face major impediments:

• a lack of political will among member states to devise conversion plans and to coordinate their conversion efforts;
• limited UN influence on decisions by sovereign states in the areas of arms trade, arms control, and disarmament;

- a growing realization of specific internal barriers to conversion in all member countries;
- doctrinal barriers – the current tendency of economists to accept only a limited role for the state narrows the possibilities for any form of non-market support for conversion;
- institutional barriers connected with reforms in the East and a shortage of investment for conversion purposes – accompanied by reluctance of leading Western members to extend the scope of projects supported by the World Bank;
- a scarcity of resources of the UN that could be spent on conversion-related research, consulting, and training;
- limited possibilities for the World Bank to deliver large-scale support for conversion in the East owing to a lack of resources and to doctrinal and political barriers;
- a revival of persistent Cold War structures of armaments dynamics;
- the development of dual-use technologies and increasing competition in arms exports as a means of preserving the military industrial base since the end of the East–West conflict.

The limited impact of UN meetings and reports on conversion has once again disclosed the "classical" limitations of the UN role in sensitive areas of international relations where consensus is often impossible to achieve. From the vantage point of 1997 it may be concluded that almost all conversion programmes, both in the West and in the East, and particularly in the former Soviet Union, have failed to achieve their goals, leaving most needs and expectations unfulfilled. As a result, the only indisputable UN contribution to global and national conversion has been the provision of the conceptual background necessary for studies and practice of conversion, along with networking of scholars, some NGOs, and a few interested officials.

5. Proposals for research and policy in the new environment

What conclusions can we draw from all the years of experience in the framework of the League Covenant and the United Nations Charter? Does the shift in the global context due to the end of the East–West conflict require a reconceptualization of security, defence, and disarmament? How relevant is UN experience with defence, disarmament, and conversion in its first five decades for the future? Are the concepts that were developed by peace researchers in response to the

East–West conflict still relevant? Based on the foregoing analysis, we offer 12 proposals.[3]

Developing the institutional framework for collective security

Any disarmament strategy requires specific analyses – in global, regional, and subregional contexts – of the international security order and of the prevailing security system. Since 1989, the disarmament successes (see table 1.1) have directly benefited from the global contextual change. However, by 1997 fundamental problems of the emerging new international security architecture, especially the specific relationship of the systems of collective security and the remaining military alliances, have not yet been resolved.

Disarmament as a diplomatic tool of security policy and as an outcome of international cooperation should also be considered in the framework of Kant's first two definitive articles: a democratic system of rule and collective security. If democracies are not fighting each other, are they also ready to reduce their armaments to the level needed for national survival? Are they willing to resist "the unwarranted influence ... by the military-industrial complex" that President Eisenhower warned against in his farewell address?

Linking disarmament with preventive diplomacy and peace-building

In the bipolar East–West context – most specifically in US–Soviet relations – arms control was a diplomatic tool to achieve arms race and crisis stability in the framework of deterrence strategy. With the passing of the bipolar system and the downgrading of nuclear weapons as weapons of last resort (NATO London summit in July 1990), but with the increase in civil wars (Amer et al. 1993; Wallensteen and Axell 1993, 1994), the four pillars of a disarmament strategy (table 1.1) may be reconceptualized in the framework of preventive diplomacy and peace-building.

Preventive diplomacy aims at conflict avoidance and de-escalation of tensions by means of good offices, mediation, and reconciliation. On the hardware side, preventive arms control (Liebert 1994; Brauch et al. 1997) should foster constraints on the process of vertical proliferation (the weapons innovation process) and horizontal proliferation (export of heavy and light conventional weapons). Both processes, along with involved domestic institutions (military R&D laboratories) and interests (arms export lobbies), have largely remained unaffected by the global context change. Rather, owing to opposition (in the United States) and the failure of conversion (in Russia and the former WTO countries), the pressure to compensate for declining national procurement with arms exports has increased. In several countries, tight export control legislation for weapons and dual-use goods has been weakened.

Daalder (1992: 9) distinguishes between traditional competitive arms control "to prevent a movement in relations towards war" and cooperative arms control "to transform political relations in a manner conducive to creating a pluralistic security community." Competitive arms control is aimed at ameliorating the security dilemma by reducing the incentives for a surprise attack or war by accident (crisis stability), taming action–reaction patterns (arms race stability), and "manipulating the military balance and limiting the quantity and quality of arms ... to achieve military stability." Cooperative arms control, in Daalder's (1992: 9–11) view,

has as its objective the improvement of political relations between states by creating, through an intensive dialogue as well as the habit of cooperation, a set of principles, norms, and rules that govern the military dimension of interstate relations.... The cooperative approach is guided by the conviction that it is possible to escape the security dilemma through a policy of common, cooperative and mutual security.... By taking steps that reassure others of one's peaceful intentions it is possible to reverse the vicious action–reaction cycle that is at the core of the security dilemma. The cooperative approach, therefore, aims to determine what actions reassure others in order to reduce the reliance on military force as a factor of interstate relations, and thus establish political stability.

Preventive arms control requires measures that take effect before the testing of new weapons and procurement. Liebert (1994: 235) refers to several suitable measures: enhanced political control over existing military technology; more openness and transparency with respect to military R&D funding decisions and a move from secret to open research; an international ban on weapons based on new scientific-technological principles; and development of sets of criteria for the evaluation of R&D project proposals and budget items. Brauch et al. (1997) discuss various institutional and procedural options for implementing such a concept in the German, European, and UN context.

41

Linking confidence-building and security architectures

Preventive diplomacy also requires a set of intersocietal and trans-national confidence-building, partnership-building, and tolerance-furthering measures (Brauch 1994a, 1994b, 1994c) to deal with historical memories and religious and ethnic enemy images that have increasingly been instrumentalized for power purposes. Peace education must address those taboos and stereotypes that sustain enemy images and thus often legitimize the use of force against minorities.

Post-conflict peace-building requires a demilitarization of both the minds and means of warring parties. Based on existing experience with the twinning of cities and youth exchanges between former enemy countries, intersocietal and transnational confidence-, partnership-, and tolerance-furthering measures must be developed – for example by peace education and reviews of history books – to counter any setback.

Implementing a non-proliferation regime and a comprehensive test ban

In order to prohibit the proliferation of weapons of mass destruction (atomic, biological, and chemical), missiles, and dual-use goods, existing treaties (NPT, BWC, CWC) and export control regimes (Australian Group, London's Suppliers Club, Missile Technology Control Regime) must be fully and tightly implemented. However, this narrow concept of non-proliferation needs to be extended to embrace the export of heavy and light conventional weapons by governments and the grey markets. Therefore, the modest reporting measures (UN Arms Export Registers) must be supplemented by a conventional arms export control regime beyond the ban on anti-personnel mines.

Since the mid-1950s, a major effort has been to achieve a Comprehensive Test Ban (CTB). After reaching a trilateral Partial Test Ban (PTB) in 1963, a bilateral Threshold Test Ban (TTB) and a Peaceful Nuclear Explosives Treaty were agreed in 1976 – although neither entered into force until December 1990. Formal negotiations for a CTB started in the Conference on Disarmament in 1994, when all five nuclear powers finally declared themselves willing to obtain a CTB. Despite the failure of the Conference on Disarmament to agree on submitting the draft Comprehensive Test Ban Treaty (CTBT) to the UN General Assembly on 25 August 1996 owing to the opposition of India, the UN General Assembly nevertheless approved the CTBT

(185-3-5) in Resolution 50/245 on 10 September 1996. By March 1997, 144 countries had signed and 3 (Japan, Fiji, and Qatar) had ratified the CTBT. Of the 44 countries required for entry into force, only four had not signed: Bangladesh, India, Pakistan, and North Korea.

Strengthening the Biological Weapons Convention

In order to restrict the use of biotechnology to peaceful purposes, the BWC must be further strengthened beyond the confidence-building measures agreed upon by the Second Review Conference (September 1986); for example by enlarging participation in the BWC; by including these new provisions in national penal law; by defining specifically what research is permitted or prohibited under the BWC; by establishing a verification regime and creating an oversight committee to supervise its implementation (Geißler 1992, 1994).

Implementing the Chemical Weapons Convention

The CWC of 1992, which entered into force on 29 April 1997 (without the two major states with declared chemical weapons stockpiles as parties), will require the solution of many legal, administrative, financial, technical, and scientific problems to assure its full and timely implementation and proper verification within 10–15 years (Altmann et al. 1994: 111–170). A specific task will be to monitor chemical and toxicological research and development closely, so as to prevent military misuse without prohibiting pharmaceutical research (Trapp 1992).

Constraining the development and deployment of anti-ballistic missiles (ABMs) and anti-satellite (ASAT) weapons

With the end of the East–West conflict, the political urgency for constraining the development and deployment of new ABM and ASAT weapons has been down-graded. Despite the end of the US–Soviet military space race, no progress has been achieved on an ASAT ban. The erosion of the ABM Treaty has continued owing to the efforts of the Bush and Clinton administrations to explore joint missile defences with Russia. In Europe, the Western European Union (WEU) increased its examination of what would be needed to provide Western Europe with protection from ballistic missiles, and both France and Germany have been exploring a joint tactical missile defence system (Spitzer 1992; Dunay 1992).

Establishing an effective global conventional arms transfer regime

For decades, peace research institutes (e.g. the Stockholm International Peace Research Institute) and groups have maintained public awareness by compiling data on arms transfers, the illegal arms trade, production licences for both heavy and light weapons, and police equipment (Wright 1994), often used for torture in severe violation of human rights. This research often sensitized concerned transnational NGOs and journalists. It became a necessary prerequisite for any preventive arms export control policy. Based on such research, the transnational NGO campaign against the export of anti-personnel mines resulted within a few years in a temporary export ban on these weapons in several countries.[4]

In February 1994, the International Committee of the Red Cross requested a ban on the spread of non-lethal laser arms, which do not kill their victims but cause permanent blindness (Sommaruga 1994). During the first Review Conference of the parties to the Inhumane Weapons Convention of 1981/83 (25 September to 13 October 1995), a Protocol on Blinding Laser Weapons was adopted, and during the third session of this Review Conference (22 April to 3 May 1996) a relatively weak "Amended Protocol on Prohibitions or Restrictions on the Use of Mines, Booby-Traps and Other Devices" was approved.

On 8 November 1995, the Centre for Disarmament Affairs organized a workshop on "micro-disarmament" as an integral part of the process preventing, mitigating, and resolving conflicts and building confidence once conflict is over.[5] Secretary-General Boutros-Ghali (1996), in a speech to the Advisory Board on Disarmament Matters, emphasized the importance of this new task.

Since 1990, light and heavy conventional weapons have been used in all the violent ethnic, national, and religious conflicts. Efforts to limit the transfer of conventional arms have not so far constrained access to these weapons: the bilateral US–Soviet Conventional Arms Transfer Talks negotiations of 1977–1979 failed; the efforts of the five permanent members of the Security Council (Paris Communiqué and London Guidelines of 1991) remained weak and inconclusive; and the UN Register of Conventional Arms was limited to a confidence-building measure, slightly enhancing the transparency of the transfers without effectively prohibiting their transfer, which could be achieved only "in conjunction with prohibitions or severe restrictions on their production."

Goldblat (1994: 187) suggests that "a start could be made with those conventional weapons the use of which is already constrained under international law. In the meantime, to avert irresponsible exports, a detailed international code of conduct in the field of arms transfers could be adopted, to bind politically, if not legally, all supplier and recipient states. Such a code must, in the first place, constrain those transfers of arms and arms-related technology that can upset regional arms balances and stimulate regional arms races."

Curbing R&D on sophisticated new conventional arms

The legal constraints on weapons use (under the 1899 Hague Declarations and 1907 Hague Conventions, the Geneva Protocol of 1925, the Genocide Convention of 1948, the 1949 Geneva Conventions and the two protocols to these conventions of 1977, and the Inhumane Weapons Convention of 1981) should be extended to a prohibition on the development and testing of such technologies and arms.

Preventive arms control as a tool of preventive diplomacy should aim at more transparency in the national weapons innovation process by enhancing the possibilities of parliamentary control. Defence technology assessments of military research, development, and procurement projects by a set of legal, financial, mission, and stability criteria could contribute to national self-control. On the international level, a new CBM regime could further enhance transparency and predictability (Liebert 1994; Brauch et al. 1997).

Developing economic strategies, concepts, tools, and financial assistance for the conversion of military production, manpower, and bases

The prospects for future UN support for conversion seem very uncertain. On the one hand, the present mediocre status of global conversion policies and the collapse of all earlier visions of conversion in the former Soviet Union make any new far-reaching recommendations difficult. Thus, lessons from the past may encourage smaller and more concrete steps aimed at supporting conversion, mainly in the new democracies of the East and in developing countries. The UN system will not be able to provide any concrete assistance for conversion, perhaps with the exception of the International Monetary Fund and the World Bank. It could, however, play a more active role in providing information for those who convert and those who could help in the process.

It can be then postulated that a Conversion Projects Register should be established at the United Nations with the following aims: (a) collection of information about conversion projects provided by governments, companies, and non-governmental organizations; (b) collection of information about experts in conversion; (c) collection of data on possible sources of assistance and investment for conversion; (d) research and training connected with the conversion projects. A Conversion Projects Register could also coordinate other efforts aimed at gathering and disseminating information on conversion, for example by the Bonn International Center for Conversion (ConverNet), or other similar initiatives undertaken by government, non-government, and international institutions (NATO, WEU, etc.). Such a Register should be associated with existing UN Disarmament and Security research units, as well as with development-oriented units (UN Disarmament Department, UNIDIR, UNCTAD, and UNIDO). Establishment of such a new body may be difficult. It needs to be more than a new forum for meetings. Initially, it should not aim at grand results but rather operate on a modest scale.

The second way in which the United Nations could help in supporting conversion stems from its unique political position as the only institution that could support new conversion programmes without raising suspicions. This advantage may also be exploited in promoting conversion in the South.

Establishing a future agenda for peace researchers

The above recommendations suggest the following research agenda:
- causes leading to intranational and international ethnic, religious, and nationality conflicts and strategies for preventive diplomacy, crisis management, and peaceful conflict resolution (anthropologists, sociologists, psychologists, historians, theologians);
- universal, regional, and subregional security systems as components of a lasting peace order (international relations specialists);

- reconceptualization of security concepts, military doctrines, future tasks, force structures (non-offensive defence), and training concepts (political scientists);
- national and international implementation of arms control and disarmament agreements (international lawyers and administrative specialists);
- economic adjustment as part of disarmament policy and of the economic transformation process (economists, management specialists);
- prospective defence technology assessments (technology assessment specialists);
- trends opposed to disarmament and conversion that may result in rearmament, qualitative enhancement of weapons, new patterns of the arms trade, development of dual-use technology, new military doctrines, revival of the latent structures and processes of armament dynamics, development of the trade of light weapons, and repression technology.

Strengthening fields of cooperation between the UN system and peace research

The analytical and practical activities of peace researchers on defence, disarmament, and conversion should contribute to education, create public awareness, and develop concepts for future actions that may contribute to a more peaceful world order. The joint interest of peace researchers and relevant bureaus in the United Nations system is to contribute conceptually to the development of new disarmament regimes and to monitor the implementation of existing disarmament treaty regimes. For both, disarmament is not an end in itself but a means to a lasting security architecture and a stable, just, and lasting regional and global peace order based on Kant's three preconditions: democracy, collective security, and human rights.

Acknowledgements

Sections 1, 3, and 5 were written by H. G. Brauch, section 2 by B. Möller, and section 4 by C. Mesjasz. H. G. Brauch acknowledges the financial support of AFES-PRESS and a travel grant by the J. W. Goethe University, Frankfurt, to participate in the IPRA Conference in Malta. C. Mesjasz's contribution relies on a research grant from the Copenhagen Peace and Conflict Research Institute (COPRI). The authors appreciate the comments received at a discussion in Malta in 1994.

Notes

1. For a survey of UNESCO disarmament activities from 1976 to 1987, see Brauch (1990: 98–103); see also the *United Nations Disarmament Yearbook* (up to 1988), the *UNESCO Yearbook on Peace and Conflict Studies* (since 1980), and UNESCO Studies on Peace and Conflict (since 1992).
2. See e.g. UNIDIR (1987); United Nations (1987).
3. A conference on the theme "Disarmament in the Last Half Century and Its Future Prospects" was held in Nagasaki, 12–16 June 1995. The papers were published in United Nations (1995).
4. See *Human Rights Watch* (1993); "U.S. Initiatives for Demining and Landmine Control," *U.S. Policy & Texts*, no. 51, 18 May 1994: 23; "U.N. Coming to Grips with Major World Problem. Land Mines," *U.S. Policy & Texts*, no. 107, 21 October 1993: 22–23.
5. For details, see the contributions by Sohrab Kheradi, Marrack Goulding, Swanesh Rana, Ivor Richard Fong, Herbert Wulf, and Edward J. Laurance in *Disarmament*, vol. XX, no. 2, 1996: 31–67. See also Laurance (1996).

References

Afheldt, Horst, 1976. *Verteidigung und Frieden. Politik mit militärischen Mitteln.* Munich: Hanser.

––––––– 1983. *Defensive Verteidigung.* Reinbek: Rowohlt.

––––––– 1992. "Conflict of Interests, Nuclear Weapons, and Flexible Response: A Critical German View." In H. G. Brauch and R. Kennedy, eds., *Alternative Conventional Defense Postures for the European Theater, Volume 2: The Impact of Political Change on Strategy, Technology and Arms Control.* New York: Crane Russak, pp. 121–148.

––––––– 1993. "Mutual Structural Defensive Superiority: A New Security Philosophy and Elements of a New Force Structure Design." In H. G. Brauch and R. Kennedy, eds., *Alternative Conventional Defense Postures for the European Theater, Volume 3: Force Posture Alternatives for Europe after the Cold War.* Washington: Crane Russak, pp. 103–116.

Albrecht, Ulrich, 1978. *Rüstungskonversionsforschung. Eine Literaturstudie mit Forschungsempfehlungen.* Baden-Baden: Nomos.

Altmann, Jürgen, Thomas Stock, and Jean-Pierre Stroot, eds. 1994. *Verification after the Cold War. Broadening the Process.* Amsterdam: VU University Press.

Amer, Ramses, Birger Heldt, Signe Landgreen, Kjell Magnusson, Erik Melander, Kjell-Ake Nordquist, Thomas Ohlson, and Peter Wallensteen. 1993. "Major Armed Conflicts." *SIPRI Yearbook 1993*, pp. 81–118.

Baudissin, Wolf Graf von, ed. 1983. *From Distrust to Confidence. Concepts, Experiences and Dimensions of Confidence-Building Measures.* Baden-Baden: Nomos.

Boulding, Kenneth E. 1960. "Economic Implications of Arms Control." In *Daedalus* Special Issue on Arms Control, pp. 846–859.

––––––– 1962. *Conflict and Defense: A General Theory.* New York: Harper & Row.

––––––– 1970. *Peace and the War Industry.* Chicago: Aldine-Atherton.

––––––– 1978. *Stable Peace.* Austin: University of Texas Press.

Boulding, Kenneth E., and Emile Benoit, eds. 1963. *Disarmament and the Economy.* New York: Harper & Row.

Boutros-Ghali, Boutros, 1992a. *An Agenda for Peace: Preventive Diplomacy, Peace-making and Peace-keeping: Report of the Secretary-General Pursuant to the Statement Adopted by the Summit Meeting of the Security Council on 31 January 1992.* New York: United Nations, Security Council, 47th year, 17 June 1992, S/24111.

———— 1992b. *New Dimensions of Arms Regulation and Disarmament in the Post-Cold War Era. Report of the Secretary General.* New York: United Nations.

———— 1992/1993. "Empowering the United Nations." *Foreign Affairs*, vol. 71, no. 5, Winter, pp. 89–102.

———— 1994a. *The Disarmament Agenda of the International Community in 1994 and Beyond.* New York: United Nations.

———— 1994b. "The Land Mine Crisis." *Foreign Affairs*, vol. 73, no. 5, September/October, pp. 8–13.

———— 1995. *An Agenda for Peace 1995*, 2nd edn., with new Supplement and related UN documents. New York: United Nations.

———— 1996. "Secretary-General's Address to the Advisory Board on Disarmament Matters. Geneva, 1 July 1996." UN Press Release, DC/96/22, 1 July.

Brauch, Hans Günter, ed. 1986. *Vertrauensbildende Maßnahmen und Europäische Abrüstungskonferenz – Analysen, Dokumente und Vorschläge.* Gerlingen: Bleicher-Verlag.

———— 1990. "Survey of Recent and Ongoing Research in the Social and Human Sciences on Disarmament." In *UNESCO Yearbook on Peace and Conflict Studies 1988.* New York: Greenwood, pp. 83–119.

———— 1993. "Globaler Strukturbruch, Systemtransformation und kein nationaler Strukturwandel: Rüstungs- und Abrüstungspolitik in den amerikanisch-sowjetischen Beziehungen 1981–1992." Mosbach: manuscript.

———— 1994a. "Confidence (and Security) Building Measures: Lessons from the CSCE Experience for the Western Mediterranean." In A. Marquina and H. G. Brauch, eds., *Confidence Building and Partnership in the Western Mediterranean. Tasks for Preventive Diplomacy and Conflict Avoidance.* Madrid: UNISCI; Mosbach: AFES-PRESS, pp. 185–228.

———— 1994b. "Partnership Building Measures for Conflict Prevention in the Western Mediterranean." In A. Marquina and H. G. Brauch, eds., *Confidence Building and Partnership in the Western Mediterranean. Tasks for Preventive Diplomacy and Conflict Avoidance.* Madrid: UNISCI; Mosbach: AFES-PRESS, pp. 257–324.

———— 1994c. "Tolerance Furthering Measures as a Political Tool of Confidence-building between Europe and North Africa." Paper presented at III Encuentro Euro-Arab de Toledo, 24–26 October.

Brauch, Hans Günter, H. J. van der Graaf, John Grin, and Wim Smit, eds. 1992. *Controlling the Development and Spread of Military Technology.* Amsterdam: VU University Press.

———— 1997. *Institutionen, Verfahren und Instrumente einer präventiven Rüstungs-kontrollpolitik.* Münster: Lit.

Brauer, Jurgen, and Manas Chatterji, eds. 1993. *Economic Issues of Disarmament. Contributions from Peace Economics and Peace Science.* New York: New York University Press.

Bull, Hedley. 1961. *The Control of the Arms Race. Disarmament and Arms Control in the Missile Age.* New York: Praeger.

Buzan, Barry. 1991. *People, States and Fear. An Agenda for International Security Studies in the Post-Cold War Era*. London: Harvester Wheatsheaf; Boulder, Colo.: Lynne Rienner.

Cortright, David. 1993. *Peace Works: The Citizen's Role in Ending the Cold War*. Boulder, Colo.: Westview.

Daalder, Ivo H. 1992. *Cooperative Arms Control: A New Agenda for the Post-Cold War Era*. CISSM Papers 1. University of Maryland at College Park, Center for International Security Studies, Maryland School of Public Affairs.

Daedalus. 1960. Special Issue: Arms Control, Fall.

Deutsch, Karl W. 1963. *The Nerves of Government. Models of Political Communication and Control*. New York: Free Press.

DiFilippo, Anthony. 1986. *Military Spending and Industrial Decline: A Study of the American Machine Tool Industry*. New York: Greenwood.

Dunay, Pal. 1992. "Constraints on the Spread of Technology Contributing to Militarization of Space: Are They Feasible, Desirable and Negotiable? The Case of Observation Satellites, GPS and Communication Systems." In H. G. Brauch, H. van de Graaf, J. Grin, and W. Smit, eds., *Controlling the Development and Spread of Military Technology*. Amsterdam: VU University Press, pp. 85–94.

Eckersley, Robin. 1992. *Environmentalism and Political Theory*. London: UCL Press.

Etzioni, Amitai. 1962. *The Hard Way to Peace. A New Strategy*. New York: Collier.

Fischer, Ronald J. 1990. *The Social Psychology of Intergroup and International Conflict Resolution*. New York: Springer-Verlag.

FRUS. 1947. *Foreign Relations of the United States, Paris Peace Conference, vol. XIII*. Washington, D.C.: US Government Printing Office.

Galtung, Johan. 1975. "Violence, Peace and Peace Research." In J. Galtung, *Peace: Research, Education, Action. Essays in Peace Research*, vol. I. Copenhagen: Christian Ejlers Forlag, pp. 109–134.

Garthoff, Raymond L. 1994. *The Great Transition. American–Soviet Relations and the End of the Cold War*. Washington, D.C.: Brookings.

Geißler, Erhard. 1992. "Molecular Biotechnology and the Third Review of the Biological Weapons Convention." In H. G. Brauch, H. van de Graaf, J. Grin, and W. Smit, eds., *Controlling the Development and Spread of Military Technology*. Amsterdam: VU University Press, pp. 95–108.

——— 1994. "Confidence-building Information from Parties to the Biological Weapons Convention." In J. Altmann, T. Stock, and J.-P. Stroot, eds., *Verification after the Cold War. Broadening the Process*. Amsterdam: VU University Press, pp. 171–177.

Gleditsch, Nils Petter, and Olav Njölstad, eds. 1990. *Arms Races: Technological and Political Dynamics*. London: Sage.

Goldblat, Jozef. 1994. *Arms Control. A Guide to Negotiations and Agreements*. London: Sage.

Gross Stein, Janice. 1994. "Political Learning by Doing: Gorbachev as Uncommitted Thinker and Motivated Learner." *International Organization*, vol. 48, no. 2, Spring, pp. 155–184.

Hartley, Keith, and Nick Hopper. 1990. *The Economics of Defence, Disarmament and Peace: An Annotated Bibliography*. Aldershot: Edward Elgar.

Hartley, Keith, et al. 1993. *Economic Aspects of Disarmament: Disarmament as an Investment Process*. UNIDIR Report. New York: United Nations.

Hilton, Brian. 1992. *Defence Conversion or Diversification, East and West: An Overview of the Literature and the Arguments*. Management Research Papers, no. 16. Oxford: Templeton College.

Hinterhoff, Eugene. 1959. *Disengagement*. London: Stevens & Sons.

IPRA (International Peace Research Association) Disarmament Study Group. 1980. "Building Confidence in Europe. An Analytical and Action Oriented Study." *Bulletin of Peace Proposals*, vol. 11, no. 2, pp. 1–17.

Kant, Immanuel. [1795] 1968. "Zum ewigen Frieden. Ein Philosophischer Entwurf." In *Kant Werke in 10 Bänden*, ed. Wilhelm Weischedel. Darmstadt: Wissenschaftliche Buchgesellschaft, pp. 195–251.

Köllner, Lutz, and Burkhardt J. Huck, eds. 1990. *Abrüstung und Konversion. Politische Voraussetzungen und wirtschaftliche Folgen in der Bundesrepublik*. Frankfurt: Campus.

Krell, Gert. 1981. "The Development of the Concept of Security." In E. Jahn and Y. Sakamoto, eds., *Elements of World Instability: Armaments, Communication, Food, International Division of Labour. Proceedings of the International Peace Research Association Eighth General Conference*. Frankfurt: Campus Verlag, pp. 238–254.

Krepon, Michael, Dominique M. McCoy, and Matthew C. J. Rudolph, eds. 1993. *A Handbook of Confidence Building Measures for Regional Security*. Washington, D.C.: The Henry L. Stimson Center, September.

Kriesberg, Louis. 1992. *International Conflict Resolution. The U.S.-USSR and Middle-East Cases*. New Haven & London: Yale University Press.

Laurance, Edward J. 1996. *The New Field of Micro-Disarmament: Addressing the Proliferation and Buildup of Small Arms and Light Weapons*. BICC brief 7. Bonn: Bonn International Center for Conversion, September.

Liebert, Wolfgang. 1994. "Verifying R & D Limitations – Relevance for Preventive Arms Control and Nuclear Non-proliferation." In J. Altmann, T. Stock, and J.-P. Stroot, eds., *Verification after the Cold War. Broadening the Process*. Amsterdam: VU University Press, pp. 234–241.

Melman, Seymour. 1970. *Conversion of Industry from a Military to a Civilian Economy*. New York: Praeger.

———— 1988. *The Demilitarized Society: Disarmament and Conversion*. Montreal: Harvest House.

Möller, Björn. 1991. *Resolving the Security Dilemma in Europe. The German Debate on Non-Offensive Defence*. London: Brassey's.

———— 1992. *Common Security and Non-Offensive Defense. A Neorealist Perspective*. Boulder, Colo.: Lynne Rienner; London: UCL Press.

———— 1994. *The Dictionary of Alternative Defence*. Boulder, Colo.: Lynne Rienner.

Osgood, Charles. 1962. *An Alternative to War or Surrender*. Urbana: University of Illinois Press.

Renner, Michael. 1989. *National Security: The Economic and Environmental Dimensions*. Worldwatch Paper, no. 89. Washington, D.C.: World Watch Institute.

———— 1992. *Economic Adjustment after the Cold War: Strategies for Conversion*. Geneva: UNIDIR; Aldershot: Dartmouth.

Richardson, Lewis Fry. 1960a. *The Statistics of Deadly Quarrels*. Pittsburgh: Boxwood Press.

———— 1960b. *Arms and Insecurity*. Chicago: Quadrangle Books.

Rittberger, Volker, ed. 1979. *Abrüstungsplanung in der Bundesrepublik. Aufgaben, Probleme, Perspektiven*. Baden-Baden: Nomos.

Roberts, Adam, and Benedict Kingsbury, eds. 1993. *United Nations, Divided World. The UN's Role in International Relations*. Oxford: Oxford University Press.

Rotblat, Joseph. 1977. *Scientists in the Quest for Peace. A History of the Pugwash Conferences*. Cambridge, Mass.: MIT Press.

Russell, Ruth B. 1958. *A History of the United Nations Charter*. Washington, D.C.: Brookings Institution.

Sandole, Dennis J. D., and Hugo van der Merwe, eds. 1993. *Conflict Resolution Theory and Practice. Integration and Application*. Manchester: Manchester University Press.

Schelling, Thomas C., and Morton H. Halperin. 1961. *Strategy and Arms Control*. Washington, D.C.: Pergamon-Brassey's.

Senghaas, Dieter. 1972. *Rüstung und Militarismus*. Frankfurt: Suhrkamp.

Sommaruga, Cornelio. 1994. "To Contain War's New Horrors." *International Herald Tribune*, 24 February.

Spitzer, Hartwig. 1992. "Constraints on the Technology Contributing to Militarization of Space: The Case of Observation Satellites, GPS and Communication Systems – Technical Considerations." In H. G. Brauch, H. van de Graaf, J. Grin, and W. Smit, eds., *Controlling the Development and Spread of Military Technology*. Amsterdam: VU University Press, pp. 75–84.

Sur, Serge, ed. 1991. *Disarmament Agreements and Negotiations: The Economic Dimension*. Geneva: UNIDIR; Aldershot: Dartmouth.

Thomas, Caroline. 1992. *The Environment of International Relations*. London: Royal Institute of International Affairs.

Trapp, Ralf. 1992. "International Constraints for Chemical Research and Development: The Prospected Chemical Weapons Convention." In H. G. Brauch, H. van de Graaf, J. Grin, and W. Smit, eds., *Controlling the Development and Spread of Military Technology*. Amsterdam: VU University Press, pp. 109–120.

UNIDIR (UN Institute for Disarmament Research). 1987. *Disarmament and Development: Some Practical Suggestions to Bypass the Present Deadlock*. New York: United Nations.

United Nations. 1970. *The United Nations and Disarmament 1945–1970*. New York: United Nations.

——— 1976. *The United Nations and Disarmament 1970–1975*. New York: United Nations.

——— 1987. *International Conference on the Relationship between Disarmament and Development. New York, 24 August – 11 September 1987. Final Document*. New York: United Nations.

——— 1988. *Study on the Economic and Social Consequences of the Arms Race and Military Expenditures*. Disarmament Study Series, no. 15. New York: United Nations.

——— 1991a. *The United Nations Disarmament Yearbook, vol. XVI: 1991*. New York: United Nations.

——— 1991b. *Conversion: Economic Adjustments in an Era of Arms Reduction, Disarmament*. Topical Papers 5, vol. 1. New York: United Nations.

——— 1991c. *Conversion: Economic Adjustments in an Era of Arms Reduction, Disarmament*. Topical Papers 5, vol. 2. New York: United Nations.

———— 1995. *Disarmament in the Last Half Century and Its Future Prospects*. Topical Papers 21. New York: United Nations.

Väyrynen, Raimo. 1992. *Military Industrialization and Economic Development: Theory and Historical Case Studies*. Aldershot: Dartmouth.

Waever, Ole, Barry Buzan, Morton Kelstrup, and Pierre Lemaitre. 1993. *Identity, Migration and the New Security Agenda in Europe*. London: Pinter.

Wallensteen, Peter, and Karin Axell. 1993. "Armed Conflict at the End of the Cold War, 1989–92." *Journal of Peace Research*, vol. 30, no. 3, August, pp. 331–346.

———— 1994. "Conflict Resolution and the End of the Cold War, 1988–93." *Journal of Peace Research*, vol. 31, no. 3, August, pp. 333–350.

Wittner, Lawrence S. 1984. *Rebels against War: The American Peace Movement, 1933–1983*. Philadelphia: Temple University Press.

———— 1993. *One World or None: A History of the World Nuclear Disarmament Movement through 1953, Vol. 1: The Struggle against the Bomb*. Stanford, Calif.: Stanford University Press.

Wright, Steve. 1994. "The Supply of Light Weapons, Repression & Refugees: The Trade in Political Conflicts." Paper for the XVth IPRA Conference in Malta, 29 October – 6 November.

2

Enforcement and humanitarian intervention: Two faces of collective action by the United Nations

Raimo Väyrynen

1. Introduction

The purpose of this chapter is to explore different faces of collective international actions undertaken by the United Nations to serve peace and save human lives. After exploring the conceptual and historical basis of collective security, the chapter contends that actions to enforce it should be separated from more limited humanitarian interventions. Thereafter, the analysis focuses on the requirements of legitimacy and effectiveness in actions to promote collective security and serve humanitarian needs. These two requirements are often in conflict with each other because effectiveness calls for the involvement of great powers, whereas legitimacy benefits from the participation of small states and non-governmental actors. A potential solution to the tension between effectiveness and legitimacy is that collective actions are carried out by a concert of major powers, while the United Nations system is reformed to become a genuine system of collective security.

The founders of the United Nations intended it to "take effective collective measures for the removal of threats to the peace, and for the suppression of acts of aggression or other breaches of the peace" (Art. 1). The determination of the United Nations to suppress aggression and other threats to peace has to be understood in the context of the preceding world war. After having defeated Germany and Japan, the victorious powers were committed to preventing the rise of new challengers to their primacy and security and thus to international stability. The leaders of these powers had fresh in their minds the fact that the League of Nations had been unable to deter the expansionist policies of the Axis powers.

The victors of World War II wanted a charter and an organization that could be used effectively to prevent the recurrence of a similar disaster. The UN Charter explicitly permitted the collective use of force to maintain international peace and security, although it preferred peaceful solutions, "and to bring about by peaceful means, and in conformity with the principles of justice and international law, adjustment or settlement of international disputes" (Art. 1). The use of economic and military force was anchored in the prominent role given to the Security Council and the establishment of the Military Staff Committee to serve as its military arm. In that sense the Charter is permeated by the culture and means of enforcement to maintain international peace.

The principles and practices of collective security are important elements of the policy of enforcement. In the United Nations they were intended to provide the building blocks for the construction of the post-war international system, while the Charter promised instruments by which its stability can be maintained. Naturally, the veto power given to the five permanent members of the Security Council made the enforcement policy selective, in the sense that it could not be used against them or in crises in which they had vital interests at stake. The outbreak and escalation of the Cold War, dividing the permanent members into two competing blocs, meant that virtually all military crises fell into that category.

The abatement of the Cold War has opened new political space for enforcement and, more generally, for collective security. The new international atmosphere permits, at least in principle, a more frequent use of enforcement measures against aggressive and expansionist powers to maintain peace and security. One of the main dilemmas is that the threats to peace do not result from military aggressions carried across state borders. Rather, instability is due to the erosion of national political systems by ethnic and religious factionalism, accumulation of repressive military power, economic failures, environmental degradation, and the delegitimization of political institutions.

These are kinds of problems that the traditional policy of collective security was not intended to manage, because internal troubles belonged to the internal sphere of national sovereignty. However, the needs to restore domestic political stability, support economic reconstruction, and alleviate human suffering have increased and the United Nations has to be able to respond to them. In addition to national efforts, their mitigation often requires external interventions, which, therefore, must be understood in a more differentiated way than before. In a "world of societies" (*Gesellschaftswelt*), both the objectives and the means of intervention differ from those of the Cold War era (Czempiel 1994).

New methods of external intervention are usually discussed under such rubrics as humanitarian intervention, conflict prevention, and peace-making. While requiring an element of enforcement to be effective, these measures often have a broader goal of ensuring the survival of people and order in societies rather than merely establishing a countervailing coalition against an aggressive power. It is this both politically and conceptually difficult relationship between collective security and humanitarian intervention to which most of this chapter is devoted.

2. Principles and problems of collective security

Collective security is a contested concept, especially in political practice. It aims to reduce the unilateral use of military force by states and counter it by the collective use of force by the international community or a coalition of states representing it. Thus, individual interests of states would be replaced by a "solidarist formula," as Hedley Bull calls it. In his definition, "the principle of collective security implies that international order should rest not on a balance of power, but on a preponderance of power wielded by a combination of states acting as the agents of international society as a whole that will deter challenges to the system or deal with them if they occur" (Bull 1977: 238–240).

This definition of collective security has five key elements: the preponderance of power, a combination of states, agents of international society, deterrence, and conflict management. There are two variants of collective security, distinguished by the different degrees of the preponderance of power. The "universal variant" refers to an ideal situation in which all other states coalesce against the aggressor and force it to desist. The "minimum winning coalition" variant appears when the coalition resisting the aggressor is able to aggregate a sufficient capability to defeat it. In both cases the states acting collectively must have a commensurate conception of security and willingness to subordinate their interests to the common good. Hans J. Morgenthau considers these requirements to be tantamount to a "moral revolution" in international relations and, therefore, unlikely (Morgenthau 1964: 412–418).

In the case of a coalition of states, a key issue is that it must represent international society and operate in its name. This requires "established norms of behavior around which a collective security regime can coalesce" and an "appropriate international cooperative framework" facilitating the identification of threats and collective responses to them (Butfoy 1993: 492–493). International norms and a cooperative framework can be established only if states give up, at least temporarily, their sovereign right to the use of force and transfer it to the international community. Therefore, collective security is "a halfway house between the terminal points of international anarchy and world government" (Claude 1971: 246).

Bull's definition of collective security is systematic and comprehensive; yet it begs a number of questions on its nature and principles, which can be summarized as follows.

First, is the preponderance of power based on a permanent international organization that has at its disposal adequate material capabilities or at least an ability to mobilize them, or are the necessary resources pooled together in each case by ad hoc actions of states? To be real, the preponderance of power in a system of collective security has to be based on either permanent or shifting coalitions of states and not on the pre-eminence of a single state; collective security cannot operate in a hegemonic international system. Thus, collective security tends to be decentralized or, if centralized, it has to rely on a workable concert of powers acting in the name of the international community.

Secondly, the establishment of a preponderant coalition of states requires a decision-making process that both is efficient in responding to aggression and commands wide acceptance as a precondition for mutual confidence. The basic questions are thus how different actors are represented in the making of decisions on collective security operations and how the legitimacy of decisions has been assured. That is, in what sense is the coalition an agent of international society in conducting the policy of collective security?

Thirdly, the composition and legitimacy of the political constellation sustaining collective security and the capacity to mobilize and use military force are pivotal for its preventive and deterrent role. The ultimate question is whether or not aggressive powers take the capabilities and readiness of the international coalition seriously enough to give up their policy of expansion. Moreover, one has to realize that collective security provides for a different type of deterrence than that prevailing in bilateral relations. Deterrence relying on collective will and capabilities "purports to establish a portable preponderance, ready to be shifted to the defense of any victim of aggression and capable of making any such victim superior to its adversary" (Claude 1971: 257–258).

Naturally, there is a host of other problems associated with the principles and practices of collective security. For example, one has to determine to what extent a working system of collective security requires the control and reduction of arms. Usually, it is assumed that the strengthening of collective security has to be accompanied by at least some arms reductions, because otherwise aggressive powers might be able to gain military preponderance. Collective security has a deterring effect only if the status quo coalition has capabilities by which the potential aggressor can be defeated beyond doubt.

A critical question is whether or not collective security is at all possible in a world with nuclear weapons. The most likely answer is that it is feasible only if the use of force is confined to conventional weapons. If violence escalates into a nuclear exchange, the basic rationale of a collective response against an attack loses its meaning. Collective security can, however, operate in a nuclear world if mutual deterrence persuades nuclear-weapon powers to refrain from using or threatening to use weapons of mass destruction and there are no threshold countries that seriously develop them as an instrument of global challenge. The more passive the political and military role of nuclear weapons, the more breathing space collective security has.

An important issue is how to define the scope of application of collective security, i.e. whether it is universal or concerns only selected countries. The standard solution is that, ideally at least, collective security should be universal in its scope. Therefore, the relationship of collective security to both military alliances and neutrality has to be resolved because they both challenge the underlying principle of universal impartiality. In fact, the idea of collective security was developed in opposition to the maintenance of international stability by military alliances, which usually have a predesignated source of threat, whereas in the system of collective security the putative enemy should not be designated in advance.

Instead of a single power or a group of powers ganging up against the aggressor, the ideal collective security calls for a universal coalition of states to restore, on the basis of a prior commitment, the status quo threatened by any revisionist power(s); i.e. collective security is "colour-blind." In terms of response, it does not matter where the military threat comes from as long as it is directed against the security and sovereignty of independent states. Then the international community must be ready to act collectively. Threats to national security by a deliberate aggressor must be checked in time if a deterioration in the situation is to be avoided. The guiding idea behind collective security is its impartial and universalistic character. It has to be underpinned with adequate resources and institutional structures available to the international community, and further supported by the determination of its members to honour the obligations.[1]

Many a political realist, believing in the primacy of national interests and military force, scorns the principles of universalism and prior commitment because of their Wilsonian origins. In Woodrow Wilson's own words: "henceforth alliance must not be set up against alliance, understanding against understanding, but there must be a common agreement for a common object."[2] For a political realist, collective security represents merely an evolution from the standard balance-of-power policy to a new method of maintaining international equilibrium. From this perspective, collective security is based on the multilateral aggregation of national power to defend the status quo.

The difference between Wilsonians and realists is not so much in the substance of power but in its form. Realists tend to be sceptical about the feasibility of collective security because states pursue independent foreign policies. In a decentralized international system, obligations are not necessarily honoured and hence the establishment of a winning coalition to counter the threat may not be feasible. Another objection to collective security by the realists is that it can make a volatile situation even worse because joint military operations to defend the status quo may escalate into a general war. On the other hand, liberals and institutionalists argue that shared values, interests, and institutions help to overcome these pitfalls and thus improve collective security (different theoretical approaches are discussed by Bennett and Lepgold 1993).

When political realists speak favourably of collective security, they often have collective defence in mind, i.e. cooperation by a limited coalition of states against an attack directed at anyone of them. Prior commitment to collective security would probably be an anathema to the realists, who regard flexible alliances in a multipolar international system and fixed alliances in a bipolar system as the best guarantee of peace. For realists in general, the commitment to collective security is a tough choice because it implies permanent common interests between states and the indivisibility of peace between major powers.

Is peace, then, indivisible or not? The empirical answer is clearly negative: some threats to peace and security are taken by the majority of states more seriously than the others. This is especially the case when threats arise from internal strife. If there is no direct risk of spillover across national borders, it is very difficult to convince governments that they should intervene early on to avert a humanitarian crisis and the potential collapse of states. It has been suggested in hindsight that decisive preventive action in 1990–1991, relying on both political and coercive means, could have reversed the deterioration of the Yugoslavian crisis. However, neither the United States nor the European states were ready to act (Väyrynen 1996).

3. Humanitarian intervention and collective enforcement

In the post–Cold War era, the notion of collective security has become more complex than ever before (or, alternatively, it has lost much of its previous meaning). Traditionally, theories and policies of collective security have been developed with inter-state wars in mind, whereas collective intervention in civil wars has largely been off limits. If the definition of the nature and seriousness of threats triggering a collective response is politically and legally a difficult task in inter-state wars, it is even more vexing in intra-state crises.

In wars between states, collective security is premised on the principle that violation of the territorial and political integrity of a sovereign state cannot go unpunished. In reality, collective security is primarily intended to protect the security of small states, because its use in a crisis involving a major power could easily lead to an all-out war. To target a collective security operation at a medium power might also lead to escalation, especially if it is allied with a great power. If an international coalition launches such an operation, the goal is usually not only to protect a particular country but also to respond to a military challenge to the very foundations of the international system, i.e. its state-centric character and the principle of national sovereignty.

Leading powers are inclined to manage risks to their national security either unilaterally or by recruiting junior members into an alliance. As a rule, they do not need or want the services of global or regional security organizations since reliance on them would impose constraints on national policies or involve other, adversarial powers in the crisis. For major powers, collective security can be a nuisance unless they are given a significant role in its decision-making and enforcement operations – which they may, on the other hand, be unwilling to assume.

In intra-state wars, the guiding principles of external intervention can be derived from either political realism or humanitarian interests. As a rule, both traditional international law and political realists have accepted intervention in a civil war only if the local government requests offsetting assistance to prevail over rebels supported by another state. On the other hand, humanitarian intervention has traditionally been considered unlawful because it involves neither self-defence (Art. 51) nor enforcement action under Chapter VII of the UN Charter. This interpretation is still in the mainstream, although legal experts are increasingly putting forward new "counter-restrictionist" arguments in favour of the permissibility of such humanitarian intervention (for a discussion, see Arend and Beck 1993: 131–136). However, intervention has been found to be acceptable in extraordinary circumstances in which the international community has been deprived of any other means to ameliorate the situation.

Some authors have submitted that the gradual legal acceptance of humanitarian intervention, calling for the use of military force to protect the victims of violence when less coercive forms of influence have failed, hinges on a paradigmatic shift from state interests (sovereignty) to human interests and international justice. This shift is said to inject a communitarian element into the protection of human rights and security and suggests that humanitarian interventions should primarily be carried out by an international police force rather than by regular military forces (Rosas 1994 and Gillespie 1993).

Humanitarian intervention is usually justified by the need to prevent disproportional loss of life and the collapse of the social and political fabric of a country. Arend and Beck define it as "the use of armed force by a state (or states) to protect citizens of the target state from large-scale human rights violations there" (1993: 113). Moreover, a humanitarian intervention occurs without the explicit consent of the target state (thus distinguishing it from peace-keeping). Pointing out that the role of humanitarian intervention in UN policy is ambiguous, Arend and Beck reach the conclusion that a humanitarian intervention *"per se* cannot be undertaken upon the authorization of the Security Council" (1993: 113–114).

This view is undermined, however, by recent political practices because both the United Nations and regional organizations have increasingly resorted to collective intervention to avert humanitarian emergencies. Thus, the "humanitarian imperative" has prompted the United Nations to undertake both preventive and enforcement actions for humanitarian purposes (Boutros-Ghali 1994: 113–125). Whereas humanitarian interventions in the nineteenth century were mostly unilateral actions to protect a country's own citizens abroad, they are now, as a rule, multilateral and altruistic, trying to rescue the people of the target country from suffering. These changes suggest that shared norms concerning humanitarian intervention are emerging (Finnemore 1995).

This conclusion is in line with the growing opinion that international law permits access to crisis areas in which egregious violation of human rights and other humanitarian imperatives can override domestic jurisdiction. Humanitarian intervention is not a panacea, but it can be an important first step in ending the human suffering. This thinking, however, runs counter to the traditional legal view, which would permit humanitarian intervention only under very restricted conditions. Interestingly, the restrictionist interpretation is in rough agreement with pacifism, which may reject the use of force even for humanitarian purposes (these disagreements are reflected in Lyons and Mastanduno 1995 and Phillips and Cady 1996).

In addition to humanitarian motives, international intervention can be used to prevent the escalation of a domestic dispute into jeopardizing the security of other states. In this case the interpretation of the UN Charter is easier. The possibility of an intra-state crisis spilling over state boundaries can be considered by the Security Council to "endanger the maintenance of international peace and security" (Art. 34) or mean a "threat to the peace, breach of the peace, or act of aggression" (Art. 39), thus justifying resort to the provisions of Chapters VI and VII of the Charter, respectively.

Legally speaking, humanitarian crises seem to "endanger" peace rather than to be a "threat" to it, calling for the use of Chapter VI provisions. Thus, by solving the underlying dispute by peaceful national and international means, the negative effects of a humanitarian crisis can be alleviated. However, neither the complexity of such crises nor various political pressures on governments to act allow enough time to negotiate a political settlement to avert the crisis. The conflict in the former Yugoslavia shows how complex the relationship between humanitarian assistance, conflict resolution, and military enforcement can be (Minear et al. 1994).

A major question is whether the system of collective security should be activated in intra-state crises only when the security of other states is threatened or whether human suffering is enough to launch a military operation to provide relief and save lives. The latter option is chosen when large-scale civil strife, famine, gross violation of human rights, and internal displacement of people are defined as threats to international peace and security and enforcement actions are subsequently initiated under Articles 40–43 of the UN Charter.

These actions range from "provisional measures ... to prevent the aggravation of the situation" to collective non-military and military sanctions. Security Council decisions to create safe havens for the Kurds in Northern Iraq (Resolution 688) and to provide humanitarian relief to Somalia (Resolutions 794 and 814) and various resolutions on the Bosnian situation testify to the readiness of the Council to undertake enforcement operations for humanitarian reasons. In all, in 1988–1994 the Security Council passed a total of 69 resolutions under Chapter VII, usually making a reference to Art. 39 as the basis for action (for a detailed study, see Chiechinski 1995).

N. D. White concludes that this tendency to stress the Charter provision on threats to the peace (Art. 39) is due primarily to the need to find a justification for rapid UN interventions in intra-state conflicts or against terrorism in situations in which the legal basis for action is limited at best. In his view, by stretching the concept of "threat to the peace" to cover such problems, members of the Security Council have developed a new political and legal justification for quick enforcement operations against "rogue" states or to meet humanitarian needs (White 1993: 38–49).

The political requirements of post–Cold War international relations have forced the Council to develop new legal interpretations applicable in humanitarian crises within states. This seems to be more a result of the political need, imposed by public opinion and the media, to be proactive in humanitarian crises than a penchant for the application of Chapter VII as such for interventionist purposes. On the contrary, the practical dilemmas of peace-keeping and enforcement seem to make states more and more wary of sending troops for UN missions in crises that look intractable.

The question of whether a humanitarian intervention can be started without the consent of the target government is contentious.

Article 2(7) of the Charter contains a ban on UN intervention "in matters which are essentially within the domestic jurisdiction of any state," but it also makes an exception in that "this principle shall not prejudice the application of the enforcement measures under Chapter VII." When the enforcement provisions of the Charter are evoked as the basis for intervention, the Security Council acquires a limited legal competence to conduct humanitarian operations without the consent of the target country. There is a major legal difference between peace enforcement and humanitarian intervention. Coercive enforcement is a collective security operation based on Chapter VII. Its task is to eliminate threats to inter-state peace and security or to reverse the aggression by restoring the *status quo ante*. Enforcement measures were used by common agreement against Iraq in 1991–1992 in order to reverse its attack on Kuwait.

Recent humanitarian interventions in Haiti (UNMIH), Rwanda (UNAMIR), and Somalia (UNOSOM) have been authorized on the basis of Chapter VII by the Security Council authorizing a group of states to deploy military forces outside the UN framework. Yet in other cases (Somalia and the former Yugoslavia), the task of enforcement has been entrusted to the Secretary-General or to another international organization, such as NATO. This practice has in some cases created a complicated situation because the outside forces, authorized by the Security Council, have operated alongside the UN forces, whose mandate for peace-keeping, peace-building, and humanitarian relief has been based on Chapter VI. It can be argued that this mixture of peace-keeping and the use of force for enforcement purposes was one of the factors that caused the failure of the international intervention in Somalia (Burci 1996: 257–263).

The carrying-out of humanitarian interventions under Chapter VII runs counter to the traditional interpretation of the Charter, which would consider such interventions to be collective security operations. This is not necessarily the case, however. But at any rate, even if humanitarian intervention relying on the enforcement rationale is considered legally acceptable, the Security Council has a special burden of proof to the international community. Matters are further complicated by the fact that the non-enforcement measures of Chapter VII are not necessarily an exception to Article 2(7) (Gordon 1994).

Conceptually, it is possible to consider the enforcement of collective security and humanitarian intervention as separate categories of international action, even if they are both based on the provisions of Chapter VII. In practice, such a distinction is more complicated, however. Inter-state wars have become less frequent and the collective use of force in them rare. On the other hand, the proliferation of intra-state crises and the deterioration of human conditions in such states have forced the United Nations to mount an increasing number of humanitarian operations, many of which have had a military dimension.

Peaceful means have proved to be inadequate to ensure the delivery of assistance to those in need in crisis areas. Their effectiveness may be stymied by the local armed units whose interests may be threatened by relief operations or who stand to profit from them. Therefore, an enforcement element easily creeps into humanitarian interventions, justifying the use of the Chapter VII mandate. Because the delivery of relief usually has a high moral priority, this "mission creep" of humanitarian interventions is difficult to oppose, although there are disagreements on its advisability (opposing viewpoints are presented in Winters 1995). In Bosnia especially, it became clear that the needs of a UN humanitarian mission can contradict the need to force the parties to refrain from the use of force.

Despite this practical intermingling of collective enforcement and humanitarian intervention, they should be considered separate legal and political categories. Their mixing up with each other clearly has undesirable consequences. For instance, small states, partly because they do not have the necessary military resources, think that the enforcement of collective security is not primarily their task and that major powers should, therefore, carry the main burden. However, if this reasoning is also applied to humanitarian intervention, the major powers would be deprived of advantages that small states could confer on them. For example, the military organizations of small states are probably more flexible than those of major powers and hence can better adjust to local conditions. In addition, small states could more easily develop a rapport with non-governmental organizations (NGOs), without which no humanitarian operation today can be effectively carried out.

It is surprising that recent debates on the relationship between peace and humanitarian intervention have largely overlooked the concept and policy of collective security. It is symptomatic that even *An Agenda for Peace* and its 1995 supplement by the UN Secretary-General barely mention collective security. Instead, Boutros Boutros-Ghali explores various political and military strategies, such as peace-keeping, peace-making, and preventive diplomacy (Boutros-Ghali

1992, 1993; United Nations 1995). This tendency to neglect collective security is not due to the lack of its need, but more to the political difficulties of persuading major powers to create an international order in which a collective response to the use of force would be prompt, effective, and predictable.

In an approach similar to that of the Secretary-General, Adam Roberts and Benedict Kingsbury (1993: 40–48) bypass a detailed analysis of collective security and are content to list various "UN variations of the collective security scheme." They consider peace-keeping, post-conflict peace-building, sanctions, and humanitarian intervention to be such variations. However, in another context Roberts suggests in an interesting way that, instead of being a "general system of international security," collective security should be regarded as a "form of action that is mobilized occasionally – and imperfectly."[3] In his view, the most common use of collective security should be in inter-state, rather than intra-state, relations "in response to especially glaring aggressive actions by military powers of the second rank" (Roberts 1993: 27–28).

Thus, Roberts supports the view that the leading powers have the main responsibility to maintain international security by stemming military challenges by aspiring medium-sized or semi-peripheral powers. Roberts' distinction between collective security as a system and as a form of action, and his choice of the latter, is consistent with Claude's conclusion that "collective security is a specialized instrument of international policy in the sense that it is intended only to forestall the arbitrary and aggressive use of force, not to provide an enforcement mechanism for the whole body of international law." Since the aim of collective security is to prevent the "arbitrary use of force" in a partially disarmed system of states, its maintenance is not expected, as a rule, to "include the large-scale use of force" (Claude 1971: 249 and 260).

Because of its focus on inter-state crises, the contribution of collective security to guide international intervention in intra-state crises is limited. In fact, the policy of collective security should also in the future be used against cross-border aggressions threatening international order and security. Coercive multilateral actions should be decided by the Security Council on the basis of Chapter VII of the UN Charter. They preferably should be conducted by forces serving under the UN flag, but the delegation of enforcement actions to coalitions of states and other international organizations probably cannot be avoided. On the other hand, the starting point of humanitarian intervention should be the use of peaceful, non-coercive, and impartial means to reconcile conflicts, protect human rights, and deliver humanitarian relief. These operations should be based on Chapter VI provisions and the Secretary-General should have primary responsibility for them.[4]

This division of responsibilities is too neat, however. In many cases, humanitarian goals cannot be attained if the international community is not prepared to use limited force to protect civilian lives and the delivery of humanitarian aid. So far, the international community has been incapable of setting up a viable system of multilateral intervention in which limited military force can be used, if needed, to promote humanitarian objectives. Often concern with the implications of violating the national sovereignty of the target country and unilateral calculations of their interests by the intervening countries have been the main obstacles to humanitarian intervention.

To overcome these obstacles, the international community should agree on a set of rules defining the goals, means, and limits of admissible humanitarian interventions. They should also be given realistic mandates in which objectives, resources, and rules of engagement match each other (see also Knudsen 1995 and Mayall 1996). In practice this means that the United Nations should develop a third category of involvement in addition to the peaceful settlement of disputes and the enforcement of collective security.

This category would contain humanitarian interventions using, if necessary, military forces for the "mini-enforcement" of human security. The mandate of such actions should draw upon Chapter VII, but the UN Secretariat would have a stronger role in conducting them than in collective security operations proper. Autonomous, volunteer UN forces would be appropriate for carrying out "mini-enforcement" actions. The idea of "mini-enforcement" shares many features of the British idea of "wider peace-keeping" in which force can be used selectively for self-defence and for tactical, but not strategic, purposes (Ruggie 1996: 99).

4. Problems of (im)partiality

Basic problems in both the enforcement of collective security and humanitarian intervention concern their political complexity and their practical effectiveness. Politics creeps into humanitarian operations in at least two different ways. As explored above, one problem is the reinterpretation of the UN Charter to permit humanitarian interventions under Chapter VII. It creates thorny legal problems, but may be needed to retain the effectiveness of multilateral actions in the new conditions of instability in the peripheries. But even if the motives and means of humanitarian interventions were broadly acceptable, their consequences can be unintended and therefore unpredictable and even undesirable. Thus, in addition to meeting humanitarian needs, interventions can "lead to two quintessentially political tasks: guaranteeing the borders of countries under challenge, and constructing an apparatus of government in places where it is absent" (Mandelbaum 1994: 5).

Neither collective enforcement nor humanitarian intervention can be judged only by legal criteria; they also call for political solutions. Politics links the legitimacy of interventions with the representativeness of the bodies (especially the Security Council) making decisions on them. For instance, by pointing to the predominance of leading Western powers in the Council, parties to a conflict can mobilize local people against it. The anti-UN attitudes of the Bosnian Serbs and the Somali clan leaders are real-world examples of this tendency. Thus, efforts to strengthen the UN role in enforcement operations cannot be separated from reform of the Security Council, although they do not necessarily require it, nor does a reform assure the success of such operations.

In traditional peace-keeping, the legitimacy of UN operations has hinged on impartiality, non-use of force, and the consent of the parties concerned. However, with the increase in the complexity and intensity of intra-state crises, impartiality has become politically more and more difficult. Too strong a commitment to impartiality may also reduce the effectiveness of the multilateral intervention for peace because it may make the international forces impotent. The paralysis may be worsened by a lack of political support and the insufficiency of resources to carry out effective enforcement operations. The failure to enforce peace also gives rise to criticism that the impotence of international agencies permits and even encourages the victimization of certain groups in the conflict area (on Bosnia, see Rieff 1995).

In enforcement missions, impartiality cannot be a main requirement, which makes the broad international acceptance of such missions even more important. According to one view, impartiality should be given up altogether. The aim of enforcement actions is not an abstract peace sought by neutral involvement of the United Nations, but an outcome in which a new political order is established by full-fledged military measures favouring one party over another

(Betts 1994). To be legitimate, such a forceful collective enforcement should enjoy broad acceptance among both governments and international public opinion. This assumption is unrealistic, however, because legitimacy would require that either a well-coordinated concert of powers or a hegemonic power carry out the intervention. A concert is difficult to organize, especially to deal with intra-state crises, while a hegemonic intervention would alienate significant segments of governments and public opinion.[5]

The more partial the UN intervention in relation to the parties of a civil war, the greater the propensity for a local backlash against it. Instead of producing a "a new political order," such an intervention will more often than not deepen the crisis. In addition, the humanitarian mission would obviously suffer from the reactions against it. Moreover, the implementation and results of relief operations can be undermined by the inability and/or unwillingness of national governments, and of the UN itself, to act early on to prevent the outbreak or the escalation of intra-state conflicts into large-scale crises (for more on these problems, see Sahnoun 1994).

Practical experience, resulting from the narrow definition of national interests and the difficulties of coordinating state actions, suggests that collective security would function better if an autonomous, voluntary UN force were established. It would be available at all times and could be promptly dispatched to conflict spots before the local situation had deteriorated beyond repair. Apart from maintaining collective security, such a multilateral intervention could also have humanitarian functions. In a larger context, it would also mean the transformation of a state-based system of collective security in a communitarian direction. In addition to being presumably quick and effective, a voluntary force would also be more legitimate because it represents the international community rather than its individual actors.

However, advocates of an international volunteer force should keep Claude's caveat in mind: "Collective security is much like Marxism, in the sense that its theory has reflected excessive preoccupation with the moment of initiation of decisive action" (Claude 1971: 279). In a multilateral intervention, a quick and decisive *entrée* into the conflict to stop violence is one of its desirable requirements. However, at least as important is the *sortie*, i.e. the way in which intervening parties can exit from their involvement. The Somali experience provides evidence on the importance of managing the *sortie* well (while in Bosnia the jury is still out). Of course, the exit from intervention does not necessarily fail, as the successful examples of Kampuchea and Namibia show.

Although a permanent UN force could be more impartial and legitimate than a coalition of national contingents, there are also reasons for leaving enforcement actions to member states. First, it would be politically difficult to establish and fund an adequate voluntary military force, under international command, to prevail in a local crisis. Secondly, whereas traditional peace-keeping has been distinguished by its impartiality in relation to warring parties, such neutrality is not possible in enforcement actions because they are carried out without the consent of a target country and may require a considerable amount of force.[6]

The bottom line of my argument is that the enforcement of collective security, and even of less ambitious objectives, is both politically and militarily so demanding that its success requires a genuine commitment by major powers to carry it out. Success can be achieved only if the major powers arrive, by mutual consultation, at a common decision to mount and finance an operation effective enough. Even a joint commitment to enforcement does not, of course, solve all practical problems. The establishment of a unified military command and logistical system may be especially difficult, in spite of their central role in a successful operation.

The preference for a multinational rather than an international enforcement force does not mean that the idea of voluntary military units under UN auspices should be discarded altogether. They could be more useful than national contingents of major powers in humanitarian operations in which only limited military force is needed and in which impartiality has its merits. Thus, two different types of international force can be envisaged: (a) an overwhelming military capacity by a multinational coalition for major ad hoc enforcement operations to maintain collective security, and (b) an autonomous UN force for more limited humanitarian interventions, especially in intra-state crises. This arrangement would obviously make the coordination of humanitarian action and its military support easier. Now the use of multinational forces for enforcement may create a need for humanitarian organizations to distance themselves from the users of military forces (Ogata 1996: 125–127).

Because impartial enforcement is a contradiction in terms, one can question whether or not the United Nations should be burdened with the political consequences of establishing an international military force for large-scale enforcement operations. For instance, the military involvement of a UN force in a local crisis could undermine the positive role of the Secretary-General's diplomatic efforts to settle it. Therefore, it might be sensible to maintain and even strengthen the current division of labour between the Security Council and the Secretary-General. A drawback of this solution is that the command of large-scale enforcement operations would in all likelihood be taken outside the United Nations, as happened in the coalition war against Iraq. The Council is in charge of mandating and raising economic and military resources for enforcement operations and bearing political responsibility for them under Chapter VII. On the other hand, the Secretary-General can concentrate on diplomatic mediation under Chapter VI and implementation of the non-enforcement provisions of Chapter VII.[7]

This solution would inevitably mean that the United Nations has to rely on individual member states and their coalitions to carry out enforcement actions in support of collective security. This raises questions about both their legitimacy and their efficacy. To be legitimate, enforcement actions have to be decided by a sufficiently broad array of member states and the troops involved must have a pluralistic political and cultural composition. To be effective, such actions should have a viable system of command and communication and adequate logistical resources. The requirement of effectiveness would, in the present circumstances, dilute the UN role and exclude troops from developing countries, which are usually more poorly trained and equipped than those from industrialized countries.

Claude has argued, primarily with reference to the Uniting for Peace resolution, that collective security can degenerate into collective legitimization. This may happen when operations are conducted in the name of the United Nations by a group of countries that has vested interests in the crisis (Claude 1971: 269–271). For example, some experts have questioned whether the UN-mandated war against Iraq was a genuine collective security operation or rather a coalition war legitimated by the Security Council. Owing to delegation of the use of force, it can hardly be considered a genuine action to uphold collective security, although it was widely supported both in the Security Council and in most national capitals.

The legitimacy of other similar enforcement operations, if they occur, will probably be more contested because the permanent members of the Security Council will be less likely to find a mutual consensus than they were in the Gulf War. This is an important reason to reform the decision-making and organization of UN operations for enforcement and humanitarian purposes to make them more acceptable and in that way more effective. This concerns both of the potential new multinational voluntary UN forces. Moreover, the training of troops from different nations to cooperate with each other and the establishment of a joint and well-coordinated command are for both political and practical reasons immensely difficult tasks (a detailed proposal is made in Whitman and Bartholomew 1994).

5. Collective security and international order

Traditionally, the functioning of collective security has presupposed that a majority of states perceives the threat to international peace and security to be comprehensive and serious. However, this condition may have existed neither during the Cold War, when an ideological consensus was lacking, nor after it, when such a consensus has been difficult to develop. Local violence seldom poses a threat to international peace and security; rather it violates people's basic needs, human rights, and democracy. Therefore, an effective, positive response to humanitarian crises requires both the perception of common security interests and shared moral standards, and the determination of governments to act.

In spite of their strengthening, legal and moral standards have not yet been internalized to the extent that a prompt, consistent, and universal response would follow from their violation in intra-state crises. This observation is consistent with the results of opinion surveys that throughout the post-war years American people have been more ready to accept the use of military force to resist cross-border aggression than to bring about internal changes in other countries (Oneal et al. 1996).

The emphasis on a common ideology as a basis for collective security opens interesting avenues of enquiry; it posits that collective security works best when basic, shared principles and values are in jeopardy. UN intervention in the Korean War was politically skewed, but perhaps this very lopsidedness of the operation was its most vital feature. Although based only on a UN recommendation and not on a binding decision, the intervention was a strong collective response by the United States and other like-minded states to the ideological and military challenge by socialist countries, especially the Soviet Union and China.

In the Korean War two competing ideologies of world order clashed with each other, and the Western one emerged victorious.

The central role attributed in the aggression to Moscow was reflected in the speech to the UN General Assembly on 20 September 1950 by Dean Acheson, who stated squarely that the "root of our trouble is to be found in the new imperialism directed by the leaders of the Soviet Union" (the text is published in Larus 1965: 236–241). A few years later Arnold Wolfers (1954) pointed out that the US-led response in the Korean War was not a collective security operation because it did not signify a departure from "power politics" and a "break with tradition," which to him were prerequisites of collective security. The dominant role of the United States defined the Korean operation as a common defence in disguise, intended to strengthen its coalition against the Soviet Union and its allies, rather than as collective security.

Wolfers observes that up until 1950 the United States had failed to obtain alliance commitments from most Asian countries. The Korean War provided a unique opportunity to expand the anti-communist coalition in the region. Thus, for the United States, "it was of paramount importance that the United Nations be made to serve as a substitute for a formal alliance of the free world." This "could only be done by demonstrating that under the Charter the United States considered itself committed to take up arms against the North Korean aggressor" (Wolfers 1954: 490). In sum, instead of proving that the United Nations is capable of undertaking enforcement operations against the violators of international peace and security, the Korean War showed that, in the absence of consensus among major powers, such operations were unlikely (Ruggie 1996: 55–57).

The war by the coalition forces against Iraq also had ideological underpinnings, even though material factors, such as the concern with oil supplies and the proliferation of weapons of mass destruction, played a major role. The war was perceived by almost all UN members to be a necessary response to Iraq's rampant violation of Kuwaiti sovereignty. The attack threatened the foundations of the traditional, state-based international order. These ideological roots of the war help to explain why most small states supported the collective operation against Iraq even though many of them had qualms about its political merits and ethical aspects of its military conduct.

It is not easy to decide whether the coalition war against Iraq was a true application of the principle of collective security. No doubt, by reversing Iraq's gains and restoring the *status quo ante*, the Gulf operation served the general goals and principles of collective security. However, if Wolfers' criterion of "breaking with tradition" is used as

73

the yardstick, the Gulf War hardly qualifies as a collective security operation. The strong unilateral element in the response hints to the continuation of traditional US policy by other means.

Thus, from a critical perspective one can argue that the Gulf War was a comprehensive collective defence (rather than security) operation legitimated by the Security Council resolutions. However, the Gulf War "broke with tradition" in the sense that some members of the Security Council, especially France and Russia, turned against their previous partner of cooperation, Iraq, and some Arab states also reversed their positions in relation to it. Thus, it may be said that the war against Iraq resembled more of a collective security operation than the Korean War, and also relied more on non-military instruments of enforcement, such as economic sanctions. Sanctions, however, were used not as an independent means to enforce collective security but rather as a prelude to the use of military force.

Another ideological question of obvious relevance for today's situation is Wilson's statement that at the heart of the common object of collective security "must lie the inviolable rights of peoples and of mankind." This can be taken to mean that a system of collective security must defend not only the sovereignty of states but also the rights and security of peoples. If this argument is accepted, then one steps on the borderline between collective security and humanitarian intervention.

To clarify the debate, it is important to define carefully the meaning of a humanitarian intervention. It should be distinguished, for instance, from pre- and post-war peace-building programmes because it is more limited in time and scope and takes place in the context of civil war. Humanitarian intervention helps people in the conflict area by protecting them by external military means against killing, harassment, and displacement as well as providing them with relief to avert starvation and diseases. As a multilateral instrument, humanitarian intervention is said to have enduring political and practical value (Haas 1994: 26–30). At the centre of the humanitarian intervention is the use of military means to attain human and social ends.

6. A concert of powers

Collective security and humanitarian intervention can be pursued by different types and coalitions of actors. Whereas humanitarian intervention may be carried out by a hegemonic power, collective security cannot rely on hegemony. It is even doubtful whether collective security can be managed by a duopoly of powers establishing condominium. In such a system, the leading powers aim to assure international stability not in the name of collective security but to protect their own privileges. Moreover, such an arrangement is historically rare and provides only a scant basis for joint actions because of the tendency of bipolarity to degenerate into mutual confrontation (Liska 1990: 355–356). While the United States and the USSR were unable to agree on some ground rules for their relations during the Cold War, their mutual competition paralysed the Security Council.

As a consequence, during the Cold War the Security Council was never able to implement UN Charter provisions concerning collective security. In addition to their bilateral rivalry, the emergence of China as a global player in the late 1960s also made the US–Soviet management of international relations impossible (Bull 1977: 225–227). The latter development was reflected in the Security Council, where Chinese views had to be taken seriously after Beijing became one of its permanent members in 1973. The erosion of bipolarity since the 1980s has not ensured, however, that an effective system of collective security has emerged to replace it.

Collective security has to be a common enterprise in which several states take part. This is possible if collective security becomes a truly global project either by a rare agreement between most states of consequence to act together or by transferring a significant amount of power and resources to a global organization. This would require, among other things, the establishment of a permanent UN military force to be available at all times for peace-keeping and peace-enforcement missions and the willingness of the major powers to abdicate their right to veto decisions that they do not like. In other words, the United Nations needs to acquire substantial supranational powers if a full-fledged collective security is to be created. Although there may be a need to move in this direction, the realization of this option looks unlikely (this is also the conclusion of Ayoob 1993: 58–59).

The remaining alternative is, then, the establishment of a concert of powers that would be primarily responsible for making decisions and carrying out operations to maintain collective security. A concert can operate only in a multipolar system in which cleavages criss-cross and have a low conflict intensity rather than divide major powers into antagonistic groups. A concert is based on consultation and accommodation of interests, leading to ad hoc joint actions to retain or restore the status quo, rather than binding commitments made by key powers (Liska 1990: 349–350). A concert also presupposes that its members shun the search for unilateral gains to the disadvantage of other members, agree by consensus on any significant changes, and in general feel common responsibility for operating the concert (Holsti 1991: 165–169).

A concert is expected to produce international public goods, such as order and stability, from which all states would benefit; in that sense it is a benevolent arrangement. However, there is also an element of rivalry in every concert of powers. For example, for de Gaulle the European Economic Community, based on the primacy of nation states, was the embodiment of the post-war concert in Europe. He expected the concert both to contain Germany and to prevent the Commission in Brussels from confiscating too much power from national governments (de Gaulle 1994). In the nineteenth-century Concert of Europe, the pervasiveness of the great power concert was tempered by balance-of-power politics and a lack of trust, which prevented one power from operating unilaterally on behalf of all others. The Concert of Europe was based on multiple power centres, which kept the continent fragmented and prevented any power from becoming hegemonic (Watson 1992: 238–242).

A concert is viable only if its members refrain from unilateral territorial, economic, or strategic actions that upset the existing equilibrium and agree on the fundamental principles of international relations. In fact, one of the main purposes of the concert is to prevent such unilateral actions. The effectiveness of a power concert is enhanced by the ideological and structural similarity of participating states, although this is not a necessary precondition for its existence and functioning. There is evidence that an effective policy of collective security does not require unanimity between major powers and that even its imperfect implementation produces positive effects (Cusack and Stoll 1994).

A concert is based on a central coalition of major powers, which must have the minimum winning capacity. Such a coalition is supposed to provide a more stable alternative to both a balance of power and deterrence alone. A concert provides for stability because states outside it are either unable to establish a countervailing coalition or consider it to be unnecessary. Recently, it has been stressed, though not agreed upon, that in the post–Cold War world a concert of powers is both politically necessary and feasible. It is a cheaper arrangement to manage inter-state relations than either deterrence or a balance of power, both of which tend to stimulate military build-ups. Furthermore, as a loose structural arrangement of power, a concert is compatible with the emerging multipolarity of international relations (Rosecrance 1992; Kupchan and Kupchan 1991).

If the establishment of a strong global organization for managing a consistent and effective collective security policy is impossible, the concert of powers remains as the only available option. This view is adopted, among others, by the Kupchans, who submit that the concert "represents the most attenuated form of collective security" in which its membership is restricted to major powers (Kupchan and Kupchan 1991: 120). Kegley and Raymond consider a concert of powers as a half-way house between various specialized relationships between states (alignment, entente, and condominium) and a full-fledged system of collective security (Kegley and Raymond 1994: 151–162).

Although the concert may be able to provide the public good of collective security, it also has its disadvantages, including a lack of equity and democracy. The concert is, by definition, an arrangement steered by major powers, which maintain their mutually consensual relations. This curtails the autonomy and influence of middle and especially small powers in international relations and may even permit interventions in their internal affairs.[8] Small states have to make a judgement on whether they value the putative stability provided by a concert more than their national political autonomy, however limited. This is a classical trade-off between security and autonomy with which both allied and non-allied states have been wrestling.

The dilemma of small states can be partially resolved by recalling the earlier distinction between military enforcement and humanitarian intervention. Stability maintained by a hegemonic power does not necessarily mean collective security, while such a power may carry out unilateral interventions. In a duopoly of power, neither of these two forms of enforcement is likely, especially if they cross the boundaries of influence spheres. In a duopoly, deterrence and balance of power rather than collective security are the names of the game, while humanitarian involvement easily deteriorates into a power-motivated intervention. In a bipolar arrangement, small states are not permitted and seldom want to become involved in conflicts overlaid by great power interests.

The concert system approaches the ideal of collective security, although it does not quite reach it; its establishment is hampered by justified doubts about the loss of national sovereignty and the dominance of great powers. On the other hand, the coordinative and consultative mechanism of a multipolar concert makes it possible for small states to participate in protective and relief operations to help the victims of violent conflicts. Together with the cooperation between major powers, this is one reason humanitarian intervention is more likely in a concert than in a duopolistic system. Owing to the limited resources of small states, the humanitarian responsibility falls mostly upon major powers; in fact, their ability to do so under the UN Charter is a measure of whether the concert works or not.

It would, however, be unwise to give a strong and specific mandate for major powers to be in charge of more limited humanitarian interventions as well. Such a mandate could degenerate into a manipulative system in which the leading powers, instead of protecting human needs and interests, mould the politics in crisis-ridden states to their own liking. The normative goals of a humanitarian intervention require that smaller states and non-governmental organizations have a meaningful role. Therefore, a concert of powers should be kept accountable to the international community and its power and policies should be collectively shaped. On the other hand, the community has an interest in the concert's continued operation, which ceases when one or more of its members differ significantly with others. At that point, the central coalition may disintegrate and international security deteriorate. Those who lament undemocratic features of a concert, should balance their criticism against the consequences of the potential deepening of global and regional instability.

If relations between major powers become riddled with political tensions and arms races, there is little safety for small states. Avoidance of this risk requires a two-track policy in which the concert would be responsible for preventing and reversing the most flagrant actions violating peace, while at the same time a genuinely multilateral system of security is strengthened. This policy should be accompanied by a legitimate doctrine and workable practice of humanitarian intervention to ameliorate social and human conditions in wars that cannot be prevented.

7. The Security Council

International relations lack an adequate theory of representation. This deficiency is becoming increasingly clear now that the international structure and the organization of the United Nations, inherited from 1945, are diverging from each other. The ensuing crisis of representation has prompted two kinds of proposals to enhance the democracy of the United Nations. One advocates the restructuring of the Security Council to correspond better to the present international distribution of power. Another proposes the establishment of a people's assembly alongside the General Assembly. Efforts to restructure the Security Council follow the state-based logic, while plans to enhance the voice of people in the United Nations reach out to international civil society and non-governmental actors.[9] An interesting effort to involve NGOs in the work of the Security Council was made in February 1997 when Oxfam, CARE, and Médecins Sans Frontières were invited to brief the Council informally on the humanitarian crisis in the Great Lakes Region of Africa. The institutionalization of such consultations would greatly enhance the timeliness and relevance of knowledge available to Council members on the crisis regions of the world.

I will focus my remarks here on the structure of the Security Council as the key forum for decision-making on security issues. One reason for the revival of interest in the Security Council is the perception that its role has become more central again. In fact, Ernst B. Haas has shown that during the second half of the 1980s both the share of international disputes referred to the United Nations and its success rate increased, and this tendency seems to have continued in the 1990s. At the same time, major regional organizations have been unable to increase their relevance and effectiveness in conflict resolution (Haas 1994: 64–67, 77–78).

The Security Council is pivotal in considering the existence and operation of a concert of powers in international relations. Coral Bell even suggests that the Council's ability to pass and implement resolutions on collective security is a key criterion for the existence of a concert: "the new activism of the Security Council is in itself *prima facie* evidence of that concert of powers" (Bell 1993: 111). Bell also argues that without such a concert the Council cannot work effectively. In her view the Security Council is "a machine that would run only on one special fuel: a concert of powers." Her formulation clarifies another point: the Security Council and a concert should not be equated with each other. A concert is a mechanism to coordinate policies, whereas the Council is a legal and political institution that may become a forum for consultations.

The current composition of the Security Council leaves much to be desired if the effectiveness of collective security is used as the yardstick. Although Western powers are overrepresented among the permanent members, the Council also bridges, at least in principle, two important gaps in international relations, that between the Western powers and Russia on the one hand and that between China and others on the other. Thus the Security Council creates a modicum of criss-crossing at the top echelons of international relations.

In the present structure of the Council, the United Kingdom, France, and the United States have borne the main responsibility for organizing multilateral operations, either within the UN framework or outside it. The effectiveness of the Western coalition has left much to be desired, though. The United States in particular has been unwilling to commit itself fully to multilateral actions because it fears entrapment after having been spurned in Somalia. On the other hand, the United States has become involved when it has not had any other option or when it has been able to advance its own political agenda. The US "intervasion" into Haiti is a clear-cut example how, under a Security Council mandate (Res. 940), multilateral interests in peace and democracy can be combined with the promotion of US interests in the "enlargement of democracy" and regional stability.

The United States has also been at odds with France, each suspecting the other of promoting primarily its own interests in various multilateral operations. There is little doubt that France has had its own agenda in Iraq, Rwanda, and, to a lesser degree, Bosnia. In Iraq, the French government wants to ease the containment strategy relying on sanctions and inspections, partly because French companies want to renegotiate oil and other sweetheart deals they made with the Baghdad regime before the war. In Rwanda, the French government showed fortitude in July 1994 by sending in *Opération Turquoise* troops under the Security Council mandate to protect civilians from genocide. On the other hand, the operation had an element of self-interest because it protected the supporters of the previous Hutu government. In Bosnia, the French have adopted a more flexible attitude towards the local Serbs than have other Western powers.

The present composition of the Security Council provides two bridges between the Western core and others centres of power. They bring Russia and China into the potential concert in the Security Council. Until 1994, Russia cooperated with the Western powers in the multilateral effort to manage and resolve new intra-state conflicts. Since then, however, it has taken a more independent course in dealing with local conflicts. For instance, Moscow worked hard and successfully to persuade Baghdad to recognize the borders of Kuwait and used this move as an argument to ease sanctions against Iraq.

This effort ultimately failed because of Iraq's decision to start redeploying troops near the Kuwaiti border.

In the name of Slavic solidarity, Russia has sought to improve its relations with Serbia, which has considered its peace-keepers to be more evenhanded than those coming from NATO or even non-aligned countries. In the former Soviet Union, Russia has started rebuilding its own empire by pushing for economic union, by engaging in joint patrolling of its outer borders, and by insisting on a *droit de regard* in the internal affairs of now independent former Soviet republics. There are Russian troops and bases in Georgia, Moldova, and Tajikistan, and Russia has intervened on both sides in the civil war in Nakorno-Karabakh between Armenia and Azerbaijan.

In his speech to the UN General Assembly in October 1994, President Yeltsin proclaimed a doctrine that "the main peacekeeping burden in the territory of the former Soviet Union lies upon the Russian Federation." Although Western powers are unwilling to give such a licence to Russia, it is likely to continue its interventionist policies, especially in areas where it senses a challenge from Afghanistan, China, Iran, or Turkey. Russian peace-keeping efforts in Nagorno-Karabakh and Abkhasia have been formally approved by the Confederation of Independent States, but in reality they are, both logistically and politically, Russian operations (Kreikmeyer and Zagorski 1994).

China has taken a principled stance against economic sanctions, war crime tribunals, and other external efforts to dilute the principles of sovereignty and non-interference in the internal affairs of states. On the other hand, as long as China's own interests have not been threatened, it has not opposed efforts at collective enforcement by the other permanent members of the Security Council. There seems to be, however, a strong unilateral streak in China's policy in terms of both continuing its military build-up and promoting its strategic interests in East and South-East Asia. There are few, if any, signs that it is planning to give up this policy of national regional interests.

In sum, the concert that emerged in the Security Council in the early 1990s will not necessarily last. First, all permanent members of the Council, except perhaps for the United Kingdom, are opting for unilateral policies within the multilateral framework or even outside it. This unilateralism has gone so far that new speculation has started on the establishment of spheres of influence in the Balkans, Caucasia, and Central Asia. The US role in protecting Haitian democracy is not regarded by France and Russia only as a disinterested action to restore democracy, but, partly for their own tactical reasons, they see it as a regional action that justifies comparable policies by France in Africa and Russia in the former Soviet Union. Thus, the concert of powers in the Security Council could deteriorate into consensual spheres-of-influence agreements permitting permanent members to promote their unilateral interests in different regions. The concert may also cease to exist altogether as a consequence of Chinese and Russian refusal to cooperate with the Western powers in enforcement operations, the US withdrawal from collective responsibilities, and the continued bickering within NATO.

Could these problems be remedied by bringing in new permanent members to the Security Council? To a degree, yes. German and Japanese membership would possibly bring new economic resources to collective security operations. With the weakening of domestic constraints on their participation in such operations, these countries might also make more tangible political and even military contributions. German and Japanese membership would not, however, eliminate the rifts that exist at the moment among the Western powers, China, and Russia. These tensions might none the less be alleviated by Germany's economic clout in Russia and by a more active Japanese participation adding a new restraint on unilateral features of China's policy.

Brazil and India, supposing that they would be the other new permanent members of the Security Council, could weaken rather than strengthen a potential concert. India, in particular, is known to pursue rather stubbornly its own political and military interests, including the acquisition of nuclear weapons. Permanent membership in the Security Council might not alter the basic orientation of India's external policy, but it would involve it in a novel way and expand the political basis of the Council. If committed to multilateral solutions, India could significantly help to resolve intra- and inter-state conflicts in South Asia. Provided that their economic growth becomes sustained, both Brazil and India could increase their financial contributions to the United Nations. It has also been submitted that permanent membership in the Security Council would diversify the international relations of new members and in that way increase their sense of regional responsibilities (Bell 1993).

8. Conclusions

This chapter is based on the premise that the United Nations would best serve the interests of international security if the Charter system of collective security were put in practice. So far, this has not happened, however. The United Nations does not have adequate logistical and military capabilities of its own to maintain collective security, and it is unlikely to acquire them in the foreseeable future. Therefore, the mounting of a strong collective response requires US political and military leadership, with which other permanent members must acquiesce. It is clear that the United States prefers to operate a "coalition of the willing" outside the UN framework, although authorized by it. In the US view, this is the only way to get rid of the operational and control-and-command problems besetting UN operations. The conclusion is inescapable that traditional collective security operations can only be decided by the Security Council and carried out, by common agreement, under US leadership.

The situation is quite different in humanitarian interventions. Their main purpose is to protect human life and rights, and to deliver humanitarian relief by the means needed for the operation (for detailed discussion, see Minear and Weiss 1995 and Roberts 1996). Depending on the nature of the crisis, humanitarian aims may be achieved in agreement with the local parties to the conflict. The "humanitarian space" is respected by the parties and minor violations can be managed impartially by peace-keeping forces deployed on the basis of a mutual consent. The situation may prove so complex, however, that traditional peace-keeping is inadequate to control the situation and an element of enforcement is needed.

Today, the main problem of the United Nations is that there is neither a clear legal basis nor a generally accepted doctrine for humanitarian interventions in civil wars. Chapter VII of the Charter has proved to be flexible enough to permit them, but at the same time its provisions have been stretched to the limits. In particular, the trade-offs between military enforcement operations and the delivery of relief, visible in Bosnia and Somalia, have turned out to be most problematic. Therefore, the world community needs a new, long-term, and comprehensive doctrine of humanitarian interventions and a new multifaceted international mechanism to carry them out (see also Ruggie 1996: 93–103).

Such a doctrine and mechanism can be best created by accepting that the enforcement of peace and human security in civil wars is a legitimate task of the United Nations. The defence of national sovereignty should not be an obstacle to a humanitarian intervention if there is a broad consensus that it should be launched. The requirement of such a consensus is, of course, a major qualification, because the international community has an unfortunate tendency to drag its feet and become involved too late in a crisis. If consensus exists, however, the operation should be started to make sure that peace can be restored and relief provided to suffering people.

The use of peaceful means should, of course, have priority, but often they are not enough. Limited military force, selectively used, may be needed to protect civilians and deliver aid. In other words, a humanitarian intervention may require "mini-enforcement" to accomplish its aims and avoid a situation in which the peace-keepers and relief workers become hostages of local warlords. It is conceivable that mini-enforcement can be handled by national contingents of a multinational force, as happened, to a degree, in Bosnia. It would be preferable, however, for the United Nations to have a permanent, voluntary force that can make sure that the humanitarian goals of an intervention can be achieved. Such a force would be independent of member states, although its mandate should probably be decided by the Security Council and its operations supported by a Military Staff Committee. Such an arrangement would be in the service of humanitarian aims.

Economic and other functional sanctions are also an instrument of collective security deserving closer scrutiny. On the one hand, economic sanctions are a moderately effective, non-violent alternative to military enforcement actions against the sources of threats and instability. On the other hand, the effectiveness of material punishments has been questioned and the use of positive economic inducements has been recommended instead. It has also been queried whether or not the human toll of economic sanctions in target countries and their adverse effects on third countries are too high to justify their recurrent application. Obviously, the time has come for a new political synthesis of the advantages and disadvantages of economic sanctions.

Acknowledgements

I am grateful to Jürgen Dedring (City University of New York) and William DeMars (American University of Cairo) for useful comments on an earlier version of the paper.

Notes

1. Many of these issues are listed in Roberts and Kingsbury (1993: 38–39) and discussed in greater detail in Roberts (1993).

2. This quotation, as well as other citations to follow, originate from a compilation of documents edited by Finkelstein and Finkelstein (1966). For another useful historical documentary collection on collective security, see Larus (1965).
3. An almost similar conclusion is offered by Inis L. Claude, Jr.: "Multilateral resistance to aggression will continue to be, as it always has been, selective, unpredictable, and, therefore, unreliable" (Claude 1996: 290).
4. A similar division of labour between the Security Council and the Secretary-General in enforcement operations and the peaceful resolution of disputes has been advocated by Picco (1994) and Claude (1996).
5. Betts (1994) does not address the problem of legitimacy, but speaks repeatedly of the United States *or* the United Nations as potential agents of intervention. Betts' emphasis on *"or"* can be construed as a reference to the US reluctance to intervene, when the United Nations (minus the United States) is supposed to carry out the enforcement measures. His neglect of this problem makes his recommendations exhortatory rather than analytical. Moreover, Betts pays hardly any attention to the tensions between the nature and impact of US and UN interventions, especially if they are partial by nature.
6. For a typology of different types of collective security operations based on the degree of consent and the amount of force, see Durch (1993: 4–7).
7. This policy of "strength in separate roles" has been advocated, among others, by Picco (1994). A positive assessment of the strong role of the Security Council in peace-keeping and enforcement is also provided by Weiss (1994).
8. See Bull (1977: 297–301). On the other hand, a concert and collective security are regarded as better than a balance of power because they contain a consultation mechanism, which is absent in the balancing system (Kegley and Raymond 1994: 162–163).
9. The restructuring of the Security Council is discussed, among others, by Wallensteen (1994) and Sutterlin (1994). The need to enhance the role of non-governmental forces within the United Nations is explored in Archibugi (1993) and Alger (1994).

References

Alger, Chadwick. 1994. "Citizens and the UN System in a Changing World." In Yoshikazu Sakamoto, ed., *Global Transformation: Challenges to the State System*. Tokyo: United Nations University Press, pp. 301–329.

Archibugi, Daniel. 1993. "The Reform of the UN and Cosmopolitan Democracy: A Critical View." *Journal of Peace Research*, vol. 30, no. 3, pp. 301–315.

Arend, Anthony Clark, and Robert J. Beck. 1993. *International Law and the Use of Force*. London: Routledge.

Ayoob, Mohammed. 1993. "Squaring the Circle: Collective Security in a System of States." In Thomas G. Weiss, ed., *Collective Security in a Changing World*. Boulder, Colo.: Lynne Rienner, pp. 45–62.

Bell, Coral. 1993. "Future Hypothesis: A Concert of Powers?" In Richard Leaver and James L. Richardson, eds., *Charting the Post-Cold War Order*. Boulder, Colo.: Westview, pp. 110–120.

Bennett, Andrew, and Joseph Lepgold. 1993. "Reinventing Collective Security after the Cold War and Gulf Conflict." *Political Science Quarterly*, vol. 108, no. 2, pp. 213–237.

Betts, Richard K. 1994. "The Delusion of Impartial Intervention." *Foreign Affairs*, vol. 73, no. 6, pp. 20–33.

Boutros-Ghali, Boutros. 1992. *An Agenda for Peace*. New York: United Nations.

———— 1993. "An Agenda for Peace: One Year Later." *Orbis*, vol. 37, no. 3, pp. 323–332.

———— 1994. *Building Peace and Development: Annual Report on the Works of the Organization*. New York: United Nations.

Bull, Hedley. 1977. *The Anarchical Society: A Study of Order in World Politics*. New York: Columbia University Press.

Burci, Gian Luca. 1996. "United Nations Peacekeeping Operations in Situations of International Conflict." In Mortimer Sellers, ed., *The New World Order: Sovereignty, Human Rights, and the Self-Determination of Peoples*. Oxford: Berg, pp. 237–272.

Butfoy, Andrew. 1993. "Themes within the Collective Security Idea." *Journal of Strategic Studies*, vol. 16, no. 4, pp. 490–510.

Chiechinski, Jerzy. 1995. "Enforcement Measures under Chapter VII of the U.N. Charter: U.N. Practice after the Cold War." Paper prepared for the 36th Annual Convention of the International Studies Association, Chicago, 21–25 February.

Claude, Inis L., Jr. 1971. *Swords into Plowshares: The Problems and Progress of International Organization*, 4th edn. New York: Random House.

———— 1996. "Peace and Security: Prospective Roles for the Two United Nations ." *Global Governance*, vol. 2, no. 3, pp. 289–298.

Cusack, Thomas R., and Richard J. Stoll. 1994. "Collective Security and State Survival in the Interstate System." *International Studies Quarterly*, vol. 38, no. 1, pp. 33–59.

Czempiel, Ernst-Otto. 1994. "Die Intervention. Politische Notwendigkeit und strategische Möglichkeiten." *Politische Vierteljahreschrift*, vol. 35, no. 3, pp. 402–422.

Durch, William J. 1993. "Introduction." In William J. Durch, ed., *The Evolution of UN Peacekeeping: Case Studies and Comparative Analysis*. New York: St. Martin's Press, pp. 1–14.

Finkelstein, Marina S., and Lawrence S. Finkelstein, eds. 1966. *Collective Security*. San Francisco: Chandler Publishing Co.

Finnemore, Martha. 1995. "Changing Patterns of Military Intervention." Paper prepared for the 36th Annual Convention of the International Studies Association, Chicago, 21–25 February.

Gaulle, Charles de. 1994. "A Concert of European States." In Brent F. Nelsen and Alexander C.-G. Stubb, eds., *The European Union: Readings on the Theory and Practice of European Integration*. Boulder, Colo.: Lynne Rienner, pp. 25–41.

Gillespie, Thomas R. 1993. "Unwanted Responsibility: Humanitarian Military Intervention to Advance Human Rights." *Peace and Change*, vol. 18, no. 3, pp. 219–246.

Gordon, Ruth. 1994. "Article 2(7) Revisited: The Post-Cold War Security Council." In Abiodun Williams et al., *Article 2(7) Revisited*. Providence, R.I.: The Academic Council on the United Nations System, Reports and Papers, No. 5, pp. 21–36.

Haas, Richard N. 1994. "Military Force: A User's Guide." *Foreign Policy*, no. 96, pp. 21–37.

Holsti, Kalevi J. 1991. *Peace and War: Armed Conflicts and International Order 1648–1989*. Cambridge: Cambridge University Press.

Kegley, Charles W., Jr., and Gregory Raymond. 1994. *A Multipolar Peace? Great-Power Politics in the Twenty-First Century*. New York: St. Martin's Press.

Knudsen, Tonny Brems. 1995. *Sovereignty under Pressure: Humanitarian Intervention in the Post-Cold War World*. Aarhus: Department of Political Science, Aarhus University.

Kreikmeyer, Anna, and Andrei V. Zagorski. 1994. "The Mechanism and Capacity of the CIS in Peacekeeping." Paper presented at the conference on Peacekeeping and the Role of Russia in Eurasia, Swedish Institute of International Relations, Stockholm, 14–15 October.

Kupchan, Charles A., and Clifford A. Kupchan. 1991. "Concerts, Collective Security, and the Future of Europe." *International Security*, vol. 16, no. 1, pp. 114–161.

Larus, Joel. 1965. *From Collective Security to Preventive Diplomacy*. New York: John Wiley.

Liska, George. 1990. *The Ways of Power: Pattern and Meaning in World Politics*. Oxford: Basil Blackwell.

Lyons, Gene M., and Michael Mastanduno, eds. 1995. *Beyond Westphalia: State Sovereignty and International Intervention*. Baltimore, Md.: Johns Hopkins University Press.

Mandelbaum, Michael. 1994. "The Reluctance to Intervene." *Foreign Policy*, no. 95, pp. 3–18.

Mayall, James. 1996. "Introduction." In James Mayall, ed., *The New Interventionism 1991–1994. United Nations Experience in Cambodia, Former Yugoslavia and Somalia*. Cambridge: Cambridge University Press, pp. 1–24.

Minear, Larry, and Thomas G. Weiss. 1995. *Mercy under Fire: War and the Global Humanitarian Community*. Boulder, Colo.: Westview Press.

Minear, Larry, et al. 1994. *Humanitarian Action in the Former Yugoslavia: The U.N.'s Role 1991–93*. Thomas J. Watson Institute for International Studies, Occasional Paper No. 18. Providence, R.I.: Brown University.

Morgenthau, Hans J. 1964. *Politics among Nations: The Struggle for Power and Peace*, 3rd edn. New York: Alfred A. Knopf.

Ogata, Sadako. 1996. "The Interface of Peacekeeping and Humanitarian Action." In Daniel Warner, ed., *New Dimensions of Peacekeeping*. Dordrecht: Martinus Nijhoff, pp. 119–127.

Oneal, John R., Brad Lian, and James H. Joyner, Jr. 1996. "Are the American People 'Pretty Prudent'?: Public Responses to U.S. Uses of Force, 1950–88." *International Studies Quarterly*, vol. 40, no. 2, pp. 261–280.

Phillips, Robert L., and Duane L. Cady. 1996. *Humanitarian Intervention: Just War vs. Pacifism*. Lanham, Md.: Rowman & Littlefield.

Picco, Giandomenico. 1994. "The U.N. and Use of Force: Leave the Secretary-General out of It." *Foreign Affairs*, vol. 73, no. 5, pp. 14–18.

Rieff, David. 1995. *Slaughterhouse: Bosnia and the Failure of the West*. New York: Simon & Schuster.

Roberts, Adam. 1993. "The United Nations and International Security." *Survival*, vol. 35, no. 2, pp. 23–26.

——— 1996. "Humanitarian Action in War. Aid, Protection and Impartiality in a Policy Vacuum." Adephi Paper, No. 305. London: International Institute of Strategic Studies.

Roberts, Adam, and Benedict Kingsbury. 1993. *Presiding over a Divided World: Changing UN Roles, 1945–1993*. Boulder, Colo.: Lynne Rienner.

Rosas, Allan. 1994. "Towards Some International Law and Order." *Journal of Peace Research*, vol. 31, no. 2, pp. 129–135.

Rosecrance, Richard. 1992. "A New Concert of Powers." *Foreign Affairs*, vol. 71, no. 2, pp. 64–82.

Ruggie, John Gerard. 1996. *Winning the Peace: America and World Order in the New Era*. New York: Columbia University Press.

Sahnoun, Mohamed. 1994. *Somalia: The Missed Opportunities*. Washington, D.C.: United States Institute of Peace Press.

Sutterlin, James S. 1994. "United Nations Decisionmaking: Future Initiatives for the Security Council and the Secretary-General." In Thomas G. Weiss, ed., *Collective Security in a Changing World*. Boulder, Colo.: Lynne Rienner, pp. 121–138.

United Nations. 1995. *Supplement to An Agenda for Peace*. United Nations, General Assembly, Fiftieth Session, A/50/60, 3 January 1995.

Väyrynen, Raimo. 1996. "Preventive Action: Failure in Yugoslavia." *International Peacekeeping*, vol. 3, no. 4, pp. 23–44.

Wallensteen, Peter. 1994. "Representing the World: A Security Council for the 21st Century." *Security Dialogue*, vol. 25, no. 1, pp. 63–75.

Watson, Adam. 1992. *The Evolution of International Society: A Comparative Historical Analysis*. London: Routledge.

Weiss, Thomas G. 1994. "Intervention: Whither the United Nations." *Washington Quarterly*, vol. 17, no. 1.

White, N. D. 1993. *Keeping the Peace: The United Nations and the Maintenance of International Peace and Security*. Manchester: Manchester University Press.

Whitman, Jim, and Ian Bartholomew. 1994. "Collective Control of UN Peace Support Operations: A Policy Proposal." *Security Dialogue*, vol. 25, no. 1, pp. 77–92.

Winters, Paul A., ed. 1995. *Interventionism*. San Diego: Greenhaven Press.

Wolfers, Arnold. 1954. "Collective Security and the War in Korea." *Yale Review*, vol. 43, no. 4, pp. 482–496.

3

Enhancing United Nations peace-keeping

Robert C. Johansen

1. Introduction

By the end of the 1980s, governments and publics throughout the world began to call increasingly upon United Nations peace-keepers to protect innocent victims of military aggression and to rescue those perishing from starvation and gross violation of human rights. Yet no sooner had a new surge of hopeful requests for Blue Helmets reached New York than a loud chorus of criticisms arose from those who felt the United Nations was doing too little too late in places such as Somalia, Bosnia, the Sudan, Angola, and Rwanda. More quietly, many UN members refused to provide the human and financial resources needed to enable peace-keepers and humanitarian workers to fulfil the mandates that the Security Council had authorized or that seemed required by alarming outbreaks of violence. This was most graphically illustrated by the Security Council decision to *withdraw* all but 270 of 1,700 UN peace-keepers in Rwanda as genocidal massacres began to erupt and spread in April 1994.[1]

Many governments have complained that UN peace-keeping needs reforms, which is true, yet these complaints often have come from the same member governments that have repeatedly hampered the United Nations' optimal functioning within its existing institutional structure and that continue refusing to pay the costs of reform. In short, new demands for UN peace operations have been quickly followed by disappointments in the United Nations' capacity to keep the peace and protect innocent victims of gross violations of human rights. These disappointments occurred because (a) UN peace-keepers were given assignments in violent contexts for which the classic UN peace-keeping formula was inappropriate and (b) no international political leadership emerged and no consensus formed to construct a global strategy of peace capable of drawing together the separate interests of diverse UN members. As a result, governments chose not to provide the material, political, and moral resources required to enable the United Nations to succeed in peace-keeping and enforcement.

For the United Nations to succeed in future peace-keeping requires a clearer understanding of what the contributions of peace-keeping have been and how they might be enhanced. To increase political support for implementing improvements in peace-keeping, UN members will need to discuss and then commit themselves to a sustained global strategy of peace. Such a commitment and strategy are essential for drawing divergent national interests together around a broader human interest in peace and security. In order to lay a few building blocks in the foundation for such a global strategy of peace, this chapter examines the role of peace-keeping as one part of such an overall strategy. The purposes of this chapter are, first, to discuss how to measure the success of UN peace-keeping operations so their utility is not misjudged, secondly to survey past contributions and problems of peace-keeping in order to facilitate wise support for its strengths, and thirdly to recommend ways to improve its future functioning by overcoming some of its past difficulties. A brief discussion of the origins and distinguishing features of peace-keeping will preface the discussion of these three topics. It should be clear at the outset that this chapter focuses on UN peace-keeping.[2] Evaluation of enforcement[3] and collective security[4] measures under Chapter VII of the Charter are discussed by Raimo Väyrynen in chapter 2 of this volume.

2. The origins and distinguishing features of peace-keeping

Although peace-keeping has become widely known as one of the United Nations' most significant contributions to the maintenance of peace and security, the Charter does not mention it, nor did the United Nations' founders anticipate it, even though they wrote scarcely a dozen years before peace-keeping's advent. The peace-keeping instrument, now so widely known and used, illustrates well the elasticity of the UN Charter when implemented by imaginative statespeople and scholars. Peace-keeping is correctly understood as a major creative invention. It is a reminder that far more can be done to implement new norms and institutions, even without Charter revisions, than is commonly acknowledged. Peace-keeping emerged almost unexpectedly through the imaginative midwifery of Secretary-General Dag Hammarskjold and his key aid, Andrew Cordier, after the stillbirth of collective security functions induced by the seemingly frozen adversarial relations between Moscow and Washington during the Cold War.

Moreover, peace-keeping reminds us that, important though the end of the Cold War may be, many significant innovations occurred long before the US–Soviet military and ideological rivalry ended. Blossoming in the 1950s, peace-keeping emerged from social forces that are no less profound than those commonly seen as bringing the end of the Cold War: the assertion of peoples' rights of self-determination and the delegitimation of colonial empires after World War II. As an instrument for keeping peace in third world contexts where the two superpowers hesitated to intervene directly but did want to keep the other one out, peace-keeping arose more from issues between North and South, most of which still remain, rather than from East–West conflicts that have now dissipated. The advent of peace-keeping should keep progressive faith alive even during times of discouraging inertia in international relations, because it demonstrates that, even in the face of daunting constraints such as the Cold War, it is possible to break through what is commonly seen as the unchanging, tradition-bound fabric of international relations.

Of course the creative innovation of peace-keeping did not just happen. Its origins lay in a much longer tradition, nurtured over time by many imaginative policy makers, scholars, and peace movement organizations, with roots in the experiments with multinational auspices for international forces during the League of Nations.[5] Peace activists in the inter-war period, many of whom did not live long enough to see the fruits of their labours, in turn stood on the shoulders of those who earlier had built the Hague system, the first international public unions, and even the Concert of Europe.[6]

From these origins, classic peace-keeping arose to become fundamentally different from conventional military combat, whether under national or UN auspices. Although peace-keeping forces normally include military as well as civilian personnel, they usually engage in non-fighting field operations to maintain peace in an area of potentially violent conflict. They implement cease-fire agreements, facilitate the withdrawal of forces, and monitor tense borders to prevent incidents from flaring into violent combat. Peace-keepers are distinguished by:

- carrying only light arms (Blue Helmets) or none at all (Blue Berets),
- operating only with the consent of the government(s) ruling the territory where they are deployed,
- maintaining strict neutrality amidst conflicting national claims regarding the disputes that threaten the peace, and
- firing weapons only as a last resort in self-defence.

In addition, peace-keeping forces are:

- created from contingents voluntarily contributed by national governments drawing upon their own national armed forces,
- placed under UN commanders often of a nationality different from the national identity of the peace-keepers in the field, and
- financed by ad hoc arrangements relying upon voluntary contributions or legally binding assessments not unlike the allocations of the regular UN budget.

More recently, peace-keepers have been invited to play roles that go far beyond the classic functions of monitoring a cease-fire, ranging from certifying that elections are fair (El Salvador, Namibia, Nicaragua) to administering governmental ministries during a transition from internal war to a newly constituted national government (Cambodia). These new functions, as recorded in the appendix, illustrate further innovation and are sufficiently different from classic peace-keeping to justify a different label of "expanded" or "comprehensive" peace-keeping. The following functions indicate a range of contemporary peace-keeping tasks that now goes far beyond the minimal task of monitoring borders or buffer zones: uncovering facts that if left in dispute will threaten the peace; verifying military disengagements or force reductions or demobilizations; monitoring cantonment of military forces and equipment; maintaining internal security conditions essential to the conduct of elections; verifying the fairness of elections; temporary or transitional administering of government ministries; repatriating refugees; providing humanitarian assistance to refugees; protecting UN personnel and humanitarian relief workers in societies without effective central authority; fielding committees of reconciliation to promote community education for reconciliation and to restore social infrastructure; and monitoring economic sanctions. Despite the growing number of functions, most remain within the classic peace-keeping formula of not using force offensively and of relying on the consent of local authorities to cooperate with the UN mandate. If the host government is unwilling or unable to give meaningful consent and approval to the UN mission, the situation begins to approximate enforcement under Chapter VII of the Charter rather than peace-keeping under "Chapter Six-and-a-half."

Chapter VII explicitly condones the threat or use of large-scale military force to resist aggression. In contrast to this military mode of collective security enforcement, peace-keepers are soldiers without an enemy. They usually are not deployed to fight against an identified aggressor. Although conceptually peace-keeping differs sharply from military enforcement under Chapter VII, in Somalia and Bosnia the two activities blended in field operations. Many consider Operation Desert Storm, which ousted Iraqis from Kuwait, as an example of enforcement, although perhaps extreme in its destructiveness and dubious in its failure to follow Charter provisions for Security Council oversight of military operations. Desert Storm was not conducted by forces put under UN command through Article 43 agreements as anticipated by the writers of the Charter.

The disinclination of peace-keepers to mount a UN fighting force that is superior to an aggressor does not mean peace-keepers are powerless. On the contrary, their power lies in contributing to an atmosphere and a set of practical facts on the ground that discourage adversaries from thinking that war is a preferable option to a UN-facilitated peace. Their powers are psychological and symbolic, as well as political and policing. When deployed effectively, these powers are usually able to maintain peace at a much lower cost than military power can. Because peace-keepers frequently can be outgunned by the disputants whom they are sent to monitor, in one sense they are similar to police operating in a domestic society: both can succeed only with the support or acquiescence of most of the established order and the surrounding population.

For this reason the international and local legitimacy of peace-keepers is more important to their success than are their arms. The same relative utilities exist in domestic law enforcement. If municipal police need to call in the armed forces, something is wrong in the governance of that society. Underlying social problems and cleavages are not being addressed, with a resulting alienation of large segments of the population. In such a context, the real problem is not that the police have insufficient weaponry, it is that the society has lost its normal quality of being governable as a civil society. Such a situation is more akin to war than to the kind of law enforcement of which UN peace-keepers are capable, as illustrated by the positive role they have played in Cyprus since 1964. In contrast, if an enforcement context seems to require great military power, it is because local and global social problems are not being addressed. To counter these problems, a long-term emphasis on UN preventive diplomacy,[7] preventive development,[8] and peace-building[9] to overcome injustices and encourage cooperation should be part of the global peace strategy that can enable peace-keeping to succeed.

Recognition that military power cannot readily solve social problems in places such as Somalia, Rwanda, and Haiti suggests caution about rushing to the conclusion that the United Nations' failures in dealing with tough peace-keeping in recent years can be solved by simply providing more military muscle and shifting from a peace-keeping (or police) enforcement mode to a military enforcement mode. A more prudent strategy would be to alleviate the underlying causes of violence, to identify the contributions of peace-keeping, and to find ways to build upon its past successes while drawing upon them to shape enforcement actions that may sometimes be required.

3. Evaluating peace-keeping

Explicit standards are necessary for conducting a careful assessment of the contributions of peacekeeping. Many observers tend to form judgements based on the belief that the utility of peace-keeping operations can be adequately evaluated by observing whether peace-keepers are successful in (a) preventing armed conflict or genocide and (b) promoting conflict resolution. Paul Diehl, for example, argues that the first criterion "for judging the success of peacekeeping operations is their ability to deter or prevent violent conflict in the area of deployment."[10] Of course peace-keepers do attempt to prevent violence where they patrol, but it is not sensible to extend this limited goal to the point of holding them responsible for preventing war in general between belligerents. Unless we attempt to distinguish between violence attributable to the shortcomings of the peace-keeping operation itself and violence resulting from other causes, we are not making a useful assessment of the contributions of peace-keeping. If one does not make that distinction, peace-keepers are devalued by any violence that erupts even if it is not caused by peace-keepers' failings.[11] The United Nations Emergency Force (UNEF I) in the Sinai peninsula from 1956 to 1967 can be judged as a successful operation even though war erupted between Israel and Egypt in 1967, immediately after Egypt asked the United Nations to withdraw UNEF I from its territory. Before the outbreak of war, UNEF I monitored the longest period of peace in the Middle East since the founding of Israel. Thus we must reject a facile criterion of war prohibition as an adequate measure of the benefits of peace-keeping.

A parallel problem arises from an analytic error rooted in the belief that a second criterion "on which to judge the success of peacekeeping is its ability to facilitate the resolution of the disagreements underlying the conflict."[12] This criterion also asks more of peace-keeping forces than reasonably can be expected. They usually are not designed for the purpose of resolving underlying conflicts, nor are they authorized to arbitrate disputes. Moreover, even if scholars intend to evaluate peace-keepers on their ability to resolve conflict, in practice their focus often slips from examining the extent to which peace-keepers facilitate conflict resolution to judging peace-keepers on the basis of whether adversarial countries actually resolve their conflicts. This is quite a different matter, over which peace-keepers usually have little or no control. With such an approach, observers measure not so much the United Nations' ability to facilitate conflict resolution as the adversaries' willingness (or unwillingness) to be facilitated. The UN operation in Cyprus (UNICYP), for example, is sometimes criticized for being unsuccessful because Greek and Turkish Cypriots have not settled their disputes despite 30 years of UNICYP's presence.[13] Yet, if judged by a different standard, the UN force in Cyprus has been an outstanding success because year after year it continues to dampen violent conflict. Despite complaints that UN peace-keeping operations are costly because they are difficult to terminate, UN members have repeatedly renewed UNICYP's mandate because it has played a vital role in keeping peace. Similarly, the local people living in the areas of southern Lebanon served by the United Nations Interim Force in Lebanon (UNIFIL) approve of its presence, despite its enormous difficulties and limited effectiveness, because their lives are more secure with UNIFIL than they would be without it.

Scholars, journalists, and politicians should no longer measure peace-keeping against an ideal state of peace (e.g. no armed conflict or no ethnic cleansing after deployment) or against an ideal form of conflict resolution (e.g. settlement of longstanding animosities). Both of these commonly employed criteria miss much of what is important about peace-keeping. They do not focus attention on the nature of the conflicts, the responsibility of the adversaries for continuing the conflicts and the peace-keeping costs, the responsibility of the surrounding world community for using preventive diplomacy, peace-building, and other options to dampen conflict, or on the broader contributions of peace-keepers. Yet these factors are central to understanding peace-keeping realities. The war-prohibition and conflict-resolution criteria are inadequate and misleading.

A third error in evaluation is to blame peace-keepers for larger UN failures, or for the failures of UN members.[14] As some critics have pointed out, surely the United Nations may be judged to have failed in preventing ethnic cleansing in Bosnia and holding Serbia accountable to prohibitions against aggressive use of force. However, this UN failure is due to the Security Council's habit of operating as an instrument of the geopolitical interests of dominant states and should not be misunderstood as a failure of peace-keeping. UN observers need to exercise care to avoid being drawn inadvertently into the great powers' scapegoating the United Nations for ineffectiveness while depriving it of the wherewithal to be effective.

To assess the utility of peace-keeping more fairly, observers should examine the effect of peace-keeping forces on local people who are affected by their work and compare the degree of misunderstanding, tension, deprivation, or violence that occurs in the presence of UN peace-keepers with the estimated results of balance-of-power diplomatic activity without peace-keeping. Observers should try to judge whether peace-keeping operations increase understanding or at least the credibility of information needed for monitoring, reduce the likelihood of violence for local people even by a modest degree or for a limited time, discourage incidents from escalating, make violence less bloody when it does occur, or postpone a seemingly "inevitable" recurrence of conflict long enough to give diplomacy a further opportunity to succeed, even if in the end it fails to prevent war completely.

In addition, evaluation of peace-keeping operations should include an appreciation of the extent to which peace-keeping precedents and successes may in the long run "teach" politicians and publics how to build a new code of international conduct based on the enforcement of global norms by increasingly authoritative and democratic multi-national agencies of the UN system attempting to represent all countries. Because such a teaching function can change global political culture, its benefits can be as important for peace-keeping and enforcement in the long run as security-enhancing functions are in the short run. The benefits of this UN teaching function should be compared in their consequences with the consequences of the negative teaching that would result from relying on traditional national military policies.

4. The contributions of peace-keeping

By these standards, peace-keeping has been remarkably successful. Indeed, despite a chronic shortage of funding, uncertain political support, and an inability to stop hostile military action, UN peace-keeping has almost always improved the lot of the people on the ground in conflict zones. One reason for this is that the UN forces do not normally engage in combat, so they cannot do great harm to local people. They also provide impartial eyes and ears for the world community.[15] Merely by being on the spot they often stabilize a situation and discourage violations of human rights or of a cease-fire agreement.

Of course UN forces in Bosnia did not succeed in discouraging genocide and ethnic cleansing. In addition, the presence and vulnerability of UN forces in Bosnia made them function as hostages in the hands of the morally unscrupulous. Concern for their safety discouraged military action by NATO against Serbian forces because the latter threatened retaliation against UN forces if air-strikes were launched against Serbian heavy guns. Croatian forces also claimed that the UN presence at cease-fire lines between them and Serbians prevented Croatian counter-attacks against Serbian forces that could enable them to re-capture land Serbians took from Croatians. In these cases UN peace-keepers were accused of doing nothing forceful against aggression and of standing between aggressors and those who would counter aggression, acting as a buffer that protects earlier aggression.

Even in these extremely difficult circumstances where UN peace-keepers have been deployed amidst hostile forces with superior fire-power, it is not clear that the most severe charges against UN peace-keeping are warranted. Although it is correct that UN officials in the region and the governments contributing troops to UN forces there discouraged NATO air-strikes against Serbians, it is not clear that violence overall would have been reduced or justice increased if UN forces had been withdrawn. In most cases, their withdrawal would probably have led to even further ethnic cleansing and an escalation of military combat. Indeed, Bosnian leaders in September 1994 decided not to press for a lifting of the UN arms embargo against them because of fear that an intensification of fighting might lead to a withdrawal of UN forces – an outcome the less well-armed Bosnians did not desire. Moreover, one should remember that peace-keepers were never deployed with the expectation that they could dominate the scene militarily to stop aggression or genocide. Thus, despite the peace-keepers' precarious situation and difficulties in the face of hostile fire, the decision to keep them there may have contributed to dampening of violent conflict. Peace-keepers also facilitated the provision of humanitarian aid, but they were often not successful in shepherding such aid through hostile lines. In any case, the Bosnian context, and to some extent the Somalia operation, also represented situations more appropriate for Chapter VII enforcement than for classic peace-keeping because the hosts either reneged on earlier consent to the UN presence or could not provide sufficient order for UN peace-keepers to act most effectively.

Despite the ambiguity of cases that are a blend of peace-keeping and enforcement, or, more accurately, that attempt to use the means of peace-keeping to achieve the ends of enforcement, they illustrate further some of the positive contributions that peace-keeping can make, even in extremely trying circumstances. Failure of UN peace-keepers to end violence should not lead one to jump mindlessly to the conclusion that they contribute nothing to dampening violence or that their presence adds to the overall violence. Only careful, case-by-case study based on an overall assessment can justify such conclusions.

Because peace-keeping has developed in response to a wide variety of conflicts, it has taken so many forms that it defies easy categorization. The functions of UN peace-keeping forces summarized below provide a basis for suggestions that would enhance peace-keeping. In examining these functions, it may be helpful to recall that a single peace-keeping function, such as monitoring national military deployments adjacent to a demilitarized buffer zone between two adversaries, might be carried out in a variety of modes in different political contexts. The Blue Helmets and the Blue Berets, for exam-

ple, may conduct similar functions in two different contexts but carry dissimilar armament. Peace-keeping functions range across several continua:
– non-violent to violent actions;
– unarmed forces to heavily armed forces;
– deployment with the consent of all parties, to the consent of one party, to the absence of meaningful consent;
– low-cost to high-cost assignments;
– small-sized, single-function forces to large, complicated forces;
– forces composed of civilian monitoring experts, to those composed of police personnel, to well-armed military forces;
– forces with a modest degree of internationalization to extensive internationalization;
– diffuse command and control exercised by contributing states to centralized control in the hands of the Secretary-General; and
– operations resulting in negative precedents and political learning to positive learning.

One of the most valuable and cost-effective peace-keeping functions has been performed by unarmed forces deployed as authoritative observers and monitors. This might be considered the first category of peace-keepers' contributions because it was chronologically the earliest and exists logically on a continuum moving from non-violent to violent action. In addition to providing the most peace-keeping bang for the scarce peace-keeping buck, this category is also the least controversial and therefore the most widely supported and politically feasible form of peace-keeping. For these reasons, it deserves high priority as an activity that might be strengthened and used more widely in the future.

Lightly armed peace-keepers have also performed a wide range of tasks with a high degree of success. Because arms are used only in self-defence, peace-keepers have often enjoyed good relations with local populations and achieved a high degree of legitimacy and support throughout the international community. This traditional form of peace-keeping therefore also deserves high priority for enhancement to deal with a wide range of security needs in both inter-state and intra-state conflicts. When civilian or military observers succeed in their missions, it is because they are armed with: the political will of the international community; the moral authority of the observers and of the community-established norms being implemented; the symbolic transformation of a conflict situation from one where war is considered normal to one where non-war is expected; and the responsiveness of the parties being monitored.

5. The problems of peace-keeping

The main difficulties encountered by peace-keeping emerge from its ad hoc nature. To be strengthened, the best features of peace-keeping need to be institutionalized to encourage the utilization of past knowledge and experience and to extend good precedents judiciously into new domains. This process simply cannot proceed without increased political and financial support. Eight problems need to be addressed.[16]

Insufficient force size

In many cases peace-keepers have been handicapped because they have not had sufficient numbers to do their tasks well. In Namibia, for example, violence broke out during the effort to demobilize fighting forces because there were insufficient numbers of peace-keepers to provide security for those who felt fearful and threatened. Shortages were faced by UN peace-keepers in Angola, Bosnia, Burundi, Cambodia, Georgia, Rwanda, and Somalia. If the lightly armed peace-keepers were deployed in sufficient numbers, heavier armament and the willingness to engage in offensive combat would often not be needed.

Inability to respond rapidly

Because there are no permanent UN peace-keeping forces, the United Nations is incapable of responding rapidly in a crisis. Preventive deployments, such as would have been helpful in Iraq in 1990 and Rwanda in 1994, are extremely difficult if not impossible. Delays that allow blood to be spilled make subsequent efforts to arrange a cease-fire difficult and often unattainable. Successful preventive diplomacy in Macedonia illustrates the deterring possibilities of a "trip-wire" UN presence.

Lack of staying power

Some UN forces have had their effectiveness compromised by the threat or actual withdrawal of contingents contributed by member nations. Miserly contributions to or precipitous withdrawals from UN operations have forced the compromise of peace-keeping functions in Angola, Bosnia, Cambodia, Croatia, and Somalia. These demonstrate that peace-keepers sometimes should remain on job longer than countries contributing forces may be willing to accept.

Uneven training

Training is now carried out by the contributing national governments, producing highly uneven results. Most national units are not well integrated with or trained to act together with forces from other regions of the world. In Somalia, loss of life increased and political support eroded because nationally separate forces had not been trained well for a coordinated response to emergencies.

Uncertain command

Relying on ad hoc forces has caused difficulties for UN commanders in exercising control over national contingents. Often in Somalia, for example, peace-keeping units waited for orders from their own national commanders before deciding whether to follow UN orders. As long as UN forces rely entirely on contingents contributed from member nations, the contributors may exercise excessive control over the UN forces, whether in a major operation such as Desert Storm where the United States command acted unilaterally or in a Somali context where Washington simply set a deadline for its forces to leave regardless of whether the tasks were completed.

Unreliable and inadequate financing

No obstacle to the effective functioning of UN peace-keepers is greater than the ad hoc nature of financing for UN forces, resulting in chronic shortages of money to pay for well-trained, well-equipped, and adequately sized peace-keeping forces. There has not been a unified UN peace-keeping budget nor has there been regular, permanent budget authority to pay for peace-keeping. Even when assessments for peace-keeping are legally binding, members often pay late or pay only part of their assessments.[17] The UN force in Rwanda, for example, was delayed for several weeks while tens of thousands were slaughtered because of lengthy negotiations growing out of US insistence that Washington be reimbursed for trucks it loaned to the

101

UN operation. The United Nations not only has lacked ready forces; it has lacked money to contract for ad hoc forces when needed.

Inadequate UN staff

As late as 1992 a UN staff of only 15 people administered tens of thousands of peace-keepers in more than a dozen locations. Subsequent expansion to 50 personnel is still not adequate to stay on top of the demanding tasks they face around the clock.[18]

Diffusion of cumulative learning

When useful peace-keeping precedents occur, it is easy for them to be forgotten or simply not followed again because ad hoc forces must be created anew whenever the Security Council defines a new mandate. Political and financial support also lack continuity and routinization because the forces themselves are ad hoc.

UN peace-keeping could be enhanced by taking institutional initiatives to address each of these eight areas of current difficulty. None of the following suggestions takes up the question of when UN forces should depart from peace-keeping in order to undertake enforcement that may involve combat under Chapter VII. Instead, the following proposals emphasize the possibility for making peace-keeping itself more effective. This in turn should make military enforcement less necessary. Moreover, many of the following initiatives, if implemented, would be assets not only in peace-keeping but also in enforcement when it may be needed.

These recommendations for the next generation of UN peace-making institutions illustrate the design of an overall strategy of peace – a strategy that is urgently needed to address the preceding problems and to enable the United Nations to play a more forceful role in upholding fundamental norms of peace[19] without increasing its reliance on violence to do so.

6. Expanding peace-keeping assets with preventive diplomacy, peace-building, and unarmed peace teams

The Security Council should take preventive diplomacy much more seriously than it has in the past so that there will be less need to deploy peace-keepers in highly violence-prone contexts. Effective preventive diplomacy not only can make peace-keeping less necessary; it also can make peace-keeping more successful when it is required. Skilled mediation and efforts at conflict resolution before a conflict erupts into violence will enable peace-keepers to conduct their work far more effectively than has been possible in the former Yugoslavia, for example, once blood has been shed. More intense preventive diplomacy has been needed for conflicts in Angola, Burundi, India, Liberia, Nigeria, Rwanda, Sri Lanka, the Sudan, several former Soviet republics, and the former Yugoslavia.

To make preventive diplomacy more effective, the Security Council and the Secretary-General need better communication and negotiation capabilities and an extensive early warning system. The Security Council should authorize the Secretary-General to employ more roving ambassadors to meet with those involved in festering conflicts. In addition, the Council and Secretary-General should establish standing conflict-resolution committees in each major region of the world. A United Nations Institute for Mediation and Dispute Resolution,[20] emphasizing early efforts at conflict resolution, should be established to mediate conflicts and provide seasoned expertise to the regional committees.

Secondly, the United Nations should establish an International Monitoring Agency to integrate diverse monitoring functions and bring the weight of the entire world community behind the effort to ensure compliance with the norms of peace, Security Council or World Court decisions rendered to settle disputes, future arms constraints, environmental standards, and other rules as these are established. Such an agency could utilize surveillance by high-altitude aircraft, satellites, and other means. In addition to monitoring arms agreements, such an agency could help UN monitors deter clandestine tests of missiles or warheads, observe cease-fire lines and UN-mandated economic sanctions, discourage illegal shipments of technology or infiltration of arms across borders, and hamper covert operations to manipulate elections or political events in small countries.

Thirdly, to counter the one-sided, fear-inspiring, inflammatory reports that people in regions of conflict often receive and the appeal to bigotry by unscrupulous political leaders bent on increasing their own political power even if it leads to ethnic cleansing, the United Nations should develop its own electronic information and education programmes aimed at reconciliation, broadcast around the world on its own radio or TV network.

An extensive peace-building programme could help ease many of the conditions that make peace-keeping difficult. Genocide in Rwanda and Burundi, for example, has been exacerbated by desperate economic conditions. The United Nations' most influential members could launch a global peace-building programme through a restructured Economic and Social Council or a new UN agency and along with cooperation from the World Bank and International Monetary Fund. Such a programme could provide economic benefits for governments attempting to lower their military spending and demilitarize their societies, develop equitable economic integration as a conflict-dampening instrument poised against both intra-state and inter-state violence, and nurture democratic institutions.

Armed UN peace-keeping could also benefit from an expansion of unarmed peace teams, organized by citizens' organizations and religious groups. As Elise Boulding and Jan Oberg spell out in chapter 4, unarmed peace teams, if well trained, efficiently organized, recruited in sufficient numbers, and wisely deployed, may carry out many potentially far-reaching functions in reconciliation, deterrence, protection, and policing.

In considering expansion of peace-keeping assets, exponents of more effective peace-keeping should always keep in mind that peace-keeping has many different modalities (the range has been indicated above). These often must be kept distinct in organization and application, but they can complement one another in field operations. As Boulding and Oberg indicate, there is enormous room for expansion and mindful experimentation in the domain of conflict mitigation. If well utilized, non-governmental peace teams could go far in relieving some of the conditions that have placed peace-keepers in their bloodiest quandaries.

7. Raising revenues for peace-keeping

A new source of financing for peace-keeping is required if it is to become more effective. The most promising proposal is to impose a tax on the roughly US$900 billion of international currency exchanges that occur *each day*.[21] These transactions are carefully recorded by banking institutions, which are already regulated by government authorities and therefore easily taxable. Each institution involved in currency exchanges could simply be required to deposit in a separate UN bank account a small fraction of each transaction at the moment it occurs. The tax would not be regressive because people who are relatively poor and do not use currency exchanges would not be taxed. Revenues would be drawn proportionally from the role that each currency plays in the world economy. A tiny 0.01 per cent tax would produce roughly US$28 billion annually, enough to finance all UN peace-keeping operations and assist in subsidizing some preventive diplomacy and peace-building operations proposed above as well.

Other sources of revenue that could be drawn from the international assets of modern life should also be exploited to defray the costs of peace-building and peace-keeping because they could provide a good return in generating political support for a global peace strategy. For example, appropriate UN agencies might study ways of renting "parking space" to national satellite systems in order to help finance the proposed UN monitoring agency.

To institutionalize more fiscal responsibility, the United Nations should establish a single peace-keeping fund to pay all peace-keeping costs. Until the proposed tax on currency exchanges or alternative financing arrangements are established, revenues for this fund should be raised through regular UN assessments. Any defaulting country should lose its vote in all UN proceedings and be required to pay interest on its overdue payments, just as governments frequently require their own citizens to do.

8. Strengthening UN forces for peace-keeping

Upgrading the Department of Peace-keeping Operations

The world community needs larger and better-prepared peace-keeping forces to enable the United Nations to meet the rising demand for its services. Toward this end, the Security Council should ensure that the Department of Peace-keeping Operations in the Secretary-General's office does not remain understaffed and short of resources. The Secretary-General should strengthen the Department's capacity for pre-deployment planning, general field support, secure communications, and command and control of peace-keepers in the field.

Establishing permanent UN forces

To be prepared for future peace-keeping needs, the Security Council should establish a permanent, individually recruited UN police or constabulary force.[22] Such a force is needed to overcome problems arising from delays that occur in deploying ad hoc forces, from fears that ad hoc UN forces will not be impartial or effective, from difficulties in recruiting and deploying ad hoc forces for hazardous duty, and from attempting to integrate nationally diverse forces under a unified UN command.

What is proposed here would differ from past UN forces not only in being permanent, but also in consisting of individually recruited persons drawn from volunteers among many countries rather than contingents sent from various national military forces. It could start as a small force of 10,000–20,000 personnel, but it could grow to ten times that size if demands for UN peace-keeping continue to rise.[23] In more contexts than are generally recognized, UN personnel could contribute more to dampening violence by increasing the number of skilled UN personnel for monitoring duty than by increasing the fire-power of the arms they carry, in part because peace-keepers' heaviest "armament" is their legitimacy and presence with symbolic authority, their power to expose misdeeds, and the political and economic clout of the world community backing them up. To nurture a healthy culture of compliance and enforcement, the proposed force probably should emulate a highly effective transnational police or constabulary force rather than an international army prepared to conduct large operations such as Desert Storm.

The proposed UN force would have the following merits: rapid deployment, reliability and effectiveness, impartiality, equitable burden-sharing, ease of coordination among UN agencies, ability to address inter-state and intra-state conflicts, and "teaching" effectiveness.

Rapid deployment
As the Iraqi invasion of Kuwait in 1990 demonstrated, the United Nations has been handicapped in its reliance on ad hoc UN peace-keeping forces because the Secretary-General cannot dispatch forces to a trouble spot immediately. If a standing UN force had existed in July 1990, it could have been moved to the Kuwaiti border before the Iraqis invaded. Faced with UN peace-keepers on his border, Saddam Hussein might have been more acutely aware that an attack against Kuwait could provoke a severe international response. At the very least, a preventive deployment of UN forces could have bought more time for diplomacy. To take a second example, it seems likely that, if a permanent UN force had been available when massacres began in Rwanda in April 1994, rapid deployment of such a force could probably have saved tens of thousands of lives by protecting safe havens to which multitudes might have fled until the fighting ceased.

Reliability and effectiveness

A permanent force could be better trained in the unusually demanding, intricate tasks of international peace-keeping and enforcement. It could be fielded with a high degree of reliability and sensitivity to ways of discouraging collective violence among people of different ethnic and religious traditions. UN political authorities would also be more certain of their ability to exercise necessary and efficient control over the use of the force,[24] a quality clearly lacking during UN operations in Somalia and occasionally in Bosnia.

When US forces were pinned down at one point during fighting in Somalia in 1993, for example, nearby relief was available to help but was delayed for nine hours because of a fragmented command structure, previous lack of cooperative training among units of different nationalities, and poor preparation to deploy quickly.[25] With an integrated, permanent force, 18 US and scores of Somali deaths might have been avoided. Moreover, the resulting erosion of US public support, which has had a lasting impact on US policies toward UN peace-keeping, would have been less likely.[26] In addition, had a permanent, well-trained force existed and been deployed for duty, it is likely that it could have been commanded with more impartiality and skill, and with less of a combative operational doctrine.[27] It possibly would not even have become engaged in a military attack on one of the Somali warlords, thereby involving itself in a partisan role that many Somalis resented and saw as a factional or an anti-Somali intervention rather than a pro-Somali enforcement operation.[28]

In addition, a permanent UN constabulary could be deployed more readily and rationally, with more ability to remain in place until it was no longer needed if it were not subject to nationally partisan political pressures that often have made governments reluctant to contribute national military contingents to UN duty.

Impartiality

If a UN constabulary were individually recruited and loyal to the United Nations, states asking for UN forces would no longer need to worry that the force would be unduly influenced by a contributing state or prematurely forced to disband because of politically induced withdrawals by contributing governments before the UN force had completed its work. Such problems have now arisen in more than a half dozen instances with ad hoc forces.

Equitable burden-sharing

Direct recruitment of UN forces from among individual volunteers drawn from many countries would enable personnel burdens to be shared more fairly than at present. Individual Japanese and German citizens, for example, could serve in UN forces without wrenching political battles at home or revising existing constitutional principles. Moreover, those peoples who have suffered from German and Japanese militarism in the past would not fear individuals recruited from those countries if they were integrated into units trained and commanded by the United Nations. Individual recruitment might also enable US citizens to serve under UN command, a condition that Congress and existing public opinion have not been willing to allow. US citizens could have volunteered to help defend safe havens in Bosnia or Rwanda in 1993–1994, for example, even though those assignments were considered too dangerous for the US armed forces to accept as long as the goal was "merely" to protect innocent civilians rather than to serve narrower US national interests.

Ease of coordination among UN agencies

A skilled, permanent constabulary would enable the United Nations to integrate its own policies more effectively. It is often necessary for diverse agencies such as UNICEF, the High Commissioner for Refugees, the Human Rights Commission, UN negotiators and mediators, and the Department of Peace-keeping Operations to work simultaneously in the same crisis. If these agencies also need to coordinate their work with several national military contingents, the task is overwhelming.[29] Occasionally during Bosnian operations in 1993–1994, UN policy was pulled in a cautious direction by the British and French, who had troops on the ground, and in a quite different direction by Washington officials who were prepared to launch airstrikes because the United States had no ground forces in Bosnia to be threatened by an escalation of the warfare. To make matters more complicated, occasionally in Bosnia the United Nations faced trade-offs between defending those being victimized by a war-making élite and obtaining concessions from the victimizing élite to arrange a cease-fire. Having its own seasoned forces would make such delicate operations more likely to succeed.

Ability to address inter-state and intra-state conflicts

Even in its infancy, a permanent force could help perform traditional peace-keeping functions more reliably than have ad hoc peace-keeping forces in dampening border incidents and small-scale aggression by militarily adventurous states. A standing UN force would also enable the idea of "UN-protected countries"[30] to become a realistic possibility. Small countries could feel some reassurance if UN forces were always ready to come to their aid in time of need. Unable to protect themselves militarily against larger, determined aggressors anyway, UN-protected countries would be able to relieve themselves of the financial burden of maintaining their own armed forces.[31] They also would be freed of the danger that their own military people might threaten democracy, or the prospects for it, at home. As the UN role in maintaining security for small states increased, the temptation for external military powers to intervene would decline; incentives for international arms sales, foreign bases, and the projection of military power abroad would also decrease.

Moreover, a UN peace-keeping constabulary often could be more effective than existing national and ad hoc UN forces in dampening intra-state conflicts and in preventing them from being exacerbated by external forces. The idea of UN-protected states might be extended to intra-state enforcement in which UN peace-keeping could help maintain order in states where the national government has failed to function effectively and shows little prospect of doing so, as occurred in Somalia in 1993. Member states could give a new mandate to the Trusteeship Council to deal with such societies and to establish procedures for helping to train indigenous police forces, promote conflict resolution, and assist in maintaining order as intra-state peace-building activities are carried out.

"Teaching" effectiveness

To have personnel of many nationalities working effectively side by side, regardless of their homelands' former or current animosities, would dramatically symbolize the ability of the world community to enforce norms established by the community without prejudice to any nationality. This is a profoundly important perception to cultivate because a UN member's fear that the United Nations might not fairly serve *its* particular interests probably constitutes the primary reason that members refuse to empower the Security Council more fully (and thereby to address the structural security dilemma of the balance-of-power system). To help overcome this fear, an individually recruited, permanent multinational force could be a potent teacher about the possibilities for transforming a culture of combat into a culture of enforcement.

Because a UN constabulary would be more thoroughly integrated and efficient, more readily available, less subject to charges of unreliability and partisanship, and better able to build useful experience and precedents over time, it is an important next step in domesticating the international system. Such a force would help set the institutional stage for educating publics and governments about the possibilities for gradually and reliably curtailing national uses of military power by impartially enforcing key rules against armament and aggression.

Preparing stand-by forces

Even if a transition is under way to a permanent UN constabulary, contingencies may arise (such as the Iraqi invasion of Kuwait) in which governments will feel a need to employ collective security of a more traditional military variety. Because a collective UN response is often preferable to national or bloc military actions in such cases, UN members should respond favourably to the Secretary-General's request that governments fulfil the provision of Article 43 calling upon members to conclude special agreements to "make available to the Security Council" armed forces and other forms of assistance to help in maintaining peace and security.

Authorizing preventive deployment

In addition to establishing a permanent UN constabulary and a stand-by force, the United Nations' deterrent strength could be enhanced by preparing several other instruments for immediate use. The Security Council should lay plans, as Secretary-General Boutros-Ghali suggested,[32] for preventive deployments of peace-keepers along borders where tensions have begun to mount but hostilities have not yet broken out. Non-governmental, non-violent peace teams, orchestrated with UN command structures, as Boulding and Oberg suggest, should be included in these conflict mitigation efforts. Although UN forces could not prevent large-scale cross-border military movements, their presence might deter such actions by signalling the strength of the world community's watchful eye and commitment to the prohibition of aggression. Preventive deployments might occur as a result of a Security Council decision on a case-by-case basis, to serve as a trip-wire for further enforcement action if the Council should decide it is necessary.

9. Democratizing and legitimizing political authority over peace-keeping

Restructuring the Security Council

To maximize peace-keeping effectiveness requires the world community constantly to nurture a climate and code of conduct that will minimize adversaries' willingness to use violence against UN personnel. For this to occur, UN peace-keeping and enforcement agencies must enjoy high legitimacy and worldwide support. Achieving these conditions requires representative decision-making structures and procedures in major organs such as the Security Council as well as in less visible committees and Secretariat structures. Perhaps the most important step that could be taken to enhance a global political culture propitious for peace-keeping would be to make the Security Council more representative. If the Council does not change its membership to reflect current political and economic realities more accurately, it gradually will be more and more severely limited in its ability to deploy peace-keeping forces successfully in violence-prone areas. It will be seen as an agent of the World War II victors and more particularly of the United States. This will render it increasingly useless as an agency capable of maximizing enforcement strength with a minimum of violence. In reflecting the power of the allies that defeated Germany and Japan in 1945 when the United Nations was founded, the Council does not adequately represent peoples of the then colonized third world or the Germans and Japanese. The democratic defects of the Council could be addressed by slightly expanding the Security Council to reflect current political and economic realities, by reorienting considerations in selecting members, and by diminishing the role of the veto power exercised by the permanent members.

To begin, a more equitable, principled basis for permanent membership should be developed. Many ingenious suggestions[33] have been made to satisfy the political demands of those additional countries seeking permanent seats without offending those who would be kept out or those who now hold permanent seats and fear being demoted. Yet these suggestions seem flawed because they give more weight to national pride and tradition than to a principled basis for membership. A better approach is to begin with objective criteria to ensure that the permanent members, or preferably those states holding reserved seats, would together include at least half the world's

111

population, economic productivity, military strength, and contributions to the UN budget.[34] This could be achieved by granting seats automatically to the world's eight most populous countries (China, India, the United States, Indonesia, Brazil, Russia, Japan, and Pakistan, in descending order) and its eight most productive economies (the United States, Japan, Russia, Germany, France, Italy, the United Kingdom, and Canada in descending order). Because three countries (the United States, Russia, and Japan) are in both groups, this formula leaves seven or eight other (non-permanent) seats to be elected from among all UN members, assuming an enlarged Council of 20 or 21. All of the original (existing) permanent members are in at least one of the two proposed groups for permanent seats, so none would need to vacate its seat. But none of the seats under this formula would be absolutely permanent; if the GNP of the ninth-place country should surpass the GNP of the country in eighth place over a period of years, for example, it would automatically take the permanent seat. A Council with such a composition would indeed represent a formidable force when it made a decision. This would take a major stride toward achieving the compelling legitimacy that a world enforcement body requires if it is to do its job with a minimum of violence.

Of course even this proposal gives too much weight to the segmentation of world society into states. People in Africa, divided into less populous states, lack automatic representation of their regions under this scheme. As a result, the preceding formula should be qualified by specifying that any of the five continental regions not otherwise represented in the permanent seats should be automatically represented through a seat reserved for the underrepresented region from among the elected seats. This reserved seat could be filled through an electoral process, with perhaps the most populous and influential states, such as Nigeria, South Africa, and Egypt, being selected on a rotating basis. In the long run, another legislative chamber or people's assembly, directly representing people on a more equitable basis, is a good idea.[35]

An optimal strategy for enhancing peace-keeping should not encourage the idea that UN members cannot gain full status or permanent membership on the Council unless they are prepared to project their armed forces beyond their shores. Such a suggestion would encourage states to develop military muscle as an admission ticket to the Council, for permanent as well as non-permanent membership, and set a poor example for others.[36] Instead, because of Japan's importance and its reservations about projecting military power, it and Germany should be invited to become permanent members without flexing military muscle because they can contribute to UN peace-keeping through other means. If the world is to demilitarize, it is wise to represent fully those who are themselves less militarized.

The veto power enjoyed by permanent members should be qualified so that the geostrategic interests of one member cannot dictate to the rest of the world community. Still, it would be foolish to pretend that the Security Council could do its work wisely and well against the intense opposition of one of the world's most powerful countries. None the less, to move away from the clearly unacceptable possibility that a government could use its veto power to act as a judge in its own case, it would be wise to aim at requiring two negative votes from permanent members (rather than simply one) to block an action that two-thirds of the other Security Council members favour. In the long run, it makes sense to implement Peter Wallensteen's suggestion that the veto be abolished and that decisions be authorized by a three-fourths vote.[37]

Encouraging states to utilize international law

The potential uses of peace-keeping could be effectively expanded if a more representative Security Council were to ask all members to expand the use in the international domain of those processes of impartial adjudication and legal settlement that are used in dispute settlement in the domestic sphere. This is particularly important because peace-keeping is more an instrument of police enforcement than it is of military combat such as has been associated with collective security operations. Increasing the role of legal settlement enables police enforcement to play a central enforcement role, whereas a global culture with an insignificant role for legal settlement leads adversaries to feel military combat is the ultimate arbiter of disputes.

When tensions rise between countries, the Security Council should encourage or require states to honour their Charter obligation to settle disputes "in conformity with the principles of justice and international law."[38] Although many conflicts are characterized as political rather than legal, any of them are amenable to legal analysis and political settlement based on treaties and custom if the parties are willing to be bound by legal standards.

In order to institutionalize an expanding role for legal settlement the Council should encourage a strong set of economic incentives[39] to induce all countries to accept without reservation the general compulsory jurisdiction of the International Court of Justice under Article 36 of its Statute.[40] The World Court could play a much larger role, for example in determining how a dispute should be settled (in order to avoid military confrontations) or when a government has violated the norms against aggression. Toward this end, the Security Council, already authorized by the Charter's sweeping but seldom utilized provisions for maintaining peace,[41] could declare that a state's refusal to submit a dispute to the World Court constitutes a threat to the peace. Any threat to international peace authorizes the Council to take whatever legally binding action it chooses to nullify the threat. Peace-keeping forces could implement Court decisions if backed, when necessary, by more forceful enforcement mechanisms, such as economic or legal sanctions focused on holding individual leaders accountable for their actions.[42]

Holding individuals accountable to the law

One of the most fundamental needs in creating a culture propitious for peace-keeping is to bring international law to bear on individuals. That instrument provides two gigantic merits: it combines legitimate coercion, when needed, with avoidance of collective violence and severe collateral damage. Although it is difficult to hold individual public officials, military commanders, and individuals in irregular forces accountable for their behaviour, practical steps in that direction are essential if the prospects for effective enforcement are to be substantially improved.[43] Law cannot be enforced on an entire society through physical force, against people's collective will, without excessive costs in violence and moral legitimacy; but it can be enforced on individuals without massive violence and with moral integrity.

The world community has hardly begun to tap new possibilities for taking steps in that direction, although efforts to use ad hoc war crimes tribunals and to establish a permanent international criminal court to hear charges against people's real misdeeds are positive measures. Theodor Meron has compellingly argued that multilateral efforts to collect information and to initiate proceedings for prosecuting war crimes can be immediately influential even though at first individual convictions may be infrequent because of an inability to apprehend those accused of crimes.[44] Surely the international community should be engaged in serious conversations to implement new ways of holding public authorities individually responsible for any actions that might violate the universally endorsed ban on all breaches of the peace.

If governments are to become serious about peace-making, they should heed evidence that the failure to prosecute genocidal killings in Rwanda from 1990 through 1993 encouraged the massive blood-letting in 1994 and created such violent conditions that UN peace-keepers were unable to function. Indeed, one Rwandan official has reported that timely investigations and convictions are the only way to halt a repeating cycle of violence. "The impunity that the killers enjoyed [in previous years] fueled the genocide more than any ethnic hatred."[45]

The creation of a permanent international criminal court would strengthen the prospects for war crimes proceedings and create precedents for impartiality. Even if alleged war criminals hoped to hide behind the protection of a sympathetic government, they should know that if they ever set foot outside of such a territory they could be subject to arrest and trial. And to strengthen enforcement, people everywhere should ask governments on the Security Council to impose sanctions on any government that refuses to extradite for a fair international trial any of its nationals who have been indicted for war crimes.[46]

Of course it is unrealistic to assume that the United Nations might suddenly succeed in apprehending the head of government who has engaged in aggression. Yet in Rwanda, for example, the problem has not been that many of the accused could not be tried because they have been shielded by a sympathetic government. Indeed, many of the genocide planners and executioners were abroad in Zaire, Tanzania, and the West.[47] The problem has been that governments live inertia-bound in a culture of combat and have failed to enforce the law even when they could. In Bosnia, a new wave of ethnic cleansing in the summer of 1994 was observed repeatedly by officials of both the United Nations and the International Red Cross, so evidence to be used in deterring future crimes is clearly available[48] but has not been well used as of this writing. If serious plans were laid now to prosecute war crimes, the picture might look quite different to commanders or soldiers in the future who might risk being indicted or captured during a conflict with UN forces.

The idea that citizens can be convicted of crimes against the peace even while carrying out superior orders of their own governments is a powerful tool that should no longer go unutilized. Any person violently opposing UN peace-keepers should be charged with crimes against the peace, just as domestic citizens may not use force against duly authorized police officers attempting to make arrests. The Security Council should immediately establish the principles (a) that any violent act against any UN peace-keeper carrying out authorized duties is *prima facie* evidence of a crime against the peace and (b) that the United Nations will attempt to prosecute as many violators of these norms as possible. The world community should insist upon extradition of government officials who claim, as have Bosnian Serb leaders, that they reserve "the right to retaliate against United Nations peacekeeping troops."[49] Toward these ends, the United Nations should establish (1) a permanent centralized office and com-munications network to gather information about war crimes and to monitor compliance with the norms of peace, (2) a permanent office for prosecuting war crimes, and (3) a permanent international crimi-nal court to provide nationally impartial trials for those accused.

Initiating a demilitarizing process

To make peace-keeping more effective, it needs to be placed within a global strategy of peace that emphasizes the importance of demilita-rizing and domesticating world society rather than militarizing UN peace-keeping. One concrete way of implementing this goal could be to reorient the now moribund Military Staff Committee. This Security Council Committee, which is made up of the Chiefs of Staff (or their representatives) of the five permanent members, was established by the UN Charter but has never functioned as intended. To reassure those who rightly object to the unrepresentative nature of the existing Security Council and Military Staff Committee, its composition should be changed. The Charter allows for any UN members to be invited to the Committee's deliberations when the "efficient dis-charge" of the Committee's responsibilities requires it.[50] This would enable other countries to be immediately represented if only the Security Council would invite them to sit on this Committee. By using a more representative Staff Committee in a serious manner, the Security Council could provide an immediate, practical bridge between the present Security Council, whose membership is out-dated, and a Security Council with membership formally changed as a result of the Charter revision proposed above.

As the Security Council democratizes its membership and seeks to strengthen its peace-keeping role, it should establish guidelines to create a permanent peace-keeping force and to govern the force's use, to begin a global demilitarizing process, and to use economic sanctions more pointedly. A reoriented Military Staff Committee could participate in the development of such guidelines and discourage the misuse of power by national officials pursuing their own goals within a UN operation, as has happened occasionally in Somalia and Bosnia. In addition, wise guidelines would encourage the broad political support required not only for an initial UN decision to use its forces, but also for their continuing successful operation.

The Military Staff Committee should begin by carrying out a Charter-mandated function that the Security Council has never exercised: to make recommendations for "the regulation of armaments, and possible disarmament."[51] A major impediment to peace-keepers' success in recent cases in Haiti, Rwanda, Somalia, and the former Yugoslavia, after all, has been the alarming abundance of arms in these societies. The Council could broadly exercise its existing authority to protect peace and peace-keepers by drawing upon multinational military staff expertise to make these prohibitions technologically sophisticated, legally binding, and subject to enforcement. It could develop and specify ways of disarming tanks and other military equipment, once it has been brought under control of UN forces, to prevent re-capture and use by hostile forces, as occurred in Bosnia in the summer of 1994. Perhaps non-lethal ways of neutralizing heavy military equipment that threatens peace-keepers also could be developed.

10. Making economic sanctions more effective

Economic sanctions have several merits. When the Security Council needs a coercive instrument, economic sanctions offer the world community substantial leverage beyond traditional diplomacy to force non-complying officials to change their behaviour. Economic sanctions can buttress peace-keeping in ways that are morally and politically preferable to military enforcement because they are almost always less costly than war in blood and treasure, even though, as sanctions in Iraq and Haiti have shown, they may contribute to the deaths of people already living on the margins of subsistence. Because they are usually less costly than war, governments and publics also are more willing to offer political support for them than for military combat.

Many observers have criticized economic sanctions both because they do not produce rapid results and because they may inflict a

117

heavy toll of suffering on innocent people who already have been victimized by their own governments. These valid criticisms of economic sanctions do not, however, lead to the conclusion that their potential has been fully explored, particularly when coupled with peace-keeping and intense efforts to protect ordinary people. They can be made far more effective by focusing their impact on élites rather than on entire populations, by applying them more strictly and universally, and by utilizing a longer-term strategy when sanctioning outlaw governments.[52] The expansion of UN peace-keeping through the creation of a naval force, particularly designed to monitor economic sanctions, could strengthen both peace-keeping and economic sanctions while possibly reducing the danger of escalation that would occur if military combat were used, even under UN auspices.

11. Supplanting a culture of combat with a culture of compliance

In conclusion, peace-keeping usually succeeds because (a) it represents the legitimate authority of the world community in maintaining peace through primarily peaceful means, (b) it helps adversaries move from war to peace, from violent relations to non-violent relations, and (c) it dampens and buffers military and social forces that otherwise might reverse the pacification process and move it toward war. Peace-keepers promote a transformation that is as much symbolic as it is physical and that invites adversaries to begin relying more on the benefits of peace than on the benefits they may anticipate would flow from attacking UN forces or each other. As a result, the enhancement of peace-keeping not only requires more money, training, and personnel, it requires nurturing an international code of conduct and a global political culture in which the expectation and legitimacy of war decline, even at some short-term sacrifice to those who might with impunity occasionally resort to arms.

The growth of an aversion to war could serve the long-term interests of the militarily strong as well as of the militarily weak countries because the former's occasionally opportunistic use of force cannot be relied upon to offset the dangerous loss of security, resources, and other values that would accompany a continuing legitimation of national military force well into the twenty-first century. For these reasons, peace-keeping should be seen not as a poor cousin to tougher UN enforcement based on large-scale military combat associated in the past with collective security, but instead as a pioneering

118

agency leading toward the enforcement of law on individuals and eventually a world without war. UN peace-keeping is closer than UN military enforcement (*à la* Desert Storm and Korea) to the form of multilateral enforcement that is truly capable of ushering in a more peaceful and just future – enforcement based on law, courts, police, and people's willing compliance with the norms established by a representative global political system.

As indicated above, UN members should support preventive development, peace-building, and revenue-raising to demonstrate unequivocal seriousness about expanding instruments for peace-keeping and non-military enforcement. The Security Council should institutionalize a permanent UN constabulary force, backed up by stand-by forces, to empower the United Nations to oppose aggression and gross violations of human rights more effectively. The Council should democratize itself to give it more legitimacy and integrative power, enabling it to encourage states and individual officials to respect the law in ways that will enable peace-keepers to function well. Finally, the Council, in part through a reoriented Military Staff Committee, should take initiatives for global demilitarization and for pinpointing long-term economic sanctions to reduce permanently the role of military force in international affairs. In taking these steps the United Nations could greatly expand the utility and effectiveness of UN peace-keeping in the twenty-first century.

Appendix: UN peace-keeping

Mission	Date	Function
UN Special Committee on the Balkans (UNSCOB)	1947–52	Monitor Greek border
UN Commission for Indonesia (UNCI)	1947–51	Observe Indonesian cease-fire and Dutch troop withdrawal
UN Truce Supervision Organization (UNTSO)	1948–present	Report on Arab–Israeli cease-fire and armistice violations
UN Military Observer Group in India and Pakistan (UNMOGIP)	1949–present	Observe cease-fire in Kashmir
UN Emergency Force (UNEF)	1956–67	Supervise troop withdrawal and provide buffer between Israeli and Egyptian forces
UN Observation Group in Lebanon (UNOGIL)	1958	Check on clandestine troop movement and aid across Syrian–Lebanese border

Mission	Date	Function
UN Operation in the Congo (ONUC)	1960–64	Maintain order in the Congo, expel foreign mercenaries, prevent secession and outside intervention
UN Temporary Executive Authority and UN Security Force in West New Guinea (West Irian) (UNTEA/UNSF)	1962–63	Maintain order during transfer of authority from Netherlands to Indonesia
UN Yemen Observation Mission (UNYOM)	1963–64	Supervise military disengagement in Yemen
UN Peacekeeping Force in Cyprus (UNFICYP)	1964–present	Prevent internal conflict in Cyprus, avert outside intervention
Representative of the Secretary-General in the Dominican Republic (DOMREP)	1965–66	Report on cease-fire between domestic factions
UN India–Pakistan Observation Mission (UNIPOM)	1965–66	Observe India–Pakistan border
Second UN Emergency Force (UNEF II)	1973–79	Supervise cease-fire and troop disengagement, control buffer zone between Egypt and Israel
UN Disengagement Observer Force (UNDOF)	1974–present	Patrol Syria–Israel border
UN Interim Force in Lebanon (UNIFIL)	1978–present	Supervise Israeli troop withdrawal, maintain order, restore authority of Lebanese government
UN Good Offices Mission in Afghanistan and Pakistan (UNGOMAP)	1988–90	Monitor Geneva Accords on Afghanistan and supervise Soviet withdrawal
UN Iran–Iraq Military Observer Group (UNIIMOG)	1988–91	Supervise cease-fire and mutual withdrawal of forces by Iran and Iraq
UN Angola Verification Mission (UNAVEM I)	1989–91	Verify withdrawal of Cuban troops from Angola
UN Transition Assistance Group in Namibia (UNTAG)	1989–90	Assist Namibia's transition to independence, ensure free and fair elections
UN Observer Mission to Verify the Electoral Process in Nicaragua (ONUVEN)	1989–90	Monitor Nicaraguan elections
UN Observer Group in Central America (ONUCA)	1989–92	Verify compliance by Costa Rica, El Salvador, Guatemala, Honduras, and Nicaragua with agreement to disarm and neutralize irregular forces in the area

Mission	Date	Function
UN Observer Mission to Verify the Electoral Process in Haiti (ONUVEH)	1990–91	Observe elections in Haiti
UN Iraq–Kuwait Observation Mission (UNIKOM)	1991–present	Monitor demilitarized zone between Kuwait and Iraq
UN Angola Verification Mission (UNAVEM II)	1991–95	Verify compliance with Peace Accord to end civil strife in Angola
UN Observer Mission in El Salvador (ONUSAL)	1991–95	Monitor cease-fire and human rights agreements in El Salvador's civil war
UN Mission for the Referendum in Western Sahara (MINURSO)	1991–present	Attempt referendum in Western Sahara on independence or union with Morocco
UN Advance Mission in Cambodia (UNAMIC)	1991–92	Assist Cambodian factions to keep cease-fire agreement
UN Protection Force (in the former Yugoslavia) (UNPROFOR)	1992–95	Monitor cease-fire in Croatia and Bosnia–Hercegovina, protect relief programmes
UN Transitional Authority in Cambodia (UNTAC)	1992–93	Demobilize armed forces of Cambodian factions, supervise interim government, conduct free elections
UN Operation in Somalia (UNOSOM I)	1992–93	Monitor cease-fire between Somali parties, protect shipments of relief supplies
UN Operation in Mozambique (ONUMOZ)	1992–95	Supervise internal peace accord, disarm combatants, establish a non-partisan army, hold national elections, conduct humanitarian programme
Second UN Operation in Somalia (UNOSOM II)	1993–95	Protect relief work and discourage domestic violence
UN Observer Mission in Uganda–Rwanda (UNOMUR)	1993–94	Monitor the border between Uganda and Rwanda and verify that no military assistance crossed it
UN Observer Mission in Georgia (UNOMIG)	1993–present	Observe cease-fire
UN Observer Mission in Liberia (UNOMIL)	1993–present	Implement cease-fire agreements
UN Observer Mission in Haiti (UNMIH)	1993–96	Restore democracy, re-train police, encourage domestic order
UN Mission for Rwanda (UNAMIR)	1993–96	Protect humanitarian assistance efforts, encourage stability

Mission	Date	Function
UN Aouzou Strip Observer Group, Chad/Libya (UNASOG)	1994	Verify the withdrawal of Libyan forces from the Aouzou Strip in accordance with decision of International Court of Justice
UN Mission of Observers in Tajikistan (UNMOT)	1994– present	Assist the Tajik government and the Tajik opposition in monitoring a cease-fire
UN Mission in Bosnia and Herzegovina (UNMIBH)	1995– present	Enhance law enforcement capabilities and stability
UN Confidence Restoration Organization in Croatia (UNCRO)	1995–96	Implement and monitor cease-fire agreements
UN Preventive Deployment Force, Republic of Macedonia (UNPREDEP)	1995– present	Monitor developments in the border areas that could undermine stability
UN Angola Verification Mission (UNAVEM III)	1995–97	Assist in restoring peace and achieving national reconciliation
UN Mission of Observers in Prevlaka, Croatia (UNMOP)	1996– present	Monitor demilitarization
UN Support Mission in Haiti (UNSMIH)	1996–97	Assist in professionalization of the police and maintenance of stability
UN Transitional Administration for Eastern Slavonia, Baranja and Western Sirmium, Croatia (UNTAES)	1996– present	Supervise demilitarization; monitor return of refugees and displaced persons; maintain peace and security in the region; the civilian component is to establish a temporary police force; train police; monitor the prison system; organize elections
UN Verification Mission in Guatemala (MINUGUA)	1997	Verify fulfilment of the cease-fire between the government of Guatemala and the Unidad Revolucionaria Nacional Guatemalteca, including demobilization of combatants
UN Observer Mission in Angola (MONUA)	1997– present	Assist in consolidating peace and national reconciliation, enhancing confidence-building and democratic development
UN Transition Mission in Haiti (UNTMIH)	1997– present	Contribute to professionalization of the Haitian National Police

Notes and references

1. Editors, "Cold Choices in Rwanda," *New York Times*, 24 April 1994, p. Y14.
2. "Peace-keeping" means the classic or traditional monitoring activities of UN peace-keeping forces made up of contingents of armed forces contributed by member nations for special UN duty to patrol borders or cease-fire lines in order to defuse misunderstandings and to prevent escalation of incidents between adversaries. The classic examples are the two United Nations Emergency Forces (UNEF I, 1956–1967; and UNEF II, 1973–1979) that served as buffers between Egyptian and Israeli forces.
3. "Enforcement" means actions, ranging from positive inducements to UN military coercion taken under Chapter VII of the Charter, to ensure that states comply with the prevailing norms of peace and Security Council decisions for the maintenance of peace and security. The term frequently refers to economic sanctions or military action against a country in accord with procedures outlined in Chapter VII of the Charter, but it also can, and in my view should, include the use of international war crimes tribunals and domestic courts to enforce international law on individuals and states.
4. "Collective security" means a system of commitments by members of the international community to come to the aid of one another when any member of the system is threatened by military aggression of another. It is summed up in the dictum: "All for one and one for all." The Charter discusses implementation of the idea in Chapter VII, but the provisions of this chapter, especially Article 43 agreements, have never been fully implemented.
5. See Alan James, *Peace-keeping in International Politics* (New York: St. Martin's, 1990), for discussion of a surprising number of efforts to plan and deploy international military forces for monitoring purposes before 1945. On League precedents see also Gunther G. Greindl, "UN Peace-Keeping Operations: History and Operational Concepts with Special Reference to UNFICYP and UNDOF," presented to United Nations University, September, 1985 (Xeroxed copy), pp. 3–5; and A. Walters, *A History of the League of Nations* (London: Oxford University Press, 1952), vol. II, pp. 538–540.
6. On these points see the important article by Chadwick F. Alger, "The United Nations in Historical Perspective: What Have We Learned About Peacebuilding?" in Richard A. Falk, Samuel S. Kim, and Saul H. Mendlovitz, eds., *The United Nations and a Just World Order* (Boulder, Colo.: Westview, 1991), pp. 87–108.
7. "Preventive diplomacy" refers to intensified diplomatic efforts by the United Nations or other third parties, focused upon a rising crisis that threatens to erupt into violent conflict.
8. This refers to forms of development that alleviate the conditions that give rise to violence and that promote social integration.
9. Secretary-General Boutros Boutros-Ghali introduced the concept of "post-conflict peace-building" in his *An Agenda for Peace* (New York: United Nations, 1992), pp. 32–34, where he defined it as "concrete cooperative projects which link two or more countries in a mutually beneficial undertaking that can not only contribute to economic and social development but also enhance the confidence that is so fundamental to peace." Although he discussed this as a post-conflict activity, the concept need not be limited to a time immediately following war. I also apply peace-building to intra-state weaving of a domestic social fabric, because in its most general sense the term describes efforts to employ economic, social, and political cooperation to alleviate underlying conditions likely to produce violence.
10. See, for example, Paul F. Diehl, *International Peacekeeping* (Baltimore, Md.: Johns Hopkins University Press, 1993), p. 34.
11. In his assessment of peace-keeping Diehl notes, "I do not distinguish violence directly attributable to the shortcomings of the peacekeeping operation itself from that resulting from other causes" (ibid., p. 34).
12. Ibid., p. 37.
13. Ibid., p. 92.

14. The United Nations has very little autonomy, and UN peace-keepers even less, so their responsibility for failures is after all quite limited.
15. One exception was the failure of some peace-keepers in Bosnia to report promptly and accurately gross violations of human rights they witnessed.
16. An excellent brief survey of weaknesses of peace-keeping is contained in Michael Renner, *Critical Juncture: The Future of UN Peacekeeping*, WorldWatch Paper 114 (Washington, D.C.: WorldWatch, 1993), pp. 29–38.
17. The United States, the biggest offender, and Russia together have accounted for 75 per cent of the unpaid regular and peace-keeping dues (Michael Renner, "A Force for Peace," *World Watch*, July–August 1992, p. 31). The Clinton administration planned to pay off the more than US$1 billion in past dues that the United States was legally bound to pay, but Republicans in Congress strongly opposed doing so (Steven Lee Meyers, "Administration Proposes Paying U.N. Debt, but Congress Resists," *New York Times*, 30 December 1996, p. A1).
18. Renner, "A Force for Peace," op. cit., p. 30.
19. Under the rubric of "norms of peace" I mean to refer collectively to international legal prohibition of crimes against the peace (military aggression), war crimes (violations of the laws governing weapons and warfare), crimes against humanity (acts of genocide), and gross violations of human rights that constitute a threat to the peace or cause scores of civilian deaths (such as ethnic cleansing in Bosnia–Hercegovina or the obstruction of efforts to avert mass starvation in Somalia).
20. See Dietrich Fischer, *Nonmilitary Aspects of Security: A Systems Approach* (Geneva: United Nations Institute for Disarmament Research, 1993), pp. 172–173. Kuman Rupesinghe recommends an Office for Preventive Diplomacy in chapter 5 of this book.
21. See Martin Walker, "Global Taxation: Paying for Peace," *World Policy Journal*, vol. 10 (Summer 1993), pp. 7–12.
22. A permanent yet relatively small UN force, perhaps the most desirable and likely next step, was recommended by the first Secretary-General, Trygve Lie, and subsequently by Robert C. Johansen and Saul H. Mendlovitz, "The Role of Enforcement of Law in the Establishment of a New International Order: A Proposal for a Transnational Police Force," *Alternatives: A Journal of World Policy*, vol. 6 (1980), pp. 307–338. On this point, see also Robert C. Johansen, *Toward an Alternative Security System: Moving from the Balance of Power to World Security* (New York: World Policy Institute, 1983), pp. 26–46; and Robert C. Johansen, "The Reagan Administration and the U.N.: The Costs of Unilateralism," *World Policy Journal*, vol. 3 (Fall, 1986), pp. 630–632. More recently Brian Urquhart has given the idea its first prominent attention in "For a UN Volunteer Military Force," *New York Review of Books*, vol. 40 (10 June 1993), pp. 3–4. An early discussion of a much larger United Nations Peace Force is contained in Grenville Clark and Louis B. Sohn, *World Peace through World Law* (Cambridge, Mass.: Harvard University Press, 1960), Annex II.
23. In Bosnia, for example, tens of thousands of UN personnel were needed simply to dampen conflict, protect relief efforts, and attempt to protect civilians from ethnic cleansing. With 13,000 peace-keepers in place in March 1994, UN commander Michael Rose pleaded unsuccessfully for 10,000 more simply to carry out the existing mandate ("Bosnian Serbs Resume Campaign of Delaying UN Relief Convoys," *New York Times*, 6 March 1994, p. Y4).
24. Retired US Admiral Jonathan Howe reported that in Somalia the coordination of the forces of 30 different nations was "the most difficult problem" (Robert M. Press, "Somalia: Use of Force Shakes UN Credibility," *Christian Science Monitor*, 6 October 1993, p. 11).
25. See Eric Schmitt, "Clinton Reviews Policy in Somalia as Unease Grows," *New York Times*, 6 October 1993, pp. Al, A7.
26. The loss of US support turned out to be highly significant because it led officials, in the face of stiff Congressional and public criticism, to revise Presidential Decision Directive 25 so

that it diminished US willingness to participate in future UN peace-keeping and reduced US support even for UN missions that operated without US troops.

27. Mats R. Berdal explains that existing US military doctrine and training for low-level military operations are not suited for Somalia-type operations ("Fateful Encounter: The United States and UN Peacekeeping," *Survival*, vol. 36, Spring 1994, pp. 41–42, 45).

28. A more experienced force with commanders trusted by the Secretariat might well have cautioned against those in New York recommending the capture of one of several warlords during what was essentially a humanitarian assistance operation. Deviation from the humanitarian mission made the United Nations appear to be taking sides among the various Somali factions. If forcible disarmament of belligerents was to become the guideline for UN operations, it should have been applied even-handedly for the United Nations to maintain its legitimacy in the eyes of the local population.

29. Thomas G. Weiss points out that "a new humanitarian delivery unit should form an integral part of a unified command." He recommends that it "be comprised of a cadre of soldiers and of civilians in possession of humanitarian expertise and body armor" ("UN Responses in the Former Yugoslavia: Moral and Operational Choices," *Ethics and International Affairs*, vol. 8, 1994, p. 20).

30. See Robert C. Johansen, "The United Nations after the Gulf War: Lessons for Collective Security," *World Policy Journal*, vol. 8 (Summer 1991), pp. 567–573.

31. Of course national police forces would be the principal agency for ensuring domestic tranquillity.

32. Boutros-Ghali, *An Agenda for Peace*, op. cit., pp. 16–19.

33. Many of these are discussed in the Stanley Foundation, *The Role and Composition of the Security Council* (Muscatine, Ia.: The Stanley Foundation, 1994) and Peter Wilenski, "The Structure of the U.N. in the Post-Cold War Period," in Adam Roberts and Benedict Kingsbury, eds., *United Nations, Divided World: The U.N.'s Role in International Relations* (Oxford: Clarendon Press, 1993).

34. See Renner, *Critical Juncture*, op. cit., especially pp. 54–57.

35. See Dieter Heinrich, *The Case for a United Nations Parliamentary Assembly* (New York: World Federalist Movement, 1992); Daniele Archibugi, "The Reform of the U.N. and Cosmopolitan Democracy: A Critical Review," *Journal of Peace Research*, vol. 30 (1993), pp. 303–309; and Frank Barnaby, ed., *Building a More Democratic United Nations* (London: Cass, 1991).

36. In addition, to encourage the extension of Japanese military power is grossly insensitive to the leaders of most Asian states who have raised strong objections to Japan sending armed forces beyond its own shores. See Nayan Chanda, "Why They Worry: Asian Neighbours Fear Military Revival," *Far Eastern Economic Review*, 25 June 1992, p. 18.

37. Peter Wallensteen, "Representing the World: A Security Council for the 21st Century," *Security Dialogue*, vol. 25 (March 1994), pp. 63–75. For an assessment of various suggestions for Security Council reform, see Raimo Väyrynen, "La Reforma de la Organización Mundial: Estructura y Eficacia del Consejo de Seguridad de la ONU," in Modesto Seara Vazquez, ed., *Las Naciones Unidas a los Cincuenta Años* (Mexico, D.F.: Fondo de Cultura Economica, 1995), pp. 63–85.

38. Article 1(1).

39. These might vary widely and include, for example, reduced UN assessments, debt forgiveness, lowered interest on international loans, and concessionary rights in the high seas, the seabed, and outer space in return for helping to initiate a demilitarizing process.

40. Shridath Ramphal has proposed that acceptance of compulsory jurisdiction of the International Court of Justice should be a requirement for UN membership (*Global Governance in the Global Neighborhood*, Waging Peace Series No. 35, Santa Barbara: Nuclear Age Peace Foundation, June 1994, p. 15).

41. The Security Council "may decide what measures not involving the use of armed force are to be employed to give effect to its decisions and it may call upon the Members of the

125

United Nations to apply such measures" (Article 41). In addition, it may take military action "as may be necessary to maintain or restore international peace and security" (Article 42).

42. The Charter also authorizes the Security Council to use its enforcement powers to ensure compliance with a Court decision if war threatens from a failure to settle the dispute through legal means. In Article 94(2) the Security Council is empowered to "decide upon measures to be taken to give effect to the [Court's] judgment."

43. See Robert C. Johansen, "Toward a New Code of International Conduct: War, Peace-keeping, and Global Constitutionalism," in Richard A. Falk, Robert C. Johansen, and Samuel S. Kim, eds., *The Constitutional Foundations of World Peace* (Albany: State University of New York Press, 1993), pp. 48–50.

44. Theodor Meron, "The Case for War Crimes Trials in Yugoslavia," *Foreign Affairs*, vol. 72 (Spring 1993), pp. 122–135. See also Payam Akhavan, "Punishing War Crimes in the Former Yugoslavia: A Critical Juncture for the New World Order," *Human Rights Quarterly*, vol. 15 (May 1993), pp. 262–289; Theodor Meron, "War Crimes in Yugoslavia and the Development of International Law," *American Journal of International Law*, vol. 88 (January 1994), pp. 78–87.

45. Wilson Rutayisire quoted by Andrew Jay Cohen, "On the Trail of Genocide," *New York Times*, 7 September 1994, p. A17.

46. This proposal rests on the establishment of an adjudicatory process that would be widely perceived throughout the world to be impartial and held in an internationally established criminal court.

47. Cohen, "On the Trail of Genocide," op. cit., p. A17. The Rwandan leader, General Paul Kagame, indicated willingness to cooperate with UN war crimes trials if held in Rwanda and to help identify those indicted. He also indicated openness to prosecuting those in his own Patriotic Front military forces accused of crimes against humanity since his political front became the Rwandan government. See Raymond Bonner, "Top Rwandan Criticizes U.S. Envoy," *New York Times*, 8 November 1994, p. A6. The world community lost an important opportunity in not responding quickly and favourably to this offer.

48. Chuck Sudetic, "In New Campaign, Bosnian Serbs Oust 2,000 Muslims from Homes," *New York Times*, 30 August 1994, p. A1.

49. Roger Cohen, "NATO Planes Bomb Serbians Near Sarajevo," *New York Times*, 23 September 1994. p. A1. The Serbian officers who said that they would target any UN aircraft attempting to land at the Sarajevo airfield should be indicted for war crimes. This decision was delivered to UN officials in a handwritten note by a Serbian officer. See Roger Cohen, "At Odds over Bosnia," *New York Times*, 2 October 1994.

50. Article 47(2).

51. Article 47.

52. For discussion of this prospect, see Robert C. Johansen, "Reforming the United Nations to Eliminate War," *Transnational Law & Contemporary Problems*, vol. 4, no. 2 (Fall 1994), pp. 455–502.

4

United Nations peace-keeping and NGO peace-building: Towards partnership

Elise Boulding and Jan Oberg

1. Perspective

Although it was governments that established the United Nations to maintain international peace and security and to "save succeeding generations from the scourge of war," those 51 founding governments had in fact all along been pushed and prodded to do this by people's associations. Transnational citizens' peace movements in Europe and Asia had already been at work for two centuries to bring about such an entity, from the time of the Napoleonic Wars.

It was transnational citizens' efforts to develop a model arbitration treaty that paved the way for the Hague Peace Conference that opened the twentieth century. A continuing lobbying process to get governments to accept arbitration, mediation, and third-party *bona officia* or good offices[1] in inter-state conflicts, and a 1913 People's Peace Congress proposal for an international police force, were rudely interrupted by World War I. However, citizens' movements – civil society's non-governmental organizations (NGOs), voluntary organizations, and grass-roots organizations – continued undaunted

127

in their efforts to strengthen the preventive diplomacy and conflict-resolution capabilities first of the League of Nations and then of the United Nations.

This analysis presents an argument and some proposals about how NGOs worldwide can contribute to the effectiveness of United Nations peace-keeping efforts by developing networks of civilian peace teams that co-function with the military and civilian peace-keepers.

Yet, from the time of the first armed operations of the UN peace-keeping forces (the largely non-violent UN Emergency Force on the Egypt–Israeli border from 1956 to 1967, and the much bloodier Opération des Nations Unies au Congo operation in the Congo, 1960–1964), it was clear that states, for all their rhetoric, were not giving up reliance on military means to enforce peace. Although the history of UN peace-keeping is filled with instances of creative thinking by early UN commanders on how to minimize the use of force and maximize opportunities for non-violent problem-solving and preventive diplomacy by civilian personnel,[2] on the whole there has been a failure seriously to develop this civilian capacity within the UN peace-keeping missions sent to areas of violent conflict. Observer missions have a better record. Military personnel on these missions are usually unarmed, although with little or no conflict-resolution training, and they are accompanied by experienced Civil Affairs officers with problem-solving skills.

Although UN Civil Police (UNCIVPOL) and Civil Affairs staff are a regular component of UN peace-keeping missions, the UN Department of Public Information tends to emphasize numbers of troops (Blue Helmets), yet the civilian police often bring important specialized skills to peace-keeping operations.[3] Furthermore, it is difficult to judge from UN reports what percentage of civilian staff are actually Civil Affairs staff who in fact work with local citizens and how many are administrative and logistical personnel. Oberg estimates that only 10 per cent of UNPROFOR's civilian staff are actually in civilian peace-building roles (Oberg 1993).

Security Council deliberations are very complex and necessarily involve conflicting considerations, but major powers are seen as driving a decision process in the direction of their own national interests rather than impartially in the world interest. As long as this situation obtains, Security Council control of the UN forces will be seen by many states as an obstacle to peace rather than a guarantor of peace. In fact a group of two-thirds world governments issued a warning at a UN Committee meeting on decolonization about unilateral, ill-planned UN peace-keeping interventions by a Western-dominated Security Council.[4]

2. Reforms

Awareness exists of the need to develop further the civilian peace-building capacity of the UN forces, especially given that the frequency and intensity of internal wars, including ethnic struggles, along with continuing incidents of inter-state wars, are creating a growing demand for UN peace-keeping forces.

The report to the General Assembly by the Special General Assembly Committee on Peacekeeping Operations (GA Doc. A/49/136, 2 May 1994) notes the growing importance of the civilian component in peace-keeping and the need for better coordination with humanitarian and other civilian aspects of peace-keeping, both at UN headquarters and in the field, and urges a system of data banks on available civilian personnel and standby civilian cohorts from member states. It is encouraging to note that we find these same recommendations in the Report of the Secretary-General to the Security Council and the General Assembly (A/48 403 S/26450, 14 March 1994), and in resolutions of the General Assembly itself (A Res. /48/42) on the same day.

However, actual UN peace-keeping deployments continue to emphasize military operations, with the unfortunate outcome that UN forces sometimes exacerbate the conflicts they are intended to bring under control.

Fortunately there are currently several proposals on how to reform and optimize the UN peace-keeping operations.[5] The focus is on organization, decision-making, control, financing, and modes of deployment and on the relations between military and civilian components and the distinction between peace-keeping and peace enforcement.

The focus of this essay is not on change in peace force operations *per se*, however, but on the possibility of increasing the effectiveness of UN peace-keeping through the further development of a civilian capability for preventive diplomacy, mitigation, mediation, and conflict resolution, closely coordinated with UN peace-keeping forces under the Department of Peace-keeping Operations (DPKO) but under the direction of another UN office, the Department of Humanitarian Affairs (DHA), rather than directly under military

129

command – a proposal that would of course necessitate that the DHA be linked to the DPKO and its mandate broadened.

3. The UN Volunteer programme

The development of an improved civilian capability is already under way. The UN Volunteer Unit (UNV) is administered by the United Nations Development Programme (UNDP), but works now also with the newly reorganized Department of Humanitarian Affairs (DHA). The UNV programme has worked closely with NGOs since it was founded in 1950, placing volunteers with special skills in various UN projects and programmes.

Now UNV has urgent requests to place experienced conflict-resolution practitioners in Angola, Burundi, Bosnia-Hercegovina, Cambodia, Liberia, Mozambique, Rwanda, Somalia, the Sudan, and wherever UN peace-keeping missions are under way. The UNV is also working closely with UNESCO, the UN Institute for Training and Research (UNITAR), the Centre for Human Rights, and a group of peace NGOs to locate and deploy well-prepared conflict-resolution practitioners in teams to work in conflict areas where UN peace-keeping forces are currently stationed. The UNV also places such teams in troubled "pre-conflict" areas where preventive diplomacy may obviate the need for UN forces. The UNV thus becomes a key locus in the UN system for expansion of a network of highly trained non-violent peace teams to undertake conflict mitigation, and for a possible eventual replacement of military peace enforcement by non-military operations carried on by conflict-resolution practitioners who can help the United Nations realize its original goal of ending the scourge of war.[6]

Because the administering agency for the UNV, the UNDP, has very limited resources at its disposal and does not have the Security Council's power to draw funds from member states, this whole project of non-violent peace teams depends heavily on both the funding and the conflict-resolution and peace-building capabilities of the peace-and-development-oriented NGO community. In the long run, the same process that builds NGO support for non-violent peace teams working in coordination with UN peace-keeping operations may also help to bring about the long-sought People's Assembly, or Citizens' Assembly, as part of the UN system. A brief overview of the interests and activities of that sector of people's associations may be helpful here.

130

4. Gandhi's peace brigades

The concept of peace armies trained in non-violence can be traced to Gandhi's programme of training young Indian women and men for village-level activity to combat communal strife and poverty and work for national independence from the British. In 1931 he spoke of the possibility of overcoming violent conflicts with "a living wall of men and women," who would interpose themselves between conflicting parties without any other weapons than themselves (Weber 1988; quoted by L'Abate 1994).

Gandhi's vision of an expanded *shanti sena*, or peace army, composed of local groups trained in non-violence across the country never came into being. However, a decade after his death a national organization was formed to promote local *shanti senas*. Though at present a weak organization, it still exists and offers training at various Gandhi centres for community development and conflict-resolution work at the village level.[7]

Gandhi's vision went beyond India, however. His prophetic eye could see every city, town, and village the world over containing local teams of trained *shanti-sainiks* to nurture the social and physical well-being of each community and facilitate non-violent conflict resolution. When local or regional conflicts got out of hand, he saw the possibility of calling in fellow *sainiks* from other communities – even from other continents.

Although Gandhi's concept never came close to realization, his vision nevertheless inspired countless efforts since then on all continents to form and train peace teams to deal with violence, aggression, and war in such a way as to create the conditions and facilitate the processes for just and peaceful settlement of disputes. The broader context for all such efforts has been an overriding call to lay the foundations for more humane and nurturant relations among peoples and with all living things, in a life course based on the practice that Gandhi called *sarvodaya*, "welfare for all."

5. International peace brigades

In the 1930s a Peace Army recruited by European pacifists[8] was offered to the League of Nations to intervene non-violently in the fighting in Shanghai. The offer was refused, and subsequent projects, including one that actually took place in the Middle East, eventually petered out owing to difficulties in organization and financing.

However, the concept kept being reborn. In Europe we find a widespread movement for a civilian peace service to provide a constructive alternative to military action through non-military methods of dealing with conflict (Drago 1994). A specific plan for such a volunteer service has been developed by the Federation for Social Defence, a German umbrella organization of the peace movement.

In 1960, the World Peace Brigade was formed on the model of the *shanti sena* with leaders from Asia, Africa, Europe, and the Americas. Between then and 1994, 21 separate peace team bodies were formed and have gone into action in conflict situations on every continent.[9] Of these 21, at least half a dozen bodies are active today in conflicts from Sri Lanka to the Sudan to the Balkans to Haiti. Among these are Peace Brigades International, reconstituted in 1981 from the original World Peace Brigade. Currently they have teams in Sri Lanka, Guatemala, Haiti, the Balkans, and Quebec, with negotiations under way for a team in Colombia. In each case the teams are invited by groups from within the country, and receive advance training to work in a variety of ways to end fighting, rebuild trust, and develop cooperation between warring parties.

Another type of group is represented by Witness for Peace, which since 1983 has trained and organized grass-roots faith-based delegations from the United States to carry out protective accompaniment for endangered individuals and groups in Central America, and works in Guatemala, Mexico, Nicaragua, and Haiti. Christian Peacemaker Teams, begun in 1986, represent a third type of group, sponsored by Mennonites and Brethren. Members have an intensive two-month training and then are on call for a three-year period to work in long-term protection and peace-building missions in Haiti, the Sudan, the Gaza Strip, and elsewhere as called.

Generally peace team operations are very small (usually 6–12 persons), though at times larger groups of several hundred people will be trained for special missions – for example, Witness for Peace delegations to Central America. Every peace team group is underfunded, but their work of protective accompaniment of endangered local peace-makers, interpositioning between hostile groups, message-carrying between opponents, and untiring mediation efforts is widely respected wherever they operate.

The heroism with which they move through extreme violence and retain the ability to communicate with leaders who organize genocidal activity, their willingness continually to jeopardize their own safety, is a heroism that goes largely unrecorded. Collectively the people who have served on these teams have built up an invaluable reservoir of knowledge, experience, and skill that could be many times multiplied if resources were available.

The gap between the scale of present violence on every continent and the reality of these small scattered teams of peace-makers is staggering. However, given the intensity of the need, it is worth paying attention to efforts to expand the number, size, and capability of non-violent peace teams through NGO coalition-building in anticipation of cooperative efforts between NGOs and the United Nations. In addition to the inherent value of such expansion, these efforts can only strengthen the possibility of moving the UN peace-keeping practices toward more civilian participation in peace-keeping missions.

Violence and war are destructive of the work of every NGO focused on human well-being. When violence is at its most intense, even those NGOs whose mission is to work in disaster areas and emergency situations cannot carry out their functions, as reports from both African and Balkan NGO operations make clear in this very year of the UN Fiftieth Anniversary.

The constituency for NGO coalition-building in support of non-violent peace team activity goes well beyond the "peace" NGOs. This is due to the fact that both professionals and activists in the NGO world are increasingly aware that peace, human and social development, protection of the environment, humanitarian activity, human rights, and the full participation of women and minorities in the shaping of society are all intimately interconnected and interdependent.

From the perspective of the humanitarian agencies already at work in these war-torn settings, such as Médecins Sans Frontières, Catholic Relief Services, and the International Red Cross, civilian peace teams are urgently needed to negotiate with local warlords and other power figures for safe space in which to carry on their work. They need personnel who can specialize in "listening around" and connecting with local wisdom, who can do neutral message-carrying to counter rumours that exacerbate violence.

It is not only the humanitarian NGOs that need the peace teams. The UN peace-keeping missions are urgently in need of civilian peace teams to do what the military are often not equipped to do: work with local groups to develop grass-roots peace-building and reconstruction activities and to develop trust and patterns of cooperation.

A point may come when UN peace-keepers are seen by one or more warring parties as part of the conflict. In such situations they may be ineffective as protectors of humanitarian workers. Unarmed peace teams trained in the non-violent creation of listening spaces in the midst of violence, neutrals who offer no threat to anyone, are urgently needed and asked for by the beleaguered humanitarian agencies that have no personnel or skills to spare for negotiating the spaces needed to carry out their work.

A number of NGOs have reluctantly had to withdraw from where they were most needed, to avoid continuing slaughter of their own workers.[10] Although peace teams would also be in danger, their skills in working with local groups are their best protection.

6. Coalition-building among the NGOs

It will be seen that coalition-building is integral to all these activities. NGO coalition-building stands at the centre of all other coalition-building, since NGOs by their very nature represent a linking of the resources of states, the United Nations, and the civil society.

Significant leadership in this coalition-building is being provided by London-based International Alert, which came into being in the 1970s to create an early warning system based on NGO networking, with the hope of preventing the kinds of wars that in fact erupted in the 1980s and the 1990s. International Alert is moving from its earlier more low-key strategy of networking and conflict-resolution training, to a more proactive strategy of more thorough-going coalition-building among a larger number of NGOs to gain the resources for a higher level of activity in each conflict area.

International Alert's focus is on middle-to-just-below-top-level preventive diplomacy, and on providing skill training in each region for locals to carry on this type of conflict-resolving activity (Rupesinghe and Kuroda 1992; Rupesinghe 1993). Local mediators, with the assistance of experienced outsiders, are currently at work in hot spots in Asia, Africa, and Eastern Europe. International Alert is also playing a key role in the development of the Intergroup on Preventive Diplomacy and Humanitarian Action of the European Parliament. It is helping that group to interface with the larger group of relevant NGOs.

Another approach to coalition-building is found in efforts to create a coordinating body for networking among existing organizations that carry out peace team work. Currently these organizations operate more or less independently of one another, though there is some informal information-sharing.

One of these bodies, a faith-based group called Global Peace Services, is facilitating this networking through a series of international consultations designed to develop partnership arrangements with local groups in conflict areas in different world regions. The focus will be on the provision of training in non-violent conflict resolution and mediation for local teams, and on the creation of international teams that can work with local teams. The vision of Global Peace Services is basically the *shanti sena* vision, that every community should have its own trained local team, known and trusted by the local community, to help with local problems – but also to be available for mobilization into larger groups for larger-scale action in more serious situations of out-of-control violence.

At present each existing peace team organization, many of them faith based, others secular, provides its own training. In addition there are independent training programmes, such as the International Civilian Peace-keeping and Peace-building Training Programme at the Austrian Study Centre for Peace and Conflict Resolution at Stadt Schlaining, which is now running four-week courses each year. It has also recently begun offering a specialized Course in Humanitarian Aid within its Civilian Peace-keeping Programme.

A new Institute for Conflict Studies and Peacebuilding has been established at Eastern Mennonite University in Virginia, United States, which will offer training for field service as well as a full M.A. programme in Conflict Analysis and Transformation. The International Peace Academy also conducts training seminars in various world regions, and shorter training opportunities exist through some peace studies programmes on college campuses and at peace centres in Europe, Asia, Africa, and Latin America.[11]

The possibility exists that by the end of the 1990s there will be a number of regional training centres on each continent, and hundreds if not thousands of trained peace team personnel. The constraints on such a development are not personnel constraints. There are always more volunteers for peace team work than there are openings. The constraints rather lie in the problem of the financing of larger-scale work, in the creation of appropriate infrastructure, and in handling the logistics of large-scale deployment of peace teams.

Further challenges lie in the problems of coordinating peace team activity with local authorities, UN missions, and relevant on-the-ground NGOs already there doing humanitarian work. It is clear that all three types of NGO coalition – those that work primarily with regional intergovernmental bodies, those that work primarily with other NGOs concerned with peace, environment, development, and humanitarian services, and those that work primarily among existing peace services and peace teams – need to coordinate with the United Nations itself.

7. NGOs and the regional cooperative organizations

NGOs, states, regional organizations, and the United Nations itself all have strong interests in developing early warning systems and shifting the focus of activity from meeting crises to preventive diplomacy.

Although NGO coalitions and NGO networking have a special role to play in crisis prevention and long-term peace-building because of their roots in civil society and access to grass-roots developments, it should also be noted that regional intergovernmental bodies working in partnership with NGOs can increase the effectiveness of both conflict-resolution and peace-building work. NGOs are important here because they link up in various ways with governments, the United Nations, and civil society.

So, for example, the Organization for Security and Cooperation in Europe (OSCE) several years ago moved to create a Conflict Prevention Centre. This and other OSCE bodies and field missions will benefit considerably from inviting NGO expertise to be optimally effective in the Balkans, the former Soviet Union, and the Mediterranean, its primary action areas.

The European Parliament in July of 1994 established an Intergroup on Preventive Diplomacy and Humanitarian Action, which already had 120 signatories, the most ever in the history of the European Parliament.[12] The Intergroup immediately dispatched a mission to Burundi and is moving toward ongoing work there.

Similarly, Parliamentarians for Global Action, a worldwide network of activist national legislators, have been sending missions for preventive diplomacy to Burundi and Haiti and are mobilizing to increase this type of activity, which uniquely links governmental and non-governmental actors.

Regional intergovernmental organizations, from the Association of South-East Asian Nations to the Organization of African Unity (OAU) to the Organization of American States (OAS), are all keenly aware of the need for "regime-building," for the development of regional and global norms and frameworks for cooperation, in order to move away from an upward spiralling of military action and towards cooperative problem-solving. One of a number of valuable resources for regional organizations is the Copenhagen-based Global Non-Offensive Defence Network, an NGO of peace researchers committed to working with governments to reduce the military component of national defence policies and promote economic conversion and differently based security.

8. UN peace-keeping operations

As a new UNV–peace team collaboration evolves and conflict-resolution professionals with area expertise and language skills are placed at the disposal of the UN peace-keeping missions, the peace-building capacities of the UN missions will be greatly strengthened. In time the Blue Helmets will once again be seen as the "peace army" they were intended to be. This can happen gradually through the substantial strengthening of the civilian component of each mission.

This civilian component includes civilian police and a civilian affairs division to coordinate, but it could develop into a multi-competent "UN peace army" responsible for tasks such as:
- conflict mitigation, mediation, and general communication with official local bodies and other groups;
- economic and social reconstruction plus rebuilding of agricultural, productive capacities, and human services;
- demobilization and retraining as necessary of soldiers to participate in reconstruction; and
- the work of social healing for the traumas of war suffered by women, men, and children.

In an area of western Slavonia in Croatia, which, until Croatia retook it in May 1995 in a military operation, was designated United Nations Protected Area (UNPA) West, precisely such activity had been going on during 1993 and 1994, organized by a Dutch peace activist in coordination with the United Nations Office, Vienna (Schultz 1994).

At present the civilian arms of UN peace-keeping missions – the Civil Police and Civil Affairs – are grossly understaffed. It should therefore be kept in mind that NGO peace teams, with logistical support from a given UN peace-keeping mission, would be able to recruit larger teams than existing NGO bodies can support unaided. When these teams can expand to larger units, their coverage and effectiveness in high-violence situations will be greatly increased.

Figure 4.1 indicates the extent of UN peace-keeping missions as of May 1997. It lists the 17 missions, how many states are contributing

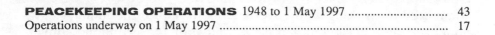

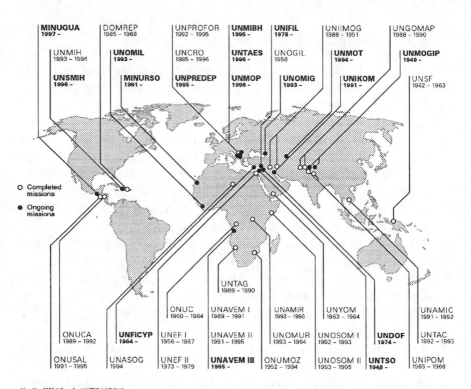

Map No. 3852.1 Rev. 8   UNITED NATIONS
February 1997

Department of Public Information
Cartographic Section

PERSONNEL
Military and civilian police personnel serving on 30 April 1997 23,874
Countries contributing military and civilian police personnel on 30 April 1997 71
Fatalities from 1948 to 30 April 1997 (military, civilian police, international and local civilian) .. 1,503

FINANCIAL ASPECTS
Estimated total cost of operations from 1948 to 30 June 1996 .... About $16.0 billion
Estimated annualized cost from 1 July 1996 to 30 June 1997 .... About $1.3 billion
Estimated cost from 1 July 1997 to 30 June 1998 not expected to exceed 1996–1997 level
Outstanding contributions to peacekeeping as of 30 April 1997 .... About $1.65 billion

Fig. 4.1 **UN peace-keeping operations, 1997 (Source: Prepared by the United Nations Department of Public Information in consultation with the Department of Peacekeeping Operations and the Peacekeeping Financing Division, Office of Programme Planning, Budget and Accounts, DPI/1634/Rev.6, May 1997).**

138

UNTSO Since June 1948
United Nations Truce Supervision Organization
Strength at 30 April 1997: 155 Fatalities: 38
Budget estimate for 1997: $23.7 million

UNMOGIP Since January 1949
United Nations Military Observer Group in India
and Pakistan
Strength at 30 April 1997: 45 Fatalities: 9
Budget estimate for 1997: $6.4 million

UNFICYP Since March 1964
United Nations Peacekeeping Force in Cyprus
Strength at 30 April 1997: 1,200 Fatalities: 168
Budget estimate (1 July 97–30 June 98): $50.3 million*
*[UN assessment on Member States ($27.8 million) and
voluntary contributions by Cyprus ($16 million) and Greece
($6.5 million)]

UNDOF Since June 1974
United Nations Disengagement Observer Force
Strength at 30 April 1997: 1,045 Fatalities: 37
Budget estimate (1 July 97–30 June 98): $32.4 million

UNIFIL Since March 1978
United Nations Interim Force in Lebanon
Strength at 30 April 1997: 4,564 Fatalities: 215
Budget estimate (1 July 97–30 June 98): $122.2 million

UNIKOM Since April 1991
United Nations Iraq-Kuwait Observation Mission
Strength at 30 April 1997: 1,082 Fatalities: 9
Budget estimate (1 July 97–30 June 98): $50.7million*
*[Two thirds of the cost is paid by Kuwait]

MINURSO Since April 1991
United Nations Mission for the Referendum in
Western Sahara
Strength at 30 April 1997: 238 Fatalities: 7
Budget estimate (1 July 97–30 June 98): $29.1 million

UNOMIG Since August 1993
United Nations Observer Mission in Georgia
Strength at 30 April 1997: 116
Fatalities: 2
Budget estimate (1 July 97–30 June 98): $19.9 million

UNOMIL Since September 1993
United Nations Observer Mission in Liberia
Strength at 30 April 1997: 92
Budget estimate (1 July 97–30 June 98): $19.7 million

UNMOT Since December 1994
United Nations Mission of Observers in Tajikistan
Strength at 30 April 1997: 23 Fatalities: 1
Budget estimate (1 July 97–30 June 98): $8.0 million

UNAVEM III Since February 1995
United Nations Angola Verification Mission III
Strength at 30 April 1997: 5,249 Fatalities: 32
Budget estimate (1 July 97–30 June 98): Unavailable*
*[No cost estimate was prepared in the expectation that the
Security Council might authorize a follow-on mission as of
1 July 1997.]

UNPREDEP Since March 1995
United Nations Preventive Deployment Force
Strength at 30 April 1997: 1,147 Fatalities: 4
Budget estimate (1 July 97–30 June 98): $44.3 million*
*[Revised cost estimates which will modify this figure are
being prepared for submission to the General Assembly in
order to reflect recent decisions of the Security Council.]

UNMIBH Since December 1995
United Nations Mission in Bosnia and Herzegovina
[Incorporates International Police Task Force (IPTF)]
Strength at 30 April 1997: 1,698 Fatalities: 4
Budget estimate (1 July 97–30 June 98): $165.6 million*
*[See remark for UNPREDEP, above.]

UNTAES Since January 1996
United Nations Transitional Administration for
Eastern Slavonia, Baranja and Western Sirmium
Strength at 30 April 1997: 5,378 Fatalities: 6
Budget estimate (1 July 97–30 June 98): $266.6 million

UNMOP Since January 1996
United Nations Mission of Observers in Prevlaka
Strength at 30 April 1997: 28
Cost included in UNMIBH [see above]

UNSMIH Since July 1996
United Nations Support Mission in Haiti
Authorized strength: 800 supplemented by
some 800 voluntarily funded military personnel
Total combined strength at 30 April 1997: 1,558
Budget estimate (1 July 97–15 Mar 98): $14.5 million

MINUGUA Since January 1997
United Nations Verification Mission in Guatemala
Strength at 30 April 1997: 188
Budget estimate (15 Feb–31 May 1997): $4.6 million*
*[Military observer component only]

NOTE: Strength figures include military and civilian police personnel. Fatality figures include military (1,387), civilian police (44) and civilian international (41) and local staff (31) as of 30 April 1997. Costs to the United Nations of 15 of the 17 current operations are financed from their own separate accounts on the basis of legally binding assessments on all Member States. UNTSO and UNMOGIP are funded from the United Nations regular budget. Budget estimates reflect the new financial periods established by the General Assembly in its resolution A/49/233A. Estimates do not include the cost of backstopping of operations at Headquarters funded from the Support Account for Peacekeeping Operations.

Fig. 4.1 **(cont.)**

139

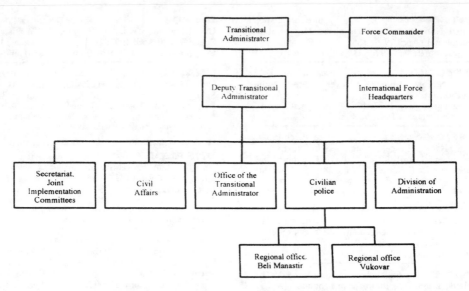

Fig. 4.2 **UNTAES organization chart (Source: UN General Assembly, Fifty-First Session, December 1996, A/51/520/Add.1, New York: United Nations, p. 25).**

personnel to each, and the number of personnel in each mission (information on the percentage civilian is not available).

To illustrate how civilian police, and Civil Affairs, have been incorporated into some UN peace-keeping missions, figure 4.2 shows an organizational chart for the United Nations Transitional Administration for Eastern Slavonia, Baranja, and Western Sirmium (UNTAES) in the former Yugoslavia. In January 1996 the Security Council authorized 5,000 troops, 100 military observers, and 600 civilian police for this operation.

9. The structure of the United Nations and the integration of peace teams

Secretary-General Boutros Boutros-Ghali instituted a major overhaul of the organization of peace-keeping operations when he assumed office, considerably reducing the bureaucratic tangle of existing operations. There is now a unified Department of Peace-keeping Operations (DPKO) with its own Under-Secretary-General (see fig. 4.3).

The missions continue to be under military command with the Secretary-General as Commander-in-Chief, at least formally. Troops and civilian personnel continue to be assigned by member govern-

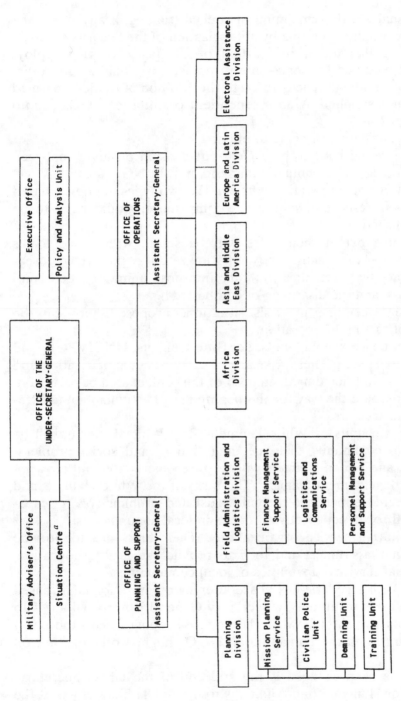

Fig. 4.3   Organizational structure of the Department of Peace-keeping Operations (Note: *a*. The designation "Centre" as used here is not derived from official organizational nomenclature standards – see General Assembly Resolution 32/204; see also A/C.5/33/6. Source: United Nations Secretariat, "Organization Manual: Functions and Organization of the Department of Peace-keeping Operations," *Secretary-General's Bulletin*, 22 March 1995, p. 15).

141

ments, usually with a minimum of special training, if any. Also, the missions continue operating by authorization of the Security Council.

Assuming that the current extent of UN peace-keeping deployment will continue for some time to come, how could a substantial new peace-building capacity through the addition of trained unarmed peace teams supplied by an independent coalition of NGOs fit into this picture?

Three considerations come to mind:

(1) There would have to be a clear-cut division of labour between UN forces under military command and the NGO teams.

(2) A pattern of cooperation between the two types of bodies, based on their respective spheres of competence, would have to be established.

(3) To some extent their roles will be serial, with peace teams expanding their activities (mediation, etc.) as the armed forces contract their activities (military interpositioning between combatants, and the disarming of combatants).

The peace-keeping in crisis situations proposed here can be thought of as a multi-operation.

- The UN peace-keeping units, i.e. Blue Helmets, UNCIVPOL, and Civil Affairs staff. Their tasks are to carry out demilitarization and disarmament (including demining) of the conflict area or parts of it, and to prepare the way for the beginnings of a civilian administrative infrastructure.
- Peace team units or White Helmets. The White Helmets will be active in community dialogue, negotiation, and social problem-solving, and Green Helmets will form reconstruction and environmental development teams.[13] The tasks of the White Helmets and the Green Helmets are to build trust and problem-solving capabilities through cooperative projects in local communities.
- Humanitarian service organizations. Their tasks are to provide emergency assistance, and then to rebuild the health, education, and social services capabilities of local communities.

Figure 4.4 is a generic UN peace-keeping organization chart based on the reforms instituted by Secretary-General Boutros-Ghali, with modifications to show how the UN peace-keeping forces, the NGO peace teams, and the humanitarian NGOs might work together on missions.

What has been changed is the addition of the Under-Secretary-General for Humanitarian Affairs, who in the UN hierarchy is at the same level as the Under-Secretary-General for Peace-keeping, to the

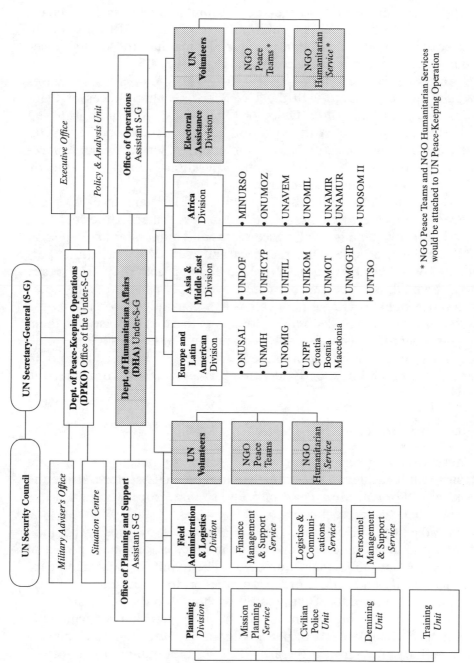

Fig. 4.4 **Proposed UN peace-keeping organization.**

* NGO Peace Teams and NGO Humanitarian Services
would be attached to UN Peace-Keeping Operation

top coordinating level of the chart. This places the work of coordination between the UN peace-keeping units and the civilian peace teams at the top command level, but leaves the administration of the peace teams under the Department of Humanitarian Affairs rather than directly under military command[14] (see fig. 4.5).

An Assistant Secretary-General for UN Volunteer Operations would then coordinate with the UN Peace-keeping Offices of Planning and Support, and its Office of Operations, while administering two Offices of Field Administration and Logistics, one for NGO peace teams and one for NGO humanitarian services. Field placement in specific UN peace-keeping operations would be done by these Offices of Field Administration.

By creating this role for the Department of Humanitarian Affairs it becomes possible to create a UN Volunteers Office at the logistical level, directly administering peace teams and humanitarian NGOs, in full coordination both with planners and with field operations personnel, wherever there is a UN peace-keeping operation. The peace teams would not necessarily serve in every UN peace-keeping operation. It would be a judgement call as to when and where they should serve but, when the decision is to serve, there is a place for them in the operation. The peace teams and humanitarian NGOs would be separate from but coordinated with the military command in any given operation, clearly identified as a civilian sector under the DHA.

10. There are other possibilities

There are a number of other ways in which the necessary coordination could be achieved, including leaving the NGO sector outside the formal UN organization chart entirely, so that cooperation would be an informal voluntary process.

Another option, possibly seen as preferable by those who look forward to major modifications in the military enforcement aspect of UN operations in the near future, would be to put the unarmed peace teams directly under the Force Commander, to work in tandem with the armed contingents. That possibility should not be ruled out.

Attention is being given to non-military, tension-reducing and conflict-resolving aspects of peace-keeping by senior military officers and military strategists in the armed forces of a number of countries, including Canada, the United States, Scandinavia, Austria, and the United Kingdom. Similar explorations are also taking place at the

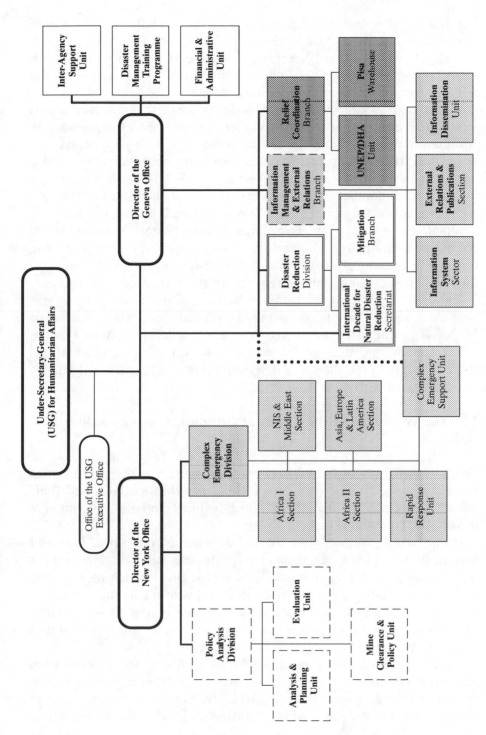

Fig. 4.5 **The proposed Department of Humanitarian Affairs.**

regional level within the CSCE, the OAU, and the OAS, and in regional bodies in the Asia-Pacific and the Middle East.

The strategy proposed here straddles the two main positions on peace teams – having them either completely integrated into the military force structure or completely outside it.

Retaining a significant degree of independence for the peace teams would help ensure that the non-violent mode of operating, obviously completely different from the military mode, will be kept intact and not eroded through incorporation into military operations that would undercut the unique contribution unarmed White Helmets have to make in high-conflict situations. Pressures for incorporation would come not necessarily from Force Commanders, but from the Security Council. However, if one is optimistic that current exploration of conflict-resolution and mediation training for UN peace-keeping forces will actually go forward in the near future, then integration of the two types of contingents might speed the transformation process.

Retaining significant relations with the UN peace-keeping operation via the DHA has the advantage of officially involving the United Nations in some of the most creative peace-building capacities of the NGO system, and thus in the long run moving the United Nations more strongly in the direction it was intended to go – toward ending the scourge of war.

11. The resources of the voluntary organizations and their tasks

From the catching of the earliest warning signals to being present at the grass roots of full-blown crises, there are things NGOs and their peace teams can do that the United Nations and its governments cannot do, and vice versa.

Professionals and activists from the peace NGOs offer, first and foremost, impartiality and experience in conflict situations and a trained capacity for conflict analysis based on decades of research and practice, plus the skills of conflict prevention in the period of early signals of a conflict. They are experienced in negotiation, mediation, message-carrying, protective accompaniment, and the creation of social spaces for rebuilding relationships.

No UN authorization is required for peace teams to carry out such activities, as long as they have an invitation from parties within a country who will respect their impartiality. Early fact-finding, conflict analysis, and the collection of information about the country/countries in conflict can, of course, be done without such an invitation. This means a speedy response capacity in early warning situations, where governments and the United Nations often get bogged down in a lengthy bureaucratic decision-making process.

Conflict monitoring is an important contribution NGOs can make through (1) reports from humanitarian agencies already at work where trouble is brewing (admittedly a very delicate process); and (2) reports from conflict analysts with process and area expertise. Conflict analysts can be sent out regularly to potential crisis areas to gather information for their constituencies – which can include local grass-roots peace-oriented groups excluded from the local power structure, NGO coalitions, the United Nations, and other concerned bodies. This type of monitoring, systematically organized, should be able to provide several months' warning of grave crisis situations.

12. Rapid Response Teams

Rapid Response Teams are another contribution that peace NGOs can make, sending out peace teams made up of trained persons available on a stand-by basis, including persons from a pool of retired or otherwise available specialists, to work with local groups who seek peace, as well as with the contending parties. The pool of trained persons will have to be enlarged, and no person would be admitted to a peace team for work outside their own country who had not already learned how to work with violence at home.[15]

Rapid Response Teams and larger peace teams in units of up to 100 persons can be planned for, with initial support coming from NGO coalitions and some governments with an impartial concern for peace-building. The Danish government, for example, funds humanitarian brigades for crisis areas.[16]

This possibility will, of course, depend on a future NGO coalition establishing a coordinating body for training and deployment of peace teams and for linkage to the United Nations in countries where UN peace-keeping missions are present or planned. Also, it will depend on the extent to which host governments will accept that they operate on their territory.

Because the larger-scale peace teams here envisaged will be a new type of venture, it will be important to gain experience in less extreme situations of violence, and not try to begin with the hardest cases, such as Rwanda at the peak of its genocidal violence.

It cannot be emphasized strongly enough that the first responsibility for peace team projects is to focus on local training in countries experiencing serious violence, for the people of that country who wish to participate in peace-building. Experience of the dozen peace teams currently at work in war-torn countries is universally that there are many grass-roots groups already at work on peace-building in apparently hopeless situations. What they need is support and resources. Any training outsiders can offer may provide additional tools, but should not replace local peace-making know-how.

The secret of peace team effectiveness lies in the partnership between locals and those who come from abroad to provide additional support. Any notion that outside peace teams can come into a country to "fix things" cannot be tolerated. Such an attitude represents "peace colonialism," which is no better than other colonialists for the long-term social health and recovery of a society in conflict.

In all the discussions of early warning systems it is easy to forget that there are a number of conflict areas from which warnings have long been emanating that the world chooses to ignore. Places such as Georgia, the Sudan, Afghanistan, and Sierra Leone have long had crisis situations that get very low levels of attention from the media and the United Nations and even from internationally minded publics in other world regions. Where this is so, the peace team efforts would be to try to prevent a long-term situation of violence from getting worse, at the same time offering new sources of support to local peace initiatives, tired and weak as these may be.

13. Cooperation between UN peace-keeping forces and peace teams

Joint action in a crisis situation that draws on the Blue Helmets, civilian police, and Civil Affairs officers of UN missions, working in tandem with peace teams and other humanitarian NGOs, can greatly enhance the specific capabilities of each of these four types of actors. In terms of UN mission stages, the Blue Helmets would have the initial task of demilitarizing a conflict area while peace teams carried out exploratory dialogue and protective accompaniment for threatened persons. Then the civilian police and the Civil Affairs officers would work with the local population to reconstruct a viable infrastructure of local and national governance, greatly aided by the contact work done with warlords by message-carrying peace teams.

If in some of the operations the stage of developing a new constitution has been reached, peace team activities of monitoring of election and post-election activities and monitoring the extent of keeping of agreements and the respecting of human rights by all parties will play a crucial role. At this stage, hundreds of therapeutic specialists may be needed to work with traumatized children, adults, and former soldiers, and UN and NGO personnel would work closely together to meet those needs. It must never be forgotten that individual human beings have been using violence in situations of civil conflict, and it is individual human beings who need help in breaking the cycles of violence they are caught in, individuals who must live with the memory of the sorrows and traumas of war.

In all of these activities, the enormity of the difference between the present reality of having peace brigades of perhaps only a dozen people in any crisis situation, as against having peace teams of a hundred people or more available to work with UN units to carry out the many tasks involved in peace-building, must not be forgotten. That realization must motivate the new developments called for in the NGO community.

At the same time, the possibility of this scale of peace team operation depends heavily on cooperation with the United Nations and the technological and logistical capabilities of the peace-keeping forces from member states. The United Nations and the NGOs each have something to offer, and each needs the other. Never has this been more true than today.

14. Implications for peace research

Studies of peace-keeping and humanitarian operations in crisis areas carried out by the Transnational Foundation (Oberg 1993; Schultz 1994) reveal that often only very few people actually structure the military operations and strategies of each party in conflict, particularly in local society. The common people are ignored, and local peace-making resources are ignored.

More on-the-ground research on conflict structures in ongoing crisis situations will enable both the United Nations and peace teams to operate more effectively. Each crisis situation in which UN peace-keeping forces are involved produces a body of experience accumulated by the mission people involved, and peace research has failed to document this experience. What is needed is a systematic recording of the experience of military and civilian, UN and NGO personnel in peace-making and peace-building in crisis situations, so that the international community can begin to learn from these experiences instead of making the same mistakes over and over.

It should be acknowledged that the peace research community has on the whole made valuable contributions to theory-building and conflict analysis in its search for the conditions of peace. It has illuminated the study of structural and behavioural violence and different types of problem-solving and conflict-resolution strategies. It has demonstrated the role of non-violence in these strategies. It has provided the evidence for the interrelationships of peace, environment, development, and human rights, thus transforming the understanding of national security as common security. Further, it has also developed conflict resolution and peace studies as a field to be taught from kindergarten to graduate school, producing citizens and policy analysts who can think in terms of alternative defence and in terms of peace and security policies and strategies at the national and international level that will contribute to sustainable peace.

What peace research has *not* paid sufficient attention to is the training of practitioners in mediation, negotiation, and conflict resolution. This rapidly growing field, although heavily dependent on the findings of peace research, has grown up largely outside the peace research community. Oberg has pointed out during the dialogue that has produced this paper that there are three underlying reasons for this. First, peace research in general has dealt far too little with conflict and non-violence and too much, by comparison, with war, arms control, and security/disarmament. Secondly, there is a surprising lack of serious attention to the study of non-violence. And, thirdly, most peace researchers still sit in laboratories, study books and travel too little (except to conferences), and do too little empirical conflict studies on the spot. They work too little with diagnosis, prognosis, and therapy, i.e. practical conflict mitigation that also involves politics.

We believe it is time for the International Peace Research Association (IPRA) to address the training process more directly, both for military and civilian peace-keeping and peace-building, and to help produce a new generation not only of conflict analysts but of conflict-resolution practitioners. It is this new generation whose task it will be to bring the slowly evolving joint UN–NGO peace-building initiatives to fruition on a scale that will make creative UN–People's Peace-making a hallmark of the twenty-first century.

150

Notes

1. "Good offices" means friendly assistance rendered by an impartial third party for the purpose of bringing disputants together so that they may seek to reach a settlement. For definitions of other key terms, see the Glossary to this chapter.

2. Among the classic studies of UN peace-keeping operations we could mention Rikhye, Harbottle, and Egge (1974); Roberts and Kingsbury (1993); and Durch (1993). Rikhye, Harbottle, and Egge are the three military commanders who helped shape the concept of the Blue Helmets. Major General Rikhye was also the founder of the International Peace Academy, whose offer to train peace-keepers for the United Nations was unfortunately turned down. Important related studies by UNITAR were also being prepared in the 1970s, including Pechota (1972) and Raman (1975).

   In Oberg (1995) – originally written for the UN Fiftieth Anniversary book – the reader will find a series of basic facts about UN peace-keeping as well as references to more recent mainly academic books. For information about the structure and organization of the United Nations, see UN Department of Public Information (1995).

3. In Cyprus, for example, General Rikhye reported that the 174 police officers from Australia, Austria, Denmark, New Zealand, and Sweden serving in one integrated unit, and working with Turkish and Greek police, had repeatedly prevented minor incidents from escalating into major Greek–Turkish clashes (Rikhye et al. 1974; note also Harbottle 1994).

4. See Life and Peace Institute (1994). See also Ferris (1992).

5. Thus, for example, *The Peacekeeping and International Relations Newsletter* of the Canadian Institute of Strategic Studies is currently filled with such proposals, and with reviews of books and special studies addressing issues of changes in peace-keeping. Note, for example, the following: Sahnoun (1994); Charters (1994); Clements and Wilson (1994). You may also consult the Transnational Foundation (1991) and Wahlgren (1996).

6. In fact, the Secretary-General specifically mentions the UNV's role in providing skilled peace-building personnel to UN peace-keeping operations in his Report to the Security Council and the General Assembly (A48 403 S/26450, 14 March 1994).

7. Their activities are reported in the quarterly journal, *Gandhi Marg*, published by the Gandhi Peace Foundation, New Delhi.

8. Among them was the British Maude Royden and it was referred to as Maude Royden's Peace Army.

9. The story of these peace teams is told in Moser (forthcoming). An excerpt from this book is found in Beer (1994).

10. An important document spelling out the criteria for humanitarian assistance in the midst of violence has been issued by the Program on Humanitarian Assistance of the World Conference on Religion and Peace (n.d.).

11. A sample list of institutions with non-violence training programmes might include the following:

    Europe: School of Peace Studies, Bradford University, Bradford, England; the Peace and Development Research Institute, Gothenburg University, Sweden; and the Department of Peace and Conflict Research, Uppsala University, Sweden.

    North America: The Institute of Conflict Analysis and Resolution at George Mason University, Virginia, USA; and the new Canadian Peacekeeping Centre in Toronto, Ontario, Canada.

    Latin America: Education, Action for Peace Program of the Centro de Estudios Internacionales, Managua, Nicaragua; and SERPAJ (Servicio Paz y Justicia) in Brazil and other Latin American countries.

    Asia-Pacific Region: Conflict Resolution Network, Chatswood, New South Wales, Australia; Network of Engaged Buddhists in Bangkok, Thailand; and the Peace Studies Program of the Faculty of Political Science in Thammasat University, also in Bangkok; India Peace Centre, Nagpur, India.

151

    Africa: Nairobi Peace Initiative Centre, Nairobi, Kenya; and Centre for Intergroup Studies, University of Capetown, South Africa.

    The Middle East: The University of Cairo and the National Centre for Middle East Studies in Marsa Matrouah, Egypt, have begun a series of training seminars in conflict resolution.

12. International Alert, *Network Update* 2, November 1994.
13. The term "White Helmets" has very recently been adopted by the UN General Assembly as a category designating national volunteers based on a draft resolution by Argentina (23 December 1994). It is used here however as referring to NGO peace teams.
14. This approach necessitates moving the UN Volunteer Unit out of the separate UN agency, the UN Development Programme, where it now sits, and into the UN Secretariat under the Department of Humanitarian Affairs Under-Secretary-General. This fits with one of the recommendations of the Childers and Urquhart (1994) report that the Department of Humanitarian Affairs should take responsibility for all humanitarian operations within the UN system.
15. This is seen as an important sensitizing process for volunteers from the one-third world.
16. One may assume that such an action would evoke more popular support than sending armed forces to the UN peace-keeping missions.

Glossary

Conflict mitigation = fact-finding, analysis, meetings, various types of empathic influencing and proposal-making – about ways to settle differences rather than suggesting final solution – all aiming at helping the parties themselves to seek solutions that fit their needs, not that of the third party.

Conflict resolution = the process of making incompatible values, interests, and expectations compatible and deciding a satisfactory distribution of such values, interests, and expectations so that the conflict never re-occurs.

Mediation = when an impartial "third" party actively participates in the discussion of substantive issues and offers proposals for settlement.

Peace-building = implementation of peace agreement but also – and sometimes before such an agreement – changing the structures, thinking, and causes that lead to violent activity in the first place. In the international system this often means underlying historical, socio-economic problems; in local communities it means reconciliation, economic reconstruction, and trust-building so that citizens can live either together in the same place or as good neighbours.

Peace enforcement = a term introduced by Boutros-Ghali in his *Agenda for Peace* (1992), meaning to employ military power beyond that of peace-keepers to enforce agreements against any party violating such agreements – however, with a high probability that the party/parties hit will perceive the United Nations as unfair, party-taking, and a participant in the conflict; should hardly be used simultaneously with traditional peace-keeping.

Peace-keeping = activities such as supervising cease-fires, serving as buffers, demilitarization, and keeping contending parties at a distance from each other, helping or protecting humanitarian transports. This is the classical activity of the United Nations and requires that the peace-keepers are impartial, are armed only with personal self-defence, and are present in a conflict area on the invitation of the conflicting parties.

Peace-making = activities such as negotiations, mediation, third party intervention, shuttle diplomacy, etc. that lead up to a peace agreement.

Preventive diplomacy = activities that aim to prevent conflicts from breaking out in various types of violence, including war. Often mistakenly termed "conflict prevention" – mistakenly because we aim not to suppress or avoid conflicts but to prevent violence from breaking out and thereby deal with conflicts effectively, i.e. with a minimum of violence.

Third party = that a neutral outside actor, e.g. the United Nations, an expert panel, or citizens' diplomats, helps parties in conflict to settle their differences; it should be observed that the term does not imply that most conflicts have only two parties.

References

Beer, Michael, ed. 1994. *Peace Team Reader: Nonviolent Third-Party Crisis Intervention by NGOs*. Washington, D.C.: Nonviolence International.

Boutros-Ghali, Boutros. 1992. *An Agenda for Peace*. New York: United Nations.

Charters, David A. 1994. *Peacekeeping and the Challenge of Civil Conflict Resolution*. New Brunswick, N.J.: University of New Brunswick Center for Conflict Studies.

Childers, Erskine, and Brian Urquhart. 1994. "Renewing the United Nations System." *Development Dialogue*, 1.

Clements, Kevin, and Christine Wilson, eds. 1994. *UN Peacekeeping at the Crossroads*. A Publication of the Peace Research Centre, Research School of Pacific and Asian Studies. Canberra: Australian National University.

Drago, Antonio. 1994. "Peoples' Diplomacy: From the Movement to a Specific State Institution." Paper presented to the International Conflict Resolution Commission at the International Peace Research Association Conference in Malta.

Durch, William J. 1993. *The Evolution of UN Peacekeeping. Case Studies and Comparative Analysis*. London: Macmillan.

Ferris, B., ed. 1992. *The Challenge to Intervene: A New Role for the UN?* Life and Peace Institute Report No. 2. Uppsala, Sweden.

Harbottle, Michael. 1994. "The Peacebuilding Role of United Nations Operations." Paper presented at session on Peacebuilding in Crisis Areas at the International Peace Research Association Conference in Malta.

L'Abate, Alberto. 1994. "Nonviolent Interpositionary Forces: Are Effective Nonviolent Interventions Possible in Armed Conflicts?" Paper presented to the International Conflict Resolution Commission at the International Peace Research Association Conference in Malta.

Life and Peace Institute. 1994. "Third World Warns UN on Interventions." *Life and Peace Review*, vol. 8, no. 2, p. 7.

Moser, Yeshua. Forthcoming. *Recurrent Vision: A History of Citizen Peacekeeping Actions*.

Oberg, Jan. 1993. "Conflict Mitigation in the Former Yugoslavia." *Peace Review: The International Quarterly of World Peace*, Winter, pp. 423–436.

——— 1995. *The UN and the Keeping of the Peace. A Conflict-Resolution Perspective*. Lund: Transnational Foundation.

Pechota, V. 1972. *The Quiet Approach: A Study of the Good Offices Exercised by the Secretary General in the Cause of Peace*. New York: UNITAR.

Program on Humanitarian Assistance of the World Conference on Religion and Peace. n.d. *The Mohonk Criteria for Humanitarian Assistance in Complex Emergencies.* Available at WCRP, 777 UN Plaza, NY 10017.

Raman, K. Venkata. 1975. *The Ways of the Peacemaker: A Study of UN Intermediary Assistance in the Peaceful Settlement of Disputes.* New York: UNITAR.

Rikhye, I., M. Harbottle, and B. Egge. 1974. *The Thin Blue Line: International Peacekeeping and its Future.* New Haven, Conn.: Yale University Press.

Roberts, Adam, and Benedict Kingsbury. 1993. *United Nations, Divided World. The UN's Role in International Relations.* Oxford: Clarendon Press.

Rupesinghe, Kumar. 1993. "Early Warning and Preventive Diplomacy." International Alert Discussion Paper.

Rupesinghe, Kumar, and Michiko Kuroda, eds. 1992. *Early Warning and Conflict Resolution.* London: Macmillan.

Sahnoun, Mohamed. 1994. *Somalia: The Missed Opportunities.* Washington, D.C.: United States Institute of Peace.

Schultz, Kerstin. 1994. *Build Peace from the Ground up.* Lund: Transnational Foundation.

Transnational Foundation. 1991. *A United Nations of the Future.* Lund: TFF.

UN Department of Public Information. 1995. *Basic Facts about the United Nations.* New York: UN DPI.

Wahlgren, Lars-Eric. 1996. *UN Peace-Keeping Towards the Year 2000.* Lund: Transnational Foundation.

Weber, Thomas. 1988. "Gandhi's Living Wall and Maude Royden's Peace Army." *Gandhi Marg*, July.

5

Coping with internal conflicts: Teaching the elephant to dance

Kumar Rupesinghe

1. Quick-step into a new era?

This chapter is both a celebration of the United Nations' achievements over the past 50 years and a reflection upon the future potential of the Organization as it pursues the cause of peace into the new millennium. Within this context I will touch upon the limitations that hitherto restricted UN involvement in intra-state conflicts, as well as outline how a new security paradigm has arisen among the fresh opportunities of the post–Cold War era.

The United Nations is no longer a fresh-faced newcomer on the world scene. Its bureaucracy spreads out across the continents and it is all too frequently caught napping by younger organizations that are more fleet of foot when it comes to grasping new ideas and creating opportunities. Like many middle-aged organizations, it is easy to believe that it has lost its cutting edge with the passage of time. In the business world, stagnant corporations are swallowed up by more aggressive, youthful competitors or dwindle into bankruptcy. But, with its monopoly on global intergovernmental organizations, the United Nations does not face that sort of competition or threat. Instead , in its attempt to remain at the centre of international affairs, the onus is on the organization itself periodically to examine and reassess its applicability to world politics.

The question that dominates contemporary debate in global affairs is what kind of world order is going to develop in the next 50 years and what part will the UN play in it? Are we standing at the edge of a new epoch characterized by new human possibilities; or are we poised on the brink of a new dark age? These questions have pushed the issue of UN reform on to the international agenda. The present system is embedded in the structures of the Cold War era and has been shown to be inadequately equipped to deal with the new global challenges. These include rising demographic levels worldwide, especially in poorer countries, widening economic disparities between industrialized and agrarian-based societies, and the problems of environmental degradation. Often these trends occur amid conditions that pose some of the most prominent challenges in the world today, namely violent conflicts inside sovereign states and between peoples. The former Yugoslavia, Somalia, Rwanda, Chechnya, read like a roll call of tragedy and human horror. Since 1989, intra-state conflicts such as these have proved themselves to be some of the most intractable and complex confrontations of the twentieth century.

By tracing the history of UN-oriented interventions, evaluating recent initiatives, and looking towards the potential for strengthening the Organization's role in preventing and resolving internal conflict, the debate outlined in the following pages focuses upon the United Nations' ability to address these problems and manage their consequences. In the past few years, the debate concerning UN reform has gathered quite a significant global momentum. This reflects two perspectives in the United Nations' position: on the one hand, the importance that many people in the international community attach to the United Nations' role; on the other hand, the new freedom and opportunity that have been presented to the Organization at the end of an era marked by the straitjacket of bipolar confrontation.

End of an era

The era of European domination and "old-style" diplomacy, which so characterized nineteenth-century international relations, finally collapsed at the end of World War II with the formation of the United Nations Organization. The spirit that propelled the establishment of the United Nations had of course already been articulated a generation before with the formation of the League of Nations at the end of World War I (1914–1918). But the idealism upon which the League of Nations was formed was quite deliberately bypassed during the formation of the United Nations. For a start, unlike the League, the United Nations was built upon a bedrock of *Realpolitik* in which the needs and interests of the great powers could be accommodated.

One of the primary objectives in establishing a successor to the League of Nations was to create a global organization that could maintain international peace and security on the basis of the inviolability of state sovereignty. The *purpose* of the new organization would be to "maintain international peace and security, encourage friendly relations among nations, and achieve international co-operation." Its *nature* would be "based on the sovereign equality of its members, in the tradition of early international organisations and the League of Nations." Its *competence* would lie principally with a Security Council, which would have the prime responsibility for maintaining peace and security, "with all decisions in this crucial area reached only by unanimous agreement of the permanent members" (Riggs and Plano 1994: 13). The central Allied powers would occupy permanent seats on the Security Council and UN effectiveness would be based upon their cooperative efforts. Indeed the spirit of wartime cooperation required to defeat the Axis powers lasted until the inaugural United Nations Conference on International Organization (UNICO) in San Francisco, which opened on 25 April 1945, and the final drafting of the UN Charter. The major tenets agreed to at Dumbarton Oaks were, with a few modifications, adopted by the United Nations' 51 founding member states, who signed the Charter on 26 June 1945.

State accountability and the UN system

Reflecting a universal determination to prevent the re-emergence of the conditions that had led to two world wars, the preamble of the UN Charter states a number of priorities for the Organization and its system: "to save succeeding generations from the scourge of war ... and to reaffirm faith in fundamental human rights." In the field of humanitarian affairs the Charter set out to "promote social progress and better standards of life in larger freedom" and to "employ international machinery for the promotion of the economic and social advancement of all peoples." However, the state-centred nature of the United Nations, designed to manage inter-state disputes, seemed to contradict the active promotion of obligations related to human security within states. Article 2(7) of the Charter stated: "Nothing contained in the present Charter shall authorise the United Nations to intervene in matters which are essentially within the domestic jurisdiction of any state or shall require the Members to submit such matters to settlement under the present Charter." UN interference in internal affairs was authorized only if the events within a sovereign entity were deemed as being a threat to international peace and security (Chapter VII).

On the question of human rights, the original Charter fell short of wartime rhetoric, in which US President Franklin Roosevelt articulated his "Four Freedoms" (Buergenthal 1988: 18): "freedom of speech and expression," "freedom of every person to worship God in his own way," "freedom from want," and "freedom from fear." However, the inclusion of provisions for the recognition of human rights, which non-governmental bodies had strongly pressed for, did, if seriously recognized and implemented, contradict the notion of non-interference in domestic issues. Article 13 mandates the UN General Assembly to "initiate studies and make recommendations for the purposes of ... assisting in the realisation of human rights." Article 56, together with Article 55, pledges all UN members "to take joint and separate action with the Organisation for the achievement of ... universal respect for, and observance of, human rights." Article 68 requires the Economic and Social Council (ECOSOC) to "set up commissions ... for the promotion of human rights."

However, the implementation of such measures was a matter that none of the principal Allied powers was keen to focus on, lest they were caught red-handed. The Soviet Union had its *Gulag*, racial discrimination was rampant in the United States as a whole, and Britain and France had their colonial empires. Moreover, Hitler's original pretext for invading Czechoslovakia in 1938, to protect the rights of Sudetenland Germans, invoked worries of future foreign interventions and violations of national integrity in a world of minorities. Of course over the years, with an increasingly proactive human rights movement developing worldwide and higher international standards emerging, the General Assembly (GA), developed a whole body of human rights legislation, based upon the legal and conceptual foundations set by these Charter articles. The Universal Declaration of Human Rights, adopted by the GA in December 1948, and the International Covenants on Civil and Political Rights and on Economic, Social and Cultural Rights, which came into force in 1976, subsequently established the basic norms for individual protection in the human rights field. Other conventions and treaties adopted by the GA over the years concentrated on specific human rights abuses and include: the Convention on the Prevention and Punishment of the Crime of Genocide (1948), International Convention on the Elimination of All Forms of Racial Discrimination (1965), International Convention on the Suppression and the Punishment of the Crime of Apartheid (1973), Convention on the Elimination of All Forms of Discrimination Against Women (1979), Convention Against Torture and Other Cruel, Inhuman or Degrading Treatment (1984), Declaration on the Rights of Persons Belonging to National or Ethnic, Religious and Linguistic Minorities (1992). Refugee law, established through various international mechanisms, most notably the Geneva Convention and the Refugees Convention (1951 and 1967), has created a body of law that establishes standards for the protection of persons. In principle, the above provide the legal basis for the international community to intervene in the affairs of states, thus further eroding the absolute nature of state sovereignty. The increase in the numbers of internally displaced persons and the need for more humanitarian assistance have also provoked a discussion regarding the right of intervention. In practice, however, upholding these Conventions and abiding by the laws are still deeply embedded in the rhetoric of most countries.

Still, gradual changes to international law and their acceptance have dissolved rigid notions of state sovereignty and, despite Article 2(7), turned them into a pool of relative principles. Furthermore, the growth of activity by non-governmental organizations (NGOs) in the human rights field and the wide body of international law has made state behaviour, to a degree, accountable to the UN body, citizens, and the international community as a whole. Indeed, some commentators have noted that "by the 1970s a considerable body of support existed for the view that grave violations of human rights were not a matter essentially within the domestic jurisdiction" of the state concerned, involving as they did breaches of that state's obligations under international law (Greenwood 1993).

The United Nations' endeavours to promote human rights were strengthened between 1966 and 1971, when successive actions by the GA, ECOSOC, the Human Rights Commission, and the Sub-Commission on the Prevention of Discrimination and Protection of Minorities fashioned the machinery for human rights protection. The principal components of this framework are Commission Resolution 8 (XXIII) of 1967 and ECOSOC Resolutions 1235 of 1967 and 1503 of 1970, which established procedures by which the UN Human Rights Commission annually considers situations of gross violations in different countries.

A number of country-specific experts or rapporteurs were appointed to investigate serious human rights violations in different countries in the world. Since the 1980s, as the result of pressure from NGOs, the UN Commission on Human Rights (and its Sub-Commission) have also established a number of thematic mechanisms to address grave violations of fundamental human rights (for instance, forced disappearances, torture, summary and arbitrary executions, religious intolerance, the sale of children, arbitrary detention, internally displaced persons, racism, censorship, violence against women). Monitoring bodies were set up under human rights treaties to scrutinize state parties' compliance with their human rights obligations. As a result, there was a significant shift in the 1970s from the development of universal human rights principles to the implementation of norms and the attempt to enforce standards already agreed upon. This implied a high level of interference by the United Nations' human rights bodies in the internal affairs of states, albeit interference by consent. Governments under suspicion of committing human rights violations were often forced by consensus to permit de facto interventions in order to protect their moral integrity within the international community. It is interesting to note, however, that, despite this shift in the concerns of the United Nations, less than 1 per cent of the Organization's budget was invested in the Human Rights Commission, and it is interesting to speculate how much more progress could have been made if the United Nations' financial commitments had matched the moral commitments of those who pressed for these changes.

Sadly, from a historical perspective the period between 1945 and the late 1980s is characterized by UN impotence in the maintenance of global peace. In the Security Council, decision-making was in effect strait-jacketed by the East–West stand-off, the veto being used frequently to block resolutions that went against the perceived strategic interests of one of the permanent members – 279 vetoes were cast during the Cold War period. Speaking in 1960, Dag Hammarskjold was frank in his comments on the United Nations' limitations and freedom of action: "With its constitution and structure, it is extremely difficult for the United Nations to exercise an influence on problems which are clearly and definitely within the orbit of present day conflicts between power blocs. If a specific conflict is within that orbit, it can be assumed that the Security Council is rendered inactive, and it may be feared that even positions taken by the General Assembly would follow lines strongly influenced by considerations only indirectly related to the concrete difficulty under consideration" (Hammarskjold 1960). In this environment, internal conflicts and, more significantly, proxy wars very rarely reached the Council's agenda, while the United Nations' humanitarian bodies and the international NGO community were left with the task of containing the consequences of these self-destructive struggles.

The post–Cold War era and *An Agenda for Peace*

With the end of the Cold War, the United Nations was able to facilitate the disengagement of a number of internal conflicts in Latin America, Africa, and Asia, many initiated by the then UN Secretary-General, Javier Pérez de Cuéllar. This employed the use of his "good offices" function in establishing a Central American peace process, the withdrawal of Soviet troops from Afghanistan, an end to the Namibian crisis, and the outlining of a series of proposals upon which a peace plan was adopted for resolving Cambodia's civil war. Perez de Cuellar's initiatives were supported by Security Council action and the establishment of a number of peace-keeping operations. These post–Cold War operations in El Salvador, Cambodia, and Namibia, for example, went beyond the traditional forms of conflict management because complex mandates were drawn up to facilitate a comprehensive peace process in each case. Perez de Cuellar was in no doubt about the potential effectiveness of the Secretary-General's good offices function and, as he put it in 1988, "No one will ever know how many conflicts have been prevented or limited through contacts which have taken place in the famous glass mansion which can become fairly opaque when necessary" (Franck and Nolte 1993: 144).

The United Nations' quick response to the Kuwaiti crisis of 1990 also gave an impression that the Organization had at last become a credible actor on the international scene. As a result, for the first time ever, on 31 January 1992 the Security Council met at the level of heads of government to decide, among other things, "the responsibility of the Security Council in the maintenance of international peace and security." The Council invited the newly elected Secretary-General, Dr. Boutros Boutros-Ghali, to prepare a report that would recommend ways to enhance the "capacity of the United Nations for preventive diplomacy, for peacemaking and for peace-keeping," covering areas such as early warning, regional organizations, resourcing of the United Nations, and the greater use of the UN Secretariat (United Nations 1992).

Although the special session of the Security Council had dictated the terms of reference for *An Agenda for Peace*, in particular preventive diplomacy, peace-making, and peace-keeping, the UN Secretariat added post-conflict peace-building to this trio of high-priority topics. Under preventive diplomacy were ranged headings on confidence-building, fact-finding, early warning, preventive deployment, and demilitarized zones. Peace-making covered the means by which the United Nations can bring parties together, such as the International Court of Justice, amelioration through assistance, sanctions, the use of military force, and peace enforcement units. The amplification of peace-keeping covered the possibility of new departures and the logistics of such operations. The chapter on the post-conflict phase dealt with joint projects between states in rather vague terms and then tackled the very specific issue of land mines. It resumed a vaguer tone with the assertion that the United Nations now had a mandate to provide "technical assistance" to transform "deficient national structures and capabilities." There was mention of cooperation between the United Nations and regional organizations. However, only in passing did it mention NGOs, which is rather odd given the sophisticated relationship that has developed between them and ECOSOC since it passed Resolution 1296 in May 1968.

Dr. Boutros-Ghali had assumed an instrumental role in the document's drafting and had resolved to create something that would be bold and comprehensive, and invite debate. Indeed, with a few close advisers he had in effect formed an inner group of the drafting committee, and some of the key proposals concerning peace-keeping emerged directly from his office. As this suggests, the Secretary-General established clear ownership of the report and it emerged, in many respects, as his own personal agenda for his tenure in office. Certainly the final document (Boutros-Ghali 1992) did not enjoy the unconditional support of the original full drafting committee. Comments made by Marrack Goulding in the months following the publication of *An Agenda for Peace* indicated that he was not a wholehearted supporter of some of the most controversial proposals on expanding the United Nations' peace-keeping capacity (Cox 1993: 4).

Preventive diplomacy

The focus on UN action to "prevent disputes from arising between parties, to prevent existing disputes from escalating into conflicts and to limit the spread of the latter when they occur" was an attempt to resurrect a concept that had been a feature of the United Nations' conflict-management mandate during the Cold War. In his 1960 Report to the GA, Hammarskjold outlined the purpose of preventive diplomacy in the context of superpower competition. Hammarskjold considered the use of UN peace-keeping forces, first deployed in 1956 after the Suez Crisis, and then in the Congo in 1960, as being an instrument to prevent the potential for US–Soviet competition in parts of the world emerging from colonialism. Dr. Boutros-Ghali adopted the concept as a method for addressing the problems of the contemporary era.

Yet even at that early stage, some observers, including Dr. Boutros-Ghali, recognized that the conflict-prevention measures described in *An Agenda for Peace* did not go far enough towards creating a comprehensive framework for preventive action. In particular it did not include potential options for addressing root causes of conflicts and possible instability, namely the social and economic problems that lie at the heart of many internal conflicts. It was becoming increasingly apparent that the thaw in the East–West stand-off was not bringing President Bush's much hailed "New World Order." Rather, a much more complex global arena was emerging in which a multitude of groups were vying for power and international legitimacy. In Afghanistan, for instance, the decade of fighting against Soviet troops erupted into an even bloodier battle between rival armed groups and militia after the Soviet departure in 1990. So the receding threat of the bipolar global nuclear war was replaced by an unstable multipolar system, manifested by an eruption of internal conflicts. By 1995, there were 30 fully fledged wars (with over 1,000 deaths per year) being fought worldwide, all of them internal.

The international community is faced with more than just the effects of these changes. It has been forced to contend with the fragmentation of conflicts and the disintegration of states. Martin Van Creveld, a leading Israeli military strategist and historian, in describing the wars of the future suggests that they will be between sub-state organizations (*Newsweek*, 17 April 1995). He argues that the state in its traditional mould is beginning to lose relevance and that global society will become more and more fragmented, as first sovereignty and then governments become less important. In this situation, wars, he says, will be fought not between states using heavy weapons and regular armies but between warlords and narrowly defined interest factions that use light weaponry and irregular forces. This warlordism, in turn, has become effective in destabilizing societies and states (*Newsweek*, 17 April 1995).

This form of warfare is characterized by the indiscriminate destruction of life and property, reflected most profoundly by the use of land mines, which by their nature have bequeathed a legacy of carnage to succeeding generations. Moreover, in these fragmented conflicts it is civilians who make up the vast majority of casualties in today's wars. According to the United Nations Development Programme, as many as 90 per cent of war casualties are civilians (UNDP 1994: 47). Furthermore, internal conflicts have created the greatest forced movements of people since 1945. In 1993, there were 18.2 million refugees and 24 million internally displaced people, according to the UN High Commissioner for Refugees. By October 1994 these figures had increased to 23 million and 26 million, respectively. Some estimates suggest that by the year 2000 the total could reach 100 million people.

The responsibility for preventive diplomacy lies principally with the Security Council and Secretary-General and to a lesser extent with the General Assembly. The Council's role derives from its position *vis-à-vis* international peace and security, and it can act of its own volition by sending missions, as it did to Burundi in August 1994 and February 1995, or it can authorize the Secretary-General to initiate measures. The Secretary-General has a responsibility under Article 99 of the UN Charter to bring to the Council's attention situations that may threaten peace and security. Over the years, different Secretary-Generals have interpreted this in different ways, but often this has encompassed a proactive approach. From 1992, Dr. Boutros-Ghali presided over some major innovations to institutionalize preventive diplomacy within the UN Secretariat. This included the structuring of regional desks within the Department of Political Affairs (DPA), which are charged with the responsibility of monitoring developments around the world, and innovations such as Task Forces on peace operations and interdepartmental working groups (Kittani 1995).

Despite these efforts, there are some severe constraints that hinder the United Nations' attempts to advance preventive diplomacy. The first of these concerns the practical challenge of managing the sheer volume of information that the United Nations has to handle. The DPA has only 70 professionals working on preventive diplomacy and peace-making and all too often the difficulty derives not from the lack of information but from being able to distinguish the relevant factors that may point to an area of concern from the inconsequential (Cox 1993: 37). Another constraint has been the lack of professional diplomatic or political personalities able to commit themselves on a long-term basis to the job of undertaking good offices missions. A third constraint is the lack of capital to support preventive diplomatic missions, because the United Nations has found it difficult to get governments to finance missions before violence has broken out.

These practical constraints, which are surmountable, are accompanied by political obstacles that, because they are issues of principle, may not be so easy to overcome. The most potent of these is the fact that for the United Nations to act preventively it still requires the consent of at least one of the parties to the potential conflict. This is particularly salient in internal conflicts, where a government that may be involved in a counter-insurgency campaign does not wish to *internationalize* the problem. Often governments will cite Article 2(7) and resist the attentions of the Security Council, which all too often is viewed as a threatening intruder, representing the interests of major powers and reassembling a form of neo-imperialism. The other key obstacle to preventive diplomacy concerns the willingness of parties to negotiate. The need to create appropriate political will is a major feature of any design to prevent conflict. It is for these reasons that non-state actors such as NGOs may be far better equipped in such situations, and the relative advantages of NGO preventive action can be used to overcome these obstacles related to issues of state consent and sensitivities regarding sovereignty.

Military and non-military dimensions

The growth in the non-military aspect of the United Nations' agenda drew upon ideas that, hitherto, had been marginal in the UN debate but were common fare among NGOs and in peace research. But these non-military concepts, such as early warning, fact-finding, peace-making, and the others detailed above, were accompanied by proposals to strengthen the United Nations' capacity for military action as well. A close reading of the text shows that the main emphasis is on the military aspects of preventive diplomacy. The latter included recommendations to establish peace-enforcement units, the preventive deployment of troops, the establishment of demilitarized zones, the expansion of peace-keeping, and the utilization of Chapter VII provisions such as the earmarking of troops and the resurrection of a Military Staff Committee.

Ironically, now that the Cold War has ended, in one way or another the world's military establishments have seized upon these military elements in *An Agenda for Peace* and have been keen to interpret the United Nations' enhanced profile in terms of a greater role for their own interests. British, French, and American military planners have developed their own Army Field Doctrines for peace-keeping, while the Department of Peace-keeping Operations has been working on plans for a rapid deployment force. At least 21 governments have confirmed a willingness to provide troops on a stand-by basis (S/1994/777). The need for restructuring within the UN Secretariat reflects the enormous expansion of activities related to peace and security since 1988. According to the Secretary-General's Supplement to *An Agenda for Peace* (Boutros-Ghali 1995), the quantitative increase in the number of disputes in which the United Nations was involved rose continually between 1988 and 1994. In the 12 months before 31 January 1988 the United Nations was involved with 11 disputes. In the same period preceding 16 December 1994, this rose to 28. Between 1988 and 1994 the number of military personnel deployed under UN auspices rose from 9,570 to 73,393, and as of March 1995 there were 16 UN peace-support operations worldwide.

What became clear during this time was that the United Nations has been unable to mobilize the resources to meet the ever-growing demands on its peace and security system. As a result, Dr. Boutros-Ghali was forced to retreat from some of his original proposals, outlined in *An Agenda for Peace*, for meeting the challenges posed by modern-day conflicts. The problems encountered in Somalia and the former Yugoslavia were instrumental in making the UN Secretary-General reassess the role of peace enforcement as a UN tool. One of the major problems that the UN Force faced in Somalia, for example, was the failure of command and control. American pre-eminence in directing the military dimension of UNOSOM II (United Nations Operation in Somalia) led to confusion and a very one-sided interpretation of the UN mandate in Somalia. The political misjudgements of American decision-makers were transformed into UN failures on the ground. In his 1993 Report to the General Assembly, the Secretary-General wrote that in UNOSOM II the "Security Council had chosen to set up an unprecedented operation involving, as necessary, enforcement action by the United Nations itself under the authority of the Security Council" (Boutros-Ghali 1993). There was at this time a feeling that UNOSOM II would become a model for future peace-support operations, where peace-keeping functions would be accompanied by options to use enforcement measures. The decision to withdraw the United Nations' military mission from Somalia in March 1995, while much of the internal conflict was still continuing, reflected in many respects the need to reassess the feasibility of such an approach. In the Supplement to *An Agenda for Peace*, Dr. Boutros-Ghali (1995: 6) indicated that at present neither the Security Council nor the Secretary-General possesses "the capacity to deploy, direct, command and control operations for this purpose, except perhaps on a very limited scale."

The retreat from peace enforcement on any substantial scale has been replaced by a new emphasis on the need to create a rapid deployment force:

I have come to the conclusion that the United Nations does need to give serious thought to the idea of a rapid reaction force. Such a force would be the Security Council's strategic reserve for deployment when there was an emergency need for peace-keeping troops ... These units would be trained to the same standards ... and would be stationed in their home countries but maintained at a high state of readiness. (Boutros-Ghali 1995: 16)

More recent departures in peace-keeping have shown how a small, highly trained group, immediately deployed at an early stage before tensions have erupted, can be more effective than a large and less well-trained force that arrives at a stage when conflict has already started. The preventive deployment of fewer than 1,000 troops in Macedonia had greater relative success than the major multinational interventions in Somalia, Haiti, and Rwanda. The most commonly cited measures for realizing such a rapid reaction arrangement include stand-by forces, possibly composed of volunteers, and proposed in *An Agenda for Peace*, or, as Sir Brian Urquhart has often proposed, a highly trained volunteer rapid response force owned by the United Nations itself (Commission on Global Governance 1995). Given the complexity of many conflicts, such a UN-owned force would have to be constituted on a multifaceted basis, encompassing a mixture of military, police, civilian, and technical personnel to reflect the scope of flexibility required to deal with the demands of modern humanitarian crises.

The present wave of conflicts has placed the concept of human security at the centre of the present debate in international affairs and the agendas of many NGOs and humanitarian agencies. In spite of this conceptual shift, *An Agenda for Peace* did not attempt to elaborate on the role of "we the peoples," set out as the ordaining feature of the UN Charter. Furthermore, the role of NGOs was, for all practical purposes, ignored, leaving a major gap in the overall strategy that the document aimed to create. Even the role of regional organizations received only passing attention. The failure to elaborate the precise nature of the relationship between regional organs or to develop the concept of a division of labour represented a crucial disjunction with the overall theme of the report. Essentially, the non-military aspect of preventive diplomacy and its associated tools and methodologies were omitted.

Clearly Dr. Boutros-Ghali became aware of this deficiency for, in his statement to the forty-seventh conference of NGOs in New York on 20 September 1994, he rejected the view of the United Nations as a "forum for sovereign States alone." NGOs were now "full participants in international life." He went on to stress the necessity for their involvement in the peace-building process. Indeed, compared with the passing references in *Agenda for Peace*, he was quite unequivocal, stating that he was "convinced that NGOs have an important role to play in the achievement of the ideal established by the Charter of the United Nations: the maintenance and establishment of peace"; and that "the vast enterprise of building peace pre-supposes that non-governmental organisations will be involved at every stage" (United Nations 1994).

The changing nature of sovereignty

Dr. Boutros-Ghali's recognition of NGO support for UN field activities is consistent with the erosion of the sovereign principle. Although in *An Agenda for Peace* he formally stated that the "time of absolute and exclusive sovereignty ... has passed," he affirmed a process that had been evident since the 1960s, in which "the theory" of sovereignty "was never matched by reality."

This conceptual shift in the sovereignty debate was, in part, motivated by precedents that occurred at the end of the 1991 Gulf War.

Principal among these was the adoption of Security Council Resolution 688 (1991), which allowed the international community to give humanitarian aid and protect the Kurds of Northern Iraq, who at the time were being attacked by the Iraqi armed forces. The subsequent military-backed humanitarian intervention, "Operation Provide Comfort," witnessed the deployment of British, Dutch, American, and French troops and the establishment of "safe havens" on sovereign Iraqi territory. As "Operation Provide Comfort" got under way, many political leaders spoke openly of a new international code of conduct in which sovereignty was no longer absolute and exclusive.[1] At the time, the then UN Secretary-General, Javier Pérez de Cuéllar, said in a speech in Bordeaux:

We are clearly witnessing what is probably an irresistible shift in public attitudes towards the belief that the defence of the oppressed in the name of morality should prevail over frontiers and legal documents. (Wilenski 1993: 465)

These precedents and subsequent interventions by the Security Council in places such as the former Yugoslavia, Somalia, and Rwanda have refocused the debate on the meaning of Article 2(7) of the UN Charter, the exact nature of the Security Council's authority, the applicability of enforcement powers, and, more precisely, what criteria should be used to judge the validity of an issue deemed to be within the domestic jurisdiction of a state. That a re-examination of this question has emerged is not surprising. As global society has become increasingly interdependent over the past 40 years, many problems that underlie the security dilemmas in the international system have become transnational. Issues such as environmental degradation, drug trafficking, and AIDS illustrate this point. The UNDP's human security concept highlights the ramifications of this evolution. What is clear is that today's problems require ever-broader approaches for resolution and often this will mean going beyond the narrow confines of the sovereignty concept. In a very real sense, sovereignty, previously the prerogative of the state, now falls within the ambit of the people. In the new era the empowerment of citizens is becoming more evident.

"We, the peoples ..."

The past 50 years have witnessed a massive expansion of the state-centred system. In 1945, 51 states signed the UN Charter. As of May

1995 there were 185 member states. While this evolution in global politics, over the past half-century, has manifested itself in various social, economic, and commercial directions, the technological revolution has had an even more profound influence in determining the relationship between these state units. The growth of global communications, and of the economic and financial interdependence that has benefited from the communications revolution, has also promoted and fostered a multi-centred system. The most concrete illustration of this "Third System" has been in the growth of non-governmental entities. From the world of global financial markets, to that of non-governmental lobbying organizations, to the shadowy world of terrorist groups, the state-centred system is being challenged by the effects of the multi-centred system.

Increasingly, the worldwide communications network is developing into a system of global interdependence. For example, the effects of the Internet are becoming ever more evident as millions of computer terminals become linked together through existing communications systems. Consequently, the advantages and disadvantages of this global communications network can be seen in many examples of information exchange. The question that emerges from these developments is how can a comprehensive peace-building paradigm be developed? At present there are a number of limitations on the role of the United Nations in advancing preventive diplomacy. This has been compounded by the logistical and financial burdens imposed by existing commitments and demands to intervene in crises. Then there is the lack of political will amongst UN member states to act to prevent or contain the growing instabilities in the international system. It becomes clear that dealing with the sheer complexity of global problems is beyond the capabilities of a single agency or organization. Addressing these problems requires a grand coalition of forces, drawn from a variety of different sectors and aimed at preventing and resolving the tensions that lead to war. Such a coalition would include, in addition to the United Nations and national governments, regional organizations, popular movements, and NGOs.

In recent years, NGOs and popular movements have grown. They have played a constantly expanding role in the advancement of human rights, in organizing and providing humanitarian assistance, in promoting adherence to humanitarian law, in fostering economic and social development, and in promoting peace with justice. This "Third System" constitutes the link between "we, the peoples" of the UN Charter and states and the intergovernmental system. Together,

170

NGOs represent a wealth of human and material resources that can be used to great advantage in complex and often perilous areas of action.

NGOs, like the United Nations, are readjusting to the new realities, while attempting to cope with some of the remaining consequences of the Cold War era. Part of that readjustment must be the building of effective coalitions that focus on the non-military aspects of pre-conflict peace-building – early warning and prevention. These networks must become more than a convenient method of information-sharing and develop an organizing principle.

The "Third System" and the growth of NGOs have facilitated the massive development of networks at all levels of the global community. These networks have in some ways been a low-cost, flexible, and efficient way of working and have tended to be a more democratic way of managing mandates. The information revolution, by means of computers, electronic mail, fax machines, teleconferencing, and other developments, will continue to facilitate networking and bring communities closer together. In this context, the "Third System" has a central role to play in advancing the concept of preventive diplomacy, facilitating conflict resolution, and being the focal point for a conflict-prevention coalition.

2. The need for a new agenda!

Preventive action

A series of measures is required to prepare the international community more effectively for conflict prevention. Central to this is the reform of the United Nations' decision-making processes and the development of mechanisms that would enable the Organization specifically to address conflicts in a preventive manner.

As I have argued here, part of this design for UN reform must include an expansion of the qualitative and quantitative role of NGOs. And in this context it is also important to make the distinction between preventive diplomacy, which is pursued by the state-centred system, and preventive action, which is the subject of the multi-centred system. Moreover, there is a distinction between the concerns of state security, which aims to protect states and their agencies, and human security, which is aimed at protecting and sustaining the lives of people. However, the changing nature of UN activities in peace and security has brought the NGO community into closer contact with the

Organization on the ground, especially in humanitarian relief and post-conflict peace-building. This has brought the two systems of state-centred interests and multi-centred interests into very close contact. What is missing, however, is a serious evaluation of the role of NGOs in conflict prevention. It is now obvious that the United Nations should assess and integrate the relative strengths of preventive action undertaken by the NGO community and the preventive diplomacy in which states and state agencies engage. Whereas the measures under preventive diplomacy have been outlined in some detail in *An Agenda for Peace* and subsequent Secretariat documents, a discussion of preventive action within the United Nations and the relationship with NGOs has not been given equal attention.

The non-state nature of NGOs and their familiarity with the societal structures that are at risk in potential conflict situations make them ideal for identifying tensions that are all too often precursors to societal violence. This closeness and the inevitable links that are created among the different sectors of civil society mean that NGOs are very well placed to influence or facilitate processes towards dialogue. The successful experience of this form of conflict resolution has demonstrated the merits of NGO action: from the Buddhist monks and peace marchers of Cambodia (Garcia 1994), to the Catholic bishops and civic organizations in Latin America; from the multisectoral peace advocates and peace zone communities in the Philippines (Garcia 1994) to the community groups and NGOs involved in improving Catholic–Protestant relations in Northern Ireland, to the tribal elders of Somaliland (Yusuf Farah and Lewis 1993), who have used traditional forms of local diplomacy to resolve resource-based conflicts in the north of their country. The requirement for a successful new agenda is the employment of these methods at an early stage before violent conflict has broken out, using the relative strengths of the international community to achieve this objective.

Just as "preventive diplomacy" is constituted of a number of principles, so "preventive action" is made up of a wealth of tools, methodologies, and approaches that are now available through the actions of citizen-based diplomacy and aimed at creating environments of non-belligerence. *Citizens' peace missions* are being used on a regular basis to define the issues better and to recommend ways forward. These should be accompanied by *special peace envoys*, who would be credible emissaries to speak to parties in conflict or establish links with an emerging peace constituency to explore the possibilities for a negotiated peace settlement. The experience of *problem-solving workshops* has illustrated the value of creating a forum in which informal consultations can take place between representatives of rival parties, local peacemakers, and sectors of civil society. The need for *capacity-building* is a necessary dimension of the structured approach to early action, where relevant actors and community leaders could be supported in becoming catalysers or mediators in a process for dialogue. Such support could also take the form of offering logistical and technical help to negotiators, providing good offices such as secure venues for talks. Mobilizing peace constituencies within countries affected by potential or actual conflict is a paramount concern for preventive action. To facilitate the evolution of such a constituency, NGOs have organized *peace conferences* or *Peace Task Forces* that, by bringing together relevant sectors of civil society, establish forums for national reconciliation. *Supporting peace initiatives* such as "zones for peace or "peace corridors" have been valued, while putting *public pressure for peace* on parties involved in conflict should be viewed as a particularly potent tool for making politicians re-evaluate their priorities and policy. Plans of action are often necessary for coordinating the international community's response to conflict situations. There will be a need to create multi-layered forums made up of eminent persons who will be responsible for designing the structured approach to early action in each situation. The creation of the *Friends of Burundi* is an example where round-table seminars attended by different NGO partners, international organizations, and representatives of states have led to a degree of coherence and structure for action. This forum provides an opportunity for different actors to brainstorm solutions and devise coordinated strategies with specific objectives. Generally this aimed at producing a "Plan of Action" for preventing humanitarian disasters, supporting a negotiated solution, and ensuring that parties to the conflict can rely on the international community for help in a post-conflict peace-building situation and help with the rebuilding of institutions necessary for sustained reconciliation in a hitherto divided society.

Multi-track diplomacy

The New Agenda needs to be based upon the concept of complementarity and a consistent design. Only through this approach is it possible to address the chaos that currently prevails through the international system. It is possible to conceptualize this and draw upon different levels, which, when brought together, present a comprehensive, mutually reinforcing network and design towards preventive action.

It is clear that the conflict arena is multi-layered and that different types of preventive action must be used to address these different dimensions. We can identify five layers: the personal, the local, the national, the regional, and the international. What is clear is that different actors, intervening at appropriate intervals and using relevant tools, can be used to construct a cohesive network for preventive action and conflict resolution throughout this multi-layered paradigm. As this chapter has illustrated, this includes the United Nations and its agencies, regional organizations, and NGOs.

At the heart of this design and preventive action plan is the concept of multi-track diplomacy. Multi-track diplomacy is the application of peace-making from different vantage points within a multi-centred network. Neither one-track nor two-track diplomacy can encompass the extraordinary values and genius of a multifaceted approach. It must reflect, first, the different levels of conflict that need to be addressed and, second, the overall design of complementarity. Eleven types of diplomacy can be identified:

- intergovernmental diplomacy, such as the United Nations;
- governmental peace-making through official diplomacy, such as the bilateral negotiations between the parties in the Middle East;
- second-track diplomacy using unofficial forums, such as the secret Norwegian negotiations that eventually led to the 1993 peace deal between Israel and the Palestine Liberation Organization;
- citizen diplomacy through private means – this can come in many forms but one of the most successful illustrations of this is in Somaliland where tribal elders have used traditional kinship networks to resolve conflicts;
- economic diplomacy, which includes donor assistance from a variety of donor agencies working towards an economic package for sustaining peace;
- peace diplomacy through religious organizations – this encompasses not only the work of local churches and religious leaders but also projects established by international religious establishments such as the Quakers or the Italian-based Catholic lay community of Sant' Egidio;
- diplomacy through women's movements, which at both local and international level have helped mobilize women in the pursuit of conflict resolution;
- communications diplomacy through the media, which has proved to

be a particularly powerful tool in mobilizing public opinion and moulding the perceptions of policy makers;

- peace diplomacy through social movements – this is a broader form of the citizen diplomacy described above and examples may include the "peace zones" and "peace corridors" created by communities in places such as Colombia and the Philippines, or the work of the Community Relations Council in Northern Ireland;
- peace education through education and training, which is seen as addressing some of the root causes of conflicts – examples include UNESCO's Programme to Promote a Culture of Peace and International Alert's training seminars and workshops in the Near East, Africa, and Latin America;
- creative diplomacy through artists and personalities from the world of entertainment, for example "Live Aid," "Band Aid," and "Comic Relief."

The need for new UN mechanisms

It is clear that there needs to be substantial reform within the United Nations to enable it to address contemporary global security. The nature of UN decision-making must be reformed to make it compatible with present realities. This will include rejuvenating the UN Security Council to make it more representative of the global polity, strengthening the Office for Preventive Diplomacy as well as the position of the High Commissioner for Human Rights. With so many conflicts centred on contending national claims there is a need to create a structure within the UN system for dealing with cases of self-determination. In addition, there is much belief in the revival of an International Trusteeship system. In cases of failed or failing state institutions, and where civilian lives may be at risk from warlordism and factional warfare, a trusteeship under UN auspices may be a viable option.

Individual components of the newly emerging global security mechanism should also be reviewed. For example, the extension of non-military intervention should be considered as part of the structured response mentioned above. The dispatch of so-called "White Helmets" with a human rights monitoring mandate could be seen as a component of any preventive action package. A long-term preventive measure is represented by a determination to control the instruments responsible for most of the killing in modern wars, namely light weapons. The monitoring and maintenance of a light weapons register would be a step in the right direction. It is within this context that justice must be seen to be done in those situations where there is evidence of gross human rights violations. Thus the establishment of a permanent international criminal court supported by the international community is a desirable legal instrument. This should be complemented by Truth Commissions that ensure reconciliation between communities and that impunity, so often practised in many states, ceases to become a pervasive feature of international society.

Strengthening financial support

Financing the United Nations has often been precarious. The various UN budgets are all too often depleted, so that the Organization is unable to furnish the resources to meet needs. Much of the problem comes from the failure of many member states to pay their dues on a regular basis. As of 1 January 1995, the regular budget was owed US$1,380,722,575, while the largest peace-keeping operation in the former Yugoslavia was owed US$1,085,361,909 (UN Budget figures, 1 January 1995). The continued inadequacy of the present financial arrangements within the United Nations has stimulated major thinking towards alternative strategies for financing the Organization. One idea that has been adopted by some lobbying organizations includes the placing of a tax on foreign exchange transactions. Although there may be problems with this, the Commission on Global Governance has urged the United Nations and the Bretton Woods institutions to explore the feasibility of such an idea.

The Commission has also urged consideration of surcharges for using the global commons, such as a charge on airline tickets, a charge on ocean maritime transport, user fees for non-coastal ocean fishing, special user fees for activities in Antarctica, parking fees for geo-stationary satellites, and charges for user rights of the electro-magnetic spectrum.

A structured response to early warning

The information revolution has many implications, particularly for early warning and conflict prevention. But how can the contributions of the information revolution advance from recording the plight of victims to victim prevention? We can address this conundrum by solving another problem: how can we route information to the right people at the right time? This means seeing that this information becomes the basis for action. It is, however, not enough merely to get the information across at the right time; also pertinent is the form in which information reaches the people who need to take action. We must remember that today we are living in a period of information overload. Every sign, symbol, magazine, journal, newsletter, bulletin, fax, or e-mail message competes for our attention. How then can we package the information so that it can have the proper impact and make people act on the basis of our information? For some there is too much early warning. The emphasis must now be upon early action.

One excellent example of a system that works well is the Urgent Action Network run by the British Section of Amnesty International. Information is sifted by the research officers in the International Secretariat and then passed on. Urgent Action then disseminates it by fax and e-mail to volunteers who have previously agreed to participate. When they receive the information, the volunteers bombard the violators of human rights with polite requests to desist, by employing a variety of high-speed media, such as telegrams and faxes. Although this system has been developed within one organization for a specific purpose and refined over a period of time, and in that sense is limited, it does serve to illustrate one avenue of development. Another example of this form of mobilization around a single issue is demonstrated by EarthAction, which has been able to pull together the resources of thousands of NGOs and focus this energy towards addressing a particular environmental concern.

Although effective early warning of potential conflicts is the backbone of a conflict-prevention strategy, the need for early action requires a new conceptual base. The relative failure of UN-based early warning and information analyses is due to the fact that the United Nations alone is unable effectively both to manage the collection of early warning signals and to act upon them in an appropriate manner. A UN Secretariat working group on early warning has pointed out that information itself is not sufficient to make political decisions. More important is the relation of information to analysis and policy decisions (Dedring 1994: 102–103).

The United Nations' limitations highlight the comparative advantages that a multi-centred network could have in developing an effective early warning to early action system. By developing a framework under which a range of agencies, each with their own expertise, cooperated in collecting, analysing, and disseminating information, there would be a multilateral system of early warning leading to early action. It could be possible to build a consortium of international agencies, each contributing personnel, resources, and expertise in information-gathering and analysis. Members could divide their responsibilities and the regions on which they focus, depending on their comparative strengths. A common methodology, including report formats and a range of conflict indicators, could be agreed upon, so that a degree of consistency could be achieved across the network. The overall objective would be local or regional cooperation with partners, including governments, NGOs, religious communities, and grass-roots organizations, in order to produce situation analyses and policy and action recommendations for key decision makers – locally, regionally, and in donor countries. UN agencies could participate in such a network by providing information on the areas in which they operate and by acting upon the analyses and recommendations that emerge. The advantages of a network over the singular UN mechanism are clear. Based on the principle of the division of labour, the consortium would be able to respond in a more structured way, with each agency utilizing its specific expertise. For example, while one group of agencies monitored the human rights situation, another group could mobilize global pressure and lobby governments, and another could build a peace constituency.

The whole point of coalition-building is to take advantage of the different relative strengths that can be offered by different agencies and to ensure that there is no duplication of effort. It represents a multi-layered approach that brings together human rights and peace-making agencies on the one hand, and environmental and developmental interests on the other. Included in this is the joining of like- and unlike-minded people, so that the coalition is truly cross-sectoral and represents all of those various interests needed for a sustainable peace-making strategy (for example, the media, the military, business, and commerce). What I am proposing is that a clearing house of agencies in each country in the developed world, focused upon a lead agency, be responsible for preventing and resolving specifically designated conflict situations. For example, in the United Kingdom, a coalition of agencies has already started the work of establishing an action plan for preventive action in Burundi. Other agencies are also working on the situation in Kenya. Consequently a situation should develop whereby each country specializes in certain conflict regions, using the multisectoral approach. Each coalition will be global in character, whereas its secretariat is located in a specific country. One of the responsibilities of each coalition will be to promote national capacity-building so that the consortium is duplicated in those states affected by the conflict.

A global coalition for war prevention

From time immemorial, one of the great dreams of humanity has been the elimination of war as a means of resolving conflicts. In celebrating the fiftieth anniversary of the United Nations, the time has come to rededicate ourselves and the international community to the first principle of the UN Charter: "to save succeeding generations from the scourge of war." However, it is clear that intergovernmental organizations such as the United Nations and individual governments have not and will not be able to meet this challenge by themselves. Nor is it reasonable to expect that undemocratic or defective governments will be ready or willing to address the underlying causes of violent conflict without sustained pressure from ordinary people, non-governmental organizations, social movements, and others concerned with peace, justice, and human rights.

We need to move into an era in which war is perceived as being so abhorrent that it is discouraged as a course of action in the global community. To do this effectively requires a global coalition for war prevention. This consortium would be a strategic umbrella, reflecting the global cross-section of those directly concerned with the elimination of war and the disastrous human and material consequences of war. It would help set an agenda for peace for the twenty-first century and would include as an essential tenet the formal link between the United Nations and the NGO community. Consequently, the "Third System" would in effect become an active and even proactive dimension of the UN system.

The global coalition for war prevention needs to develop a strategy for peace in which there is contingency planning for preventing disputes and violence and for promoting conflict resolution. It would involve the complementary division of labour between different strands of the war-prevention coalition, and would employ a structured approach to preventive action. Each component would act in a strategic manner, according to its own unique strength, within the overall system, while working in concert towards the same end – preventive action.

This approach requires the formulation of frameworks for sustainable peace and the establishment of mechanisms for the prevention of violent conflicts. A global non-governmental alliance for peace should necessarily comprise humanitarian agencies, development agencies, human rights groups, humanitarian law agencies, military representatives, local and international peace groups, social movements, the media, business leaders, parliamentarians, municipal leaders, religious groups, scholars, and artists. In former times, before electronic networks were able to connect like-minded individuals whatever the physical distance between them, such an alliance would have been inconceivable. Now it is the stuff of television interviews, such as that given by the Secretary-General in New York on 20 October 1994 when he pointed out that "a new opportunity is offered to the United Nations to get in contact directly, and we are trying this with the parliamentarians, with academia, with non-governmental organizations, with the grass-roots organisations, with the public as such."

It would be politically naive to expect that, without concerted pressure from NGOs and "we, the peoples of the United Nations," UN member states will put aside their concerns over the dangers of fragmentation, grasp the nettle, and work expeditiously to develop the necessary processes to ensure that claims for degrees of greater representation, autonomy, and even independence can be managed peacefully. If an effective range of mechanisms is to be developed, NGOs can and must serve as a catalyst for launching the process and as the "honest broker" between the intergovernmental community and minorities worldwide.

3. Conclusion

War is a disease. Violent conflicts are infections of the international system. The international community must develop an ethic of war and conflict prevention. Just as epidemiology is the science of epidemics and the prevention of disease, so the war consortium must represent a global movement towards eradicating the scourge that is modern warfare. During the nineteenth century, when many American cities were regularly consumed by conflagrations, fire trucks were invented as the first systematic attempt at intervention. Over time, a preventive perspective grew and smoke detectors, fire exits, and laws about the use of materials in buildings were introduced, heralding the dawn of a preventive ethos. In terms of advancing the concept of preventive diplomacy, the coordinating elements of the strategic alliance represent the fire detectors and fire-resistant materials.

As the millennium approaches, it is best to remind ourselves of the great achievements of this century: medical progress in combating disease and prolonging human life, astounding economic and technological growth, which has increased the well-being and security of millions of people around the globe, advances in education, communications, transportation, and the arts. Over the centuries, humankind has resolved and overcome many problems: the outlawing of slavery, the elimination of feudalism, an end to duelling as a means of settling disputes, and the abolition of capital punishment in many countries. Although many of these problems still persist in some areas of the world, they are no longer accepted forms of conduct. And, although wars may continue in different forms, it must become the mission of the United Nations and the international community at large to promote a global culture in which wars and violence are no longer accepted as being a normative relationship between people.

Note

1. Sadly the outbreak of conflict between rival Kurdish factions and subsequent Iraqi government attacks in the summer of 1996 rendered this operation a failure in the eyes of many international observers.

References

Boutros-Ghali, Boutros. 1992. *An Agenda for Peace*. New York: United Nations Department of Public Information, DPI/1247.
——— 1993. *Report to the General Assembly*. New York: United Nations.
——— 1995. *An Agenda for Peace 1995*, 2nd edn, with new Supplement and related UN documents. New York: United Nations (S/1995/1, 3 January).
Buergenthal, Thomas. 1988 *International Human Rights in a Nutshell*. Minnesota: West Publishing Company.
Commission on Global Governance. 1995. *Our Global Neighbourhood*. Oxford: Oxford University Press.
Cox, David. 1993. *Exploring An Agenda for Peace: Issues Arising from the Report of the Secretary-General*. Aurora Papers 20. Ontario: Canadian Centre for Global Security.
Dedring, Juergen. 1994. "Early Warning and the United Nations." *Journal of Ethno-Development*, vol. 4, no. 1.
Franck, M., and G. Nolte. 1993. "The Good Offices Function of the UN Secretary-General." In Adam Roberts and Benedict Kingsbury, eds., *United Nations, Divided World*. Oxford: Clarendon Press.
Garcia, E., ed. 1994. *Pilgrim Voices: Citizens as Peacemakers*. International Alert/ Manila: Atheno de Manil a University Press.
Greenwood, Christopher. 1993. "Is There a Right to Humanitarian Intervention?" *The World Today*, vol. 49, no. 2.

Hammarskjold, Dag. 1960. *Report to the UN General Assembly*. New York: United Nations.

Kittani, I. 1995. "Peacemaking and Peace-keeping for the Next Century." Paper prepared for the 25th Vienna Seminar co-sponsored by the Government of Austria and the International Peace Academy, 2–4 March.

Riggs, Robert E., and Jack C. Plano, eds. 1994. *The United Nations: International Organization and World Politics*. Belmont, Calif.: Wadsworth.

UNDP. 1994. *United Nations Development Report*. Oxford: Oxford University Press.

United Nations. 1992. *High Level Meeting of the Security Council: Note by the President of the Security Council on Behalf of the Members*. Doc. S/23500. New York: United Nations.

——— 1994. *47th Annual DPI/NGO Conference Final Report. We the Peoples: Building Peace*. New York: United Nations.

Wilenski, Peter. 1993. "The Structure of the UN in the Post-Cold War Period." In Adam Roberts and Benedict Kingsbury, eds., *United Nations, Divided World*. Oxford: Clarendon Press, Chapter 13.

Yusuf Farah, A., and I. M. Lewis. 1993. *Somalia: The Roots of Reconciliation*. London: ActionAid.

Part II
Peace-building: Creating economic and social structures that sustain human fulfilment

6

Moving norms to political reality: Institutionalizing human rights standards through the United Nations system

Clair Apodaca, Michael Stohl, and George Lopez

> At present, the human rights apparatus of the United Nations is badly overburdened and unable to respond adequately to the flow of appeals on human rights abuses. (United Nations 1996)

1. Introduction: Before the Universal Declaration

As the tragedies of Bosnia and Rwanda (among numerous others) unfold in the fifty-first year of the United Nations, it would appear that any assessment of the United Nations with respect to human rights would easily conclude that the organization has failed in this important area. To do so without examining the context within which the organization began, the history of United Nations human rights activities within those 50 years, and its impact on the world's governments and peoples would be a major error. Those who are interested in the United Nations can empathize with Katerina Tomasevski's statement: "In discussing the problems and prospects of United Nations work it is much easier to criticize it than to make it function well" (1994: 82).

In this chapter we will review the situation with respect to human rights in the period before the founding of the United Nations, the drafting and signing of the Universal Declaration of Human Rights, and its acceptance as a "legitimate" international standard. We will argue that the Universal Declaration and the successive family of international human rights instruments have, despite numerous violations, reshaped the context of the conduct of state behaviours within and between states.

Although debate will continue about the missed opportunities and lack of enforcement capability of the varied agencies and agents of the United Nations, at the outset of this chapter it is well worth noting that without the United Nations there would not be a human rights regime within which discussions of shortcomings could take place. Whatever its shortcomings, it is because of the United Nations and the development of the Universal Declaration of Human Rights that a human rights regime has become a reality and that legitimate expectations of judging governments and behaviours and enforcing standards of human rights compliance and violation even take place. This is due, in part, to the shift in sentiment, among member states, about what best promotes international peace and security. Earlier, the United Nations and its member states emphasized a narrow interpretation of sovereignty, that of juridical sovereignty. Juridical sovereignty is where "states recognize each other's existence and honor the principle of non-interference" (Barnett 1995a: 413). Since the end of the Cold War, the interpretation of sovereignty has been expanded to include empirical sovereignty, where the state's legitimacy is the result of its internal order, which allows the state to uphold the standards of the international community (Barnett 1995a, 1995b). External peace is a consequence of internal peace and regard for human rights. Thus, to echo the opinion of two prominent UN scholars, "If nothing more had been done in forty-five years at the United Nations than the negotiation and adoption by from 61 to 180 states of the nearly 70 instruments of the International Bill of Human Rights, this alone would fully justify the existence of the organization" (Childers and Urquhart 1994: 64). This optimism is also mirrored by the words of Tomasevski, who states that "the fact that virtually all governments cooperate with the UN on human rights issues, that more than half of them have been held accountable for violations, represents a genuine success" (1994: 82).

It is important to acknowledge just how far the world community has come in the development of the comprehensive body of law and institutions that has protected human rights over the past 50 years, beginning with the adoption of the Charter of the United Nations. Certainly, prior to the Charter there existed international norms that protected the individual, but international law, commonly, treated individuals as "bearers not of personal rights but of rights belonging to their governments ... the individual was nothing more than a symbol and a capital asset" (Farer 1993: 240).

In the aftermath of the devastation of World War I, the first general international organizational experiment of the century was embodied in the Covenant of the League of Nations (1919), which was part of the Treaty of Versailles ending the war. Within this context, the League was "basically designed to maintain the international order that was created at the conclusion of World War I" (Jacobson 1984: 42) and made no direct provision for human rights. Yet the League did play a preliminary role in the promotion of human rights protection. The League guaranteed the protection of minorities, even though this guarantee covered only specific minorities and "did nothing to create general obligations to respect fundamental human rights" (Brierly 1963: 292). This protection did, nevertheless, place limited restrictions on how a state may treat its own nationals. Jan Herman Burgers (1992) argues that the minority clauses, which pertained to only a handful of states, did include guarantees that extended to all inhabitants, such as the protection of life and liberty without distinction of any type. Furthermore, the clause decreed that all nations would be equal before the law and would enjoy the same political and civil rights. The minority clauses further guaranteed that nationals belonging to minorities would be free to use their own language and practise their own religion.

Secondly, under the aegis of the League several labour conventions protecting workers' rights were concluded by the International Labour Organization (Brierly 1963). Huaraka (1991) notes that the Covenant of the League of Nations did protect, under Article 22, the "freedom of conscience and religion" for mandated territories.[1] Furthermore, the mandate system provided for limited individual petition, albeit through the administering authority.

As we know, although World War I provided the impetus for the development of the League, it was the failure of the League, a critical analysis of its shortcomings, and the horrors of World War II that provided the impetus and political will for the establishment of the United Nations. In that context, it is useful to note the important role played by the Roosevelts not only in the development of the United Nations, but also for generating international standards for human rights.

In a speech to Congress in January 1941, President Franklin

Roosevelt announced that the United States would face the risk of war to ensure the "Four Freedoms" for all those who struggle to gain or keep these freedoms. The Four Freedoms comprise the freedom of speech and expression, freedom of worship, freedom from want (economic security), and freedom from fear (a reduction in armaments). Burgers, reading the history of the Four Freedoms, concludes that the freedom from want "must be understood ... [as] the responsibility of governments actively to promote the well-being of their citizens" (1992: 469),[2] whereas the freedom from fear was for Roosevelt "protection of people against oppression by their own state as well as protection of people against aggression by other states" (Burgers 1992: 469). For Roosevelt, international peace and security were undeniably entwined with human rights. Roosevelt's concern for human rights as both a condition and consequence of international peace is apparent by its inclusion in the Atlantic Charter (1941). The Atlantic Charter, signed by Roosevelt and Churchill in the middle of the Atlantic Ocean in August of 1941, was an outline of the war aims of the Allied forces in World War II, and was inspired by Roosevelt's "Four Freedoms."[3] Roosevelt's goal for the Atlantic Charter was:

[not a] vision of a distant millennium. It is a definite basis for a kind of world attainable in our own time and generation. That kind of world is the very antithesis of the so-called new order of tyranny which the dictators seek to create with the crash of a bomb .... This nation has placed its destiny in the hands and heads and hearts of its millions of free men and women; and its faith in freedom under the guidance of God. Freedom means the supremacy of human rights everywhere. Our support goes to those who struggle to gain those rights or keep them. Our strength is in our unity of purpose. (Quoted in Nagan 1992: 402)

President Franklin Roosevelt was successful in establishing human rights as one of the war aims of World War II.

The atrocities of the Nazis against humanity during World War II led the Nuremberg Tribunal, and the world at large, to view the deliberate mistreatment and suffering of human beings as violations against the moral order. In spite of the overwhelming support for the protection of individual human rights, the sacrosanct principle of national sovereignty nearly derailed the incorporation of human rights provisions in the Charter. The relevance of human rights and fundamental freedoms within the Charter was secondary to the concept of an international community of states. For quite different reasons, the British and Soviets were particularly determined that human rights receive only a passing reference.[4]

The initiative to include human rights in the UN Charter was the result of the persistent determination of non-governmental organizations (NGOs). John Humphrey (1967), the first Director of the Division of Human Rights at the United Nations, maintains that human rights would have obtained "only a passing reference" in the Charter had it not been for the exhaustive lobbying of a few dedicated delegates and consultants. At the San Francisco conference, the coalition of NGO consultants attached to the US delegation strongly supported the incorporation of human rights in the Charter. By arguing that respect for human rights was essential for international peace, a legion of US-based NGOs was successful in having "respect for human rights" included as one of the four main purposes of the United Nations.[5] Of course, to have its argument heard the alliance had to do a little political arm-twisting. Joseph Proskauer, of the American Jewish Committee, pointedly advised the US Secretary of State, Edward Stettinius:

I said that the voice of America was speaking in this room as it had never spoken before in any international gathering; that voice was saying to the American delegation: "If you make a fight for these human rights proposals and win, there will be glory for all. If you make a fight for it and lose, we will back you up to the limit. If you fail to make a fight for it, you will have lost the support of American opinion – and justly lost it. *In that event, you will never get the Charter ratified.* (Proskauer 1950: 225; emphasis added)

In part as a result of this thinly veiled threat, human rights were specifically incorporated into the Charter of the United Nations. Once the US Secretary of State was convinced of the importance of including human rights into the Charter, it took less than a day before all the great powers (Great Britain, France, China, and the Soviet Union) agreed (Gaer 1996). Whereas the Covenant of the League of Nations failed to mention concern for human rights, the Charter of the United Nations makes explicit reference to human rights seven times. Field Marshal Smuts, of South Africa, believed a document of such historical importance should be introduced "by a Preamble setting forth, in language which should appeal to the heart as well as the mind of men, the purposes which the United Nations were setting themselves to achieve and the nobility of intention of the founders" (quoted in Russell 1958: 912). The prominent position accorded human rights is evident by its inclusion in the second sentence of the Charter's preamble, where member states "reaffirm [their] faith in fundamental human rights, in the dignity and worth of the human person, in the equal rights of men and women."[6] Furthermore, the promotion of and respect for human rights are listed as one of the four purposes and principles of the Charter.

Yet, the Charter of the United Nations addresses "human rights and fundamental freedoms" without defining or enumerating them. Specifically, Article 1(3) requires states "to promote and encourage respect for human rights and for fundamental freedoms for all without distinction as to race, sex, language or religion"; and Article 13(1)(b) compels the General Assembly to "assist in the realization of human rights and fundamental freedoms."

The standards set by the Universal Declaration of Human Rights are in large part due to the efforts of Eleanor Roosevelt. Eleanor Roosevelt served as the first Chairperson of the United Nations Human Rights Commission from 1946 to 1951. Owing to Mrs. Roosevelt's ceaseless work and persuasion, she is credited as the driving force behind the adoption of the Universal Declaration of Human Rights and with preparatory work on the Covenants. Johnson refers to her tenure as Chairperson of the Human Rights Commission as:

a period of great significance in the attempt to develop international structures of the protection of human rights. The Universal Declaration of Human Rights was adopted by the General Assembly in December 1948. The basic work on the binding covenants on Civil and Political Rights and Economic, Social and Cultural Rights was also done in their [*sic*] period although they were not finally approved by the General Assembly until 1966. (1987: 28)

Although her appointment to the United Nations was intended to be a symbolic gesture, Mrs. Roosevelt did have the ear of Washington leaders and was able to influence US policy with regard to human rights.

2. From the Universal Declaration to the international covenants and beyond: Standard-setting

Although the Charter of the United Nations laid the conceptual framework for the development of a legally binding human rights law, it failed to clarify the substance of human rights. The Universal Declaration of Human Rights (1948) is a non-binding proclamation that represents the international acceptance of proper standards of conduct. The Declaration was intended to clarify "a common standard of achievement for all peoples and all nations." The Universal Declaration inventories an extensive catalogue of rights all people possess as members of the human family. For the first time, human rights and fundamental freedoms were given explicit meaning.

It has been argued that the Universal Declaration, by delineating an international standard of conduct, has exerted the most significant influence in modifying state behaviour regarding the treatment of citizens. As the instrument that interprets and particularizes the provisions on human rights and fundamental freedoms of the UN Charter, some believe that the Universal Declaration derives an ancillary binding authority (Henkin 1981; Sohn 1982). Therefore, the Universal Declaration has become the prevailing explication of rights and obligations. In the words of Tom Farer, the Universal Declaration has evolved into a legally binding document: "in part because it had passed without a negative vote, in larger part because many of its provisions subsequently found their way into formal international agreements or were incorporated in national constitutions, it has acquired a legal aura, the appearance of stating, if not having by its existence created, binding norms of state behavior" (1993: 249). The Universal Declaration is consequential because its standards are widely accepted as the legitimate measure of human rights achievement. As the defining measure, the provisions of the Universal Declaration are included in many international documents and national constitutions modifying the behaviour of states.

Furthermore, asserts Burns Weston, "representatives from many diverse cultures endorsed the rights therein set forth 'as a common standard of achievement for all peoples and all nations'" (1992: 17). Based on the wide acceptance of the rights listed in the Universal Declaration, coupled with the fact it was passed with a vote of 48 to 0, with 8 abstentions, it is often argued that the Universal Declaration has acquired the status of customary international law binding on all states.[7] McDougal et al. (1980: 274) assert that the principles of the Universal Declaration, once a mere aspiration of human rights standards, having been "affirmed and reaffirmed by numerous resolutions of United Nations entities and related agencies; invoked and re-invoked by a broad range of decision makers, national and transnational, judicial and other; and incorporated into many international agreements and national constitutions," have gained the standing of customary law "having the attributes of *jus cogens* and constituting the heart of a global bill of rights." The principles set forth in the Universal Declaration are now part of international law because they are widely recognized and incorporated into the legal systems of civilized nations. The consensus of the international community regarding the Universal Declaration is evident from the unanimous affirmation by the delegates to the International Conference on Human Rights (Teheran, 1968) that the Universal Declaration "states a common understanding of the peoples of the world concerning the inalienable and inviolable rights of all members of the human family and constitutes an obligation for all members of the international community" (UN Doc. A/CONF.32/41). Thus, Sohn concludes, "The Declaration, as an authoritative listing of human rights, has become a basic component of international customary law, binding on all states, not only on members of the United Nations" (1982: 17).

In order to give the principles articulated in the Universal Declaration of Human Rights greater clarity, the United Nations drafted a Covenant on Human Rights. The ensuing debates about whether or not economic and social rights are of the same character as civil and political rights resulted in two separate and overlapping documents: the International Covenant on Economic, Social and Cultural Rights; and the International Covenant on Civil and Political Rights. The Covenants are legally binding treaties, which entered into force in 1976 after ratification by the required number of states (35). The Covenants impose different national and international obligations. Although the indivisibility and interdependence of political/civil rights and economic/social rights are repeatedly affirmed by the various groups and committees of the United Nations, many scholars, political leaders, and human rights defenders have built an artificial barrier between these sets of rights. Whereas civil and political rights have gained widespread recognition as human rights, there is still substantial disagreement among Western scholars and political leaders in the debate whether social, economic, and cultural rights are "rights" or goals. The debate on whether economic and social rights are genuine human rights or merely national aspirations is virtually non-existent outside the West. For many third world leaders, scholars, and human rights activists, economic rights are the most fundamental whereas political and civil rights are considered non-crucial, "luxury" rights.

A second tension exists between human rights and people's rights. Supporters of the former claim that human rights belong to the individual, as opposed to the group. For those who give priority to individual rights, the rights of people threaten to infringe individual rights in the name of preserving culture, tradition, and customs even if those institutions are repressive and outmoded. Advocates of people's rights, on the other hand, believe that society (a group of people) has rights that the individual, the state, and the international community must respect and submit to. Donnelly and Howard report,

In traditional society, one's worth, rights, and responsibilities arise from and remain tied to differential membership in a particular society.... [T]he idea that one is entitled to equal concern, respect and a wide range of inalienable personal rights simply because one is a human being is utterly foreign.... Although most people in traditional societies have at least some rights and privileges, these are contingent on the proper fulfillment of social roles. (1986: 808)

Individuals, as members of society, have a responsibility to society and to those who constitute that society. Their rights are determined by their place in society.

To explain the dynamic process of human rights, with elements of change and continuity, Karel Vasak introduced the concept of the three generations of human rights, *liberté* (liberty), *égalité* (equality), and *fraternité* (solidarity). First-generation rights are claims to liberty, based on a principle of individual freedom (as noted in Claude and Weston 1992). The first generation of human rights includes political and civil rights, which can trace their origin to classical Western thought of liberal individualism and the social doctrine of laissez-faire. They provide protection to individuals from the state. Political and civil rights are negative rights. Negative rights deny state control over individuals in particular areas and can easily be secured through the legislative process. The government simply refrains from certain activities for the realization of these rights. The duty to comply with the obligations in the Political Covenant is immediate. Since they belong to the individual, the rights of the first generation have been championed by the Western powers as being the only authentic human rights. Political and civil rights include the right to life, the prohibition against torture and inhuman treatment, the right to a fair trial, the right to choose the form of government one lives under, the right to association, freedom from arbitrary execution, freedom from unreasonable detention, and the right to freedom of thought, conscience, and religion.

Tunguru Huaraka (1991) illustrates how the changing composition of the General Assembly transformed the Political Covenant. Although the Political Covenant is based upon the precepts enunciated in the Universal Declaration, the Political Covenant was altered by the growing cultural and religious diversity of the member states of the United Nations. Huaraka notes that the first draft of the Political

Covenant included a "colonial clause" by referring to the "general principles of law recognized by civilized nations," which, at the insistence of the newly independent states, was replaced by a fundamental principle of decolonization. The Political Covenant declares the right of peoples to self-determination and requires states that control Trust and Non-Self-Governing Territories to promote and respect that right. The modification of Article 18 of the Political Covenant was also the result of the change in the General Assembly's configuration. Article 18 of the Universal Declaration includes the guarantee of the right to change one's religion. This clause was dropped from Article 18 of the Political Covenant at the request of Muslim states. They believed that, in states whose legal systems were based on Islam, the right to change one's religion would undermine domestic law (Huaraka 1991).

Second-generation rights are claims to social equality. These rights originate in the socialist tradition. It has been claimed that the second-generation rights were, until recently, relegated to secondary status. Although the Universal Declaration of Human Rights does not explicitly differentiate between economic/social and political/civil rights, or give priority to one set of rights over the other, only 6 of the 30 articles (Arts. 22–27) of the Universal Declaration make mention of economic and social rights. Imre Szabo states that, "although mention is made in the Declaration of economic, social and cultural rights, they are referred to only in passing, and they are not examined in a manner comparable to that of other [political and civil] rights" (1982: 25). With the influx into United Nations membership of third world states, the second generation of human rights has gained prominence. Economic, social, and cultural rights are viewed as positive rights, in that they require the provision of goods and services and the expenditure of scarce resources for their realization. Therefore, it is often argued that the obligation to fulfil economic and social rights is progressive in character (Alston and Quinn 1987; Trubek 1984). Unlike political and civil rights, which seek to limit state authority, economic and social rights often require active state involvement for their fulfilment. Economic and social rights include the right to work, the right to an education, the right to basic health care, and the right to an adequate standard of living.

The third-generation rights, solidarity rights, are those rights we hold as humans collectively. The evolution of a third generation of rights reflects the interests of the newly independent states, which constitute a voting majority in the General Assembly. Watson explains that these rights comprise six claimed rights:

Three of these reflect the emergence of Third World nationalism and its demand for a global redistribution of power, wealth, and other important values: ... self-determination; the right to economic and social development; and the right to ... benefit from the "common heritage of mankind" ... The other three third-generation rights – the right to peace, the right to a healthy and balanced environment, and the right to humanitarian disaster relief – suggest the impotence or inefficiency of the nation-state in certain critical respects. (Weston 1992: 19)

Satisfaction of third-generation rights requires a holistic, global approach by the United Nations and its member states. Third-generation rights require both governmental abstention from certain activities dictated by first-generation rights and governmental action in the provision of goods and services obliged by second-generation rights. Thus, the third-generation rights are based on the solidarity between people and states and can be achieved only through collaboration and cooperation.

The role of the United Nations in the protection, promotion, and enhancement of human rights for the past half-century is a complex evolutionary topic. Glancing back from the vantage point of the mid-1990s we might make a number of observations in succinct summary form.[8] Although dynamically constrained by the Cold War in numerous ways, the human rights work of the United Nations did proceed in somewhat identifiable phases. As explained by Farer:

It is a commonplace of scholarship to discern three phases in UN human rights activities during which the main focus was, in turn, standard setting (conventions and declarations); promotion (advisory services, broad studies, and an incipient reporting system); and protection (establishment of procedures for assessing information received from private persons and groups concerning possible gross violations and reporting thereon to the general membership, fact-finding in certain cases where member states allege grave violations and efforts to mitigate or terminate violation in particular cases). (Farer 1992: 235)

In the immediate post–World War II environment, the United Nations, often through General Assembly action, produced a series of important covenants and standard-setting treaties that slowly increased the expectation of the minimal-level human rights performance of states. In some regional areas, such as Europe in the work of the Helsinki process or Latin America in the work of the Inter-American Human Rights Commission, these standards were sharpened and often more strictly applied, the result being an intersection of human rights concerns with a variety of other international issues. Perhaps the most developed regional system for the protection and promotion of human rights is that of the Council of Europe. Under the authority of the Council of Europe, the European Convention for the Protection of Human Rights and Fundamental Freedoms was drafted. The European Convention establishes three bodies for the enforcement of the Convention's provisions: the European Commission of Human Rights; the Council of Ministers; and the European Court of Human Rights. The European Convention is unique in that it not only provides for inter-state complaints but also allows individuals to bring complaints against their governments to the Commission and the Court (Art. 25).[9] Additionally, with the acceptance of Article 46 of the European Convention, the European Court of Human Rights has compulsory jurisdiction to hear cases brought before it. Unlike the International Court of Justice, where state parties must agree to appear before the court, the European Court can summon a state to answer the complaint. All 30 members of the Council of Europe have agreed to Article 46.

The standard-setting action of the United Nations begged for greater attention to monitoring for compliance and thus prompted the creation and use of institutional mechanisms, the most prominent of which was the UN Commission on Human Rights. Although the Commission would have a mixed historical record, notably because of its reluctance to condemn publicly the worst rights violators, it none the less served as the structural foundation for the UN "system" of rights monitoring. In light of the nature and number of nations where gross violations of human rights were taking place, the Commission relied rather heavily on the work of various international non-governmental organizations to provide reliable information about violations. Although this interactive system might appear to work well in theory, over time it has led to increasing controversy, about which we will comment briefly below.

Beyond the formulation and monitoring phases of the UN work for human rights, various parts of the UN family of institutions would further the cause of human rights by focusing attention on particular categories of violations (such as torture or extra-judicial execution) or the denial of rights to particular population segments (certain races, ethnic groups, women, workers, etc.). Thus, according to Donnelly

(1993), a series of human rights "regimes" followed, which complemented, and in most cases surpassed, the capacity of the United Nations Commission. Beyond the six principal human rights treaties (the International Covenant on Civil and Political Rights, the International Covenant on Economic, Social, and Cultural Rights, the International Convention on the Elimination of All Forms of Racial Discrimination, the Convention against Torture and Other Cruel, Inhuman, or Degrading Treatment or Punishment, the Convention on the Rights of the Child, and the Convention on the Elimination of All Forms of Discrimination Against Women), human rights are well represented in the specialized agencies: workers' rights by the International Labour Organization, the right to food and access to medical care by the World Health Organization (WHO) and the United Nations Children's Fund (UNICEF), the right to an education by the United Nations Educational, Scientific and Cultural Organization (UNESCO), and the right to asylum from persecution by the Office of the United Nations High Commissioner for Refugees. The International Covenants provide that the specialized agencies of the United Nations Organization receive country reports on matters within their competence. The specialized agencies were allowed to submit reports and attend public Committee meetings.

Furthermore, human rights issues were included in recent United Nations world conferences, such as the Fourth World Conference on Women (Beijing, 1995), the World Summit for Social Development (Copenhagen, 1995), and the Habitat II meeting (Istanbul, 1996). In view of the relevance human rights has to issues of development, women, and adequate housing, it was necessary for the conferences to include human rights on their agendas. Human rights were also prominent on the agendas of the summit meetings of the Group of Seven and the Non-Aligned Movement, as well as the Organization of American States, the Organization of African Unity, the Rio Group, the Association of South-East Asian Nations, the European Union, and the Commonwealth of Independent States (UNHCHR 1996). This diversification in substance and structure meant that the human rights landscape was poised to spread to new areas of activity as the Cold War began to wind down.

Another arena in which the United Nations has contributed to the development of standard-setting with respect to human rights is in the area of the humanitarian law of armed conflict. General Assembly resolutions for the purposes of creating new treaties for the regulation of the conduct of armed hostilities may be found in GA

197

Resolutions 2444 of 19 December 1968 and 2675 of 9 December 1970. Luise Doswald Beck (1987: 255) argues that "United Nations General Assembly Resolutions may be a reflection of customary law if they are passed with a sufficient majority, including that of the developed nations, and if they are meant to be statements of existing law (rather than mere exhortations); such was the case here." Oliver Durr (1987: 271) noted the transition: "in its early years, the UN concentrated on maintaining peace and respect for human rights. Since 1968 it has been turning its attention to respect for IHL (International Humanitarian Law)."

3. The human rights machinery

The General Assembly and, under its authority, the treaty supervisory committees bear the primary responsibility for the promotion of human rights. The General Assembly is the final arbiter of the standards adopted and the issues addressed and controls the amount of resources (money, time, staff) granted to the human rights organs. The UN Charter establishes, under the authority of the General Assembly, the Economic and Social Council (ECOSOC) as the principal organ for the promotion and protection of human rights (see fig. 6.1). ECOSOC coordinates the activities of the specialized agencies, organizes world conferences, and obtains reports from member states on their compliance with the will of the General Assembly. Furthermore, the UN Charter empowers ECOSOC to "make suitable arrangements for consultation with non-governmental organizations which are concerned with matters within its competence" (Art. 71). ECOSOC Resolution 1296 (1968) defines an NGO as any organization not created by intergovernmental agreement. To receive consultative status an NGO must meet several qualifications: the NGO must have an expressed purpose that falls within the scope of economic and social concerns; the NGO must be representative of the members it claims to speak for; its members must participate in the NGO's agenda in a democratic fashion; the NGO must not advocate the use of violence; the NGO must not be a political party; and the NGO must be international in character. Furthermore, NGOs must submit data on their budgets and sources of finance to the ECOSOC. After meeting these criteria, an NGO will be categorized into one of three groups. Category I NGOs have large memberships and broad economic and social interests and are geographically inclusive. These NGOs generally have greatest access to UN personnel. Category II

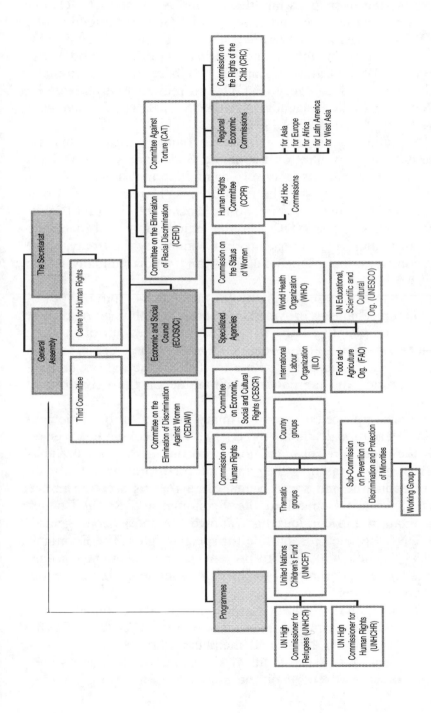

Fig. 6.1 **The United Nations human rights machinery (Note: The majority of UN bodies are concerned with some aspect of human rights; this chart covers only those bodies directly related with the promotion and protection of human rights).**

are more limited in scope, while those listed as "roster" NGOs are occasional or narrowly focused groups. All NGOs can attend public ECOSOC meetings, submit written statements on their subject of competence, and, if invited, attend hearings (Gordenker and Weiss 1996; Willetts 1996). Category I and II NGOs can petition to make oral statements, and Category I NGOs can request that an issue be placed on the ECOSOC agenda. As of 1995, 1,003 NGOs have consultative status, up from 90 in 1949.

Both the International Covenant on Civil and Political Rights and the International Covenant on Economic, Social and Cultural rights establish an independent supervisory committee that monitors signatory states' compliance with the treaties. The Human Rights Committee and the Committee on Economic, Social and Cultural Rights, subsidiary bodies to ECOSOC, examine official state reports on the situation of human rights in each country bound by the treaty, make general comments or recommendations, and report annually to the General Assembly.

These treaty supervisory committees make use of three types of enforcement mechanisms provided by international human rights law: the right of complaint by one state against the behaviour of another; the requirement that states report to an international committee on the extent of their compliance with a treaty; and the right of an individual to petition an international committee on the behaviour of their own state.

The reporting procedure is the primary mechanism of implementation of international human rights law. The Economic Covenant outlines the procedure for mandatory reporting in Article 16. States submit reports on measures they have adopted to achieve the realization of economic and social rights. State reports are transmitted from the Secretary-General to the Economic and Social Council for examination and consideration, and to the specialized agencies (WHO, UNICEF, etc.) responsible for specific rights. The Economic and Social Council is allowed to present general recommendations, known as General Comments, to clarify or illuminate general problems or observations.

The Covenant on Civil and Political Rights created a Human Rights Committee to hear complaints and review reports. The Human Rights Committee consists of 18 elected members who act in a personal capacity. Article 40 of the Political Covenant outlines the states' obligations to submit reports on the measures they have adopted to ensure the political and civil rights of those persons within their jurisdiction. The Human Rights Committee examines the reports and subjects the state representative to scrutinizing questions. The Committee makes specific recommendations to states based upon their reports and makes general comments to clarify provisions within the Covenant. Article 41 provides for the jurisdiction of the Human Rights Committee to hear complaints made by one state that another state is not fulfilling its obligations under the Political Covenant. Under Article 41 both states must recognize the competence of the Committee to receive and hear the communications. Once the Committee has jurisdiction, it will hold closed meetings in an attempt to promote a friendly settlement between the states. The Optional Protocol to the International Covenant on Civil and Political Rights permits the Human Rights Committee to consider individual petitions. The Optional Protocol is separate from the Political Covenant, so a state may ratify the Political Covenant without accepting the Optional Protocol, thus disallowing the victim the right to protest. The Optional Protocol bars individual complaints if the victim has not exhausted all domestic remedies, or if the matter is being examined under another procedure of international investigation or settlement. Unfortunately, the Economic Covenant does not provide for individual complaints.

The 1503 Procedure was established to handle the many complaints of human rights violations that fall outside the mechanisms outlined in the Political and Economic Covenants.[10] Complaints of human rights violations are summarized and sent to the 53-member Commission on Human Rights, the Subcommission on Prevention of Discrimination and Protection of Minorities, and to the state named as violator. The complaints are anonymous. If a consistent pattern is detected, the Commission can investigate the situation. The Commission employs "special procedures," that is thematic (working groups) and country mechanisms (special rapporteur), to investigate human rights abuses. The working groups enquire into specific types of human rights abuses, such as enforced or involuntary disappearances, torture, or religious intolerance, whereas special rapporteurs examine the human rights situation in specific countries.

The reporting procedure is confronted with three main problems: the non-submission of reports, inadequate reports, and the repeated postponement of reports. The lack of time to review and deliberate on state reports, along with a grossly inadequate number of staff, has resulted in a backlog of incomplete and fragmentary reports. This administrative handicap is often overcome by the dedication and determination of NGO personnel. NGOs provide the treaty supervisory committees with detailed reports on a country's human rights situation, allowing the reviewing committee to ask pointed direct questions on situations the reporting country may wish to conceal. Gaer reports that NGOs often provide "treaty committee members with the facts about the human rights record of countries scheduled to present reports. Committee members eagerly look for NGO materials before each country review, because it helps make their questioning more precise, factual and less abstract" (1996: 56).

Not surprisingly, the inter-state complaints procedure has proven to be a remarkably ineffectual method of upholding human rights.[11] States seldom protest against rights violations in other states unless there is a political axe to grind. Ofuatey-Kodjoe (1995) explains that inter-state condemnation of human rights abuse is often a political tool. Whereas the United States supported resolutions against Iran, Iraq, and Cuba, it remained oddly quiet when attempts were made to censure the activities of Guatemala or Israel. Similarly, "the Commission has been unable to address gross violations of human rights in China due to the unwillingness of its Third World allies to condemn it" (Ofuatey-Kodjoe 1995: 329). This failure in the inter-state complaints procedure also extends to the court systems. Several conventions on human rights provide that inter-state complaints be submitted to the International Court of Justice for adjudication.[12] The regional conventions on human rights, the European Convention for the Protection of Human Rights and Fundamental Freedoms and the American Convention on Human Rights, contain an optional clause under which a state party agrees to accept the jurisdiction of the regional court (the European Court of Human Rights and the Inter-American Court of Human Rights, respectively).

After intense lobbying by NGOs, an additional UN mechanism was introduced to protect and promote human rights. In 1994, the post of High Commissioner for Human Rights was created. The general duties of the UNHCHR include making recommendations to UN agencies for the promotion and protection of human rights, responding to human rights crises, coordinating human rights activities throughout the United Nations, expanding and strengthening international cooperation in the area of human rights, and promoting education and public information programmes regarding human rights (Gaer 1996).

4. The human rights dimensions of the 1990s

With the dawn of the post–Cold War world a number of global trends converged in a way that continues to make a significant impact both on our understanding of human rights and on policy discussions about human rights within the United Nations system. A few of these trends had been evolving for quite some time, but others developed in large part because of the demise of the East–West ideological power blocs whose global competition often affected human rights in other states rather adversely. What is clear is that these trends dynamically reinforced one another in ways that created a somewhat bitter irony: whereas the underlying purpose of the United Nations Commission on Human Rights and other UN human rights organs was to prompt more nations to respect human rights, this system was absolutely unprepared for the unprecedented demand for human rights training and monitoring and services related to human rights issues created by the end of the Cold War.

Increase in member states

The first evolutionary trend to place such pressure on the system has been the dramatic increase in the number of new governments and new states entering the UN system. This has occurred in a range of locales and often for quite distinct reasons. In its most gradual phase, it involved the demise of military rule and a wave of liberalization and democratization of authoritarian governments, especially in Latin America, in the late 1970s and early 1980s.[13] By the end of the early 1990s, Gorbachev's liberal policies toward the Soviet spheres of influence in Eastern Europe and dramatic internal change in the former Soviet Union itself meant that these communist governments were on their way to becoming new governments/states. These new states exhibited democratic leanings and the human rights aspirations that accompany such tendencies. Finally, in a number of states, including cultures as different as Angola, Cambodia, and El Salvador, negotiated conclusions to brutal civil wars led to the formation of new governmental institutions aimed at greater rights protection.

These developments have placed more states and governments

than ever before in rather tentative and unanticipated "transitional" stages to full-fledged democracy. In such transitions, the protection and enhancement of human rights in practice often lag behind the desire of transitionary governments to accomplish these tasks. This has created the need for more local monitoring and greater international attention and action to ensure full compliance with the UN-based covenants and standards to which the new states themselves claim they subscribe.

Intra-state conflicts

Although many states are transforming into democracies, a second trend challenging the United Nations system is the disintegration of several states into fighting factions. Erika Burk warns that "the worst abusers today are apt to be not recognized governments at all but fighting factions or mercenaries, such as in Afghanistan, Bosnia, Somalia, and Haiti" (1995: 216). An additional, unanticipated consequence of the end of the Cold War was a reduction in the authoritarian constraints that dampened and hid many of the ethnic tensions that are often today's brutal headlines. Intra-state conflicts are being fought by militias and armed civilians with poorly defined chains of command and no knowledge of the rights of non-combatants as granted by the Geneva Conventions. Human rights protection is all the more necessary, yet more problematic, when there is no functioning central government to hold accountable, pressure, or persuade. In these situations the collaboration between human rights and peace-keeping agencies is critical. The protection of human rights requires the separation of the warring groups and the imposition of internal order.

Increase in human rights NGOs

Thus, a third trend that has developed over time has been a substantial increase in the number and role of NGOs engaged in human rights monitoring. States are both instruments of protection and the principal violators of human rights. This incongruity has led to the development of scores of non-governmental organizations formed to champion the rights of individuals. Thakur (1994: 143), for example, argues that, when comparing the United Nations and Amnesty International (AI), "[h]uman rights puts the welfare of individuals first, the UN puts the interest of member states first. AI is of, by, and for individuals; the United Nations is of, by, and for governments." The Universal Declaration of Human Rights does make provision for the legal abridgement of human rights in extreme and extenuating circumstances. Article 29(2)[14] states that rights and freedoms may be limited "for the purpose of securing due recognition and respect for the rights and freedoms of others and of meeting the just requirements of morality, public order and the general welfare in a democratic society." Similarly, the International Covenant on Civil and Political Rights, Article 4(1), expressly allows a state to derogate from its obligations in cases of public emergencies. Thus, in the opinion of Jack Donnelly (1986), reasons of state triumph over the rights of individuals. This opinion is, perhaps, a bit too harsh since the treaty allows no derogation in any circumstances from: Article 6, the right to life; Article 7, the prohibition against torture, inhuman, or degrading treatment or punishment; Article 8, the forbiddance of slavery or servitude; Article 11, no debtors' prison; Article 15, outlawing the imposition of penalties for conduct that in the future is made criminal; Article 16, the right to be recognized as a person before the law; and Article 18, freedom of thought, conscience, and religion. These rights are absolute. Thus, Amnesty International and other human rights NGOs, "[i]n dealing with human rights violations ... have relied principally upon the Universal Declaration of Human Rights and the International Covenant of Civil and Political Rights" (Weissbrodt 1987: 297–298). Those active in human rights work are quite aware of the political nature of the United Nations. Although often frustrated by the pace of work within the United Nations and the lack of power of their own organization, human rights activists recognize that "AI and the UN play competing roles, and AI is more willing to investigate possible human rights abuses by governments while UN confines itself to selected governments" (Thakur 1994: 151). Amnesty International has an active, dedicated, vocal membership of 1 million working for human rights worldwide. Its strength, and that of other NGOs, lies in its ability to mobilize public opinion, disseminate information, and pressure governments.

Both local and international NGOs have engaged in human rights advancement, through monitoring or other activities, for over three decades. The accuracy and in-depth character of information on rights violations in particular countries as reported by organizations such as Amnesty International have long been dependent on such national groups. And quite often, as in the case of the growth of Servicio Paz y Justicia (SERPAJ) in Latin America, local groups have joined forces across national boundaries to strengthen their work.[15] By the early 1990s, there were more than 200 NGOs whose human rights work had taken on a transnational character. In practice, much of the work of the UN Human Rights Commission itself became dependent on the information provided it by such groups.[16]

In 1968, and even while human rights work was still in an embryonic state, the UN Economic and Social Council formally recognized that much of the work of the UN Human Rights Commission was dependent on the information provided by NGOs. ECOSOC bestowed on these national and transnational NGOs the designation of consultative status to UN bodies.[17] From the beginning this consultative arrangement faced a structural dilemma in two ways. First, ECOSOC's procedural arrangements held that national human rights groups, and most often their transnational extensions, had to receive some level of approval from their national governments as being "representative" of the views of the nation's population on the issues of their expertise. Thus, nations engaged in systematic rights abuses regularly stifle reporting of violations by these NGOs simply by complaining to ECOSOC that the rights group is a "fringe" institution. Secondly, although an NGO may have "status" in the UN community and thus the UN Human Rights Committee, this does not guarantee access to each and every hearing of the UN agency. As the number of NGOs has grown, this has further distanced many of these organizations from being able to provide the input they would like to critical Committee discussions.[18]

Recent world conferences have shown that the 1968 provisions for NGO participation are inadequate. Frustration with the structure and outcomes of this UN–NGO relationship peaked at the Second World Conference on Human Rights in Vienna (also known as the Vienna Conference) in June 1993. To deflect some of the exasperation, ECOSOC created an Open-Ended Working Group on NGO relations earlier in February. But its progress was slow and it failed to reach any agreement in Vienna on a revision of Resolution 1296 and the rules it had codified. Subsequent meetings have made more progress on issues of access and the independence of NGOs, but it is unlikely that a final draft of rules will be complete before 1996 (Comeau 1994). ECOSOC's Open-Ended Working Group is drafting revisions to Resolution 1296 to accommodate the increased number, function, and prominence of NGOs. Unfortunately, China and the Group of 77 are actively working to block the expansion of NGO participation (Spiro 1994).

In June 1993, representatives of 171 governments met upstairs at the World Conference on Human Rights in Vienna, while over 2,000 representatives from 841 ECOSOC-accredited NGOs met downstairs with several thousand representatives of non-accredited NGOs. The work upstairs was limited to the general principles of human rights, conspicuously avoiding debate on country-specific rights behaviour (with the exceptions of Bosnia, Kashmir, and the Middle East). Downstairs, specific charges of human rights abuses from a myriad of countries were depicted in horrifying detail. Perhaps one of the most beneficial aspects of the Vienna Conference is that it allowed NGOs to network, thus strengthening their ability to press governments on human rights concerns.

The most celebrated accomplishment of the work of human rights NGOs in the 1990s came to fruition in Vienna in the resolution to create a new office, the UN High Commissioner for Human Rights (UNHCHR). As can be easily understood, expectations for what such an office might provide the UN human rights system ran rather high. Some hoped for a high-profile and powerful office akin to the UN High Commissioner for Refugees. Other groups hoped for an alternative to the UN Human Rights Commission, which too often narrowly defined both the human rights problem before it and the options available for redressing it. Still others saw the office as a new vehicle for NGO contact and influence that was not present in existing mechanisms. Perhaps the most important duty assigned to the UNHCHR is that of an early warning system, taking initiatives to pre-empt human rights crises and, failing that, to bring the relevant human rights machinery into immediate play. Soon after the creation of the UNHCHR, Secretary-General Boutros Boutros-Ghali named Ecuadorean José Ayala Lasso as the first UN High Commissioner for Human Rights. In 1995 the High Commissioner for Human Rights issued his first report (featuring the crises in Chechnya, Rwanda, and Burundi) and appeared before the Human Rights Commission to answer questions, thus setting a precedent.

5. Recommendations for the future

Progress in human rights standard-setting and compliance-seeking drafted in the international Bill of Rights has been unable to solve some of the inherent contradictions involved in the promotion and protection of rights within the UN framework. As many scholars have noted, human rights are held by the person and require protection from states, whereas the United Nations is an organization of states. Thus, the United Nations is "biased" in favour of putting the interests of member states ahead of individuals who seek its protection. In human rights, as in everything it does, the United Nations is only as good as its member states. When it fails, it is not simply a failure of the United Nations as an organization but also a failure of its states as constituent members, as recognized by the UN High Commissioner for Human Rights (1996):

the effectiveness of the United Nations human rights programme depends on the political will of Member States and other partners in this endeavor, accompanied by adequate economic and financial support. In the final analysis, the programme can work successfully only with the full commitment of Member States and their willingness to assume the corresponding political and financial responsibilities.

The following recommendations are cognizant of the weakness inherent in the United Nations. The United Nations is a political organization that answers to its member states. Both the United Nations' funding and its mandate are reliant upon member proclivity. Our recommendations are of two categories: improving the machinery of the United Nations; and enhancing the environment of human rights protection. Finally, we examine the prospects of utilizing the regional human rights systems to enhance state acceptance and compliance with the international human rights standards. We propose a few refinements in the regional systems to increase their ability to address human rights grievances.

Improving the machinery of the United Nations

Improving the machinery of the United Nations would include increasing the human rights budget, developing on-site human rights field offices, and improving coordination and communication between human rights agencies. Effectively using the offices of the newly created UNHCHR to provide guidance and direction among the many human rights bodies is integral in fostering a coherent human rights system.

We would first recommend an **increase in the budget allotment assigned to human rights programmes**. Childers and Urquhart (1994) report that the High Commissioner for Human Rights is reliant upon the inadequate number of staff members and technical resources that already exist for human rights programmes. The High Commissioner is further burdened by the lack of monetary resources. Childers and Urquhart conclude: "The allocation to date of less than one per cent of the UN regular budget to human rights is at variance not only with the vast mandates for human rights that governments have so creditably adopted for the world body, but with the intense interest of the peoples of the world in human rights"(Childers and Urquhart 1994: 110). We do realize that this recommendation will, in all probability, fall on deaf ears and tight wallets.

Our second recommendation is the **establishment of human rights field offices** (Burk 1995). At present there are only five such offices, all in the former Yugoslavia. Staffed by UN fact-finders, country experts, human rights interns, and concerned citizens, field offices would permit a more thorough continuing investigation into the human rights situation within a country. NGOs would have a large role in the works of the field office. NGOs have a tradition of impartial investigation regarding human rights abuses and enjoy the confidence of worldwide support for their endeavours. Additionally, NGOs, because they are not affiliated with any state, will be less politicized than a United Nations Commission.

It has been argued that there is a problem of coherence and co-ordination in the human rights machinery, in that states have to endure the burden of reporting to several human rights committees and there is little follow-up on reports (Childers and Urquhart 1994). Given that the major weakness in the reporting system is states' failure to present complete, comprehensive, or sufficient reports, it seems foolhardy to ease their obligations. Only by being examined and questioned by several human rights committees will a true picture of a country's human rights situation develop. Our third recommendation is thus that **committee reports be shared between human rights supervisory committee members**. In this way a state's overall performance can be evaluated. Even with the best of intentions, owing to the lack of training and experience, a state's human rights performance will be uneven. Moreover, because of the backlog of cases and the limited investigation time allotted to a committee, only a small number of states are required to report to a committee each year. Rarely would a state be required to report to several committees in a single year.

The spirit of coordination ought to extend to other UN organizations. Our fourth recommendation is to **use the office of the UNHCHR to direct and coordinate the human rights machinery**. Figure 6.1 is only a partial chart of the human rights machinery of the United

Nations. One is immediately struck by the enormity and complexity of the structure of committees, commissions, working groups, and agencies involved in the protection and promotion of human rights. For example, human rights protection and promotion are part and parcel of the work done by UNICEF, the UN High Commissioner for Refugees, and UNESCO. The work done in the regional Economic Commissions certainly falls within the purview of third-generation human rights. Mandating the authority of the UNHCHR to oversee and coordinate human rights activities would reduce the chance of duplication or contradiction in activities. In addition, coordination and cooperation among UN bodies would allow the vastly under-funded human rights organs to utilize the resources, skills, and facilities of other agencies.

Childers and Urquhart's charge that there is little follow-up on reports is well taken. This is the direct result of inadequate staffing and outmoded technology. Again, NGOs have often filled the void by keeping an unforgiving eye on human rights violations in recalcitrant states.

Enhancing the environment of human rights protection

Enhancing the environment of human rights promotion and protection would include greater protection for NGO personnel and increasing collaboration between NGOs and UN agencies.

Our fifth recommendation is granting **greater protection for the local members of accredited NGOs**. These watchdogs of human rights take great personal risk when collecting data, documenting cases, petitioning their governments, demonstrating on behalf of those abused, and going public with accusations of human rights abuses. It is well known that members of NGOs suffer a high rate of kidnapping, disappearances, detention, and murder. Recalcitrant governments often resort to intimidation and reprisals against NGO officials to silence accusations of human rights abuses. We would recommend a quasi-diplomatic status for these foot-soldiers in the battle to secure human rights protection. If an NGO official is detained or kidnapped, the government would be under strict scrutiny to explain and investigate the circumstances. This added standard would help assure the free flow of authentic human rights information.

We would further recommend a more **explicit partnership between NGOs and the United Nations**. Frederick Cuny (1993) noted that the United Nations can act as a protecting and coordinating body for

NGOs in a post–Cold War era. Under the United Nations' protective umbrella, NGOs can more easily and safely act in regions plagued by violence. Whereas NGOs enjoy the trust and respect of the common citizen needed to gather and document cases of human rights abuses, the United Nations can intervene to deter or remedy a humanitarian crisis. Linking the two systems would create a comprehensive humanitarian structure. As it stands, NGOs serve as unofficial researchers, documenting evidence, exposing abuses, and writing reports used by UN agencies. The partnership is already well under way, as evidenced by a statement made in the fifth coordinating meeting of the six supervisory committees established to monitor compliance with the human rights treaties:

The chairperson recommends that each treaty body examine the possibility of changing its working methods or amending its rules of procedure *to allow non-governmental organizations to participate more fully in its activities.* Non-governmental organizations could be allowed, in particular, to make oral interventions and to transmit information relevant to the monitoring of human rights provisions through formally established and well-structured procedures. In order to facilitate the participation of non-governmental organizations, the chairpersons recommend that information about States parties' reporting be made available ... [and] advance information on the topic of proposed general comments should be made available to encourage non-governmental organizations to provide input to the drafts ... Attention should be given to securing a stronger, more effective and coordinated participation of national non-governmental organizations in the considerations of States parties' reports. (UN Doc. A/49/537, 19 October 1994, para. 41)

There is some concern that, as an explicit partner of the United Nations, the NGO might lose some of its political neutrality, objectivity, and independence. To believe that individuals who risk life and limb to protect and promote human rights would suddenly bow to governmental or intergovernmental demands is unjustified. Felice Gaer (1996) notes that the United Nations already draws heavily upon experienced NGO personnel to staff UN human rights monitoring missions.[19] As acknowledged partners, NGOs could still maintain their independence and political neutrality with, perhaps, a bit more safety and recognition.

This partnership should actively incorporate smaller, national human rights NGOs. Many NGOs, particularly from the underdeveloped regions, lack contact with UN bodies owing to the cost of travelling to New York or Geneva. Furthermore, the system of NGO "consultative status" disenfranchises small, local, or poorly funded

NGOs. These NGOs must work through the intermediary of an international NGO to be heard. Such a procedure often produces a detrimental "paternalistic dependency between front-line national organizations and international human rights NGOs" (Wiseberg 1991: 542).

Utilizing regional human rights systems

There has been much talk recently of the new regionalism of the post–Cold War world. In the settlement of disputes the United Nations encourages regional efforts, as long as these arrangements are consistent with the purposes and principles of the United Nations.[20] UN Secretary-General Boutros Boutros-Ghali recognizes that, "[j]ust as no two regions or situations are the same, so the design of cooperative work and its division of labour must adapt to the realities of each case" (Boutros-Ghali 1995: 63). Yet the concept of regional efforts at human rights enforcement holds both future promise and potential tragedy. With many states still adhering to the belief that human rights have a cultural or regional aspect to their interpretation and promotion, a regional regime would help ease the acceptance of the legitimate enforcement of human rights. This is not to say that we would endorse claims of cultural relativism to justify acts of repression. But distancing human rights from claims of Western domination and neo-colonialism is important in securing universal acceptance (rather than rhetorical acceptance) of human rights and fundamental freedoms. And, in the words of Jack Donnelly, "to insist that all human rights be implemented in precisely identical ways in all countries would be wildly unrealistic, if not morally perverse (Donnelly 1993: 36). Donnelly advocates a "weak relativism" of human rights. We concur with this position, which upholds the universality of human rights but allows for minor cultural variability.[21]

The effectiveness of international human rights is based in large part on its harmony with domestic law and local customs. Perhaps regional interpretations of the protection and promotion of human rights would add greater legitimacy and acceptance to these norms. Europe, Latin America, and Africa have fine regional human rights conventions that mirror or complement international human rights standards. Yet these documents allow for the inclusion of customary norms. For example, the African Commission on Human and Peoples' Rights can utilize "African practices consistent with international norms on human and peoples' rights, customs generally accepted as law, general principles of law recognized by African states as well as legal precedents and doctrine."[22] Meron (1989) believes that the incorporation of regional customary law that is consistent with international standards can expand the protection of human rights.

The difficulty lies in securing adequate enforcement of human rights norms. Many developing countries govern under similar conditions: a pluralistic society made up of several ethnic or religious groups; a falling GNP coupled with rising demand for goods and services; a huge increase in population with a growing demand for democratic participation. Will neighbouring states censure governmental excesses when they can imagine being in the same situation sometime down the road? As Ofuatey-Kodjoe (1995) reminds us, China's human rights violations went unsanctioned owing to the reluctance of many third world states to condemn China's actions. A further example of the danger of regionalism involves the Human Rights Commission resolution on the human rights situation in Nigeria, which failed by 17 votes to 21, with 15 abstentions. The vote split along regional lines: the African group voted no as a block, whereas the majority of Latin American states abstained (Crook 1996).

Regional efforts to secure human rights must be consistent with UN standards, otherwise the universality of human rights will give way to expediency and limitations of local governments. Furthermore, cultural variations in the implementation of human rights must never cloud the conviction that human rights are universal, inalienable, and held equally by all people simply because they are human beings. In order to ensure that regional systems of human rights protection correspond with the goals and standards of the United Nations, several revisions are required.

First, using the offices of **UNHCHR as an oversight agency** to ensure that the principles and purposes of the United Nations are observed is a possible solution for combining the universality of human rights with the need for cultural sensitivity. By coordinating regional components, the UNHCHR will improve the human rights machinery's efficiency and effectiveness, thus fulfilling the UNHCHR's mandated responsibility to strengthen and streamline international and national human rights machinery. The UNHCHR has given the coordination of international machinery with national and regional machinery the highest priority, stating, "national institutions as mechanism ... can bridge the gap that frequently separates the most vulnerable and disadvantaged individuals from traditional means of protection" (UNHCHR 1996: 6). The development and coordination of regional institutions are vital for safeguarding human rights.

A second refinement for the use of regional human rights systems to promote and protect human rights is the **development of regional conventions** to establish human rights courts and fact-finding commissions. Regional conventions of human rights protection would have to be brought in line with international standards. This is not a problem for the regions of Europe, Latin America, and Africa because they already have exemplary human rights documents. The regions of Asia and the Middle East will need to draft conventions upholding international standards while integrating their unique cultural characteristics.

All regional, and international, courts must be **granted compulsory jurisdiction** over any alleged breach of human rights standards. Compulsory jurisdiction is well established in the European Court of Human Rights (Art. 46). All 30 members of the Council of Europe have accepted the Court's authority. The American Convention has a similar provision for compulsory jurisdiction (Art. 62). The Inter-American Court of Human Rights' jurisdiction is compulsory for the 11 states that have made special declarations of acceptance. In contrast, the International Court of Justice is granted, through treaty provision, compulsory jurisdiction only over disputes concerning the interpretation or application of several human rights conventions. The Human Rights Committee is granted compulsory jurisdiction regarding breaches of human rights treaties only if both the offending state and the reporting state have accepted, without reservation, the Committee's authority (Meron 1989). Would states be willing to relinquish a parcel of sovereignty in order to replicate the European model of compulsory jurisdiction? This appears unlikely in the short run, yet there are optimistic indications that compulsory jurisdiction may become a commonplace. As mentioned earlier, all the states of Europe and 11 of the Latin American states have accepted compulsory jurisdiction in the regional courts; they represent approximately one-quarter of the world's states, which is a substantial beginning!

Finally, all regional commissions or courts for human rights protection must be **open for individual petition**. Again, the European Commission and Court are the forerunners in the protection of human rights. Both the European Commission (Art. 25) and the European Court (as of October 1994) are open to individual complaints against governments. The American Convention allows individual victims to lodge complaints with the Inter-American Commission (Meron 1989). Some, but not all, international human rights treaties grant individual petition when a state accepts the specific treaty provision. Could the European model of individual petition be used to strengthen the international machinery for the protection of human rights? It is difficult to believe that international human rights organs could handle individual complaints when there are 6 billion people in the world. According to Janis et al. (1995), the European model is suffering a breakdown owing to an overburden of work.[23] Perhaps the right of an individual to seize an international court is unrealistic but the right of a collective (ethnic, religious, female, minority) to petition is feasible.

The United Nations' mandate to respect state sovereignty and to honour the principle of non-interference is often at odds with its mandate to protect and promote human rights. The solution is not necessarily to reduce state strength but to encourage a respect for human dignity. Indeed, a strong state is needed to safeguard the human rights of the vulnerable and less powerful groups within society (minorities, women, the poor). But the protection of human rights is too serious a cause to be left to the political agenda of states. Although the United Nations is dedicated and sincere in promoting and protecting human rights, it is imperative to remember that the United Nations remains an organization of and for states. Neutral, non-partisan monitoring of human rights remains critical. NGOs played an enormously important role in the drafting of human rights standards, and later as the vigilant sentinel and global town-crier for the protection of human rights.

The United Nations' family of international human rights instruments has, despite numerous violations, modified state behaviour. In addition, the United Nations has institutionalized the role of NGOs in detecting, investigating, and responding to human rights violations. There is much work still left to be done, but it would be a mistake to ignore the accomplishments of the United Nations.

Notes

1. To illustrate how far human rights have come in the past century, Huaraka (1991) goes on to note that the inclusion of a clause for freedom of religion in the general provisions of the Covenant was withdrawn when Japan introduced a clause for racial equality.
2. As evidenced in a later speech to Congress, 20 June 1941: "Our Government believes that freedom from cruelty and inhuman treatment is a natural right. It is not a grace to be given

or withheld at will by those temporarily in a position to exert force over a defenseless people" (as quoted in Burgers 1992: 469–470).

3. The Atlantic Charter made eight points concerning democratic principles in international relations: (1) both parties agreed not to seek territorial expansion; (2) no territorial modifications were to be made without the support of the indigenous people; (3) indigenous people were to be allowed to freely choose their own governments; (4) all states would have the right to access primary resources; (5) the signing parties agree to cooperate for the development of economic and social programmes; (6) after the destruction of the Nazi forces a peace guaranteeing international security will be enforced; (7) freedom of the seas; and (8) a global reduction in armaments (Duroselle 1985). It is interesting to note that the origin of the right to development (a third-generation right) is found in points 4 and 5, while points 6 and 7 clearly found the right to live in peace (also a third-generation right).

4. The British were concerned that the issue of human rights would be used to attack their imperial power, while the Soviets were worried that human rights provision would protect fascist governments. Both countries shared the US apprehension that human rights would transgress domestic jurisdiction (Johnson 1987).

5. The alliance was led by Frederick Nolde of the Federal Council of the Churches of Christ, Joseph Proskauer and Jacob Blaustein of the American Jewish Committee, Clark Eichelberger of the American Association for the UN, and James Shotwell of the Carnegie Endowment. The call to include human rights in the Charter was also taken up by civic groups as diverse as the League of Women Voters, the American Bar Association, the National Association of Manufacturers, and the National Council of Farmer Cooperatives (Gaer 1996).

6. Charter of the United Nations, done at San Francisco, June 26, 1945; entered into force Oct. 24, 1945; for the United States, Oct. 24, 1945, 59 Stat. 1031, T.S. No. 993, 3 Bevans 1153, 1976 Y.B.U.N. 1043.

7. International law is generated by treaties and customary law, that is "the general principles of law recognized by civilized nations" (Statute of the International Court of Justice, Article 38). Customary law is behaviour or practices that are accepted as law owing to common or long-standing usage or consensus.

8. For a much more detailed treatment of the work and success of the United Nations in the human rights area, see Donnelly (1993), especially chapters 1, 4, and 6; and Weiss et al. (1994), especially chapters 5, 6, and 7.

9. Article 21 provides for individuals to petition the European Commission for action on a human rights complaint. In October 1994, the Convention was amended so that an individual may seize the Court; prior to that time individuals did not have the authority to petition the Court directly.

10. In May 1970, the UN Economic and Social Council adopted Resolution 1503 which authorized the Commission on Human Rights to conduct confidential investigations of communications of patterns of gross violations of human rights and fundamental freedoms. The course of action required to get a complaint to be heard by the full Commission is called the 1503 Procedure.

11. As examples, Driscoll (1979) states that, although the European Convention for the Protection of Human Rights grants the right and obligation to states to complain against other states that violate the Convention, there had been only eight inter-state complaints in the 25 years prior to the writing of his article. The International Labour Organization allows for member states and trade unions to issue complaints of human rights abuses. Yet inter-state complaints totalled six within the past 60 years, whereas trade unions lodged 808 complaints between 1951 and 1975.

12. Most notably, the Convention on the Prevention and Punishment of the Crime of Genocide and the Convention on the Political Rights of Women.

13. For an analysis of such trends and country studies, see Lopez and Stohl (1987); O'Donnell et al. (1986); Sorenson (1993), especially pp. 25–62.

14. Universal Declaration of Human Rights, GA Res. 217(III)A, UN Doc. A/810 (1948).
15. For a good historical account of this see Pagnucco and McCarthy (1992).
16. As discussed in Smith (1993) – winner of the section award for best student paper from the Section on Collective Behavior and Social Movements.
17. ESC Resolution 1296 (XLIV) on Consultative Agreements, UN ESCOR, 44th Session, 1520th meeting, UN Doc. E/4548/Supp. 1 (1968).
18. For a useful discussion of the access problem see Posner and Whittome (1994).
19. For example, Ian Martin, the former head of Amnesty International, for the Haiti mission; Diego Garcia Sayan, of the Andean Commission of Jurists, along with Reed Brody, International Human Rights Law Group, for the Salvador mission. According to Gaer, many of the names on the "'international roster of specialized staff' available at short notice for human rights field missions" belong to NGO-affiliated human rights activists (Gaer 1996: 63).
20. Article VIII of the UN Charter provides for regional arrangements in dealing with matters of international peace and security. The Cold War, in the opinion of Boutros-Ghali, "impaired the proper use of Chapter VIII" (Boutros-Ghali 1995: 63).
21. Using Donnelly's example, the right to political participation is universal yet the form of participation is open to cultural interpretation.
22. African [Banjul] Charter on Human and Peoples' Rights, adopted 27 June 1981.
23. Protocol No. 11 calls for the merging of the Commission and the Court into a single body. The merger would, its proponents claim, streamline the procedure and reduce duplication of work. Opponents of Protocol No. 11 state that a single body would not reduce the caseload and the advantages of a two-stage procedure would be lost (for example the fact-finding function of the Commission or its ability to mediate friendly settlements).

References

Alston, Philip, and Girard Quinn. 1987. "The Nature and Scope of States Parties' Obligations under the International Covenant on Economic, Social and Cultural Rights." *Human Rights Quarterly*, vol. 9, pp. 156–229.

Barnett, Michael. 1995a. "Partners in Peace? The UN, Regional Organizations and Peace-Keeping." *Review of International Studies*, vol. 21, pp. 411–433.

——— 1995b. "The New United Nations Politics of Peace: From Juridical Sovereignty to Empirical Sovereignty." *Global Governance*, vol. 1, pp. 79–98.

Beck, Luise Doswald. 1987. "The Civilian in the Crossfire." *Journal of Peace Research*, vol. 24, no. 3, pp. 251–262.

Boutros-Ghali, Boutros. 1995. *An Agenda for Peace, 1995*. New York: United Nations.

Brierly, James. 1963. *The Law of Nations: An Introduction to the International Law of Peace*. Oxford: Clarendon Press.

Burgers, Jan Herman. 1992. "The Road to San Francisco: The Revival of the Human Rights Idea in the Twentieth Century." *Human Rights Quarterly*, vol. 14, pp. 447–477.

Burk, Erika. 1995. "Human Rights and Social Issues." In John Tessitore and Susan Woolfson, eds., *A Global Agenda: Issues Before the 49th General Assembly of the United Nations*. Lanhamm, Md: University Press of America.

Childers, Erskine, and Brian Urquhart. 1994. "Human Rights." In B. Urquhart and E. Childers, eds., *Renewing the United Nations System*. Uppsala: Dag Hammarskjold Foundation.

Claude, Richard, and Burns Weston. 1992. *Human Rights in the World Community: Issues and Action*. Philadelphia: University of Pennsylvania Press.

Comeau, Pauline. 1994. "Mood Is Positive as the UN Begins Review of NGO Status." *Tribune des Droits Humains*, September/October, pp. 24–27.

Crook, John. 1996. "Changing the Charter: The UN Prepares for the Twenty-first Century." *American Journal of International Law*, vol. 90, pp. 115–138.

Cuny, Frederick. 1993. "Humanitarian Assistance in a Post-Cold War Era." In Thomas G. Weiss and Larry Minear, eds., *Humanitarianism across Borders: Sustaining Civilians in Times of War*. Boulder, Colo.: Lynne Rienner.

Donnelly, Jack. 1986. "International Human Rights: A Regime Analysis." *International Organization*, vol. 40, no. 3, pp. 599–642.

——— 1993. *International Human Rights*. Boulder, Colo.: Westview Press.

Donnelly, Jack, and Rhoda Howard. 1986. "Human Dignity, Human Rights, and Political Regimes." *American Political Science Review*, vol. 80, pp. 801–817.

Driscoll, Dennis. 1979. "The Development of Human Rights in International Law." *The Human Rights Reader*. Philadelphia, Pa.: Temple University Press.

Duroselle, Jean-Baptiste. 1985. *Histoire Diplomatique de 1919 à nos Jours*. Paris: Dalloz.

Durr, Oliver. 1987. "Humanitarian Law of Armed Conflict: Problem of Applicability." *Journal of Peace Research*, vol. 24, no. 3, pp. 263–273.

Farer, Tom. 1992. "The United Nations and Human Rights: More Than a Whimper, Less Than a Roar." In Richard Claude and Burns Weston, eds., *Human Rights in the World Community*. Philadelphia: University of Pennsylvania Press.

——— 1993. "The UN and Human Rights: At the End of the Beginning." In Adam Roberts and Benedict Kingsbury, eds., *United Nations, Divided World: The UN's Role in International Relations*. Oxford: Clarendon Press.

Gaer, Felice. 1996. "Reality Check: Human Rights NGOs Confront Governments at the UN." In Thomas Weiss and Leon Gordenker, eds., *NGOs, the UN and Global Governance*. Boulder, Colo.: Lynne Rienner.

Gordenker, Leon, and Thomas Weiss. 1996. "Introduction." In Thomas Weiss and Leon Gordenker, eds., *NGOs, the UN and Global Governance*. Boulder, Colo.: Lynne Rienner.

Henkin, Louis. 1981. "Introduction." In *The International Bill of Rights*. New York: Columbia University Press.

Huaraka, Tunguru. 1991. "Civil and Political Rights." In Mohammed Bedjaoui, ed., *International Law: Achievements and Prospects*. Paris: Martinus Nijhoff (UNESCO).

Humphrey, John. 1967. "The UN Charter and the Universal Declaration of Human Rights." In Evan Laurd, ed., *The International Protection of Human Rights*. New York: Praeger.

Jacobson, Harold. 1984. *Networks of Interdependence: International Organizations and the Global Political System*, 2nd edn. New York: Alfred A. Knopf.

Janis, Mark, Richard Kay, and Anthony Bradley. 1995. *European Human Rights Law: Text and Materials*. Oxford: Clarendon Press.

Johnson, M. Glen. 1987. "The Contributions of Eleanor and Franklin Roosevelt to the Development of International Protection for Human Rights." *Human Rights Quarterly*, vol. 9, pp. 19–48.

Lopez, George, and Michael Stohl, eds. 1987. *Liberalization and Redemocratization in Latin America*. Westport, Conn.: Greenwood Press.

McDougal, Myres, Harold Lasswell, and Lung-chu Chen. 1980. *Human Rights and World Public Order*. New Haven, Conn.: Yale University Press.

Meron, Theodor. 1989. *Human Rights and Humanitarian Norms as Customary Law*. Oxford: Clarendon Press.

Nagan, Winston. 1992. "'Looking and Thinking' about Human Rights and Revolution." In Richard Claude and Burns Weston, eds., *Human Rights in the World Community: Issues and Action*. Philadelphia: University of Pennsylvania Press.

O'Donnell, Guillermon, et al. 1986. *Transitions from Authoritarian Rule*. Baltimore, Md.: Johns Hopkins University Press.

Ofuatey-Kodjoe, W. 1995. "The United Nations and the Protection of Individual and Group Rights." *International Social Science Journal*, vol. 47, pp. 315–331.

Pagnucco, Ron, and John d. McCarthy. 1992. "Advocating Non-Violent Direct Action in Latin America: The Antecedents and Emergence of SERPAJ." In Misztal and Anson Shupe, eds., *Religion and Politics in Comparative Perspective*. Westport, Conn.: Praeger, pp. 125–147.

Posner, Michael H., and Candy Whittome. 1994. "The Status of Human Rights NGOs." *Columbia Human Rights Law Review*, vol. 25, no. 2, pp. 269–290.

Proskauer, Joseph. 1950. *A Segment of My Times*. New York: Farrar, Strauss.

Russell, Ruth B. 1958. *A History of the United Nations Charter*. Washington, D.C.: Brookings Institution.

Smith, Jackie G. 1993. "Transnational Political Processes and the Human Rights Movement." Paper delivered at the annual meeting of the American Sociological Association.

Sohn, Louis. 1982. "The New International Law: Protection of the Rights of Individuals Rather Than States." *American University Law Review*, vol. 32.

Sorenson, George. 1993. *Democracy and Democratization*. Boulder, Colo.: Westview Press.

Spiro, Peter. 1994. "New Global Communities: Nongovernmental Organizations in International Decision-Making Institutions." *The Washington Quarterly*, vol. 18, pp. 45–56.

Szabo, Imre. 1982. "Historical Foundations of Human Rights and Subsequent Developments." In Karel Vasak and Philip Alston, eds., *The International Dimensions of Human Rights*. Paris: Martinus Nijhoff (UNESCO).

Thakur, Ramesh. 1994. "Human Rights: Amnesty International and the United Nations." *Journal of Political Research*, vol. 31, pp. 143–160.

Tomasevski, Katerina. 1994. "Human Rights and Humanitarian Challenges." In Erskine Childers, ed., *Challenges to the United Nations: Building a Safer World*. New York: St. Martin's Press.

Trubek, David. 1984. "Economic, Social and Cultural Rights in the Third World: Human Rights Law and Human Needs Programs." In Theodore Meron, ed., *Human Rights in International Law*. Oxford: Clarendon Press.

UNHCHR (United Nations High Commissioner for Human Rights). 1996. Report of the United Nations High Commissioner for Human Rights, "Making Human Rights a Reality," electronic edition.

United Nations. 1996. *The United Nations in Its Second Half-Century*. Report of the Independent Working Group on the Future of the United Nations.

Weiss, Thomas, David R. Forsythe, and Roger A. Coate. 1994. *The United Nations and Changing World Politics*. Boulder, Colo.: Westview Press.

Weissbrodt, David. 1987. "Humanitarian Law in Armed Conflict: The Role of International Non-governmental Organizations." *Journal of Political Research*, vol. 24, no. 3, pp. 297–306.

Weston, Burns. 1992. "Human Rights." In Richard Claude and Burns Weston, eds., *Human Rights in the World Community*. Philadelphia: University of Pennsylvania Press.

Willetts, Peter. 1996. "From Stockholm to Rio and Beyond: The Impact of the Environmental Movement on the United Nations Consultative Arrangements for NGOs." *Review of International Studies*, vol. 22, pp. 57–80.

Wiseberg, Laurie. 1991. "Protecting Human Rights Activists and NGOs: What More Can Be Done?" *Human Rights Quarterly*, vol. 13, pp. 525–544.

7

The struggle in the UN system for wider participation in forming global economic policies

Ho-Won Jeong

The development of the United Nations economic system has been influenced by challenges arising from the international political environment. It also reflects changing perceptions of economic development in a rapidly integrating global economy. In considering that policy is made in certain political and cultural contexts, normative values cannot be separated from technocratic decision-making (Jeong 1995: 79). One of the main issues in United Nations reform has focused on how the system can better serve the basic needs of poor and vulnerable social groups, with a stress on investment in human resources. On the other hand, the issues of human needs are not equally represented in the different economic development strategies subscribed to by various agencies. The struggle over reform represents changing relationships between poor and rich countries as well as the internal dynamics of the system.

Functionalist ideas based on cooperation on social and economic problems for the promotion of peace and human welfare facilitated the establishment of networks of UN specialized agencies after World War II. The increased number of independent states in former European colonies and the need for economic assistance led to the initiation of the UN Development Decade in the early 1960s. The dissatisfaction of third world countries with the Western-dominated economic order brought about the declaration of a New International Economic Order (NIEO), which emphasized changes in the international economic structure toward the goal of reducing the gap between the rich and the poor. Ever since, developing countries have been disappointed with the lack of any progress in their negotiations with industrialized countries, whereas developed countries have moved serious economic discussion to institutional mechanisms that they can easily control, such as the Organization for Economic Cooperation and Development (OECD) and the Group of Seven (G7).

Over the past several decades, changes in the United Nations have been directed toward expansion of the system by adding new units and organs, in response to the emergence of new issues such as environmental pollution and a lack of development in the third world. In addition, non-governmental organizations (NGOs) have begun to play a significant role in the global policy-making process, as has been demonstrated in various multilateral conferences discussing economic and social issues (Ramphal 1996). Although the significance of NGOs has been recognized, no new structure has emerged for incorporating NGO activities into the larger UN system.

No policy centre has been successfully installed for coordinating economic development policies in the system. More significantly, the absence of consensus on the role of the United Nations has resulted in illusions of the United Nations' capacity and influence as well as misperceptions of the present role of economic cooperation and international development. One of the main purposes of this chapter is to analyse how the UN system has evolved in response to changes in the international political economy. On the basis of this analysis, the chapter discusses questions concerning major aspects of economic cooperation under the UN system. Finally, various reform proposals are considered in the context of how to strengthen the UN economic system in serving the majority of the global populations.

1. Functionalism and specialized agencies

After World War II, the theory of functionalism inspired the creation of a system of specialized agencies at the world level responsible for economic, social, cultural, educational, health, and related fields. In Chapter IX of the UN Charter, on International Economic and Social Cooperation, there is a strong emphasis on a general pledge for the promotion of "higher standards of living, full employment, and conditions of economic and social progress and development."[1] Technical experts may easily agree on international standards, rules, or other recommendations for enhancing economic development. It was believed that the agencies constitute building blocks towards the construction of an orderly world system. The essential goal of the institutional framework was to prevent future problems of liberal capitalism (Mayall 1988: 53).

The economic and social system of the United Nations was based on loose relationships between separate organizations. According to Article 57 of the Charter, "The various specialized agencies, established by intergovernmental agreement and having wide international responsibilities, as defined in their basic instruments ... shall be brought into relationship with the United Nations." In Article 63(2), the Economic and Social Council (ECOSOC) "may coordinate the activities of the specialized agencies through consultation with and recommendations to such agencies and through recommendations to the General Assembly and to the Members of the United Nations." The role of ECOSOC is consultative and advisory only, and, right from the outset, no central authority was accorded ECOSOC. Specialized agencies undertake to submit regular reports to ECOSOC, to send representatives to each other's meetings, and to exchange information. However, they are not in any sense under ECOSOC's jurisdiction or control (Muller 1992: 7).

Specialized agencies are also loosely coordinated by other mechanisms. The Administrative Committee on Coordination (ACC), chaired by the Secretary-General and attended by the heads of specialized agencies, was given a mandate to manage and coordinate general activities in economic and social fields of the UN system. Later, such institutions as the Consultative Committee on Substantive Questions (CCSQ) were created to assist the tasks of the ACC. In addition, specialized agency budgets were, albeit superficially, reviewed in the Fifth (Administrative and Budgetary) Committee of the General Assembly. The Committee can visit the specialized agencies once every two years to review budgets (Taylor 1993: 134).

The autonomy that the 1945 Charter accorded to the specialized agencies was a deliberate attempt to encourage them to build confidence in their functional fields. The various specialized agencies were set up as separate institutions, with their own membership, intergovernmental institutions, budget, staff, executive head, and policies. It was envisaged that the agencies would not be formally supervised by ECOSOC, nor would their secretariats be formally accountable to the Secretary-General. No matter whether development issues, administration, or financial methods are concerned, the agencies cannot be obliged to adopt policies laid down by the Secretariat or other bodies of the United Nations. The dangers and disadvantages of having one monolithic organization were considered to outweigh the dangers and disadvantages of having a dispersed network. However, the main problem of the system, it was later pointed out, is the absence of a central body that can coordinate or control independent sectoral policies of specialized agencies. For instance, in the Capacity Study of 1969, also known as the Jackson Report, the specialized agencies were called "principalities," and the organization of the system was considered to be the equivalent of "some prehistoric monster" (United Nations 1969: v).

2. Technical assistance and the creation of the United Nations Development Programme

The core of the technical assistance concept at an early stage focused on the development of human capital, and this was viewed as a natural task for the United Nations. To meet the urgent need of investment in human resources, the Economic and Social Council subsequently established the Expanded Programme of Technical Assistance (EPTA), to be financed by voluntary contributions. Although the EPTA was only coolly received by industrialized countries, it was later supported by President Truman's address in 1950, which emphasized the need to provide large-scale assistance to developing countries, preferably through the United Nations. In considering the optimism of those first years after World War II, the EPTA represented the belief that the transfer of knowledge, skills, and technology would help recipient countries achieve economic independence in a decade or so. Long-term experts and grants for fellowships were the two main instruments to achieve these objectives (Kaufmann et al. 1991: 88).

Later it proved that "technical assistance alone was inadequate in solving the problems of the poor countries. The work of the experts in the field could be made much more effective if supplemented with long-term low-interest loans to finance investments in schools, hospitals, agricultural equipments and industrial plants" (Weiss et al. 1995: 179). In response to this challenge, a Special UN Fund for Economic Development (SUNFED) was recommended by a committee appointed by the UN Secretary-General. However, the recommendation was not adopted owing to strong opposition from the ministers of finance of developed countries, led by the United States (Weiss et al. 1995: 179). They argued that the primary responsibility for international lending activities belonged to the World Bank. As a compromise, the UN Special Fund was set up in 1958 with a broader mandate than the EPTA. The Special Fund focused on large projects that could yield immediate results. In addition to offering technical assistance, it would support pre-investment studies and demonstration projects (Kaufmann and Schrijver 1990: 19). The pressure for financing development also led to the creation of the International Development Fund, which has since been affiliated to the World Bank.[2]

The First UN Development Decade was inspired by President John F. Kennedy's address at the General Assembly in September 1961. It was designed to promote development worldwide in accordance with a set of targets laid down by the United Nations. This increased the need for coordination, and in 1965 the General Assembly decided to merge the EPTA with the Special Fund to create the United Nations Development Programme (UNDP). The role of the UNDP was soon recognized to be as a central coordinating agency by the 1969 Jackson Report. In accordance with a "Consensus Resolution" of the General Assembly in 1970 (based on the Jackson Report), the UNDP adopted the partnership principle and the five-year development cycle.[3] The scheme was supposed to enhance coordination between the various parts of the UN system because they all had to work within the framework of the country programme.

This phase in UN efforts to strengthen international cooperation for economic development was led by the American belief that a second Marshall Plan could bring a rising curve of economic development to the newly independent states of the third world.

This appears to have been a mixture of arrogance and naivete. It was arrogant to take it for granted that the Western model of economic development had universal validity. It was naive to believe in instant modernization. It was naive, too, to idealize the politics of liberation and ignore the diversity of cultural backgrounds in the Third world. (Jakobson 1993: 136)

As indicated by the appointment of Paul Hoffman, former administrator of the Marshall Plan, as the head of the UNDP, American enthusiasm for the First UN Development Decade was part of the great ideological contest between capitalism and communism (Jakobson 1993: 136).

In the past 25 years, the reality has substantially changed from that of 1970. The central funding principle was seriously undermined by the emergence of "multi-bi" projects executed by specialized agencies. Donor countries began to prefer projects that allow them to influence the selection of the beneficiary. This new practice led to the disintegration of the country programme process. Independent financial resources enabled agencies to implement a technical assistance project without any direct link with the country programme (Kaufmann et al. 1991: 94). The sudden rise in funding for technical cooperation by the World Bank since the 1970s has also seriously weakened the function of the UNDP.[4] Compared with US$38 million in 1968, the Bank, by the early 1990s, attained a level of about US$1.5 billion, surpassing the contributions to the UNDP, and this marked the end of the central funding principle (Kaufmann et al. 1991: 93).

3. Response to the NIEO

By the end of the First Development Decade, third world countries themselves began to lead the discussion of economic development in the UN system. This inevitably resulted in a new approach to the development issue. "It was not enough for the developed countries to provide assistance; the structure of economic relations in the world also had to be changed before developing countries could have a genuine chance to improve their economic performance" (Jakobson 1993: 137). The restructuring of the international economic system required planned policy actions on a wide range of issues, including commodity prices, trade in manufactured products, international shipping, the international monetary system, the transfer of technology, transnational corporations, etc. For this objective, the United Nations became the principal forum for negotiations.

Representing the interests of third world countries, the UN Conference on Trade and Development (UNCTAD) attempted to facilitate the coordination of the activities of other institutions within the United Nations system in the field of international trade and related problems of economic development. In a similar manner, all activities of the United Nations system in the field of industrial development were promoted by the United Nations Industrial Development Organization (UNIDO). However, to press their demand, developing countries soon switched their battleground to the General Assembly during the second half of the 1970s. The Sixth UN Special Session of 1974 dramatized these efforts of developing countries by adopting the Declaration and Programme of Action for the Establishment of a New

International Economic Order (NIEO).[5] The Declaration recognized the demands of the Group of 77 in the areas of trade, commodities, aid, industrialization, the transfer of technology, and similar matters. Developed countries accepted it, but only with many reservations.

Some argue that the NIEO was never concerned with protecting the economic and social interests of people. It was rather a reflection of the demands of the governments of the new countries.[6] "By basing its normative propositions on the principle of the sovereign equality of all states, it has afforded the cover of its ideology to all political regimes, even those which systematically violate civil and political rights and pay no heed to social justice" (Bertrand 1989: 48). Moreover, it offered only a limited analysis of the economic relations between developed and developing countries. Thus, it is not surprising that "it has not won support either from the representatives of the rich countries or from all of the defenders of the Third World" (Bertrand 1989: 48).

4. Stalemate in dialogue

The North–South dialogue has not been successful in many areas since the failure to launch a new round of global negotiations in the 1980s and 1990s, including UNCTAD VI in Belgrade (1983), UNCTAD VII in Geneva (1987), and UNCTAD VIII in Cartagena (1992). The frustration with multilateral cooperation soon led to an attack on the United Nations' function as a platform for North–South dialogue. The situation was worsened by changes in the political environment of major Western governments, which put the emphasis on free market solutions and opposed collective action often called for by UN and specialized agency resolutions. Bilateralism and regionalism replaced multilateral efforts to achieve economic development through the UN system.

Meanwhile, the global debt of developing countries doubled in the 1980s to more than US$130 billion, while official development aid transfers did not increase. Moreover, capital flight and high interest rate payments caused a reverse net capital movement from developing to developed countries. Thus, the 1980s witnessed stagnation in the economic growth of the planet's poor regions. In contrast, despite a few economic problems such as unemployment and inflation, the average income of rich countries has at least quadrupled since World War II. This international situation was reflected in the politics of the UN system.

The General Assembly's Eighteenth Special Session, from 23 April to 2 May 1990, focused on the world economic situation and international economic cooperation. It discussed conditions for growth and development in developing countries, but the atmosphere was completely different. Ten years earlier, the dominant issues were how to achieve the goals of the NIEO, and discussions focused on launching a new round of global negotiations for supervising and controlling transnational corporations. Instead of these issues, the 1990 Special Session heard of domestic economic policy failures, the need for a free market approach, the significance of human rights, etc. The Session revealed the increasing marginalization of developing countries and their peoples. The Session was unable to reach agreement on a substantive debt relief paragraph in its Resolution.

Especially since the 1980s, operative control over international development policy has been taken over by the International Monetary Fund (IMF) and the World Bank, whereas various other UN agencies superficially discuss global economic and social issues without any action. The end of the Cold War led Washington to believe that the Bank and the Fund should serve as major international institutions to promote a free market economic order. Reflecting this view, the United States and some other Western countries adopted policies that deny the United Nations any significant role in the discussion of international economic policy matters. The best example is the US government's reluctance to participate in the Special General Assembly Session on development questions in April 1990. This Western position contributed to the failure to initiate a new round of global negotiations on international economic policies in the United Nations (Kaufmann and Schrijver 1990: 17).

5. Structural divisions and political realities

The UN system has expanded in an ad hoc manner as new institutions are established on the basis of newly perceived needs (Donini 1988: 292). For example, in response to the needs of third world countries, more than two dozen new agencies and special funds were created in the UN system between the middle of the 1960s and the early 1980s. These agencies include the International Fund for Agricultural Development (IFAD), the United Nations Population Fund (UNFPA), the United Nations Institute for Training and Research (UNITAR), the World Food Programme (WFP), the United Nations Development Fund for Women (UNIFEM), as well as the United

Nations Conference on Trade and Development (UNCTAD) and the United Nations Industrial Development Organization (UNIDO). Compared with the IFAD, UNFPA, UNITAR, and WFP, a few agencies, including UNCTAD and UNIDO, clearly represented the dissatisfaction of poor countries with Western-dominated agencies such as the General Agreement on Tariffs and Trade (GATT) and the International Labour Organization (ILO). Even though the goals of the NIEO were never achieved, its supporting institutions remain. Now the UN system "resembles an army equipped and deployed to fight an enemy that has vanished" (Jakobson 1993: 149).

UNCTAD and UNIDO have different economic theories and organizational ideologies from those of such agencies as the Bretton Woods institutions (the World Bank and the IMF) and the World Trade Organization (WTO), formerly GATT. Contrary to a free market economic approach, the UNCTAD and the General Assembly supported an interventionist approach. In the views of the interventionists, "the division of the benefits of economic interchange between the rich and the poor countries must be reviewed as a consequence of the relative bargaining strengths of the two groups rather than be left to the working of normal market forces" (Williams 1987: 145). Thus, interventionists argue that poverty is caused by the drain on their resources that results from the powerful entrenched institutional position and bargaining power of developed countries. Institutional mechanisms are needed to redress the balance (Williams 1987: 145).

Because the UNCTAD Secretariat primarily promotes the interests of less developed countries, developed countries have a tendency to bypass UNTCAD (Weiss 1986). Unlike other organs in the UN system, the IMF and the World Bank are like corporations in which each member holds a certain number of shares. Their decision-making process is based not on majority vote but on the amount of financial contributions. Another character of those agencies is that they maintain a technocratic approach to economic problems.[7] The power and influence of the Bank, the Fund, and the WTO come from the sufficient financial support of rich Western industrialized countries. On the other hand, the Fund is widely resented in developing countries as "a stern custodian of financial rectitude." This dichotomy between agencies oriented to the needs of third world countries and the Bretton Woods institutions has been detrimental to the functioning of the UN economic system.[8]

The third world does not have the political and economic strength needed to restructure the world economy, but it does have the voting power to influence the UN General Assembly and the assemblies of the specialized agencies. Marginalization of third world countries and the renewed emphasis on a free market approach have weakened the role of the UN system in major international economic decision-making. The reality is that industrialized countries discuss world economic problems through G7 and the OECD. They are not interested in strengthening the UN system, where third world countries can have a majority vote. For industrialized countries, the role of UN agencies is minimal except for the World Bank, the IMF, and the WTO. Other UN agencies are not viewed by rich countries as having any influence on their prosperity. This significantly undermines the function of such UN organs as the Second Committee of the General Assembly, the Economic and Social Council, UNCTAD, and UNIDO.

The resurgence of free market economic approaches since the early 1980s strengthened the role of international financial institutions in economic policy-making in poor countries. Given the fact that the concern with human welfare is certainly less distinctive in the World Bank and the IMF than in other major UN agencies, development goals would be better served both when no single foreign source of ideas and finance has disproportionate power and when indigenous technical capacity is built to the point that genuine policy dialogue, based on mutual respect, takes place between external donors and local people.[9] A single model of development cannot be recommended as a universal norm because the circumstances, possibilities, socio-economic preferences, and political values of developing countries are so varied.[10]

6. Institutional inadequacies for economic cooperation

Ever since the drafting of the UN Charter, defining common objectives for all member states at the world level has been a difficult task. Consensus on the role of international coordination is more difficult to attain now than at any time since 1945. Before the 1970s, developed and developing countries could agree on broad development goals and some important policy strategies. In the 1960s, a major role for government in achieving growth through economic planning was widely recognized, and state action was encouraged to stimulate and direct economic growth. International policies generally supported the efforts of third world governments to develop technology and industrial skills. However, the consensus that had earlier emerged over major principles of economic development has broken down.

Since the early 1980s there has been more emphasis on strengthening existing social, economic, and cultural structures of a free market economy.

Economic development policies have been influenced by conflicting interests in the world, which comprise a mass of organized and unorganized economic, social, and political forces. There are different perceptions, expectations, and interests between industrialized and developing countries. However, no reliable methods or structures for multilateral negotiation have been adopted. The most serious obstacle is inequality between the member states. Poor countries have little influence in addressing the problems that are important to their economies. Their efforts have been mainly concentrated on building majorities in UN bodies (Renninger 1989: 249). But success in gaining the majority on the executive boards of various UN agencies has not produced any meaningful dialogue between the North and the South. The paragraphs of resolutions are couched in fine words simply to "conceal the fact that no agreement has been reached, either because there were no genuine negotiations or because the positions of the various governments are so far apart that there is no chance of a true rapproachment" (Bertrand 1989: 29).

The absence of procedures designed for binding agreements is related to the failure to define negotiation structures that are suited to the problems and are accepted by all participants. Binding solutions cannot be achieved in the weighted voting system of the Bretton Woods organizations. The system does not allow the weak to make themselves heard by permitting member states to take decisions jointly. On the other hand, the majority votes of the Group of 77 are of limited importance, since the majorities formed by poor countries are not taken seriously by rich countries. Resolutions that are adopted have no practical consequences. Thus, the lack of realistic representation has resulted in a preference for bilateral negotiations that produce agreements that can be implemented (Bertrand 1989: 50).

7. Proposals for reform of the UN economic system

Most UN reform proposals have paid attention to coordination among agencies and cooperation between rich and poor countries. Unmanageable intergovernmental decision-making and negotiation apparatuses are responsible for the lack of systematic resource-allocation procedures and effective accountability mechanisms.[11] However, building a consensus on new mechanisms for economic assistance has not been easy. New financial and institutional arrangements can influence power relations between UN agencies with different economic priorities. The discussion about a more coordinated policy-making structure cannot be separated from how to reconcile different economic strategies such as the promotion of a free market and the satisfaction of basic human needs.

One of the most important tasks for the United Nations is to ensure an economic dialogue between rich and poor countries. In most UN reform proposals (United Nations 1969, 1975, 1985), there has been an emphasis on strengthening ECOSOC.[12] Recently, the Secretary-General suggested that ECOSOC, a body of 54 member states, should be transformed into a Council of Ministers supported by a policy-planning staff for development at UN headquarters. In this proposal, the Council of Ministers for Economic and Social Affairs would be given the authority to review the medium-term plans and documents of the organizations of the UN system. Thus it would contribute to a rational utilization of resources in the light of global priorities as defined by the Council and bring about greater strength and coherence to the system as a whole (Bertrand 1989: 125–26).

The report of the Nordic UN Project presented to the General Assembly in 1991 also proposes the establishment of a high-level international development council to discuss development issues and bring general guidance for the UN system.[13] The function of the council could be undertaken by a reformed ECOSOC. The report also suggests "strengthening and enlarging ECOSOC so it becomes a universal body in session in parallel with the General Assembly, while the Second and Third Committees of the General Assembly should be abolished" (Seufer-Barr 1993: 40).

The UN working group established in October 1992 suggests the transformation of the governing bodies of the UNDP, the UNFPA, and UNICEF into smaller executive boards under the overall authority of the Economic and Social Council (Seufer-Barr 1993: 39). Similar arrangements would apply to the Committee of Food Aid Policies and Programmes, which sets policy for the World Food Programme (WFP). Some believe that improved leadership is required to cope with the urgent tasks of the United Nations and propose creating three deputies to the Secretary-General, one of whom would assist in the areas of economic and social matters with a stress on sustainable development (Urquhart and Childers 1990).[14]

Several proposals, including reports of a study group of the World Institute for Development Economics Research (WIDER), suggest the creation of a World Economic Council, equivalent to the Security Council, in order to carry out a reform of existing global multilateral institutions and, more generally, supervise and coordinate "global macroeconomic policy" (WIDER 1989). According to the UNDP and the North–South Roundtable proposals, a new Development Security Council needs to design a global policy framework in all key economic and social areas (UNDP 1992; ul Haq et al. 1995).[15] More specifically, it should reach political agreements on specific policy responses to such issues as global poverty, unemployment, food insecurity, and ecological pollution. These proposals recommend that smaller industrial countries and developing countries join forces and delegate authority to a representative group that would participate in the world summit. In particular, the WIDER report presents an elaborate scheme for a voting system based upon three objective criteria, reflecting their economic and political weight in the world: GNP, trade, and population. Two former UN civil servants have also proposed an Economic Security Council that would be able to formulate macroeconomic policy that can be supported by the North and the South (Urquhart and Childers 1994). They believe that a new Economic Security Council is needed because the current ECOSOC does not function at a high enough level of representation (Urquhart and Childers 1994: 61).

On the other hand, others propose regional approaches to development by strengthening the regional Economic Commissions. The United Nations could still remain as a forum for generating concerns and ideas for development; but the structure is not adequate for producing agreements. Specific negotiations should be based on a collective bargaining process at a regional level. Operational structures of the UN system should be reconverted into regional development agencies or enterprises (Renninger 1987: 90).

In a special report for the 1985 UN anniversary, the Joint Inspection Unit of the United Nations proposed the transformation of the UN system into a European Community-style decision-making body based on the structure of commissions and councils (United Nations 1985: 52). In its view, an expansion of this type of structure on a global scale could require the establishment of two or even three commissions. Commissions would include people who were chosen by national governments but who would act in accordance with the interests of the community. Though this proposal indicates that consensus can be more easily reached in the structure of councils and commissions, this approach may not solve North–South problems.

Unlike in the European Community, economic disparities between poor and rich countries in the world would make it difficult to reconcile different views on economic development strategies and redistribution of global wealth.

Some believe that the best hope for coordination is to be found at the country level. They suggest use of the Country Strategy Note (CSN), voluntarily created by recipient countries.[16] This would identify programmes that are compatible with a country's development needs. It would facilitate a coherent approach by identifying plans and priorities that are unique to a specific country (Stanley Foundation 1995: 27). The CSN could strengthen the status and capacities of the UN resident coordinators who coordinate policies at the sectoral as well as the project level. On the other hand, the CSN might not represent the needs of people if it relied too heavily on the government in identifying development goals.

8. The role of NGOs and human needs development

The UN system should not any longer play a peripheral role in global economic management but take greater responsibility for development policy formulation. However, the alternative to present problems is not to be found in a type of centralization, which would produce a bureaucratic monster and could in no way respond to present shortcomings. In discussions of UN reform, most attention has been paid to improving administrative and management practices between and within UN organs. But what is needed is a comprehensive view, with a programme that represents local needs. Problems must be dealt with on the spot, in close collaboration with grass-roots organizations. NGOs tend to emphasize autonomy and sensitivity to the needs and aspirations of poor communities (UNCTAD 1990). Local participation would help to overcome vested bureaucratic interests at state and international levels of organization.

Some NGOs have been granted consultative status with ECOSOC, and they can attend UN meetings, request the opportunity to speak at them, distribute documents to governmental delegations, and meet delegates informally in the UN lounges.[17] In 1975, the United Nations established its Non-Governmental Liaison Service (NGLS) in Geneva and New York to enhance contacts between the United Nations and NGOs. One of its functions is to advise small local NGOs on how to make use of the UN system's information facilities. However, even NGOs in consultative status with ECOSOC are too slightly represented at intergovernmental meetings.

More active involvement of NGOs is essential to building a democratic process in economic policy-making and strengthening a local capacity to manage economic programmes. More specifically, efforts need to be made to increase the role of indigenous NGOs and diverse cultural and ethnic groups in the formulation and implementation of community projects, as well as in facilitating open and efficient communication between development agencies and local people.[18] The creation of a Popular Chamber or a UN Parliamentary Assembly, which was proposed by A More Democratic United Nations (CAMDUN) and the World Federalist Movement, might enhance more grass-roots input into UN economic policy-making.

Since the 1980s, many UN agencies have made more efforts to engage local NGOs in various stages of project development. However, the process has not always been positive. In the case of World Bank projects, broad participation of NGOs in policy-making is the exception rather than the rule (Adams and Rietbergen-McCracken 1994: 37). Local NGOs are more heavily involved in the implementation of projects than in decision-making. More importantly, the imposition by the Bank and the IMF of neo-classical economic policies on many developing countries as conditionalities for loans has led to cuts in government spending on basic social service programmes, elimination of government subsidies on food, and retrenchment of government workers (Jeong 1995). These policies have alienated the majority of NGOs, including Oxfam and local NGOs in Africa and Latin America (George 1994).

In its 1992 annual report on global dimensions of human development, the UNDP argues that "the existing framework of global governance is weak, ad hoc and unpredictable," while numerous international institutions and forums, mostly dominated by rich countries, leave developing countries powerless and vulnerable (UNDP 1992). The reform of the UN economic system needs to be based on the recognition of development oriented to human needs.[19] NGOs operate at a level that "tries to interweave the social, human, and economic aspects of development" (Stanley Foundation 1995: 10). The participation of grass-roots organizations would be required for the construction of development programmes that fully and unambiguously reflect the needs of specific communities.[20] The alliance between the United Nations and NGOs could be formed by the transnational expansion of democratic ideas such as participation and equity.

Some UN specialized agencies such as UNESCO, the FAO, and the ILO have excellent NGO representations. Recently the FAO took a bold initiative to link the popularly organized Freedom from Hunger Campaign to its headquarter programmes. UNESCO has been very successful in mobilizing citizen support through its National Commissions composed of various grass-roots groups and professionals. The ILO has a unique tripartite structure, which includes trade unions, representatives of states, and employers' associations in its governing body. These systems have contributed to building supportive relationships between UN agencies and NGOs.

9. The need for new institutional arrangements

The recognition of development oriented to human needs in various international forums has generated demand for a radical reform rather than minimal changes to the existing system. Although an Economic Security Council could be organized to seek to design a global policy framework in all key economic and social areas, it would be very difficult to create such a body given the objections to a more centralized UN system.[21] It is politically unrealistic to expect Western industrialized countries to pay more attention to the elimination of poverty in third world countries than to the maintenance of an international economic order based on principles of free market economies. Most importantly, the creation of a new central organ would address only the interests of government élites and international economic bureaucrats.

There is fairly general professional, governmental, and popular consensus within third world countries that the relative influence of the IMF and the World Bank, particularly the latter, has grown too large. How to address the imbalance in decision-making power between different regions of the world has not been seriously considered in most official UN proposals. Despite the need for a policy framework to promote basic human needs, there is little agreement about what should or can be done about it. For example, should third world governments seek to reform ECOSOC or to strengthen a regional policy-making framework such as the UN Economic Commissions for Africa or Latin America? How should they press for more diversified sources of external assistance while somehow still seeking to minimize dependency and improve aid coordination?

In what ways should they improve various forms of South–South exchange and cooperation within the UN system?

In considering problems with and opposition to the current role of the Bretton Woods institutions in the third world, human development is likely to be best served when mutual respect is built between donors and local policy makers, and where development programmes are fully and unambiguously locally constructed. The reduced role of the IMF and the World Bank, the larger influence of UN technical agencies, and economic integration and cooperation within the South will remain the major items on the agenda for the reform of global economic governance.

In pursuing global policies to deal with economic insecurity, such as deteriorating living standards and a lack of social welfare, the Vice Executive Director of UNICEF, Richard Jolly, believes that various UN technical agencies are more appropriate for the development of programmes. This is because they are multidisciplinary and already concerned with a variety of the broader, but often neglected, areas of development such as women's concerns, children's needs, urban problems, and the environment. The common element among UN technical and regional agencies is their human focus and concern, which are certainly "less distinctive" in the World Bank and the IMF. It would be helpful "to bring the U.N. agencies together in support of some form of special and coherent commitment to the human dimension of economic development, not merely as a short term, stopgap arrangement, but as a means for strengthening long-term survival and development on a new basis" (Jolly 1986: 395).

On the issues of satisfying the basic social and economic needs of the poor, there has been discussion on the role of WHO, UNICEF, the ILO, and other UN agencies and ways to create more effective international collaboration with other international groups. One of the main issues in this area has been the lack of a clear definition of links between development agencies of the United Nations and the Bretton Woods institutions, and their respective roles. Many officials in other agencies in the UN system believe that their merger with programmes funded by the World Bank and the IMF is neither desirable nor needed. The discussion of cooperation should focus on institutionalizing human development issues in macroeconomic planning.

More active involvement of UN agencies in the development of third world countries should be related to strengthening the democratic process in economic policy-making and local capacity to manage economic programmes. More specifically, efforts need to be made to recognize sustainable development initiatives and to involve diverse cultural and ethnic groups in the formulation and implementation of community projects. The participatory decision-making process can facilitate open and efficient communication between development agencies and local groups engaged in the promotion of basic human needs projects. In this context, it is essential to redefine the relationship between international financial institutions, UN technical agencies, and grass-roots development groups. Non-governmental organizations should be strengthened, given the fact that they are more actively involved in the human aspects of development than are governmental or intergovernmental agencies.

10. New roles for the UN agencies and regional institutions

The current systems for development coordination are compartmentalized. To avoid duplication and overlapping, various agencies need to have greater collaboration. The relationships between UN specialized agencies vary, and cooperation is often based on individual and ad hoc relationships. Effectiveness has been a major concern in the discussion of reform. Yet the efficient management of the UN economic system should be considered in the context of the creation of a more participatory process. In particular, the consultative process could emerge more easily on a regional basis. Specific development issues such as food and health should be coordinated by the relevant UN technical agencies. Initiatives for development planning could be led by UN regional Economic Commissions, given the fact that each region has its own set of economic problems. The voice of NGOs would be represented better in a regional planning process. To have more impact on policy-making, NGOs should organize a consortium or a network on a regional basis. They should interact with each other as well as with regional Economic Commissions.

In establishing an appropriate framework for the coordination of development aid, I would suggest different roles for the UNDP. One approach is that, because the UNDP has greater technical expertise in economic planning and project development, UNDP offices could play a key role in identifying development problems in certain countries, allocating resources, and linking projects of various UN agencies to overall planning. This approach might guarantee efficiency in resource allocation but could create an undesirable bureaucratic process with concentration of more planning and decision-making power at one or a few offices. In addition, it would not be politically feasible given the fact that other UN agencies would not sacrifice their perceived missions and roles for better aid coordination.

The UNDP could engage in policy dialogue on employment, poverty, and human resources development, which tend to be neglected because of the present focus on crisis management and financial imbalances. The UNDP could cultivate its special relationships with the planning ministries in developing countries and work as a major funding agency for technical assistance. The UNDP could also assist in reducing the institutional divide between the finance ministries, which negotiate with the financial institutions, and the planning and sectoral ministries, in order to reintroduce into the dialogue concerns about the real economy and society. The UNDP could also mobilize the energies and thinking of UN specialized agencies in order to bring coordinated analysis and advice to the developing countries.

An alternative role for the UNDP puts stress on communication rather than planning activities. The UNDP currently has a resident representative system in many countries and has organized many round-table meetings designed to coordinate the development assistance programmes of various donors. It also tries to help economic planning ministries of third world countries build indigenous economic planning capacities through its technical aid programme. Thus the UNDP is in a good position to develop communication networks to link various UN and government agencies. They also need to extend their relationships to grass-roots development groups. By actively organizing round-table meetings in developing countries and utilizing the system of resident representatives of its own or other UN agencies, the UNDP can gather information about the aid programmes of various UN agencies and provide analysis of the economic requirements of specific countries. In addition, it could identify similar projects initiated by different agencies to help avoid any waste of resources, and improve communication among agencies that may intend to develop common projects. In this approach, although UNDP needs to be more active in promoting communication, aid planning should be made in each agency but in consultation with other agencies. Most importantly, however, if necessary, other UN agencies should also play a leading role in their areas of concern, as UNICEF did in programmes to reduce the social impact of government austerity programmes on the poor.

With respect to regional coordination, few reform proposals in the past emphasized strengthening the regional Economic Commissions.

The United Nations can still remain as a forum for generating concerns and ideas for development; but the structure is not adequate for producing agreements. It is very difficult to reach consensus in a global setting, no matter whether discussion is made by a council, committee, or parliamentary structure. Thus, specific negotiations should be based on a collective bargaining process at a regional level. The operational structures of the UN system should be reconverted into regional development agencies or enterprises (Renninger 1987: 90).

The UN Economic Commissions for Africa, Latin America, and Asia should participate more in economic planning. The regional Economic Commissions have special knowledge and focus on the specific regions of the world and could share planning functions with the UNDP. The role of regional banks, such as the African Bank, in financial mobilization needs to be strengthened, especially considering that Bank/Fund loans have strict conditions that may actually have a negative impact on poor regions of the world. In addition, self-reliance can be achieved only by increased lending activities of the regional banks rather than by external funding.

In the context of economic policy reform in third world countries, regional cooperation and efforts to build an economic community are important. For example, the OAU (Organization of African Unity) summit, which took place in Abuja, Nigeria, 3–5 June 1991, proposed an African Economic Community. Reflecting experiences of existing West African and South African Economic Communities, African countries are gradually recognizing the need for regional self-reliance, which requires utilization of indigenous technology and exchange of resources within the region. The OAU proposal envisions, within the first quarter of the twenty-first century, the eventual creation of a free trade area in the region, which will be developed from existing regional economic communities (*West Africa*, 1–30 June 1991, pp. 10152–4). The influence of regional agencies will grow if current efforts to build mechanisms for regional economic cooperation such as an African Economic Community are realized.

Another issue for future reform, perhaps the most important, is participation of local NGOs. One of the most ignored concerns is the involvement of NGOs in economic policy-making within the UN system. NGOs should be part of a consultation and decision-making network. NGO liaison offices in UN agencies should gather information about indigenous, home-grown NGO projects. It is desirable for UN agencies to avoid initiating any programmes or projects in areas where NGOs are actively involved. It is also desirable that NGO projects be supported or complemented by UN agency programmes. Consultative policy-making mechanisms need to be built to strengthen the ties of the United Nations to local NGOs.

The most complicated issue is how to define relations with the World Bank and the IMF. Almost 30 years ago, one of the most influential UN studies on reform for international aid coordination suggested that the UNDP should be more engaged in preliminary research and initiation of development aid programmes, whereas the World Bank should take more responsibility for formulating programmes (United Nations 1969). The introduction of structural adjustment, which emphasizes devaluation of currency, removal of price controls, and elimination of government subsidies on basic necessities, has placed many UN agencies at odds with the Bank since the early 1980s. Given their interest in human development, some of the most important UN agencies, including UNICEF, the ILO, WHO, and UNCTAD, have criticized, either directly or indirectly, various aspects of Bank/Fund-sponsored adjustment programmes and shown concern about the increase in Fund and Bank influence. The most vivid and direct criticisms so far have been made by the Economic Commission for Africa. The World Bank even had to issue an internal memorandum to defend its policies. Though the UNDP cooperated with the Bank on the production of a document in support of structural adjustment in 1989, its annual reports on Human Development clearly point out problems with the human dimensions of Bank/Fund adjustment programmes. Overall, as many UN agency officials argue, any cooperation with the Bank should not be on its terms, and its financial support of UN development projects should be carefully reviewed.[22]

Reform could start with promoting cooperation between UN agencies involved in basic human needs projects and building coalitions with government agencies and local groups interested in human needs issues. One interesting example is the role of UNICEF in the formulation of programmes to mitigate the social impact of structural adjustment in Ghana. Structural adjustment programmes based on macroeconomic balance often sacrifice the needs of the poor and the vulnerable in society. Since the beginning of structural adjustment in Ghana in 1983, UNICEF has conducted research on human welfare conditions in Ghana in cooperation with the University of Ghana. This research was quickly supported by the ministries of health and education, but was ignored by the World Bank and the ministry of finance. Later, the impact of adjustment policies on the economically marginalized groups became clear, and the significance of UNICEF research was recognized even by Bank officials. Subsequently, a programme to deal with the negative impact of structural adjustment in Ghana was launched in 1987. Given the small budget of the programme, and its complementary nature to orthodox adjustment programmes, the programme may be considered insignificant, but the UNICEF study has had some impact on the policy orientations of the Bank and the Fund.[23] Even though UNICEF's efforts did not produce any tangible outcome, they did lead to meetings among some UN agencies, including WHO and the ILO, to discuss the impact of liberal economic reform on the urban and poor populations.

11. Conclusion

Reform in UN social and economic activities has become an important issue over the past few decades. More than a decade ago, a UNITAR study by Martin Hill (1978) warned of the danger of the United Nations being bypassed and rendered ineffective. Currently, the Bretton Woods organizations are perceived as being the places where the real action takes place, and other UN economic agencies are left with the management of residual functions. In addition, no one can ignore "the significance of the rapidly growing importance of the OECD, and the tendency of the EEC to take independent action. This trend seems to have been intensified with the Western economic summits and the preference of some donors for bilateral rather than multilateral development assistance" (Renninger 1987: 99–100).

Reform of the United Nations requires efforts to build consensus on the management of global economic issues. States cannot undertake joint activities in fields in which they are not able to agree. Economic cooperation would not be brought about by action programmes devoid of any substance. On the other hand, independent national strategies in the economic and social fields cannot be effective if they do not take into account the strategies, methods, and principles accepted by other countries. The principle of reciprocal support at the United Nations could help to build the needed solid world political framework.

The role of the United Nations is to organize an international debate that would allow the North and the South to explore, jointly, their differences in perception and to find a common ground at a time when there is no international consensus on development and the working assumptions about the nature of the world economy. International economic decision-making toward the twenty-first century will, without doubt, require much broader vision (Jolly 1995: 191). UN agencies need to be brought together in support of some form of special commitment to the human dimension of development, not merely as a short-term arrangement but as a means to strengthen the long-term survival of the poor. The inclusion of NGOs in policy-making and implementation would be especially beneficial in periods of economic deterioration in many parts of the world.[24]

Acknowledgements

I wish to thank members of the IPRA Global Political Economy Study Commission for their support. The valuable comments from Miles Wolpin (USA), Imtiaz Ahmed (Bangladesh), Imre Levai (Hungary), and Rainer A. Ibana (the Philippines) on an early draft of this chapter especially need to be recognized. Martin Rochester (USA) also offered valuable comments.

Notes

1. The emphasis on economic cooperation in the UN Charter reflects, in part, learning from the mistakes of the League of Nations. The League Covenant contained only a single reference to economic affairs. The intellectual hegemony of liberal economics since World War I led to the rejection of any regulatory role of economic institutions. It was also believed that welfare would be optimized by the free operation of international markets.
2. In addition, the United Nations Capital Development Fund was created under the auspices of the UN General Assembly in 1966 and has become fully operational since 1974. It has been administered by the UNDP. The Fund supplements other sources of capital assistance for the least developed countries by offering grants and loans on concessionary terms.
3. The UNDP's governing council (on which 45 industrialized countries and 50 developing countries are represented) has a consensus rule. Decisions on aid are based on the need of recipients. The council calculates the population and per capita GNP, and decides the amount of funding needed for a country. It also uses a five-year plan to estimate the medium- and long-term needs of the recipients.
4. This view is shared by a report presented to the Second Committee of the General Assembly. As "a consequence of the shortcomings of the United Nations system, the World Bank group and the regional development banks have become more prominent, in the field of technical assistance, than was the case when the present system was conceived. There are, thus, clear tendencies of a marginalization of the United Nations" (United Nations 1991: 2).
5. The Charter of Economic Rights and Duties of States adopted by the United Nations later in the year helped third world countries extend the scope of the NIEO. This document includes, in detail, the principles and practices needed to implement the NIEO.
6. In his comments on this paper, Miles Wolpin (Professor, State University of New York, Potsdam) suggests that the UN system itself is composed of nation-states that are represented by government élites. The economic interests of people are not well represented by a system that does not lend significance to the welfare of grass-roots people. The NIEO can be criticized for the lack of the dramatic structural change that is necessary to deal with poverty and the inequitable distribution of wealth in the world. The comments were received in August 1994.

Similar views about the structure of the United Nations are suggested by other scholars. "As the United Nations attempts to deal with global problems, there are contradictions between its basic structure and the tasks it is called upon to perform. It is fundamentally a union of states founded to preserve the system of states. Its relationships with the peoples of the world are normally carried out through state officials, who naturally wish to preserve the prerogatives of states, including their own positions in the state system" (Alger 1995: 27).

7. In the international financial institutions, ministers of commerce and finance are represented, and the use of technical language by them contributed to their reputation as serious institutions. This can be compared with the discussion of broad economic issues at the General Assembly by representatives of governments who do not have deep economic knowledge.

8. Though the Bretton Woods institutions are associated with ECOSOC under the terms of Article 57 of the UN Charter, the relationship is mostly symbolic. The institutions are not subject to substantive coordination at ECOSOC or ACC meetings. Their link is limited to the occasional appearance of their chief executive officers before ECOSOC and their participation in some other meetings (Adedeji 1995: 70).

9. Development, defined as the full development of individual human potential, can be achieved only by "a highly decentralized global policy process" (Alger 1990: 167).

10. In the view of Imre Levai (Senior Researcher, Hungarian Academy of Sciences, Hungary), the "political difficulties inherent on the (long) existing and 'amortised' system" should be more explicitly recognized. "We may speak of development in general but the newly emerged world develops in a particular way and even the questions relating to the paradigms are not asked." The present UN economic system needs to take into consideration pragmatic aspects in this context. These comments were offered by Dr. Levai in October 1994.

11. In his comments on the early draft of this paper, Imtiaz Ahmed (Professor, University of Dhaka, Bangladesh) points out that it would be unwise to "take a positivist approach (i.e. isolating 'economic system' from other systems) in the understanding of the problem at hand. A more holistic and dialectical approach would be better." In this connection, we need to ask to what extent the UN economic system has served and failed. His comments were received in November 1994.

12. ECOSOC's failure can be attributed to the complexity of issues, inadequate size, resistance of the specialized agencies to giving up their autonomy, the shift of major discussion to UNCTAD, the General Assembly's Second or Third Committee, and the Group of Seven, etc. (Rochester 1993: 138–139).

13. The report was jointly prepared by the governments of Denmark, Finland, Iceland, Norway, and Sweden.

14. The most recent efforts to strengthen the leadership capacity to streamline and rationalize development activities led to the creation of the Department for Policy Coordination and Sustainable Development, the Department of Economic and Social Information and Policy Analysis, and the Department of Development Support and Management Services within the UN Secretariat. This resulted from consultation by the Secretary-General with a panel of independent high-level advisers in 1992.

15. Similar proposals were also made by the US World Federalist Movement. They call for the creation of "an Economic Security Council reorganized out of the current UN Economic and Social Council" that would coordinate monetary stabilization and trade programmes as well as development programmes. This body would also assist nations with non-military economic conversion and support the role of women in development (Allen 1991: 87).

16. The CSN was adopted in General Assembly Resolution 47-199 in 1992, which is intended to create a demand-oriented method of coordination. It describes a recipient country's expectation of the role of the UN agencies in development. It is to be used to evaluate how UN projects help to satisfy a country's development needs.

17. The NGO consultative status is determined by a governmental committee that meets every two years. NGOs may also be less formally associated with the UN Department of Public Information (DPI) for the purpose of distributing information to members about UN work. A DPI committee of officials determines which NGOs may become associated with it. An NGO with this status may designate an observer to the United Nations, who will be given access to the United Nations' NGO lounge, UN documents, press releases, and weekly NGO briefings by senior UN officials and experts. Over 1,500 NGOs have either ECOSOC consultative status or DPI association status. Finally, specialized agencies, UN programmes, and UN information centres (based in many capital cities all around the world) have their own ad hoc arrangements for consulting with NGOs. This means that thousands of NGOs have one form or another of consultative arrangement with the United Nations.

18. As the priorities of development shifted to the satisfaction of basic human needs, more non-governmental organizations and local governments have been involved in the policy-making process (Alger 1994: 319).

19. In that sense, the demand for reform should be generated by the recognition of the need for human welfare rather than bureaucratic efficiency.

20. The role of NGOs in the United Nations can be considered in the following context: (1) NGOs serve as mediating structures between the unorganized masses and the global eco-political order, while cushioning the impact of oppression and marginalization; (2) NGOs have a dual function in development by influencing the state and the economy as indirect forms of governance – this includes judicial processes and campaigns for free and clean elections within democratic contexts, and street rallies and mass media politics to struggle against repressive regimes; (3) NGOs demonstrate a "politics of identity" that is specific to particular interests, although this does not exclude the more universal issues of the environment and human rights. These views were presented in the comments of Rainer A. Ibana (Professor at Ateneo de Manila University) on the earlier draft of this paper.

21. For further discussion about constraints of the international system on the development of international organizations, see Rochester (1996: 69–72).

22. Interviews with WHO officials in Geneva on 20 July 1990, and with UNICEF and UNDP officials in New York on 19 December 1990.

23. Interviews with a high IMF official in Washington, D.C., 12 December 1991.

24. There is a growing belief that "it is no longer enough to coordinate international organizations. NGOs play a role in filling gaps left by the relative loss of power of the state" (Stanley Foundation 1995: 29).

References

Adams, James, and Jennifer Rietbergen-McCracken. 1994. "Participatory Development: Getting the Key Players Involved." *Finance and Development*, vol. 31, no. 3, pp. 36–37.

Adedeji, Adebayo. 1995. "An African Perspective on Bretton Woods." In Mahbub ul Haq et al., eds., *The UN and the Bretton Woods Institutions*. New York: St. Martin's Press, pp. 60–82.

Alger, Chadwick. 1990. "Grass-roots Perspectives on Global Policies for Development." *Journal of Peace Research*, vol. 27, no. 2, pp. 155–168.

——— 1994. "Citizens and the UN System in a Changing World." In Yoshikazu Sakamoto, ed., *Global Transformation: Challenges to the State System*. Tokyo: United Nations University Press, pp. 301–329.

——— 1995. "The United Nations in Historical Perspective." In Chadwick Alger, Gene Lyons, and John Trent, eds., *The United Nations System: The Policies of Member States*. Tokyo: United Nations University Press.

Allen, Anthony. 1991. "Development: Are New Institutions Needed?" In Walter Hoffmann, ed., *A New World Order: Can It Bring Security to the World's People?* Washington, D.C.: World Federalist Association, pp. 83–90.

Bertrand, Maurice. 1989. *The Third Generation World Organization*. Dordrecht: Martinus Nijhoff.

Donini, Antinio. 1988. "Resilience and Reform: Some Thoughts on the Processes of Change in the United Nations." *International Relations*, vol. 9, no. 4, pp. 289–315.

George, Susan. 1994. "The Bretton Woods Institutions at 50 Years: A Critical Appraisal." In Janet Brian, ed., *The Proceedings of the South and the Bretton Woods Institutions Seminar*. Geneva: United Nations Office, 20–21 June.

Hill, Martin. 1978. *The United Nations System: Co-ordinating Its Economic and Social Work*. New York: Cambridge University Press.

Jakobson, Max. 1993. *The United Nations in the 1990s: A Second Chance?* New York: UNITAR.

Jeong, Ho-Won. 1995. "Political Economy of Structural Adjustment: A Critical Review of World Bank and IMF Policies." *Journal of International Studies*, no. 36, pp. 77–94.

Jolly, Richard. 1986. "Adjustment with a Human Face." In Khadija Huq and Uner Kirdar, eds., *Human Development: The Neglected Dimension*. Islamabad, Pakistan: North–South Roundtable, pp. 386–400.

——— 1995. "Poverty Eradication and Human Development: Issues for the Twenty-First Century." In Mahbub ul Haq et al., eds., *The UN and the Bretton Woods Institutions*. New York: St. Martin's Press, pp. 185–195.

Kaufmann, Johan, and Nico Schrijver. 1990. *Changing Global Needs: Expanding Roles for the United Nations System*. Hanover, N.H.: Academic Council for the United Nations System.

Kaufmann, Johan, Dick Leurdijk, and Nico Schrijver. 1991. *The World in Turmoil: Testing the UN's Capacity*. Hanover, N.H.: Academic Council for the United Nations System.

Mayall, James. 1988. "The Institutional Basis of Post-War Economic Cooperation." In Paul Taylor and A. J. R. Groom, eds., *International Institutions at Work*. London: Pinter, pp. 53–74.

Muller, Joachim W. 1992. *The Reform of the United Nations*, vol. 1. New York: Oceana Publications.

Ramphal, Sir Shridath. 1996. "Peace in Our Global Neighborhood." *Peace and Conflict Studies*, vol. 3, no. 1, pp. 79–84.

Renninger, John P. 1987. "Improving the United Nations System." *Journal of Development Planning*, no. 17, pp. 86–111.

——— 1989. "The Failure to Launch Global Negotiations at the 11th Special Session of the General Assembly." In Johan Kaufmann, ed., *Effective Negotiation: Case Studies in Conference Diplomacy*. Norwell, Mass.: Kluwer Academic Press, pp. 231–254.

Rochester, J. Martin. 1993. *Waiting for the Millennium: The United Nations and the Future of World Order*. Columbia: University of South Carolina Press.

——— 1996. "The United Nations at Fiftysomething: Challenges and Dilemmas in the Post-Cold War Era." *Peace and Conflict Studies*, vol. 3, no. 1, pp. 68–78.

Seufer-Barr, Nancy. 1993. "Towards a New Clarity for UN Work." *UN Chronicle*, vol. 30, no. 4, pp. 38–41.

Stanley Foundation. 1995. *United Nations–Bretton Woods Collaboration: How Much Is Enough?*. Muscatine, Ia.: Stanley Foundation.

Taylor, Paul. 1993. *International Organization in the Modern World.* London: Pinter.

ul Haq, Mahbub, et al., eds. 1995. *The UN and the Bretton Woods Institutions.* New York: St. Martin's Press.

UNCTAD (United Nations Conference on Trade and Development). 1990. "Report of the UNCTAD Meeting on the Role of Non-Governmental Organizations in the Development of the Least Developed Countries, 1989." *Transnational Associations,* no. 1, pp. 31–35.

UNDP (United Nations Development Programme). 1992. *Human Development Report.* Oxford: Oxford University Press.

United Nations. 1969. *A Study of the Capacity of the United Nations Development System.* E.70.I.10. New York: UN.

———— 1975. *A New United Nations Structure for Global Economic Co-operation.* E/AC.62/9. New York: Group of Experts on the Structure of the United Nations System.

———— 1985. *Some Reflections on Reform of the United Nations.* JIU/REP/85. Geneva: UN Joint Inspection Unit.

———— 1991. *Operational Activities for Development.* A/C.2/46/7. New York: UN.

Urquhart, B., and E. Childers. 1990. *A World in Need of Leadership, Tomorrow's UN.* Uppsala: Dag Hammarskjold Foundation.

———— 1994. *Renewing the United Nations System.* Uppsala: Dag Hammarskjold Foundation.

Weiss, Thomas G. 1986. "International Secretariat or Servant of the G77?: A Portrait of UNCTAD." In David Pitt and Thomas G. Weiss, eds., *The Nature of United Nations Bureaucracy.* Boulder, Colo.: Westview Press, pp. 84–102.

Weiss, Thomas G., et al. 1995. *The United Nations and Changing World Politics.* Boulder, Colo.: Westview Press.

Williams, Douglas. 1987. *The Specialized Agencies and the United Nations.* London: C. Hurst.

WIDER (World Institute for Development Economics Research). 1989. *World Economic Summits: The Role of Representative Groups in the Governance of the World Economy.* Study Group Series no. 4. Helsinki: WIDER.

8

The UN system in the vanguard of advancement of women: Equality, development, and peace

Hilkka Pietilä and Jeanne Vickers

What can women expect from the manifestation of patriarchy as presented by the 185 member governments of the United Nations? Strangely enough, it is in fact the United Nations system that, in recent decades, has been in the vanguard of efforts to improve the status of women, well ahead of its member governments. It has spearheaded a process that still awaits implementation within the states of UN members.

The Organization's fiftieth anniversary in 1995 coincided with the twentieth anniversary of International Women's Year 1975 and the tenth anniversary of the World Conference on Women in Nairobi in 1985. The Fourth World Conference on Women in Beijing in September 1995 was thus one of the major events being organized to celebrate the United Nations' fiftieth birthday.

1. The early years of the United Nations

The principle of the equality of men and women is already recognized in the Preamble of the UN Charter, which states: "We, the peoples of the United Nations, determined ... to reaffirm faith in fundamental human rights, in the dignity and worth of the human person, in equal rights of men and women and of nations large and small ... have resolved to combine our efforts to accomplish these aims." It also stipulates that one of the purposes of the United Nations is "to achieve international cooperation ... in promoting and encouraging respect for human rights and for fundamental freedoms for all without distinction as to race, sex, language or religion."

At the very first session of the UN General Assembly, a Commission was appointed to draft a Universal Declaration of Human Rights, presided over by one of the most outstanding women of the time, Eleanor Roosevelt. When adopted in 1948 the Declaration contained the words: "All human beings are born free and equal in dignity and rights." The Declaration's Second Article is even more specific: "Everyone is entitled to all rights and freedoms set forth in this Declaration, without distinction of any kind, such as race, colour, sex, language ..."

Based on the principles of the Charter and the Universal Declaration of Human Rights, much work has been done to produce more binding, more concrete, and more precise provisions on the equality of the sexes. In the early years of the United Nations, women's issues were mainly debated in bodies concerned with human rights, but as early as 1946 a Commission on the Status of Women was established with a mandate to study and prepare recommendations on human rights issues of special concern to women. Its first task was to determine under what conditions and situations, worldwide, the most severe forms of discrimination against women occurred, with four areas forming the point of departure for its work:
- political rights and the possibility of exercising them;
- the legal rights of women, both as individuals and as family members;
- access of girls and women to education and training, including vocational training;
- working life.

During the past 50 years, recommendations and conventions have been prepared and adopted by the United Nations, the United Nations Educational, Scientific and Cultural Organization (UNESCO), and the International Labour Organization (ILO) in all these fields. Table 8.1 lists the most important of those relating directly to women.

A sad reflection on the crucial problems of women still prevailing during the latter half of the twentieth century, these conventions also serve to measure the achievements of the UN system with regard to the advancement of women. The first, the *Convention for the Suppression of Traffic in Persons and the Exploitation of the Prostitution*

Table 8.1 **Selected Conventions of concern to women**

Adopted		In force	Ratifications (as of Sep. 1993)
1949	Convention for the Suppression of Traffic in Persons and the Exploitation of the Prostitution of Others	1951	70 (Dec. 1995)
1951	Equal Remuneration for Men and Women Workers for Work of Equal Value (ILO No. 100)	1953	120
1952	Convention on the Political Rights of Women	1954	105 (June 1996)
1958	Discrimination in Respect of Employment and Occupation (ILO No. 111)	1960	118
1960	International Convention against Discrimination in Education (Unesco)	1962	82
1962	Convention on Consent to Marriage, Minimum Age of Marriage, and Registration of Marriages	1964	44 (June 1996)
1979	Convention on the Elimination of All Forms of Discrimination Against Women	1981	154 (June 1996)
1981	Convention Concerning Equal Opportunities and Equal Treatment for Men and Women Workers: Workers with Family Responsibilities (ILO No. 156)	1982	20

of Others, dates already from the time of the League of Nations, to which the women's movement and a number of non-governmental organizations had submitted a proposal concerning prohibition of sexual slavery. Given the situation today, it is also an example of an international effort, in the form of a Convention in force, that has failed to eliminate or even diminish the problem concerned. On the contrary, prostitution has become a big business, and "traffic in persons" has become an ever more evident part of the flourishing and expanding industry of intercontinental tourism, extending even to under-age girls and boys .

A more encouraging example is the *Convention on the Political Rights of Women*. When the UN Charter was signed 50 years ago, political rights of women were in force in only 30 of the 51 signatory states. By 1996, 105 countries had ratified this Convention, and in fact the countries where such rights do not exist are now rare.

Also pointedly evocative of the situation of women were the reasons that led to the adoption of the *Convention on Consent to Marriage, Minimum Age of Marriage and Registration of Marriages* in 1962. At that time, women in much of the world still had no say in the choice of their marriage partners or the age at which their marriages took place; they were mere commodities in the hands of their parents and families, who had full power to decide upon their fate. Obligatory registration was a necessary means to ensure that the rights of the wife were officially recognized.

But perhaps the single most important step to improve the situation of women in the twentieth century has been the recognition, as a basic human right, of the right to family planning and access to the information and practical means necessary to exercise it. Mentioned for the first time in this form in the Declaration of Teheran, 1968, and included in the General Assembly's 1969 Declaration on Social Progress and Development, it was included as an obligatory provision in the *Convention on the Elimination of All Forms of Discrimination Against Women*, adopted in 1979.

Changing perspectives

In the past 50 years, issues concerning and of interest to women have gone through a process of varying treatment by the United Nations and its specialized agencies. Although during the 1950s and 1960s women's issues were seen primarily within the context of human rights and thus not related to the big issues of development and peace, in the 1970s the perspective changed decisively. The key role of women, especially in the fields of population and food, became apparent, and in 1972 a decision was taken to declare 1975 International Women's Year.

Throughout the 1970s women's issues came to the fore in several of the world conferences convened by the United Nations to study and adopt specific plans of action for the solution of major problems of world development, and the UN agenda began specifically to address the concerns of the female half of humankind. Seen earlier as mere objects, for whose protection and rights recommendations were made and conventions enacted, in the 1970s the formula became "to integrate women into development." Characteristically, women were seen as resources and their contributions were sought to enhance the development process and to make it more efficient. For this purpose it was necessary to improve the status, nutrition, health, and education of women.

It was often claimed to be "a waste of human resources" if women were not fully integrated into development efforts. Their dignity and rights were not yet seen as a cause in its own right. The perennial nature of their contribution to the well-being of every country's population was still unrecognized within the development context.

But at last, in the International Development Strategy for the United Nations' Third Development Decade (the 1980s), a trend towards seeing women as equals, "as agents and beneficiaries in all sectors and at all levels of the development process," finally emerges, and the year 1985 became a turning point in the history of women's issues in the UN system. For in that year the World Conference to Review and Appraise the Achievements of the UN Decade for Women took place in Nairobi, adopting unanimously the Forward-looking Strategies for the Advancement of Women Towards the Year 2000 (commonly known as the FLS). These specifically recognize women as "intellectuals, policy-makers, planners, and contributors and beneficiaries of development" and require implementation by both member governments and the UN system.

"Herstory" in the United Nations

The milestones in this process can be seen as follows :
- International Women's Year (IWY) 1975;
- the World Conference of the IWY in Mexico City, 1975, and adoption of the Declaration and World Plan of Action for Implementation of the Objectives of International Women's Year;
- the United Nations Decade for Women (UNDW) 1976–1985: Equality, Development and Peace (proclaimed by the General Assembly in its Resolution 3520 (XXX), 1975);
- the World Conference of the UNDW in Copenhagen, 1980, and adoption of the Programme of Action for the Second Half of the UNDW;
- the World Conference to Review and Appraise the Achievements of the UNDW: Equality, Development and Peace, in Nairobi in 1985; adoption of the Forward-looking Strategies for the Advancement of Women (FLS), for the period 1986–2000.

– the Fourth World Conference on Women in Beijing, 1995; adoption of the Platform for Action (PFA).

Another, partly parallel and equally important, process in the UN system was the preparation and adoption in 1979 of the most important international legal instrument for women, the Convention on the Elimination of All Forms of Discrimination Against Women. This Convention, as well as the FLS[1] and the Beijing PFA,[2] thus constitute the main UN accords for the advancement of women. The UN system has committed itself to implement these accords by adopting the System-wide Medium-term Plan for Women and Development for the period 1990–1995[3] as well as a corresponding plan for the years 1996–2001.[4]

A legal instrument to prevent discrimination against women

By far the most important of the UN conventions on women's rights, the Convention on the Elimination of All Forms of Discrimination Against Women, was adopted in 1979 without any dissenting vote and entered into force in 1981, following ratification by the required 20 countries. It is a concise and comprehensive conclusion to the long process that had taken place within the UN system during some 30 years to incorporate the principles of gender equality in the provisions of international law, covering all relevant provisions of previous, separate conventions and complementing them with regard to issues not yet covered.

The fact that a special convention was needed on this subject is revealing. All the human rights conventions speak about universal human rights, meaning equal rights of men and women, but they are still not applied equally anywhere, thus requiring this particular Convention. It provides also for the establishment of a Committee on the Elimination of Discrimination Against Women (CEDAW) to monitor its implementation, i.e. implementation of human rights conventions from the point of view of women.

CEDAW, composed of 23 elected experts nominated by the states parties to the Convention, meets once a year to consider progress made in implementation of the Convention and to review the periodic reports of governments. Each government must submit its initial report within one year after entry into force of the Convention in the country concerned, then at least once every four years. CEDAW even has the power to subject governments, one by one, to public scrutiny, and can also request additional or specific reporting whenever this appears necessary.

This Convention gained ratifications more rapidly than any other international convention before it, with ratification by about 100 countries within the 10 years up to 1990. Its impact has been significant, even in a country such as Finland where, together with the FLS, it speeded up the adoption of a general Equality Act and prompted the establishment of an Office of Equality Ombudsman in 1986. Ratification of the Convention also required reforms in legislation concerning family relations, in particular provisions concerning family name, marriage, guardianship, and citizenship of a married woman. Finland and other Nordic countries do not ratify international conventions before rectification of national legislation to become compatible with the convention concerned.

2. En route to Beijing: The Nairobi Forward-looking Strategies

The final document of the UN World Conference to Review and Appraise the Achievements of the United Nations Decade for Women: Equality—Development—Peace, *The Forward-looking Strategies for the Advancement of Women Towards the Year 2000* (the FLS), was adopted unanimously in Nairobi in 1985. The mere fact that this document was adopted by consensus is an important achievement, since the world conferences in Mexico City (1975) and Copenhagen (1980) were not able to reach unanimity in their deliberations. It is also an indication of the success of the Nairobi Conference, and of the growing common understanding among governments on issues of concern to women as a result of the UN Decade for Women and women's intensive efforts in many countries during the Decade.

The main purpose of the Conference, however, was to develop strategies for the next 15 years that would realize objectives that had not been achieved during the Decade as envisaged by declarations and plans of actions adopted in earlier world conferences of the UNDW, the United Nations' International Development Strategy for the 1980s, and the Convention on the Elimination of All Forms of Discrimination Against Women, and which would be based upon the review and appraisal of progress achieved and obstacles encountered during the Decade. An essential part of UN preparations for the Conference was the compilation of the first World Survey on the Role of Women in Development (1984),[5] the first review and appraisal of global development – not only in developing countries – ever under-taken from women's perspective, which gave baseline data on the situation of women worldwide upon which the FLS could be based.

In principle, the FLS document aims to express women's views on world affairs. And because all human affairs are women's affairs, the FLS covers everything human – issues of peace and war, development, human rights, natural resources and environment, culture, participation in politics and the economy, relations between men and women, family and children, and much more. It is an ambitious document of almost 100 pages of cramped UN language, in some 400 paragraphs; and more than half of the operative paragraphs deal with development.

Definition of the concepts

While making an interesting normative contribution to the discussion on advancement of women and development, the FLS also gives hundreds of operative recommendations. The document begins by defining the basic concepts – equality, development, and peace – in a way that is relevant to the development discussion in general, not only in relation to women. The following formulations are taken directly from the text of the FLS (paras. 11–13):

– **Equality** is both a goal and a means whereby individuals are accorded equal treatment under the law and equal opportunities to enjoy their rights and to develop their potential talents and skills so that they can participate in national political, economic, social and cultural development, both as beneficiaries and as active agents.

  For women in particular, equality means the realization of rights that have been denied as a result of cultural, institutional, behavioural and attitudinal discrimination.

– **Development** means total development, including development in the political, economic, social, cultural and other dimensions of human life as well as the development of the economic and other material resources and the physical, moral, intellectual and cultural growth of human beings.

  More directly, the increasingly successful participation of each woman in societal activities as a legally independent agent will contribute to further recognition in practice of her right to equality.

  Development also requires a moral dimension to ensure that it is just and responsive to the needs and rights of the individual and that science and technology are applied within a social and economic framework that ensures environmental safety for all life forms on our planet.

255

– **Peace** includes not only the absence of war, violence and hostilities at the national and international levels, but also the enjoyment of economic and social justice, equality and the entire range of human rights and fundamental freedoms within society.

It also embraces the whole range of actions reflected in concerns for security and implicit assumptions of trust between nations, social groups and individuals. It represents goodwill toward others and promotes respect for life while protecting freedom, human rights and the dignity of peoples and of individuals.

Peace cannot be realized under conditions of economic and sexual inequality, denial of basic human rights and fundamental freedoms, deliberate exploitation of large sectors of the population, unequal development of countries, and exploitative economic relations. Without peace and stability there can be no development. Peace and development are interrelated and mutually reinforcing.

Peace is promoted by equality of the sexes, economic equality and the universal enjoyment of basic human rights and fundamental freedoms. Its enjoyment by all requires that women be enabled to exercise their right to participate on an equal footing with men in all spheres of the political, economic and social life of their respective countries, particularly in the decision-making process, while exercising their right to freedom of opinion, expression, information and association in the promotion of international peace and cooperation.

The FLS also defines **woman** in a new way compared with all previous UN documents: "The attainment of the goals and objectives of the [UN] Decade [for Women] requires a sharing of this responsibility by men and women and by society as a whole, and requires that *women play a central role as intellectuals, policy-makers, decision-makers, planners and contributors and beneficiaries of development*" (para. 15; emphasis added).

How do these definitions relate to the concepts and interpretations of peace research? What is the impact of peace research on these new definitions of terms? These FLS formulations could well help to advance thinking among peace researchers.

The impact of peace research on the FLS, and vice versa

The United Nations was founded before the emergence of peace research. How are its work and actions seen in the light of the values, theories, and aims of peace research? Does peace research help in the conceptualization of the relationship between women and peace, and of violence against women? The basic concepts of peace research

256

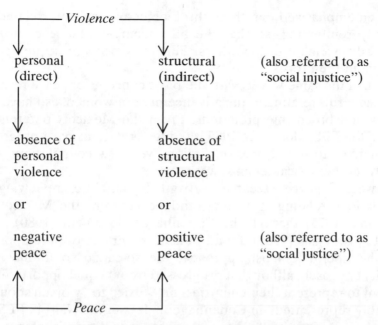

Fig. 8.1 **The extended concepts of violence and peace (Source: Johan Galtung,** *Essays in Peace Research*, **vol. I, Copenhagen: Christian Ejlers, 1975, p. 130).**

– violence, peace, development – can each be understood in both a narrow and a broad sense. Violence can be understood as both direct, physical violence and indirect, structural violence; peace taken both as negative peace and positive peace; and development seen as material, economic development as well as social and human development.[6]

Figure 8.1 recalls the well-known presentation of two ways of eliminating violence, ending in two different concepts of peace.[7] This can be applied to the activities of the United Nations in general: the left-hand alternative relates to peace-making and peace-keeping and the right-hand road relates to development in the broader sense, aiming to eliminate or at least diminish structural violence. Thus, all functions of the UN system can be seen, in the broad sense, as endeavours towards peace, the original and paramount purpose of the United Nations.

The overall objectives of IWY and the UNDW, "Equality—Development—Peace," are also the objectives of the Nairobi FLS as well as of the Fourth World Conference on Women in Beijing in 1995. Ever since the emergence of the new approach in the 1970s it has been emphasized that these three objectives are interrelated and mutually reinforcing, so that the advancement of one contributes to the advancement of the others. This integrative principle appears throughout the process since 1975.

In much the same way as with the basic concepts of peace research, the basic terms relating to the advancement of women also have both narrow and broad interpretations. From the Mexico Conference in 1975 to the FLS adopted in 1985, the interpretations have progressed from narrow to broad ones, including even new connotations stemming from the radical feminist approach.

Norwegian peace researcher Birgit Brock-Utne, reviewing the formulations relating to women and peace from the Mexico Plan of Action (1975) through the Copenhagen document (1980) to the Nairobi Strategies (1985), found that in the first two there appeared only the liberal feminist approach, the so-called traditional plain equality approach, although it progressed from "equal opportunity [of women] to represent their countries" in Mexico to "women should be equitably represented" in Copenhagen.[8] It is in the Nairobi FLS that the new definitions of the basic concepts (equality—development—peace) demonstrate "forward-looking thinking." The definition of peace is clearly based on the concept of *structural violence* as developed originally by Johan Galtung in the 1960s. Paragraph 13 on peace is even more comprehensive than cited above; it is perhaps the most inclusive definition of peace so far adopted in intergovernmental documents, bringing in the dimension of gender equality as a basic element in peace – an element that has been missing in peace research all along.

The concept of violence is also broadened in the FLS beyond the interpretations of peace research to make clear that violence at all levels, personal, social, and international, stems from the same roots and should be seen as symptoms of the same phenomenon. Sustainable peace cannot be achieved without eliminating violence at all levels, including violence against women. This approach is further clarified in paragraphs 257 and 258:

The questions of women and peace, and the meaning of peace for women, cannot be separated from the broader question of relationships between women and men in all spheres of life and in the family.

Violence against women exists in various forms in everyday life in all societies. Women are beaten, mutilated, burned, sexually abused and raped. Such violence is a major obstacle to the achievement of peace and other objectives of the Decade and should be given special attention.

This is the first time that the interrelationship between personal and international violence and its consequences has been recognized by an intergovernmental, worldwide conference, which adopted it as a definition; it can thus be claimed as generally valid and relevant, and has already had wide-ranging consequences within the UN system during the past few years.

This interpretation of violence was included in the text of the FLS exclusively owing to the fact that, this time, it was women themselves who drafted the text. It should also be mentioned that several women peace researchers, members of the Women and Peace Study Group of the International Peace Research Association (IPRA), were involved directly or indirectly in drafting the FLS passages on peace, peace education, and peace research. The approach reflects the thinking and ideas already developed at the time among IPRA women and the international women's peace movement.

The FLS concept of development is also broadened, even from the one used generally by peace research, to encompass a moral dimension. The concept of equality too is much broader than that used in the traditional (liberal feminist) equality debate, being applied to all individuals in a way that can even be equated to a general concept of justice.

The definition of "woman" in the FLS is a decisive new step in the recognition of women as subjects rather than as objects, not only in UN terminology but in the general language. According to this formula, women can no longer be seen as mere labour or human resources but are independent, self-aware, dignified persons defining their goals and aspirations themselves, and equal partners whenever their society and development are being designed, planned, or decided upon, as well as in the private sphere.

The need for women's perspective on human development is critical, according to the FLS, "since it is in the interest of human enrichment and progress to introduce and weave into the social fabric women's concept of equality, their choices between alternative development strategies and their approach to peace, in accordance with their aspirations, interest and talents. These things are not only desirable in themselves but are also essential for the attainment of the goals and objectives of the Decade" (para. 16).

This definition makes it clear that equality is not only a cause in its own right and a legitimate right of women, but a social and political necessity to bring about a more just, balanced, and sustainable development for all. Above all, it is a necessity for bringing about a more *humane* development, as stated in the first UN World Survey on the Role of Women in Development.

Peace education and peace research in the FLS

In the FLS chapter on peace there is fairly extensive discussion about education for peace and peace research, and although the recommendations are conventional it is important that these issues are dealt with. The following passage illustrates the way in which the substance of peace education is discussed:

suitable concrete action should be taken to discourage the provision of children with games and publications and other media promoting the notion of favouring war, aggression, cruelty, excessive desire for power and other forms of violence, within the broad processes of the preparation of society for life in peace. (Para. 273)

Material for peace education "should include case studies of peaceful settlements of disputes, nonviolent movements and passive resistance and the recognition of peace-seeking individuals" (para. 274). (Interestingly enough, the continuation of this idea as drafted, "rather than the glorification of war heroes," was deleted at the last stage!)

There is, however, an interesting, rather subtle passage in the FLS that can be interpreted as encouragement for women to claim resources and opportunities to organize their own studies on peace issues according to their own views and perceptions of reality, different from ordinary peace studies in schools and universities:

Opportunities should be provided for women to organize and choose studies, training programmes and seminars related to peace, disarmament, education for peace and the peaceful settlement of disputes. (Para. 275)

Another important recommendation directly concerns women in peace research:

The participation of women in peace research, including research on women and peace, should be encouraged. Existing barriers to women researchers should be removed and appropriate resources provided for peace researchers. Cooperation amongst peace researchers, government officials, non-governmental organizations and activists should be encouraged and fostered. (Para. 276)

These well-meaning words may have remained unknown even to peace researchers themselves, thus being untested in practice as arguments for strengthening peace research and the status of women among peace researchers.

3. The United Nations leads the way

In contrast to its member states, the United Nations itself seems to have been more active and faithful to its own promises and resolutions to make the work of the institution more gender sensitive. Two World Surveys on the Role of Women in Development, in 1984 and 1989, called for more human-centred development and claimed that development would become more humane if the aspirations and needs of women were listened to. The third World Survey on the Role of Women in Development, *Women in a Changing Global Economy*, was one of the principal documents for the Fourth World Conference on Women in Beijing in 1995.[9]

Learning gender-language

The 1994 Survey indicates the gradual advance of thinking behind this follow-up process; the Survey is not only a progress report on the implementation of the Nairobi Strategies, but at the same time a guiding tool for the evolution of principles and policies for planning and programming development within the UN system and in the member states. The following quotations are from the Introduction to the preliminary version of the 1994 World Survey:

The approach to the World Survey has evolved as a response to economic and social changes, the questioning of existing development models, and new thinking on the implications of gender equality. It implies that the concept of "women in development" should be given broader meaning and be refocused within a new theoretical framework....

Policies that target women only cannot achieve the best results, nor can those which assume that public actions are gender-neutral in their effects. Hence, promoting gender equality implies a profound change in the socio-economic organization of societies: not only in the way women work, live and care for other members of their households, but also in the way men do, and in the way their respective roles in the family and community are articulated with the need to earn a living.

In the past few years, UN documents have started to speak "gender-language" fluently, changing the emphasis from women as an artificially homogeneous group to the relations between the sexes.

261

The basis of the gender-analysis is to examine how gender relations, defined as the relative positions in the society of men and women, affect their ability to participate in development. These positions are defined by the socially constructed and culturally variable roles that women and men play in their daily lives. At the heart of this definition of roles is a sexual division of labour around what are termed the "productive" and "reproductive" functions of society.[10]

This emphasis on the need to change the role, behaviour, and attitudes of men as well in order to promote equality has grown stronger from one survey to the next. Another increasingly emphasized principle is the need to use double strategies, i.e. both women-specific policies and plans as well as integration of a gender perspective in all plans and decision-making, mainstreaming the gender approach.

The need to change the role of men as well as that of women is emphasized in the Secretary-General's report on the follow-up to the UN Conference on Environment and Development (UNCED, 1992):

The idea that the role of men in sustainable development is as important as the role of women should be taken into account in the monitoring process. This would give an opportunity to examine how men's roles could be modified to facilitate sustainable development. Indeed, no sustainable development can be obtained without a change in men's gender roles as well as women's.[11]

The report also criticizes *Agenda 21*[12] for shortcomings in certain aspects of changing gender roles in connection with unsustainable patterns of consumption and production: "In this, the relative role of women and men in industrialized countries is largely missing, especially the present role of women in socializing consumption values and their role as consumers." Instead, *Agenda 21* "focuses on the role of women in population programmes, which is less explicit about the role men should play for the success of family planning programmes."[13]

There is a growing awareness that a healthy environment is a prerequisite for the healthy life of people. "The new World Survey will view all the implications of sustainable development through a gender lens, and provide policy recommendations about environmentally sound patterns of development. This theme should permeate each chapter of the World Survey."[14] This is how advancement of women and ecologically sound development can go hand-in-hand, as many eco-feminists have claimed (Rosemary Ratford Ruether, Hazel Henderson, Mary Daly, Ariel Salleh, and others).

Human development – the ultimate aim

The World Surveys on the Role of Women in Development have had as a leitmotif the idea of making development "more responsive to human needs" and "incorporating the human dimension into economic planning and policy-making," i.e. looking for more humane development. In 1990 the United Nations Development Programme (UNDP) used this thread to knit the first of its new annual *Human Development Reports* (HDR),[15] whose basic point of departure is development of the people, by the people, and for the people. This in many ways closes the circle in the development discussion; UN thinking has finally placed the human being, as both subject and object, at the centre of development policy.

It comes naturally to women to consider the natural aim of development to be human development, human well-being, and favourable conditions for human advancement, but it took 30 years – three International Development Decades – for the (almost entirely male) authorities and leaders of the UN system to come to this conclusion. But better late than never! The most important departure for the *Human Development Reports* is the development of new criteria for measuring the level of development through the Human Development Index (HDI) and its three components: longevity, level of knowledge, and decent living standards. In other words, human development is defined as the process of increasing people's options to live a long and healthy life, to acquire knowledge, and to find access to the assets needed for a decent standard of living.

The second HDR in 1991 gave statistics and rankings of countries according to the gender-sensitive HDI, which reflects gender disparities. The 1995 HDR focused on women and development issues, with a view to the World Conference in Beijing and the fiftieth anniversary of the United Nations. The HDR assesses development according to criteria of which most women would approve, and represents a very welcome new approach – in spite of some doubtful aspects and shortcomings in the philosophy behind it.

Success in Beijing

Just a few weeks before the Fourth World Conference on Women in 1995, the prospects were very gloomy, with almost half of the draft Platform for Action (PFA) still in brackets. It was felt that if only the achievements of the World Conference on Human Rights in Vienna,

1993, the International Conference on Population and Development in Cairo, 1994, and the Summit for Social Development in Copenhagen, 1995, could be retained, that would be a victory. Many problems emerged with the change of site of the Forum for non-governmental organizations (NGOs) to the remote town of Huairou, about 60 kilometres from the centre of Beijing, and with other Conference logistics, which significantly reduced the number of participants.

In the event, however, the Conference turned out to be a success, in both size and outcome. The number of participating governments was 189, the highest ever in a UN world conference. The Conference was attended by some 17,000 participants, including about 6,000 official delegates, over 4,000 representatives of accredited NGOs, a host of international civil servants, and almost 4,000 media representatives. And the NGO Forum attracted about 30,000 participants from outside China and some 5,000 from the host country itself. Altogether about 50,000 people took part in the events, making it the largest UN gathering in history.

The outcome of the Conference, *The Beijing Declaration and Platform for Action*, is a document of 361 paragraphs covering the critical areas of concern to women. The strategic objectives and actions are structured under 12 headings: poverty, education and training, women and health, violence against women, armed conflicts, the economy, power and decision-making, human rights, the media, the environment, and the institutional and financial arrangements needed, at both intergovernmental and national levels, for implementation of the plan. One chapter is devoted to the girl-child, so as to draw adequate attention to the fact that still, in many parts of the world today, discrimination and violence against women, beginning often before birth, continue unabated throughout their childhood and for the rest of their lives.

However, the focus of the PFA is no longer only on equality and non-discrimination but on empowering women to become full and equal partners in all decision-making and policy formation in their societies. The issue is not only equality with men in a male-dominated culture and society but full power to contribute the values and insights of women to influence the setting of development priorities in all walks of life. "The Platform for Action, an agenda for women's empowerment," begins the document.[16]

The success of the Conference was very much due to the expertise and effectiveness of the women participating in the work of issue caucuses before and during the Conference, and skilful coordination by the Women's Linkage Caucus in Beijing. Their work was facilitated by the UN representatives, with their new approach *vis-à-vis* the NGOs, and government delegations willing to cooperate with the women and to utilize their expertise. The final analyses show that some 85 per cent of the bracketed recommendations were adopted by the Conference in the form in which women had wanted them in the preparatory process.

The Beijing Platform for Action advances the process that started in Mexico City in 1975, was updated in Copenhagen in 1980, and was reviewed and appraised in Nairobi in 1985, where the Forward-looking Strategies were adopted. The Beijing Conference consolidated the gains for the advancement and empowerment of women made in Vienna, Cairo, and Copenhagen in this decade. But it achieved even more. It produced an affirmative and consistent Platform for Action for member governments, and thus a concrete base for the practical policies and programmes to be implemented by all countries in the years to come.

4. The issue of the 1990s: Violence against women

Violence against women is a universal phenomenon, with us since the beginning of time. It has ranged from the ancient, often public and collective, practice of raping women or using them for "comfort" in wars, to the private, intimate practice of violence within the family, including rape in the marital bed. Yet it has been most efficiently silenced, eliminated as a subject for discussion, excluded from all scientific and historical records. Even the Nairobi FLS had little to say about violence against women, as seen earlier in this chapter. However, what it did say was enough to become a basis, perhaps the necessary legitimation, for more thorough UN studies on violence against women.

Now a priority issue

Soon after the Nairobi Conference, the subject of violence against women became one of the priority issues on the agenda of the Commission on the Status of Women (CSW) and in the work of the UN Division for the Advancement of Women, which published *Violence Against Women in the Family* in 1989.[17] This thoroughly documented book, which followed a companion report by the CSW to ECOSOC in the spring of 1988 entitled *Efforts to Eradicate Violence against*

Women within the Family and Society,[18] remains one of the most informative sources for further study on the subject.

The attention given to violence against women has continued to grow within the UN system, leading to resolutions of the UN General Assembly and Security Council in the 1990s. By far the most important so far is the Declaration on the Elimination of Violence Against Women, adopted by the General Assembly in 1993.[19] The definition of the issue in this Declaration is an important clarification:

"Violence against women" means any act of gender-based violence that results in, or is likely to result in, physical, sexual or psychological harm or suffering to women, including threats of such acts, coercion or arbitrary deprivation of liberty, whether occurring in public or in private life. (Art. 1)

This crosses from the outset the threshold between public and private domains, which until now had been the limit of the mandate of public laws. The issue is then more concretely defined in Article 2:

Violence against women shall be understood to encompass, but not be limited to, the following:
(a) Physical, sexual and psychological violence occurring in the family, including battering, sexual abuse of female children in the household, dowry-related violence, marital rape, female genital mutilation and other traditional practices harmful to women, non-spousal violence and violence related to exploitation;
(b) Physical, sexual and psychological violence occurring within the general community, including rape, sexual abuse, sexual harassment and intimidation at work, in educational institutions and elsewhere, trafficking in women and forced prostitution;
(c) Physical, sexual and psychological violence perpetrated or condoned by the State, wherever it occurs.

This Declaration, clarifying the issue so decisively, complements the Convention on the Elimination of Discrimination Against Women and the Nairobi FLS in an essential way. It presents a comprehensive list of measures for combating violence against women, protecting women, and redressing the wrongs caused to them, creating preventive measures of all kinds, improving legislation, training personnel in the appropriate organs and institutions to sensitize them to the needs of women, and so on. Nevertheless, it is problematic in its approach; it names the victims – women – but does not say who commits the crime, and why. What can possibly be the psychological, social, political, or cultural reasons for such acts? Advice on these aspects is lacking.

Rape as a war crime

The atrocities in former Yugoslavia have for the first time brought rape in war under the public spotlight. For the first time women have given their testimonies – some of them, for thousands remain silent. Although women have been raped, mutilated, and humiliated in all wars before and during the existence of the United Nations, it is only now that the Security Council has adopted a resolution on the issue.

Resolution 798, unanimously adopted by the UN Security Council on 18 December 1992, made history by being the first in which the United Nations condemns the rape of women in wartime. In it, the Security Council says that it is "appalled by reports of the massive, organized and systematic detention and rape of women, in particular Muslim women, in Bosnia and Herzegovina," demands that "all the detention camps and in particular camps for women should be immediately closed," and "strongly condemns these acts of unspeakable brutality."

Resolutions by the General Assembly and Security Council are immensely important steps on the way to making violence against women officially visible. In fact, with this Resolution, the Security Council has recognized rape as a war crime. In May 1993 the Security Council went further by deciding "to establish an international tribunal for the sole purpose of prosecuting persons responsible for serious violations of international humanitarian law committed in the territory of the former Yugoslavia" after 1 January 1991, its mandate to include the "massive, organized and systematic detention and rape of women." Thus, this International War Crimes Tribunal is the first ever to deal with rape as a war crime: such crimes were not an issue at the Nuremberg Tribunal after World War II.

Violence among men?

This process of making violence against women visible in the UN system is the result of a dialogue between the official system and the unofficial, non-governmental one. Passages in the Nairobi FLS were given prominence through cooperation between women peace researchers, UN officials, and delegates of various countries. Perhaps the most dramatic form of this dialogue was the Global Tribunal on Violations of Women's Human Rights organized by the International Women's Tribune Centre and others at the NGO Forum "All Human Rights to All" during the World Conference on Human Rights in

Vienna in June 1993. The testimonies of survivors of attempted wife-burning, wife abuse and police collusion, vindictive burning, incest, sexual slavery, genital mutilation, and many other violations made hard listening for the audience, none of whom remained untouched.

A good question was asked in this Tribunal by one of the judges, Edward Broadbent of Canada: "Those making war are not women; those who rape are not women. When we speak about the rights of women, where are the men?" Although progress has been made in the elimination of violence against women, another big question arises: Will it ever be possible to eliminate violence against women as long as male culture as such continues to be as violent as it is? As long as men consider beating each other an act of manliness, and aggressivity is seen as an admirable trait in the eyes of their fellow men? As long as war remains legitimized violence in our patriarchal society?

The decisions and actions of the international community indicate a turning of the pages of history concerning violence against women. The time has now come to turn the pages of male history too, so that men cease to violate their own human dignity by acting inhumanly.

6. Women's future with the United Nations

Documents such as the Nairobi FLS, the five-yearly World Surveys, the system-wide Medium-term Plans, the annual *Human Development Reports* and the Administrative Instructions for the promotion of women in the Secretariat represent very advanced thinking in comparison with that in the United Nations generally and in member governments. Follow-up and reporting from women's viewpoint has now become a regular practice in many of the UN bodies in connection with the implementation of the FLS and all new policies of the UN system, not just in particular reports but also as specific chapters in their annual reports.

Women in the Secretariat

Secretary-General Boutros Boutros-Ghali – in spite of opposite impressions at the beginning of his term – issued a very encouraging Administrative Instruction in March 1993 on "Special Measures to Improve the Status of Women in the Secretariat," his goal being to bring the gender balance in policy-level positions as close to 50–50 as possible by the fiftieth anniversary of the United Nations.[20] His instructions require "exceptional measures to recruit, promote and deploy women who fully meet the requirements of Article 101 of the Charter, in the shortest possible time." In departments and offices with less than 35 per cent women overall, and in those with less than 25 per cent women at levels P-5 and above, vacancies should always be filled by a woman whenever there are women candidates who match the required qualifications of the post.

These instructions indicate an unforeseen degree of affirmative action in favour of women, with preference always given to women and a post being made available for male recruitment only after it has been open for a year in the absence of a qualified woman. These measures are enforced in order "to bring the composition of the Secretariat into harmony with the fundamental principles of equality for which the Organization stands" and will remain in effect until the Secretary-General is satisfied that substantial progress towards parity has been made. However, these instructions did not prevent the Secretary-General appointing a new International Council to the University for Peace in Costa Rica in the spring of 1994 with only 2 women among 17 members. Women in Costa Rica and elsewhere reacted furiously to the fact that the Secretary-General himself did not respect his own rules.

Serious doubts

Along with positive achievements there are, however, some very alarming trends to be seen in the UN system. South-oriented and women-friendly institutions such as the UN Conference on Trade and Development (UNCTAD), the UNDP, UNICEF, and the Food and Agriculture Organization (FAO) are running into difficulties owing to the fact that industrialized countries are gradually shifting their political and monetary support from aid institutions to the banking and lending institutions. This is so even in the Nordic countries, which have been solid supporters of multilateral development aid for years. This shift in emphasis reflects a trend in the world economy that has gained momentum subsequent to the collapse of the socialist system. Faith in market forces, free trade, and competition has gained ground. Even UNDP's *Human Development Reports* believe in the free functioning of the markets as the best way of creating resources for human development.

There are also, however, seriously warning voices: "What markets can do – allocate scarce goods according to purchasing power – they will do efficiently, but they cannot decide a society's priorities," says Susan George of the Transnational Institute in the Netherlands.

Competition is a polite word for war. Over the past decade competition has become the rule at every level. Like markets, competition can be healthy if it is not allowed to become the *only* rule of society; but carried to its present extremes it prevents cooperation and solidarity; it undermines links between individuals, countries, peoples; it encourages an "every man for himself" mentality and disregards the rights of others. It encourages domination of winners over losers and discourages a culture of responsibility.[21]

Well known to peace researchers, Susan George speaks of "economic apartheid," describing the world economy as "a pyramid with a transnational elite at the apex, a more or less secure middle class below, and under them the vast and growing underclass of people who are unimportant both as producers and consumers and for which the system has absolutely no plans. This is a model of economic apartheid."

Market mechanisms and competition work automatically and unavoidably to the benefit of the rich and strong, giving the poor and weak no chance. The continued widening of the gap between rich and poor brings increasing flows of migrants and refugees from South to North as a consequence. This is a potent recipe for increasing human misery, conflicts, and disruption of social structures in both South and North. It turns the wheel of development backwards and sweeps away the positive achievements of recent decades.

Voice of women in the South

On the eve of the Nairobi Conference, an organization and network called DAWN (Development Alternatives with Women for a New Era), established by women in the South, made its successful entry on to the world scene. In their 1993 Asian and Caribbean regional meetings, DAWN women also expressed their concern about the upswing of neo-liberalism as a leading ideology of the moment:

The neo-liberal market model appears to have won a resounding ideological victory, reinforced by the collapse of the Soviet system and the growth of capitalist economies in East and South East Asia. Development thinking is now dominated as never before by a restructured World Bank, within which the greatest emphasis is placed on short-term, sectorally narrow projects that will pay off quickly.

There is silence on gender issues, yet human reproduction, including both biological and social relations, is a central factor in defining gender relations, which in turn impacts on sexual divisions of labour and patriarchal authority and control, and is encoded in all economic, political, cultural and religious orders.[22]

In their assessment of the world situation and of the development arena, DAWN women found three major changes:

(1) A decline in military budgets and the changing face of war, following the shift from anti-communist ideology. Wars are now waged in relation to resources (e.g. Iraq), subversion (e.g. Angola), and "ethnic" conflicts (e.g. Yugoslavia), all of which provide fodder for fundamentalists, communal gangs, and criminal activities. The implications are fragmentation and disruption of social networks, food supplies, and health services, and traumatized populations.

(2) The incorporation of the newly industrialized countries (NICs) into competitive Northern trading blocs, which is likely to cause further fragmentation of third world solidarity and lead to segmented labour markets in which employers take full advantage of existing gender and ethnic hierarchies of power.

(3) The changing role of multilateral institutions: the decline of UNDP and UNCTAD and the strengthening role of the World Bank and the International Monetary Fund. They point out that, although providing a different model from that of the World Bank, UNDP for example endorses market efficiency in its latest *Human Development Report* as almost the only way forward.

DAWN's conclusion is that, for third world women, "conditions are not improving. They continue to be incorporated into the global economy through labour-intensive exports and migration as domestics or entertainers. In national economies their participation in 'informal' trade, domestic service and prostitution has grown."

Instead of the current question, "What kind of human development would promote economic competitiveness and growth?" DAWN poses a different question: "What kind of economic development is best suited to the promotion of human development?" This would more suitably lead to a new approach, with gender being integral to the ongoing search for a people-centred economic alternative. This was DAWN's main research theme in preparation for the Fourth World Conference on Women in Beijing in 1995, for which it drew up a platform document on alternative economics.[23]

Women on the alert

In recent years women have given convincing proof of their competence and capacity to influence intergovernmental conferences with
success. This has been seen at UNCED in Rio in 1992 and at the
World Conference on Human Rights in Vienna in 1993, as well as
at the International Conference on Population and Development
(ICPD) in Cairo (1994) and in particular at the Beijing Conference in
1995, where the women's caucuses with their well-coordinated operations saved the whole Conference. Charlotte Bunch, leader of the
Women's Caucus for the Human Rights Conference, underlines the
need for women's participation in all major UN conferences:

It is important to see this work as part of a move occurring with women
internationally to claim all issues as women's issues and to claim a women's
voice in shaping global policy. It isn't just human rights that women have
targeted, but a kind of collective understanding on the part of women that
we have to be more present in all the discussions of peace, democracy,
development, environment, human rights, etc.[24]

In the case of UNCED, a successful lobbying operation was conducted by the Women's Environment and Development Organization (WEDO) – which in fact emerged in this form during the process
– in cooperation with women's groups and organizations in 31 countries.[25] WEDO was again coordinator of women's caucuses from all
regions during the preparations for the ICPD in Cairo in 1994 and for
the World Social Summit in Copenhagen in March 1995. In Beijing,
then, the lobbying operation was crucial to saving the achievements
of the previous conferences and to bringing about a long leap forward, in spite of the coordinated efforts of the Holy See and a group
of conservative governments to undermine earlier joint resolutions.
    Women worldwide are now alert to the importance of making their
voices heard with regard to all major issues discussed and pro-
nounced upon in intergovernmental conferences – even without the
consent of their own governments.

We have to recognize that there is no women's agenda as such. There is just
one national, one global agenda. But women will put different emphases and
different priorities on the issues based on where they come from and where
they want to go. The result will be that societies will be different, but build
equally on the visions of men and women ... The problems of women are
not different from country to country or region to region. They only differ in
intensity.[26]

These words of Gertrude Mongella, Secretary-General of the Beijing Conference (whose theme was again Equality—Development—Peace, as it was for the conferences in Mexico City in 1975, Copenhagen in 1980, and Nairobi in 1985), reflect her vision of the commonality of women wordwide and set the tone for the whole process of the preparations for Beijing.

7. The UN system, spearhead of change

The record of the advancement of women during the 50 years since the United Nations was established – and particularly during the past 25 years – is astonishing. The times are indeed changing when women can be seen taking their legitimate role in decision-making on all issues of humanity, at global as well as national levels. Though much remains to be done, these years will mark an epoch in women's history, and the changes that have taken place are irreversible.

In all of this, the UN system has taken the lead. On average it represents significantly more advanced norms and practices concerning women than those of its member states. Fortunately, this progress seems to trickle down from above, in contrast to the development process, which needs to trickle up from below. But the normative impact of the United Nations in the advancement of women could be vastly more efficient if its information and education programmes were better.

Implementation: A government responsibility

The United Nations is, after all, simply an instrument of governments. In reality the implementation of UN resolutions depends decisively on the governments of member states. They are the agents that put UN decisions into effect, making those decisions part of their policies in legislation, in economic and social planning, in culture, education, and training, as well as in public discussion and communication at the national level.

Thus, the Fourth World Conference on Women constantly reiterated its call in the Platform for Action for commitment of the governments to implement what had been adopted. Accountability and transparency were other demands repeated over and over again in the PFA, which required from governments "the establishment and strengthening of mechanisms at all levels for accountability to the world's women." Governments were obliged to prepare a national plan for implementation of the PFA by end-1996 at the latest.

The Beijing Conference was even called a "Conference of Commitment," emphasizing implementation and action and inviting governments to state their commitment to the advancement of women in their statements to the plenary. By the end of the Conference more than 100 governments had made public promises about their particular commitments to the empowerment of women in their countries. NGOs registered these commitments and evaluated them on a public "scoreboard" as a way of creating pressure on governments to keep their promises after returning home. The NGOs will also use these lists of commitments in advocacy and follow-up activities in their respective countries.

The key actors within each country are, after all, women themselves as citizens and their national and local organizations. They must have access in their own languages to the PFA and other programmes, provisions, and conventions of the UN system, adopted by governments on their behalf, in order to be able to monitor implementation in each country. The first thing for governments to do is to translate the documents into the national language wherever UN official languages will not do. In India, for instance, the PFA has been translated into 18 major languages of the country. And, in order to exercise their influence as citizens, the basic prerequisite is that women enjoy full political rights in their countries, in both letter and practice. There is much to do at the national level to create the firm political will required to get UN decisions implemented.

But the obligations of governments do not end at the national level. The question also arises: how many governments are systematic and consistent in their actions and policies within the UN system, where it is they who make the decisions and allocations for implementation? Without active government support, the UN bodies and organs are powerless to carry out their part of the responsibility. On the other hand, governments at the United Nations also have to monitor implementation of the PFA and other decisions at the global level.

The advancement and empowerment of women is an issue whose implementation is not limited to any particular organ or agency of the UN system. The PFA and other programmes and conventions on women have implications for each one of the bodies in the system. Thus the supporting and monitoring functions of member governments need to be effectively coordinated at the preparatory level in the countries themselves and in their policies and actions throughout the UN system. Without systematic coordination in this respect, governments may act in very haphazard – even contradictory – ways in various UN agencies and organs.

We present a model for the effective coordination of actions and policies on women by a member country in international organizations on page 276. The model is loosely based on the System-wide Medium-term Plans for Advancement of Women created by the UN Administrative Committee on Coordination for the UN system itself and on models already existing in a few member countries.

Strengthening "institutional memory" and continuity

The economic and social activity of the United Nations system, which covers most of the issues of concern to women, is seriously handicapped by lack of continuity and learning from past experience. This problem, which affects national administrations in member countries as much as the United Nations, is due mainly to generation shifts in personnel and the lack of training and retraining in international activity in this field.

Because neither UN officials nor the new generations of diplomats are benefiting from the lessons of the past in relation to development and economic issues, there is inevitably a great deal of "reinventing the wheel" within UN bodies. There is hardly any training in the economic and social activities of the UN system, either as entrance training for new UN employees or civil servants or as courses in universities and colleges. UN studies are primarily undertaken only within the faculties of political science and international law. It is a question not only of whether information about UN programmes for women is reaching those for whom it is intended, but of whether enough is being done in the educational world to ensure that UN actions in this field are included in the learning process at different stages.

In general, the lack of an "institutional memory" within the UN system is catastrophic. Because of it, UN bodies are doomed to learn the same lessons over and over again. It is urgently necessary for a full, analytical review of UN activities since its inception in 1945 to be undertaken, even beginning with the first attempts at international action under the League of Nations.

Competence tests and entrance examinations should be undergone by new entrants to the UN system (recommendations by national authorities, formal qualifications, and ordinary academic degrees

A proposal for the coordination of international women's programmes in national foreign policy

If a government wishes to behave consistently in its policies on a specific subject matter, such as the advancement of women, it has to present and promote the same logic in a corresponding manner in all of the specialized agencies and bodies of the UN system.

In order to promote the advancement of women and implementation of jointly adopted strategies systematically at international forums, the government needs to have a coherent policy, to train and brief its diplomats and representatives in all international bodies accordingly, and to have a coordinating system within the domestic administration to manage and facilitate the systematic policies and representation of the country concerning these issues.

Such coordination and systematic conduct of policies could be organized in different ways in different national administrations. The following is one possible model.

To develop an integrated, system-wide approach, and manifest the country's firm commitment to the advancement of women and the elimination of gender-based discrimination, an *International Equality Unit* or a *Principal Officer* could be established within the national administration (in the Ministry of Foreign Affairs, Office of the Prime Minister, or other appropriate structure) with the mandate to:

(a) draw up strategic guidelines for the implementation of international measures outlined in jointly adopted strategies;

(b) follow up the implementation of these strategies in the international system and instruct the decision makers and representatives of the country accordingly;

(c) ensure the substantive input of the country to advancement of women's issues at key international meetings and conferences;

(d) coordinate and guide the responsible departmental officials in respective ministries and national boards, as well as the permanent missions of the country to the UN agencies and organs;

(e) propose appropriate and necessary allocations of funds for the United Nations institutions and organs for advancement of women, and for the necessary functions to promote these issues in the domestic administration;

(f) establish and chair a national ad hoc interdepartmental steering committee to facilitate the accomplishment of these aims.

The Unit or Officer should be assisted by corresponding contact officials/focal points/links in different departments, ministries, and national boards. This is particularly important in the case of the Ministry or Agency for Development Cooperation/Planning, to guide and monitor programmes and policies on women and development.

This kind of coordinating system at the country level corresponds to the UN Administrative Committee on Coordination and would facilitate its role in the implementation of the FLS, Beijing PFA, and other jointly adopted programmes within the UN system. The System-wide Medium-term Plans for Advancement of Women 1990–1995 and 1996–2001 provide a comprehensive frame of reference also for the national coordination of policies on international issues of concern to women.

276

do not guarantee competence at the international level). In addition, the United Nations should set up really effective in-depth training courses for new entrants that will emphasize the role and the voice of women and draw the essential linkages between peace, development, and the environment. Refresher courses on women and development issues should be given at regular intervals to professionals of both sexes working in economic and social sectors of the United Nations, as well as within states.

Member states should ensure that international studies, particularly in the economic and social activities of intergovernmental organizations, are available in national universities and diplomatic and civil service training colleges and institutions for future officials in both national and international administrations. Courses in women's studies and experience in national machineries for the advancement of women, as well as training in UN economic and social activities, should be required for professional posts concerned with women's issues within the system.

The main channel for informing citizens in UN member states about their rights and entitlements is currently the "Third System" – the non-governmental organizations and institutions of learning. The development research community has done very little to teach about the United Nations' economic and social work or multilateral development cooperation, or to influence and improve the UN system in this field. And little has been done in women's studies with regard to what is done for women within the system. The peace movement and the peace research community have done much in this field but their work has been limited primarily to the political part of the UN system.

The contribution of the peace research community

It is clear that there is still much to be done to ensure that women's voices are heard in discussions concerning the future of the United Nations system and that the peace research community could make a considerable contribution in this direction.

As we have noted above, the Nairobi Forward-looking Strategies have already pointed the way, insisting that "peace includes not only the absence of war, violence and hostilities at the national and international levels, but also the enjoyment of economic and social justice, equality and the entire range of human rights and fundamental freedoms within society." They state that "peace cannot be realized under conditions of economic and sexual inequality," and that its "enjoy-ment by all requires that women be enabled to exercise their right to participate on an equal footing with men in all spheres of the politi-cal, economic and social life of their respective countries, particularly in the decision-making process" (para. 13). The Strategies even sug-gest that women must "play a central role as intellectuals, policy-makers, decision-makers, planners and contributors and beneficiaries of development" (para. 15).

These FLS formulations, together with the provisions of the Bei-jing PFA, could help to set the parameters for new thinking among peace researchers who are concerned with the future shape of the United Nations. Much could be done to analyse and explore the deep roots of violence, alienation, and destructiveness in human society.

The links between structural and physical violence, domestic and other, and the unequal role of women in society need to be clarified. The lack of women's voice in decisions relating to war and peace remains startling compared with the growing tendency to bring women into the decision-making process with regard to development, the environment, population, and other economic and social issues. The disasters in Bosnia, Rwanda, Somalia, et al. show that women not only have had no voice in the decisions taken to unleash such violence but, as always, have been its major victims.

As we move into the twenty-first century, one of the main purposes of peace research should be to show that women's empowerment can make a difference – to the maintenance of peace, to the success of development, to social and economic security – and lead to interna-tional and national action to this end. Peace education must ensure not just training in the practices of mediation, negotiation, and con-flict resolution – i.e. knowledge and skills – but concern for produ-cing people with an understanding of and reverence for life and the values of non-violence, humanity, and nature, and of the practices required for the encouragement of corresponding behaviour and policies.

The importance of peace research, and of international conven-tions, resolutions, and decisions, lies in the impetus and legitimation they give to the struggle of people – and particularly women – at the national level and to their work in claiming equal rights and oppor-tunities in their own societies and in their own lives. They provide leverage and assistance to women around the world in claiming their share of power. The equitable participation of women in all walks of life, nationally and internationally, is no longer just their legitimate right but a social and political necessity in achieving a more balanced, humane, and sustainable future.

In all of the events and conferences convened under the auspices of the United Nations, peace has been the paramount aim and aspiration of women, and will be so in the future. In the words of Rosiska Darcy de Oliveira, leader of the Brazilian women's group in charge of Planeta Femea at the '92 Global Forum in Rio:

At Planeta Femea, the longing for peace was a refrain as insistent as life itself, repeated in different languages. This is our lot and our luck: it is we who are to prepare the New Year's Eve festivities for the year 2000. We who live this mix of anguish at the past, perplexity at the present and obstinate infatuation with the future (and responsibility for as much happiness as possible).[27]

Huge progress has been made in the past two decades with regard to women's rightful place in world society, but an equally huge amount remains to be done. It is essential to maintain the impetus given by the world conferences: by strengthening the UN Division for the Advancement of Women and the special women's sections of UNDP and the specialized agencies; by mainstreaming the empowerment of women in all programmes and policies of the UN system; by greatly increasing cooperation between the UN system and nongovernmental organizations working on women, peace, and development issues; by strengthening national bodies devoted to advancement of women and increasing the amount of time devoted to women's studies in universities and training colleges; and – last but by no means least – by intensifying peace education and peace research into the essential relationship between women's equal rights and the achievement of a just and peaceful world.[28]

Notes

1. *The Nairobi Forward-looking Strategies for the Advancement of Women* (New York: United Nations, 1985). The text is available in all official languages of the United Nations through UN Information Centres and the Department of Public Information, United Nations, New York.
2. *Beijing Declaration and Platform for Action* (New York: United Nations, 1996). The texts are available in all official languages of the United Nations through UN Information Centres and the Department of Public Information, United Nations, New York.

3. *International Cooperation and Coordination within the United Nations System. Proposed System-wide Medium-term Plan for Women and Development for the Period 1990–1995*, E/1987/52 (New York: United Nations).
4. *Advancement of Women. Proposed System-wide Medium-term Plan for the Advancement of Women for the Period 1996–2001*, E/1996/16, 16 April 1996.
5. *1984 World Survey on the Role of Women in Development*, A/CONF.116/4/Rev. 1, Sales No. E.86.IV.3 (New York: United Nations, 1986).
6. Johan Galtung, "The Changing Interface between Peace and Development in a Changing World," *Bulletin of Peace Proposals*, vol. 2 (1980).
7. Johan Galtung, *Peace: Research–Education–Action. Essays in Peace Research*, vol. I (Copenhagen: Christian Ejlers, 1975), p. 130.
8. Birgit Brock-Utne, "The Peace Concepts through Three UN Women Decade Conferences," PRIO Working Paper 1/86.
9. 1994 World Survey on the Role of Women in Development, *Women in a Changing Global Economy* (New York: United Nations, 1995).
10. *Development and International Economic Cooperation: Effective Mobilization and Integration of Women in Development*, Report of the Secretary-General, A/48/393, 20 September 1993.
11. Ibid.
12. *Agenda 21: The United Nations Programme of Action from Rio* (New York: United Nations, Sales Section, Room DC2-0853, NY 10017).
13. Report of the Secretary-General, A/48/393, op. cit.
14. Ibid.
15. UNDP *Human Development Reports*, annually since 1990 (New York: Oxford University Press). Available through UN sales agents in member countries and UN depositary libraries around the world.
16. See note 2 above.
17. *Violence Against Women in the Family*, ST/CSDHA/2, Sales No. E.89.IV.5 (New York: United Nations, Centre for Social Development and Humanitarian Affairs, 1989).
18. Commission on the Status of Women, *Efforts to Eradicate Violence against Women within the Family and Society*, E/CN.6/1988/6, Spring 1988.
19. Declaration on the Elimination of Violence against Women, UN General Assembly, 20 December 1993.
20. Administrative Instruction ST/AI/382, 3 March 1993.
21. Susan George, Talk at the 25th PSI (Public Service International) World Congress, Helsinki, 5 August 1993.
22. "In Search of a People-centered Alternative," *DAWN Informs*, vol. 2 (1993).
23. Ibid.
24. Charlotte Bunch, "Women's Rights as Human Rights: An International Lobbying Success Story," *Human Rights Tribune*, vol. 2, no. 1 (June 1993), Special Issue.
25. *Women Making a Difference: An Action Guide to Women's Gains and Goals* (WEDO, 845 Third Avenue, 15th floor, New York, NY 10022).
26. Gertrude Mongella, Secretary-General of the Fourth World Conference on Women, 1995, at a press conference in November 1993.
27. Rosiska Darcy de Oliveira, "Memories of Planeta Femea," *Terra Femina*, vol. 2 (May/June 1993), IDAC (Institute of Cultural Action), Lopes Quintas 211, Jardim Botanico 22460-010, Rio de Janeiro, R.F. Brazil.
28. For more extensive coverage of issues briefly summarized here see:
    (1) Hilkka Pietilä and Jeanne Vickers, *Making Women Matter: The Role of the United Nations*, London: Zed Books, 1994; second (updated and expanded) edition with a foreword by Gertrude Mongella, Secretary-General of the Fourth World Conference on Women, Beijing, 1995; third, post-Beijing updated edition, 1996.
    (2) Jeanne Vickers, *Women and War*, London; Zed Books, 1993.

(3) Betty A. Reardon, *Women and Peace: Feminist Visions of Global Security*, Albany, N.Y.: State University of New York Press, 1993.

(4) Katarina Tomasevsky, *Women and Human Rights*, Women and World Development Series, London: Zed Books, 1993.

(5) The Women and World Development Series published by Zed Books, London, includes the following 10 books prepared by the UN/NGO Programme Group on Women and Development: *Women and the World Economic Crisis, Women and Disability, Women and Health, Women and the Environment, Refugee Women, Women and Literacy, Women and Human Rights, Women and the Family, Women and Work, Women and Empowerment: Participation and Decision-making.*

9

Generating the political will for protecting the rights of refugees

Lucia Ann McSpadden and Anthony Ayok Chol

> Once we were somebodies about whom people cared, we were loved by friends, even known by landlords as paying our rent regularly ... Contemporary history has created a new kind of human being – the kind that are put in concentration camps by their foes and internment camps by their friends. (Arendt 1978: 56, 60)

> INTERNATIONAL PROTECTION: *Protection* which it is *UNHCR's duty* to provide to refugees individually or as a group in substitution for the denial or lack of protection from the country of origin; it aims to ensure that *refugees' rights are respected* and that a *solution is found* to their problem. (ITRT 1989: 42; emphasis added)

1. Introduction

When, 50 years ago, the nations of the world established the United Nations Organization, the "refugee problem," although acute, pressing, and urgently calling for attention (partly for humanitarian reasons and partly to "close the book" on World War II), was understood as both clearly bounded and temporary. *Who* was a refugee was defined in a Euro-centric, limited fashion with exclusions, which today haunt the search for global peace (for example, Palestinian Arab refugees were outside the mandate of the United Nations High

Commissioner for Refugees). That the situation of the then-recognized 1.25 million refugees could and would be settled expeditiously in a globally supported fashion was clearly assumed in the original three-year limited mandate of the Office of the United Nations High Commissioner for Refugees (UNHCR) created in 1951.[1]

Today it is painfully clear that the definition of who is a refugee is extraordinarily complex, most frequently controversial, often politically influenced, and increasingly narrowly defined by nation-states. The expectation that the refugee problem would "go away" was, without question, misplaced. The increase in the number of recognized refugees, estimated today to be in excess of 20 million, is a horrifying and painful witness to injustice, persecution, oppression, and the inability of people to live safely in peace and stability in their native lands.[2]

The reasons for refugee flight are complex and intertwined, as many scholars and activists convincingly describe and analyse.[3] Images of the recurring and massive movements of people with no other viable options for living are captured through haunting and fleeting pictures on our TV screens. These pictures, which often offer little more than simplistic explanations, conjur up images of national sovereignty being compromised, of "hordes" on the move, of continued and extraordinary national and international financial burdens, and, perhaps most importantly, of an unending dynamic that does not seem to be amenable to solution. They elicit the response, "We can't take all the refugees in the world!" There is talk of compassion fatigue. With increasingly protectionist national legislation and processing procedures, the very notion of the world as a "global village" is undermined.

Scholars, as Ferris notes (1993: xviii–xxiv), have analysed the issues of refugees, or, more expansively, uprooted peoples, in various ways: as a humanitarian and emergency issue; as a foreign policy and security issue; as a human rights issue; as a development issue; as an international systemic issue. How the problem is analysed sets the framework for what are judged to be effective solutions. And the debate continues.

Clearly, however it is approached, the global complexity of the refugee reality and the more restrictionist responses of governments are a challenge to both justice and peace. Responding to this forced displacement of people is beyond the capacity of any one organization. Therefore, the challenge to the international community – intergovernmental, governmental, and non-governmental – to work cooperatively is both enormous and compelling if justice and consequent peace are to prevail. Refugees are a peace issue because of the national and global forces that impel them to flee their native lands and because of the action of refugees on their own behalf, actions that push governments and intergovernmental organizations to deal with the refugees' presence and pressure.

It is the aim of this chapter to set the work of the UNHCR in historical and current context in order to relate it to the concerns for justice-based peace and the search for just solutions to the root causes and the subsequent conditions in which these refugees find themselves.

people become refugees because of human actions and ... these human actions can be changed, ought to be changed, and sometimes actually are changed. (Carens 1991: 19)

2. Historical background to the international responses to refugees and the creation of the United Nations High Commissioner for Refugees

Refugees as we know them – as a social category – were basically unknown in pre-modern times (Marrus 1988: 3). According to Marrus (1988: 3–5), four factors produced the social position of refugees in the nineteenth and twentieth centuries:
(1) the emerging consciousness of national identity, usually traced to the French Revolution;
(2) in the age of revolutions, the perception of refugees as the carriers of alien and subversive doctrines;
(3) the increasing acceptance by states of responsibility for the physical welfare of the indigent and helpless citizen, which meant that refugees could become a financial and social burden;
(4) the size and destructiveness of international warfare, which has expanded to include civilian populations, eliminating, for practical purposes, the distinction between combatant and non-combatant and uprooting people well beyond the end of actual fighting.

These factors contribute to the current crisis in the international protection of refugees. They also highlight the urgency of the international community addressing the root causes of flight, especially causes that precipitate the mass movements of people.

Long before intergovernmental organizations accepted specific responsibilities to protect refugees in the global context, churches and other humanitarian non-governmental organizations (NGOs) were caring for refugees (Ferris 1993: 4). For example, in response to the Armenian genocide of 1915, a consortium of private groups called Near East Relief raised millions of dollars, sent relief teams, fed thousands of people, cared for thousands of orphans, and established and administered hospital services for Armenia (Nichols 1988: 32–33; Marrus 1985: 83–84, cited in Ferris 1993: 4). The League of Red Cross Societies responded, in the early 1900s, to the refugee phenomena produced by the Balkan Wars (1912) and the Russian Revolution and the failure of the Counter-revolution (1917) (UNHCR 1993).

The willingness of the international community to accept, through the establishment of an intergovernmental office, the responsibility to protect and meet the life-sustaining needs of refugees can, according to some scholars, be traced back to the work and the resultant pressure from such NGOs between the end of World War I and the formation of the League of Nations.

[B]y keeping so many alive, the private organizations helped to maintain the pressure of the refugee crisis. In the long run, this activity helped to elicit a response from governments and from the international agencies set in place after the first world war. (Marrus 1985: 83, cited in Ferris 1993: 4)

The actual concept of "refugee" was established as a separate category in 1921 by the League of Nations in response to a request from the International Committee of the Red Cross (ICRC) on behalf of the NGOs of that time (League of Nations 1921: 227–228, cited in Jaeger 1993: 143, 147, 148).

The above quotation illustrates the underlying difficulty that international institutions have had when confronted, during times of intense global crises and change, with the need to address refugee problems (Loescher 1994: 351). The history of the development of international laws identifying refugees as "a unique category of human rights victims to whom special protection and benefits should be accorded" (ibid.) has been fraught with ambivalence and tensions. The need and self-interested desires of states to promote and ensure international and regional stability, concerns about burden-sharing and coordination, and the protection of the very nature of the state, which, by definition, controls its boundaries, continue to be inter-twined. These concerns express themselves in the difficulties that states have in

> yield[ing] authority to international refugee agencies and institutions and consequently, [states] impose considerable financial and political limitations on ... the activities of [international refugee institutions] ... The great powers were unwilling to commit themselves to indefinite financial costs and large resettlement programs. (Ibid.: 352)

However, as Loescher notes, in spite of these tensions, "significant intergovernmental collaboration on the refugee issue did ... occur and the [international refugee] responsibilities steadily expanded" (ibid.: 352).

In 1921, the League of Nations, confronted with the enormous numbers of people displaced in the aftermath of World War I, the breakup of multi-ethnic empires, and the reluctance of the European governments to accept these homeless wanderers (Loescher 1994: 353; Simpson 1939), nominated Dr. Fridtjof Nansen of Norway as High Commissioner for Refugees. Dr. Nansen coordinated massive refugee humanitarian operations, including a difficult and contro-versial population exchange of Turkish and Greek refugees, as well as assistance for Russians, Armenians, and Bulgarians. Importantly, he introduced the "Nansen passport," internationally recognized identity papers for refugees and the forerunner of today's Conven-tion Travel Document for refugees. This was the first in an evolving series of international legal protection measures for refugees and other stateless persons (UNHCR 1993: 4; see also Loescher 1994; Skran, forthcoming; Marrus 1985). However, the amount of protec-tion Dr. Nansen and his office could provide was limited by the fact that the ongoing administration was carried out by national govern-ments. Thus the League could observe, persuade, and propose solu-tions, but action was in the hands of governments. The tension be-tween the mandate of the international, intergovernmental agency and the sovereignty of nation-states continues to this day and is especially problematic in the challenge to protect refugees.

Since 1921, the intergovernmental and international response to and responsibilities for refugees have brought into being, often briefly, various cooperative ventures and organizations. For example, in 1925 part of Dr. Nansen's office was transferred to the Interna-tional Labour Organization (ILO) in an attempt to find employment for Russians and Armenians (UNHCR 1991: 90).

The 1930s and the desperate situation of Jews in Europe brought into bold relief the limitations of the League of Nations and international organizations to protect refugees in the absence of governments' willingness to cooperate. The Intergovernmental Committee on Refugees (IGCR), created in 1938 mainly to respond to the flight of Jewish refugees, is today known "for the refusal of Western governments to admit more Jewish refugees into their territories, in spite of growing evidence of the scale of persecution in Germany" (Ferris 1993: 5).[4] Loescher cites the following three beliefs as being pervasive during the 1930s in the United States, Canada, and Australia, beliefs that blocked effective international cooperation towards refugees, including the Jewish refugees.

1. that tight fiscal constraints and high unemployment levels limited any humanitarian initiatives on behalf of refugees;
2. that no particular foreign policy benefits would accrue from either putting political and moral pressure on refugee-generating countries, or accepting their unwanted dissidents and minority groups;
3. that national interests were best served through rigid limits on immigration. (Loescher 1994: 354–355)[5]

In 1943, in the midst of World War II, the United Nations Relief and Reconstruction Administration (UNRRA) was established to work with NGOs to organize and coordinate the successful repatriation of 7 million (out of over 30 million) displaced people in Europe. UNRRA, which was in existence for four years, became embroiled in controversies about the voluntariness of many of the repatriations and, for example, came under pressure from the Soviet Union forcibly to repatriate USSR citizens from Germany to the Soviet Union.

In 1948, the International Refugee Organization (IRO) was temporarily put in place by the UN General Assembly in order to facilitate permanent solutions for the remaining European refugees (see Holborn 1956). Its basic emphasis during its four-and-a-half-year existence was not upon repatriation but upon resettlement – "distributing refugees and refugee costs among a number of North and South American and Western European nations ... Australasia and [some] African countries" (Loescher 1994: 356). The work of the IRO was also strongly affected by the developing hostile political realities of the Cold War[6] and the lack of effective international legal documents for the protection of refugees.

Another temporary refugee agency, the United Nations Relief and Works Agency for Palestine Refugees in the Near East (UNRWA), was created in 1950. UNRWA was charged with managing camps for Palestinian refugees. The 600,000–800,000 Palestinians, refused as repatriates by Israel and unwanted as new immigrants by the Arab countries, remained, for the most part, in what became permanent camps. They became pawns in the battle between the Arab states and Israel. When the UNHCR was created, the Palestinian refugees remained outside its mandate and hence its protection. "Temporary" camps became a permanent way of life for several generations of Palestinians, fostering and undergirding the struggles being played out today in Gaza and the West Bank (Morris 1988: 267–269).

UNRWA provides a case study of an agency set up to provide a durable solution in the ordinary meaning of that term – to eliminate the Palestine refugee problem – which later became a durable solution in the ironic, second sense of the term, where the solution applied continued on and on but the refugee situation was perpetuated. (Adelman 1988: 296)

According to Adelman (1988), UNRWA was an attempt to integrate aid with long-term development without, by implication, attempting a political solution to an apparently intractable refugee problem.

The Office of the UN High Commissioner for Refugees was created in 1951 by the General Assembly and, as Loescher notes, "reflected the political and strategic interests of the European powers and specifically, the United States" (1994: 357). Its mandate was temporary – three years – and has since been renewed every three, then five, years. Its mission was to *protect* refugees[7] and *find solutions*[8] to their situation on behalf of the international community. It had a budget of US\$300,000 and 33 Geneva-based staff and was responsible for 1.25 million refugees. This responsibility was to be exercised by working through NGOs. The UNHCR was not permitted to raise its own funds. Not only did it have limited funds, a limited mandate, and limited staff; it also had limited support from the most powerful Western states (Ferris 1993: 25; Loescher 1994: 357).

Beginning with the flight of Hungarians in 1956 and continuing through the exodus of Algerian refugees, the UNHCR mandate expanded to meet new demands. With the mass flight of refugees from conflicts fuelled by the Cold War – Viet Nam, Laos, Cambodia, Afghanistan, Salvador, Chile – the UNHCR increased its operations. The ongoing wars in the Horn of Africa caused hundreds of thousands of people to flee, primarily to the Sudan. The politically volatile nature of most of these refugee situations in light of East–West animosities put the UNHCR in an often confrontational position as

Table 9.1 **Top contributors to UNHCR per capita, 1994**

Country	Per capita contribution (US$)
1. Norway	10.49
2. Sweden	9.29
3. Denmark	7.42
4. Netherlands	4.04
5. Switzerland	3.21
6. Finland	2.27
7. United Kingdom	1.22
8. Luxembourg	1.02
9. United States of America	0.99
10. Japan	0.98
11. Canada	0.89
12. Ireland	0.87
13. European Commission	0.67
14. Australia	0.60
15. Italy	0.27
16. Belgium	0.22
17. Germany	0.21
18. France	0.18
19. Austria	0.12
20. Spain	0.06

Source: UNHCR (1995: 255).

it sought to protect individuals, to obtain asylum, and to develop orderly ways to handle mass movements within short periods of time (UNHCR 1991).

The combination of these new and expanded demands and the highly politicized nature of the conflicts[9] has put extraordinary pressures upon UNHCR and the total international refugee system. UNHCR's expenditures expanded from US$5.52 million in 1965 to US$500 million in 1980 to US$1.167 billion in 1994 (UNHCR 1995: 255). Funding for the administrative costs of the UNHCR comes from the UN regular budget, but the funding of assistance programmes comes from voluntary contributions, primarily (approximately 90 per cent) from governments, followed by intergovernmental and non-governmental organizations (UNHCR 1995: 255; table 9.1 lists the top 20 contributors per capita in 1994). Funding is almost totally from Western countries (see table 9.2); in 1993, 97.7 per cent of UNHCR funding came from the top 14 governmental donors (UNHCR 1995: 255).[10] This, of course, has severe complications: the UNHCR is dependent upon a small number of politically

Table 9.2   **Major contributors to UNHCR in absolute terms, 1994**

Contributor	Contribution (US$m.)
1. United States of America	232
2. European Commission	225
3. Japan	121
4. Sweden	81
5. United Kingdom	68
6. Netherlands	60
7. Norway	45
8. Denmark	38
9. Canada	26
10. Switzerland	21
11. Germany	17
12. Italy	15
13. France	11
14. Australia	11
15. Finland	11
16. Other governments	15
17. NGOs, United Nations, and private sector	38
Total contributions	**1,065**

Source: UNHCR (1995: 255).

and financially powerful governments and is vulnerable to political pressure, and the money does not come in a necessarily systematic or adequate fashion. The UNHCR is consistently and increasingly underfunded, which is a rather academic way of saying that there has been and continues to be a funding crisis for the UNHCR. Given that refugee movements are not predictable and that the needs within mass movements of people are urgent, the funding situation becomes dangerous for refugees. In these circumstances there has been pressure for UNHCR to set its budget in response to what money it thinks it will receive rather than in response to refugee and programmatic needs – a morally and ethically compromised position for a humanitarian agency. This may underlie the concern expressed by a number of refugee advocates when the UNHCR estimated the need for resettlement places in 1995 to be 45 per cent lower than those needed in 1994 at a time when intra-state conflicts were erupting and the number of refugees worldwide steadily increasing (USCR 1995: 7–9)!

Before moving on to examine further the challenges now facing the UNHCR, it is instructive to reflect upon the lessons embedded in the history of the international struggle to respond to refugees. Ferris (1993: 8–10) suggests the following:

(1) From 1921 to 1951, the refugees to be protected were specifically named groups, e.g. Armenians, thus the process carried out was a mass determination procedure that did not distinguish victims of war from victims of individualized persecution (see also Keely 1991).

(2) The international refugee protection system that developed grew out of the *European* experience and was designed to "meet specific Western needs in Europe during the immediate post-war era." It specifically avoided dealing with the very present, non-European refugee realities of that time, for example the mass movements of people due to the partitioning of India. Individual persecution defined who was designated as a refugee, thus persons fleeing war or generalized civil chaos were outside the mandate for protection.

(3) In the creation of the UNHCR and the development of the UN Convention Relating to the Status of Refugees, Western governments were interested in "limiting their financial and legal obligations to refugees" (Loescher 1994: 357–358).

(4) The United States, as the principal world power, "controlled the political environment in which the negotiations on refugees took place." Thus, issues of national security, anti-communism, and US foreign policy objectives were of central concern.[11] One consequence was that the criteria for recognizing refugee status were often highly politicized, with the needs of the refugee in tension with the perceived national interests of specific states, especially countries of asylum or potential resettlement (UNHCR 1993: 5).

(5) The international refugee protection system was developed without the participation of the USSR or any of the East European countries.[12] In fact, with the United States' strong anti-communist shaping of refugee recognition, the refugee protection system was often used internationally to highlight the human rights abuses of East European countries in particular, as well as other designated communist countries, e.g. Cuba (Matas with Simon 1989: 16–17).

(6) The NGOs and the churches were essential in providing concrete assistance to refugees in the early years. They were a primary force pushing for governments to assume their responsibilities to assist and protect refugees and other forced migrants through an international organization.

Overall, the acceptance of and commitment to national sovereignty was the international framework in which the UNHCR developed and within which it continues to function. As Ferris notes, in the international refugee system it is the governments that are the main actors (1993: 24). National sovereignty provides the context in which the UNHCR struggles to devise innovative and effective ways to respond to the ever-changing and expanding international refugee reality. At a very basic level, the struggle can be seen in the definition of who will be recognized by the international community as a refugee and thus entitled to protection and assistance.

3. Who is a refugee?

Hand in hand with the creation of the UNHCR[13] was the signing of the 1951 Convention defining who is a refugee.[14] According to the 1951 Convention, a refugee is any person who,

owing to well-founded fear of being persecuted for reasons of race, religion, nationality, membership of a particular social group or political opinion, is outside the country of his nationality and is unable, or owing to such fear, is unwilling to avail himself of the protection of that country, or who, not having a nationality and being outside the country of his former habitual residence, is unable or, owing to such fear, is unwilling to return to it.

The 1951 definition was founded upon and limited to events occurring prior to 1 January 1951. Subsequent events demonstrated the limitation of this restriction. The adoption of the Protocol Relating to the Status of Refugees in 1967 eliminated the time-limit contained in the Convention.[15] In addition, the Convention provides the right to refugees not to be forcibly returned to their country of origin (*non-refoulement*). It is this right that is basic to the UNHCR's primary mandate, i.e. the *protection* of refugees.

Evolving conditions outside of post–World War II Europe showed the limitations of the refugee definition as contained in the 1951 Convention and 1967 Protocol. For example, as early as 1956 in Europe and in Africa the UNHCR was confronted not just with individual claims of persecution but with mass movements of people fleeing general situations of conflict – the Hungarian crisis resulted in approximately 180,000 Hungarians seeking asylum in Austria and 20,000 in Yugoslavia. After the outbreak of the Algerian war of independence, approximately 200,000 Algerians sought protection in Tunisia and Morocco, and between 1959 and 1961 nearly 60,000 Tutsi left Rwanda to seek refuge in Zaire (UNHCR 1991: 123–124). In all these cases the "good offices" of the UNHCR were called upon, outside of the strict mandate of the 1951 Convention (Loescher 1994: 360–361).

In response to these realities of widespread conflict, several regional instruments have been developed that broaden the definition of who is a refugee. As early as 1963 the Organization of African Unity (OAU) recognized that a regional refugee treaty was essential. The OAU Convention Governing the Specific Aspects of Refugee Problems in Africa enlarged the refugee definition to include people who were compelled to leave their country "owing to external aggression, occupation, foreign domination or events seriously disturbing public order in either part or the whole of his country of origin or nationality" (UNHCR 1993: 12).

In 1984, Central American states, joining with Mexico and Panama and building upon the OAU definition, adopted a definition that added the criterion of "massive violation of human rights." This Cartagena Declaration on Refugees with its expansion of the refugee definition has been included in the laws of several states (UNHCR 1993: 12).

These regional broadenings of the refugee definition have allowed a needed flexibility and response to regional realities. They have also produced a situation in which persons considered refugees in one part of the world are not so considered somewhere else.

None of these instruments deals with the ever-present and threatened situation of over 24 million internally displaced persons. The internally displaced are often in even more danger than refugees but are denied international protection because they have not fled across state borders – an inhumane situation.[16] As Jaeger notes (1993: 144), recent developments put this issue in bold relief. The UNHCR has been asked to protect internally displaced Kurds and others in Iraq as a consequence of the Gulf War, and the displacement of hundreds of thousands of people from the former Yugoslavia has received varying responses by Western governments. Currently Europe adheres to the notion that Bosnians can and should be returned or should be "protected" in temporary "safe havens" outside of Western Europe (Ferris 1995: 25). The mass killings in July 1995 by the Bosnian Serb army of Bosnian Muslims living in Srebrenica, a UN-designated "safe haven" inside the Bosnia-Hercegovina region of the former Yugoslavia, are a tragic example of the moral and ethical vacuousness of such a position.

4. Asylum, safe haven, and solutions

Everyone has the right to seek and to enjoy in other countries asylum from persecution. (Universal Declaration of Human Rights, Art. 14(1))

No Contracting State shall expel or return ("refouler") a refugee in any manner whatsoever to the frontiers of territories where his life or freedom would be threatened on account of his race, religion, nationality, membership of a particular social group or political opinion. (1951 Convention and 1967 Protocol Relating to the Status of Refugees, Art. 33)

Being recognized internationally as a refugee implies an entitlement to protection, immediate assistance, and efforts to find a permanent solution. Protection has several basic conditions: asylum in a second country without threat of return, and provision of the basic necessities required to live.

Indeed, the basis of *non-refoulement* is time honoured (for example, Grotius 1625, de Vattel 1758, as cited in Grahl-Madsen 1983). It is inherent in the Mosaic religious codes that form the social framework for Judaism, Islam, and Christianity. Plato developed the concept of asylum as an ethical precept based on the defencelessness of the foreigner because of isolation from family and nation (see *The Laws*). *Non-refoulement* reflects "a basic principle of civilized government – and thus one of the cornerstones of international law" (Grahl-Madsen 1983: 14).

However, most states that grant asylum weigh up the need of the refugee against the perceived need of the state. That perceived need is strongly influenced by economic conditions, current political sentiment, and social conditions. Sadly today, in country after country there is a growing trend toward a more restrictive interpretation and application of asylum provisions, sometimes even outright disregard of international law.[17]

Although any person has the "right" to flee persecution and threat to life, that person does not have the "right" to enter any given country (Martin 1991: 31). The basic understanding of national sovereignty implies the state's right to control its borders and to decide who is a citizen, who may enter and under what conditions they may enter, who may stay and under what conditions they may stay. It is precisely here that the definition of who is a refugee becomes so important. It is here that, in 1997, Western countries, traditionally countries of both asylum and resettlement, were "closing the door" on persons who, a few years ago, they would likely have admitted as refugees and granted asylum to.

Ironically, the entitlement to asylum embedded in the guarantee against forced return, which should be recognized for the remarkable international achievement that it is, makes the granting of asylum "fragile," i.e. potentially a scarce resource in the political sense (Martin 1991: 34). For if asylum is an entitlement to those who are deemed refugees, the government and, in the current and increasingly anti-immigrant, xenophobic social climate, the general public become concerned that the persons granted asylum might not be "true" refugees (ibid.: 35). This was forcefully illustrated in US Senate hearings held in January 1995 on proposed, more restrictive immigration legislation, where Senator Alan Simpson (R–Wyoming), chairperson of the US Senate immigration subcommittee, stated:

Thousands of people are admitted each year as refugees, with all the special privileges and immunities of that unique and cherished status, even though their claims of political persecution are questionable, at best. Claims of persecution made by persons from certain countries are judged by different standards, with the result that many are granted a status not possibly available to others who come from elsewhere. I call them State Department refugees. (USCR 1995: 2)

Senator Simpson also called for a 50,000 ceiling on refugee admissions, citing "the abuses of the country's humanitarianism" (ibid.), and proposed including a refugee admissions provision in a bill on illegal immigration.

Such a mixing of the ajudicating of asylum for refugees with illegal immigration graphically illustrates that the line between refugee and voluntary migrant is often, in fact, a fine one.[18] Therefore, the confusion can easily be manipulated for political ends. The potential for political manipulation is compounded by the fact that understanding when and how extreme economic inequities are typically maintained by direct political oppression requires a sophisticated analysis that goes beyond the TV screen or the front page of the newspaper.

When the refugee–asylum system appears to be overwhelmed, when there is a perception that there is less and less distinction between refugees whose lives would be in danger if they were to be returned and economic migrants who could safely return, the backlash grows and the procedures and laws become more restrictive. That such a perception can be valid or false and can be politically manipulated is obvious. The rhetoric leading up to the passage in November 1994 in California of Proposition 187 (which prohibits the provision of publicly funded services to persons who are not US citizens or legally admitted immigrants, and requires state and local agencies to report suspected illegal immigrants to the Immigration and Naturalization Service of the US government) is a blatant example of the manipulation of public perceptions in a climate of economic uncertainty and sense of threat.[19]

Western governments are increasingly restrictive in granting asylum. For example, many now use the "first country of asylum principle," which asserts that refugees should apply for asylum in the first asylum country they enter. Sweden states that "a refugee who, before arriving in Sweden, has been in a 'first asylum country' of this kind [protected from persecution and from forcible return] will ... as a rule be returned to that country" (Swedish Ministry of Culture 1994: 7).[20] The United States used the same approach in the 1980s, saying that refugees from El Salvador or Guatemala should apply for asylum in Mexico not the United States, although it was routine for Mexican police to apprehend and jail such refugees as illegal migrants. In February 1995 Canada and the United States agreed to conclude a "border management accord," which would, in part, state:

The Parties intend that any person who: (a) makes or attempts to make a refugee status claim in Canada or in the United States, and (b) has arrived in Canada directly from the United States, or in the United States directly from Canada, will have the refugee status claim examined by and in accordance with the refugee status determination system of the country of first arrival.[21]

Such harmonizing of refugee-determination procedures in Europe and North America is based on controlling the numbers of asylum claims. As such, these procedures tend to weaken the protection for refugees because refugees are pushed from country to country. "These types of agreements generate downward pressure to the lowest common denominator of refugee protection."[22]

As Grahl-Madsen notes (1983: 21), some countries have adopted policies that essentially assign "not eligible" status collectively, i.e. to all members of certain ethnic or national groups (e.g. Haitians or Bosnians). Uganda has stated that it would not allow persons fleeing from Rwanda and Burundi to enter Uganda. Such collective judgements can easily be inaccurate, either by not making distinctions between members of the group or by misjudging the situation entirely on the basis of political "need" or a wish to diminish the numbers entering the country. For example, in 1995 a group of Bosnians were forcibly deported from Sweden back to the former Yugoslavia. They were accompanied on this journey by Swedish police. Upon arriving at the airport in the former Yugoslavia, the returning Bosnians were threatened by the local authorities. The Swedish police brought the Bosnians back, and their cases are being reconsidered by the Swedish government.[23] In the meantime the Swedish government has suspended deportations of the approximately 5,000 Bosnians with Croatian passports currently in Sweden.

The granting or withholding of asylum makes clear the assertion noted above that in the international refugee system it is the national governments that are the main actors. The agreements by European countries to harmonize their immigration and refugee policies are decisions made outside of the UNHCR and its Executive Committee (which establishes customary international law regarding refugee protection) (Ferris 1995: 25). Such decisions weaken the role of the UNHCR and put it in the position of trying to persuade governments (perhaps the very countries that fund the UNHCR programme) to change policies. Having the responsibility of being the primary agency protecting refugees while also being the client in a donor–client relationship puts the UNHCR in a difficult and delicate position. Indeed, the UNHCR has asserted that:

The protection challenge of the 1990s is how to retain and strengthen the international protection regime, painstakingly established over four decades around the key concepts of asylum and *non-refoulement*, while also developing a new regime able to provide a principled conceptual and operational base to protect civilians uprooted in conflict and post-conflict situations ... This "new protection" ... is *the major challenge facing UNHCR as we approach the 21st century....* Major reversals in the commitment to providing asylum in many areas of the world, where victims of war and human rights abuses are confronted with legal and other obstacles in their search for asylum, are of great concern. (UNHCR Briefing Note 1995: 2; emphasis added)

5. Durable solutions

Asylum is just one of the three "durable solutions," the others being resettlement in a third country (the least preferable and least used) and voluntary repatriation to one's native land. Although these are the classic three solutions, it is not clear in what ways any of the three solutions are, in fact, durable.

Asylum

Asylum for peoples who have fled *en masse* to neighbouring countries typically means camps, relief, environmental destruction. People are often in desperate circumstances, in poor health, psychologically wounded, physically wounded, searching for family. The most vulnerable are most in danger: deaths of children and the elderly are exceptionally high during flight and in the early period in camps. Even minimal food, health care, water, and sanitation require large sums of money. When camps are situated close to borders, asylum does not necessarily mean safety, as the killing of scores of Rwandan refugees in a camp in Uganda illustrates. The UNHCR has over the years given significant material assistance to refugees in camps, including digging wells, building schools, health clinics, and hospitals, and providing basic infrastructure to maintain the camps. The approval of the host country must be obtained for this assistance to proceed (Kalumiya 1981: 21).

Voluntary repatriation

Voluntary repatriation is, today, considered to be the preferred option. The UNHCR is committed to repatriation being completely voluntary, but it is not clear what "voluntary" means when the options are limited and the future seems hopeless. December 1996 saw the previously unacceptable: UNHCR support for the forced repatriation of refugees.[24] Human rights organizations fear that more forced repatriations are likely.

Assuming that the repatriation is, in fact, voluntary in the best sense of the word, the process raises pervasive and longstanding questions about what is called the "relief to development continuum." Which is to say, if repatriation has been, as one UNHCR official stated, "tools, seeds, and a handshake," or, as a representative of a donor country commented, "donors and governments understand repatriation as moving refugees from 'here' to 'there' not as development,"[25] how can peace and stability be achieved? How can people truly settle down and rebuild their lives? The UNHCR itself put the case plainly:

[I]t is now clear that relief assistance [to refugees being repatriated] and longer-term development programmes are separated by a wide gap, which threatens the successful reintegration of returnees and the viability of their communities. (UNHCR 1993: 173)

Do not such limitations upon repatriation set the stage for future refugee movements or, at the least, the movement of migrants searching for a place that is liveable in the most basic sense? The development and sustaining of community are a critical issue in repatriation. As an Eritrean government official stated when discussing the plans for repatriating 500,000 Eritreans from the Sudan to Eritrea,[26]

How do you solve ... this problem? How to bring these people what they deserve – a decent living, a bright future, especially the children? How do you go towards this? Do you look at them as a separate people or as part of the people? Bring them back and reintegrate them in the society where they have been before. They are part and parcel of the Eritrean people, therefore they should share what the Eritrean people have. They should be integrated into the overall development of the country.

But what does it mean to be "part and parcel" of the people? What does it mean to bring people back to a war-devastated country with no infrastructure and tremendous development needs? Humanitarian aid is about helping individuals; development is about building the capacity of communities and of governments to care for communities and, hence, for their own people. In either case it means money, and a great deal of money. Moreover, development aid implies long-term commitment on the part of donors, a commitment many are reluctant to engage in, and certainly seem unwilling to commit themselves to as part of funding repatriation, even though in the long run it builds sustaining capacity rather than dependency.

The relief–development gap brings up essential money issues. It also puts into bold relief the well-documented and frustrating lack of coordination between UN agencies, in this case most basically between the UNHCR and the United Nations Development Programme (UNDP). The mandates of the different UN agencies are distinct; they do not overlap. This may seem efficient on paper, but in operation it means that there are tremendous and important gaps in the funding and delivery of what everyone agrees is essential. Such gaps and lack of coordination within the United Nations are matched by similar disjunctures within the agencies of donor governments; i.e. one office funds repatriation and another office deals with development. Because NGOs and other international agencies are also involved in organized repatriation, the process is complex and intricate indeed.[27]

Resettlement

Resettlement in a third country is the least-used durable solution. Resettlement has been the main option for South-East Asian refugees, especially since the mid-1970s, as well as significant for East European refugees in the 1980s. However, resettlement is under the same pressures as discussed above regarding asylum in Western countries. The US linkage of resettlement to foreign policy objectives has already been noted. In Canada, which has been until recently quite generous in its resettlement programme, preference has been given to refugees who can most easily integrate into Canadian society. Even though some Western countries have resettled significant numbers of refugees over the past two decades, the number resettled as a percentage of the need is quite small.

The UNHCR has been criticized for giving resettlement a low priority as a mechanism for responding to those in need. This low priority is linked to the UNHCR's primary emphasis upon facilitating voluntary repatriation and local integration (USCR 1995: 8–9). The UNHCR acknowledges that resettlement is the solution of "last resort" and is concerned that resettlement would undermine support for voluntary repatriation. Critics note that there are few UNHCR field staff working with resettlement and even fewer of such staff with appropriate experience in assessing resettlement needs. However, the UNHCR responds that this, in part, reflects the reluctance of Western governments to resettle refugees. "If you know there is no pay-off in the end, there is not much point to starting at the beginning" (USCR 1995: 9). The concerned reader searches in vain for discussions of solutions that would be in the best interests of the refugees concerned; the tone of the discourse often reflects the political reluctance of resettlement countries discussed above and the pressure from asylum countries to move the refugees out. As Bill Frelick asserts:

It became evident [in 1993] that the easiest and cheapest course of action was simply preventing the flow of refugees that threatened to "upset stability" or "create a burden" on the international community. The goal, ultimately, appeared not to be to protect the persecuted, but rather to protect potential host countries from them, in effect, punishing the victims. (1995: 2)

6. Fifty years later: The challenges facing the UNHCR

Peace is more than just absence of war. It is rather a state in which no people of any country, in fact no group of people of any kind, live in fear or in need.[28]

In 1995 the refugee challenges facing the UNHCR and the international community seemed to have reached crisis proportions. The end of the Cold War, which appeared to offer the promise of a diminution of the global refugee crisis, has revealed long-suppressed intra-state ethnic tensions and, apparently, fuelled the drive toward national self-determination. This drive has, in many cases, been sought through intense armed conflict targeting and displacing thousands of civilians, thrusting them into an increasingly unreceptive global context. The 1990s is, thus, a "new era for refugees" (Loescher 1994: 363; see also UNHCR 1993).

UNHCR must confront refugee emergencies in rapid, sometimes over-lapping, succession. Refugee crises in Iraq, Bosnia, Croatia, Kenya, Somalia, Bangladesh, Nepal, the Caucasus, Tajikistan, Benin, Ghana, Rwanda and Burundi strain the capacities of the organization almost to the breaking point. At the same time, UNHCR is trying to resolve the long-standing refugee problems of the previous decade primarily through repatriation in the context of continuing instability and insecurity. (Loescher 1994: 364)

The UNHCR as the centrepiece international organization responding to the urgent and expanding (in number and type) refugee crises is clearly confronted with daunting challenges to the effective building and sustaining of peace. It is likely that the global refugee crisis will continue and even increase. Many of the specific issues have been discussed above: increasing and seemingly intractable intra-state conflicts; increasing economic disparities within and between states, disparities often enforced through state repression; the closing of the doors to asylum and resettlement by Western nations in the domestic context of employment insecurities and rising xenophobia and racism; increasing demands to protect the internally displaced while at the same time assisting in large-scale repatriation to war-devastated countries; inadequate funding for even the basic UNHCR responsibilities; the dependency of the UNHCR on donor countries for funding; the inadequacy of the refugee definition in light of current realities and yet the reluctance to open it up to change owing to the fear that the Western nations would make the definition even more restrictive; the difficulties in separating out refugees from migrants in asylum decision-making; the need to develop long-term solutions to what have been treated as short-term emergencies, integrating refugee repatriation, for example, into development aid. The list is overwhelming and often confusing. As Ferris asserts: "The international system for refugee assistance and protection is falling apart or, in more academic terms, undergoing a transformation the direction of which is unknown" (1993: 277).

There are without question enormous challenges facing the UNHCR and other international actors in this system, most especially state governments and NGOs. The following seem to be the most critical and most in need of attention.

Situations of internal conflict

The challenge that receives most visible attention is that of working in situations of internal conflict.

[The UNHCR] focuses on meeting the immediate needs of refugees, returnees and internally displaced people who live in conditions of inter-communal violence, shifting borders and on-going conflict ... [I]n countries undergoing civil wars UNHCR staff ... [are] working with governments ... [and] opposition groups, guerrilla forces and political factions ... Their duties include protecting civilians against reprisals and forced displacement; relocating and evacuating civilians from conflict areas; and assisting besieged populations ... who are either unable or unwilling to move from their homes. Frequently, however, UNHCR lacks any firm institutional and legal basis for this work. (Loescher 1994: 365)

In such a situation there is a clear need to identify and respond to the root causes of the refugee flights. As Kalumiya notes (1981: 19), there is very little that the UNHCR can do by itself, given its mandate, to tackle root causes. This is a difficult challenge, involving early warning, protecting human rights, and new types of peace-building and diplomacy. It translates into working within countries in conflict, not just with refugees after they flee. Thus the UNHCR is faced with intervening politically when its founding mandate was framed to be non-political and its staff experience and training reflect that non-political framework.

Protecting the internally displaced

The UNHCR has been assisting the internally displaced in certain circumstances but does so without a specific mandate. In fact, there are no international organizations with the mandate to protect the internally displaced. As Loescher states, "the political issues involved, particularly state sovereignty and non-intervention in domestic affairs, make the issue of the internally displaced one of the most challenging problems confronting the international community" (1994: 368).

The internally displaced are under the same threat, experience the same or similar persecution that causes refugees' flight, are in "refugee-like" circumstances, but without the protection that refugees can claim under international law.[29]

Inadequate funding

The funding for both the basic and expanding duties of the UNHCR has been (as noted frequently above) and continues to be inadequate.[30] The UNHCR is in the double bind of holding the visible and institutional responsibility for refugees yet being dependent upon national governments for voluntary contributions to provide the funding to carry out such responsibilities. The political agenda of many donor countries results in funds coming sporadically and/or "with strings attached."

The end of the Cold War has meant that donor countries' concerns have shifted to internal, domestic matters. Refugees do not have the political importance that they previously held.

The apparent intractableness of the current conflicts also means that donor countries sense a "deep black hole in which the call for funds is never-ending, but the conflicts are also never-ending."[31] To be effective, both the strategies and the funding have to be long term, with consistent support and ongoing cooperation among and between a variety of agencies and institutions.

The often ineffective use of traditional diplomatic intervention in international conflicts calls for new approaches based within the warring populations themselves, using social structures and more traditional local leadership to guide and sustain peace-building (Normark 1994). This is, however, not within either the mandate or the expertise of the UNHCR.

Coordinating development with repatriation

Repatriation has become the durable solution most preferred in the 1990s. Yet, as the UNHCR itself notes, successful repatriation necessitates development as well as relief.[32] The UNHCR does not have a mandate to do development work, whereas the UNDP does. There is thus a strong need to coordinate the work of the UNDP with that of the UNHCR so that UNDP-organized long-term development goes hand in hand with the UNHCR-organized physical return of refugees.[33] In fact, without such development it is likely that economic pressures will compromise political stability, with the possibility of renewed refugee flows.

The implementation of Quick Impact Projects (QIPS) has shown that the UNHCR and the UNDP can, in fact, work jointly and coordinate repatriation-related development projects. However, QIPS are small scale and implemented on a more or less ad hoc basis. There is clearly a need for a much longer focus and a more broad-scale development plan to respond adequately to the realities of repatriation to war-devastated countries such as Eritrea, Mozambique, and Cambodia. The assertions of the UNHCR that repatriation operations must ensure that refugees return in safety and dignity (UNHCR 1994, 1992) require that the mandates of UN agencies, other international organizations, and NGOs be re-evaluated and restructured, that repatriation plans be developed in close cooperation with the receiving countries, that staff be trained in human rights and in development, and that ongoing monitoring of human rights be structured into the repatriation negotiations and plans.

The safety of repatriated refugees

With repatriation being considered the most preferred durable solution, it is essential that the UNHCR ensures that the repatriation is, indeed, voluntary and that the refugees will be safe upon their return. This is often a highly politicized task, especially in situations where repatriation is being proposed to solve the problems of the host country rather than the needs and wishes of the refugees.

Human rights protection

Effective human rights protection for refugees and the internally displaced requires both adequate funding and effective coordination between the UNHCR and the UN Centre for Human Rights. Such coordination is being developed and needs to be strengthened. However, current funding for the UN human rights programme is seriously inadequate (see, for example, Cohen 1990, 1992; Loescher 1994). Human rights protection also requires an increased capacity to monitor human rights abuses and to bring the strength of the international community to bear in order to stop abuses. In both these tasks coordination with NGOs will likely increase the flow of information and the effectiveness of the responses.

Restrictionist attitudes and policies

The basic need, recognized in international law, for refugees to be protected faces increasing challenges, which are especially pertinent to individuals and organizations committed to peace with justice. Increasingly the distinctiveness of refugee status is being blurred by incorporating refugees into "migration" and using terms such as "economic refugees" and "economic migrants," without making appropriate distinctions. Given the current and increasing restrictionist attitudes and policies in Europe, the United States, Canada, and Australasia, there is an urgent need for education and advocacy programmes to be implemented in local communities as well as focused upon national governments. Public rhetoric as well as a growing body of legislation are aimed at keeping "them" (i.e. foreigners) out; as such, the conditions are dangerously similar to those during the 1930s. Such beliefs must be countered locally; international organizations such as the UNHCR are not effective in this local arena of debate.

The refugee problem as a political problem

All of these challenges illustrate graphically that:

[The] global refugee problem is not a humanitarian problem requiring charity but is a political problem requiring political solutions, and ... cannot be separated from other areas of international concerns such as migration, human rights, international security and development assistance. (Loescher 1994: 376)

The hard truth ... is that solutions are ultimately dependent on political, military and economic factors which lie beyond the control of any humanitarian organization. (UNHCR 1995: 234)

Thus, the conditions that propel people to flee their homes and native land must be confronted if the "refugee problem" is to be addressed in a long-lasting, effective manner based on the protection of human rights and the dignity and safety of individuals.

However, a tremendous worldwide effort is developing to remove refugees from view, or at least from consideration as *bona fide* refugees. There are attempts to close doors, to redefine the people on the move as economic migrants rather than persons in flight, to create more restrictive laws and procedures, to deny the urgency and thus to shrug off the responsibility.

One of the consequences of the refugee crisis being inherently political is that effective responses are equally political. The work of the peace research community (scholars and activists) needs to keep the refugees in view and be available for advocacy. Perhaps more basically, peace research needs to be formulated in such a way that issues are investigated with the intention of addressing root causes and encouraging conditions that could lead to a sustainable just peace. In a global situation that is as complex as described briefly above, advocacy needs to be based on adequate knowledge, to recognize the real pressures upon the major actors in the system, to take into account the forces and legal measures already present, to be humane as well as achievable. The solutions discussed by scholars,[34] by the UNHCR, by NGOs, by governments, and by intergovernmental agencies are numerous, ranging from reform of the United Nations itself, to increasing coordination between UN agencies, to expanding the refugee definition, to formulating new and humane international legislation, to regional solutions, to developing more open and responsive national legislation, to reforming the international economic order, which sustains economic inequities, to addressing the causes of conflict and war, i.e. the root causes.

Throughout the work of the many scholars cited in this chapter is the awareness that a greater international will is necessary to address the crisis in refugee protection and assistance. International will is developed from the interaction of many forces and is significantly affected by the informed advocacy of non-governmental agencies and local citizens. The world desperately needs a humanitarian vision backed by concrete action that rises above parochial self-interests; it needs a vision that recognizes the responsibility to save lives, the responsibility implicit in our common humanity, and the reality that the welfare of the global community cannot be separated from the welfare of the refugee. We all – the intergovernmental community, governments, non-governmental agencies, and individuals – are finally "known" and essentially shaped by how we treat the most vulnerable in our midst.

Because the international response to refugees is critically linked to the political and financial support of governments, informed advocacy by non-governmental agencies and individual citizens regarding the specific policies and practices of their own countries is the avenue of greatest potential effectiveness. Peace research has a significant responsibility to undergird and shape an advocacy that can propose effective actions and workable solutions with the overall aim of creating a more humane and just world.

Appendix: States party to the 1951 Convention and/or the 1967 Protocol Relating to the Status of Refugees, as of 19 January 1996

Albania	Ethiopia	Papua New Guinea
Algeria	Fiji	Paraguay
Angola	Finland	Peru
Antigua/Barbuda	France	Philippines
Argentina	Gabon	Poland
Armenia	Gambia	Portugal
Australia	Germany	Romania
Austria	Ghana	Russian Federation
Azerbaijan	Greece	Rwanda
Bahamas	Guatemala	St. Vincent and the
Belgium	Guinea	Grenadines (C)
Belize	Guinea-Bissau	Samoa
Benin	Haiti	São Tomé and
Bolivia	Honduras	Príncipe
Bosnia/Hercegovina	Hungary	Senegal
Botswana	Iceland	Seychelles
Brazil	Iran	Sierra Leone
Bulgaria	Ireland	Slovak Republic
Burkina Faso	Israel	Slovenia
Burundi	Italy	Solomon Islands
Cambodia	Jamaica	Somalia
Cameroon	Japan	South Africa
Canada	Kenya	Spain
Cape Verde (P)	Korea (South)	Sudan
Central African	Lesotho	Suriname
Republic	Liberia	Swaziland (P)
Chad	Liechtenstein	Sweden
Chile	Luxembourg	Tajikistan
China	Macedonia	Tanzania
Colombia	Madagascar (C)	Togo
Congo	Malawi	Tunisia
Costa Rica	Mali	Turkey
Côte d'Ivoire	Malta	Uganda
Croatia	Mauritania	United Kingdom
Cyprus	Morocco	United States (P)
Czech Republic	Mozambique	Uruguay
Denmark	Namibia (C)	Venezuela (P)
Djibouti	Netherlands	Yemen
Dominica	New Zealand	Yugoslavia
Dominican Republic	Nicaragua	Zaire
Ecuador	Niger	Zambia
Egypt	Nigeria	Zimbabwe
El Salvador	Norway	
Equitorial Guinea	Panama	

Source: USCR (1996).
(C) – Party to the Convention only.
(P) – Party to the Protocol only.
Note: Non-UN members Switzerland, Tuvalu, and the Holy See have also signed the UN Convention and Protocol; Monaco has signed the Convention only.

Notes

1. The most complete description of the work of the UNHCR is contained in the two-volume history of UNHCR written by Louise Holborn (1975). The history briefly outlined in this chapter is intended to point to current issues with which the UNHCR and the global community must deal, issues which affect lasting peace. Except where noted the information is compiled from UNHCR publications (1991, 1993), Holborn (1975), and Ferris (1993).
2. This extraordinarily high and disturbing number of refugees currently recognized by UNHCR does not include internally displaced persons. Their numbers, although difficult to calculate precisely, are conservatively estimated by the UNHCR to be some 24 million persons. Thus the number of people displaced within the borders of their own countries and in "refugee-like" situations exceeds the number of recognized international refugees!
3. See, for example, Gilad (1990); Ferris (1993); Loescher and Scanlan (1986); Adelman and Lanphier (1990); Matas with Simon (1989); Adelman (1991); Kibreab (1985); Bramwell (1988); Loescher and Monahan (1989); Moussa (1993); Zucker and Zucker (1987); Stein (1981); Mayotte (1992).
4. Loescher's analysis of the lack of response to Jewish refugees cites the following: Wyman (1985, 1968); Abella and Troper (1986); Wasserstein (1979).
   By 1939 it was estimated that 226,000 persons had fled Germany itself; see Chol (1983).
5. It is disturbingly obvious in the 1990s that the same beliefs are again strongly held and increasingly pervasive in Europe, the United States, Canada, and Australia.
6. The United States provided over two-thirds of the funds to operate IRO.
7. The UNHCR's international protection to refugees is not conditional upon prior governmental consent. In the protection role, the UNHCR seeks to ensure that no one is forcibly returned to a country where he or she may have reason to fear persecution and, secondly, that persons claiming to be refugees are identified as such and granted legal status in the asylum country. See, for example, Kalumiya (1981).
8. The primary, and by now classic, durable solutions that UNHCR seeks to promote are, in order of preference: voluntary repatriation; local integration in the country of first asylum; resettlement in a third country.
9. Loescher notes that during this time the Western governments used refugee assistance as part of their foreign policies.
10. The top five contributors to the UNHCR programmes in 1994 in absolute terms were the United States, the European Community, Japan, Sweden, and the United Kingdom. Table 9.2 lists the major contributors in 1994.
11. It was only with the passing of the Refugee Act of 1980 that the explicit references to preference being given to persons fleeing communism were removed from the operational US refugee definition. Ironically, since that time the percentage of refugees fleeing "communist countries" admitted for resettlement to the United States has actually increased!
12. As of March 1989 the only East European countries to have signed the 1967 Protocol Relating to the Status of Refugees were Hungary and Yugoslavia.
13. The Statute of the UNHCR states that the UNHCR "shall assume the function of providing international protection ... to refugees who fall within the scope of the present Statute and of seeking permanent solutions for the problem of refugees by assisting Governments and, *subject to the approval of the Governments concerned*, private organizations to facilitate the voluntary repatriation of such refugees, or their assimilation within new national communities" (emphasis added).
14. The Convention covered almost all aspects understood to relate to refugees at that time. It is made up of 46 articles on items such as refugee rights and juridical status, including such basic issues as freedom of movement, travel documents and identity papers, protection from deportation, freedom of religion, and a right to an education. The Convention also imposes obligations on the contracting states for the welfare of refugees.

15. A list of countries that have ratified the 1951 Convention and/or the 1967 Protocol is found in the appendix to this chapter.
16. This issue has been debated both within and outside of the UNHCR for many years. Since the early 1970s, the Economic and Social Council and the General Assembly of the United Nations have in various ways instructed the High Commissioner for Refugees to provide assistance to "displaced persons." See Jaeger (1993) for a more complete discussion, and refer to UN documents, ECOSOC Resolution 1705 (LIII) of 27 July 1972, ECOSOC Resolution 2011 (LXI) of 2 August 1976; also *Protection of Persons of Concern to UNHCR Who Fall Outside the 1951 Convention: A Discussion Note* (Executive Committee of the High Commissioner's Programme, Sub-Committee of the Whole on International Protection, 18th meeting, EC/1992/SCP/GRP.5, 2 April 1992).
17. The interdiction of Haitian refugees by the US government being a case in point. There is ongoing discussion and criticism of governments' ways of stopping the entrance of asylum-seekers (see, for example, Bramwell 1988; Matas with Simon 1989; Grahl-Madsen 1983).
18. Senator Simpson's statements are unfortunately reinforced by the fact that the US refugee resettlement policy has, from its conception, been politically shaped, i.e. people fleeing communist countries have been granted almost automatic refugee status by the US government irrespective of the validity of specific claims to persecution. Although the United States grants refugee status to large numbers of people, very few of them are those whom the UNHCR has identified as vulnerable persons of "special interest" to the UNHCR.
19. Gov. Wilson directly stated in 1993 that immigrants (refugees and migrants were lumped together) were the cause of California's economic problems. He continued to push for the development and the subsequent passage of Proposition 187.
20. Ferris (1995: 24) notes that, as asylum seekers are being turned away from West European countries, East European countries are being used as a buffer between Western Europe and much of the "third world."
21. Memorandum of Understanding (MOU) originally negotiated in 1993. The MOU does not take family reunion into consideration in determining which country would handle the asylum procedures.
22. Annie Wilson, Lutheran Immigration and Refugee Service, USA, quoted in USCR (1995: 12).
23. Private conversation with Swedish refugee advocates.
24. The highly controversial expulsion of more than 200,000 Rwandans from camps in Tanzania in which "the UNHCR has departed from its long-standing opposition to forced repatriation of refugees" was described by one UNHCR official as "a bow to the 'new realities'," including "Western governments ... tightening the purse strings" (Booner 1996).
25. Personal communications.
26. Personal communication.
27. It is well to note that significant numbers of refugees repatriate voluntarily outside of organized programmes, often to areas still in conflict.
28. G. J. van Heusen Goedhart, first High Commissioner for Refugees, in a lecture given on the occasion of the award of the Nobel Peace Prize to the UNHCR in 1954.
29. Current human rights laws offer little protection and are not adequate to cover forcible displacements and relocations (see Norwegian Refugee Council and the Refugee Policy Group 1993; *Refugees: Dynamics of Displacement* 1986; Keely 1991).
30. For example, as Loescher reports (1994: 367), 1991 expenditures, because of the emergency operations in northern Iraq and the Horn of Africa, were almost 60 per cent higher than 1990 expenditures.
31. Interviews with donor-country staff and UNHCR staff, Geneva, 1995.
32. Interviews with UNHCR staff, Geneva, 1995.
33. See UNHCR (1994: 8–9) for a discussion by Professor Barry Stein regarding the difficulties in coordinating UNHCR and UNDP activities in repatriation.
34. See Ferris (1993) for an elaboration and discussion of many of the proposed and/or possible solutions.

References

Abella, I., and H. Troper. 1986. *None Is Too Many: Canada and the Jews of Europe, 1933–1948*. Toronto: Lester & Orpen Dennys.

Adelman, H., 1988. "Palestine Refugees, Economic Integration and Durable Solutions." In A. C. Bramwell, ed., *Refugees in the Age of Total War*. London: Unwin Hyman.

––––––– ed. 1991. *Refugee Policy: Canada and the United States*. Toronto: York Lanes Press.

Adelman, H., and C. M. Lanphier, eds. 1990. *Refuge or Asylum: A Choice for Canada*. Toronto: York Lanes Press.

Arendt, H. 1978. *The Jew as Pariah: Jewish Identity and Politics in the Modern Age*. New York: Grove Press.

Booner, R. 1996. "Refugee Agency's Rwanda Policy Is Assailed." *International Herald Tribune*, 23 December, p. 7.

Bramwell, A. C., ed. 1988. *Refugees in the Age of Total War*. London: Unwin Hyman.

Carens, J. H. 1991. "States and Refugees: A Normative Analysis." In H. Adelman, ed., *Refugee Policy: Canada and the United States*. Toronto: York Lanes Press.

Chol, Ayok. 1983. *Refugee Law and Practice in Africa, with Emphasis on the Tanzanian Experience*. University of Dar Es Salaam, Tanzania.

Cohen, R. 1990. *Introducing Refugee Issues in the United Nations Human Rights Agenda*. Washington, D.C.: Refugee Policy Group.

––––––– 1992. *United Nations Human Rights Bodies: An Agenda for Humanitarian Action*. Washington, D.C.: Refugee Policy Group.

Ferris, E. 1993. *Beyond Borders: Refugees, Migrants and Human Rights in the Post-Cold War Era*. Geneva: World Council of Churches Publications.

––––––– 1995. "The Politics of Containment: Asylum in Europe and Its Global Implications." In *World Refugee Survey 1994*. Washington, D.C.: US Committee for Refugees, pp. 20–25.

Frelick, B. 1995. "The Year in Review." In *World Refugee Survey 1994*. Washington, D.C.: US Committee for Refugees, pp. 2–9.

Gilad, L. 1990. *The Northern Route*. St. John's, Newfoundland: Institute of Social and Economic Research.

Grahl-Madsen, A. 1983. "Identifying the World's Refugees." In G. Loescher and J. Scanlan, eds., *The Global Refugee Problem: U.S. and World Response*. Annals of the American Academy of Political and Social Science, vol. 467, May.

Grotius, H. 1625. *De jure belli ac pacis*. Bk. 2, ch. 2, sec. xvi.

Holborn, L. 1956. *The International Refugee Organization. A Specialized Agency of the United Nations: Its History and Work, 1946–1952*. London: Oxford University Press.

––––––– 1975. *Refugees, A Problem of Our Time: The Work of the United Nations High Commissioner for Refugees*, 2 vols. Metuchen, N.J.: Scarecrow Press.

ITRT (*International Thesaurus of Refugee Terminology*). 1989. International Refugee Documentation Network, Martinus Nijhoff Publishers.

Jaeger, G. 1993. "Refugees or Migrants?" In M. Kjaeru, K. Slavensky, and F. Slumpstrup, eds., *NGOs and Refugees: Reflections at the Turn of the Century*. Copenhagen: Danish Centre for Human Rights, pp. 143–167.

Kalumiya, K. 1981. "The Role of UNHCR in Protecting and Assisting Refugees." *Horn of Africa*, vol. 5, no. 1, pp. 19–23.

Keely, C. 1991. "Filling a Critical Gap in the Refugee Protection Regime." In *World Refugee Survey 1991*. Washington, D.C.: US Committee for Refugees.

Kibreab, G. 1985. *African Refugees*. Trenton, N.J.: Africa World Press.

League of Nations. 1921. *Official Journal*, March–April.

Loescher, G. 1994. "The International Refugee Regime: Stretched to the Limit?" *Journal of International Affairs*, vol. 47, no. 2.

Loescher, G., and L. Monahan, eds. 1989. *Refugees and International Relations*. New York: Oxford University Press.

Loescher, G., and J. Scanlan. 1986. *Calculated Kindness: Refugees and America's Half-Open Door, 1945 to the Present*. New York: Free Press.

Marrus, M. R. 1985. *The Unwanted: European Refugees in the Twentieth Century*. New York: Oxford University Press.

————— 1988. "Introduction." In A. C. Bramwell, ed., *Refugees in the Age of Total War*. London: Unwin Hyman.

Martin, D. 1991. "The Refugee Concept: On Definitions, Politics, and the Careful Use of a Scarce Resource." In H. Adelman, ed., *Refugee Policy: Canada and the United States*. Toronto: York Lanes Press.

Matas, D., with I. Simon. 1989. *Closing the Doors: The Failure of Refugee Protection*. Toronto: Summerhill Press.

Mayotte, J. 1992. *Disposable People? The Plight of Refugees*. Maryknoll, N.Y.: Orbis Books.

Morris, B. 1988. "The Initial Absorption of the Palestinian Refugees in the Arab Host Countries, 1948–1949." In A. C. Bramwell, ed., *Refugees in the Age of Total War*. London: Unwin Hyman.

Moussa, H. 1993. *Storm & Sanctuary: The Journey of Ethiopian and Eritrean Women Refugees*. Dundas, Ontario: Artemis Enterprises.

Nichols, B. 1988. *The Uneasy Alliance: Religion, Refugee Work and US Foreign Policy*. New York: Oxford University Press.

Normark, S. 1994. "Grass-Roots Peace Building: Lessons from the Horn of Africa." *Conflicts, Peacemaking and Development: Research and Action*. Conference Report. Uppsala: Life & Peace Institute.

Norwegian Refugee Council and the Refugee Policy Group. 1993. *Human Rights Protection for Internally Displaced Persons*. Washington, D.C.: Refugee Policy Group.

Refugees: Dynamics of Displacement. 1986. A Report for the Independent Commission on International Humanitarian Issues. London: Zed Books.

Simpson, J. H. 1939. *The Refugee Question*. London: Oxford University Press.

Skran, C. Forthcoming. *The International Refugee Regime and the Refugee Problem in Interwar Europe*. Oxford: Oxford University Press.

Stein, B. 1981. The Refugee Experience: Defining the Parameters of a Field of Study." *International Migration Review*, vol. 15, nos. 1–2: 321–330.

Swedish Ministry of Culture. 1994. *Immigrant and Refugee Policy*. Stockholm.

UNHCR (UN High Commissioner for Refugees). 1991. *An Instrument of Peace: For Forty Years, UNHCR Alongside Refugees*. Italy: UNHCR.

————— 1992. "Bridging the Gap Between Returnee Aid and Development." UNHCR Executive Committee.

————— 1993. *The State of the World's Refugees 1993: The Challenge of Protection*. New York: Penguin Books.

311

——— 1994. "Returnee Aid and Development." Eval/Rad/15, UNHCR Central Evaluation Section, May.

——— 1995. *The State of the World's Refugees: In Search of Solutions.* Oxford: Oxford University Press.

UNHCR Briefing Note. 1995. Informal Meeting of the Executive Committee of the High Commissioner's Programme, Geneva, 17 January.

USCR (US Committee for Refugees). 1995. "U.S. Refugee Resettlement Program Debated at Senate Hearing." *Refugee Reports*, vol. XVI, no. 3, 31 March.

——— 1996. *World Refugee Survey 1996: An Annual Assessment of Conditions Affecting Refugees, Asylum Seekers, and Internally Displaced Peoples.* Washington, D.C.: Immigration and Refugee Services of America.

Vattel, E. de 1758. *Le droit des gens ou principes de la loi naturelle; appliqués à la conduite et aux affaires des Nations et des Souverains* [Washington, D.C.: Carnegie Institution, 1916], 3: 92, sec. 231.

Wasserstein, B. 1979. *Britain and the Jews of Europe, 1939–1945.* New York: Oxford University Press.

Wyman, D. 1968. *Paper Walls: America and the Refugee Crisis, 1938–1941.* Amherst, Mass.: University of Massachusetts Press.

——— 1985. *The Abandonment of the Jews: America and the Holocaust, 1941–1945.* New York: Pantheon Books.

Zucker, N., and N. F. Zucker. 1987. *The Guarded Gate: The Reality of American Refugee Policy.* San Diego: Harcourt Brace Jovanovich.

Part III
Sharing and protecting the commons

10

Ecological security and the United Nations system

Patricia M. Mische and Mauricio Andres Ribeiro

1. Introduction

Ecology is a new scientific and cultural force that is altering concepts of security and challenging political, economic, and social systems, including the United Nations system. The United Nations Charter made no provision for ecological security. Its framers never anticipated that environmental issues would accelerate in scale and complexity until they constituted global threats. Once environmental threats did erupt on the global scene, many UN agencies and programmes responded from their area of competence. In turn, ecological concerns have altered discourse, policies, programmes, and structures within the UN system, and are affecting concepts of security at the core of the United Nations' purpose.

The UN system's response to environmental threats shows that it is a living organism with the capacity to learn, adapt, and act on unforeseen problems. It also shows the potential of scientific, civic, and non-governmental organizations (NGOs), as well as governments, to affect the UN agenda and collaborate in solving global problems. But whether UN responses to date have been effective enough or whether the United Nations can develop the capacities and structures needed to respond effectively to the added environmental strains anticipated in the coming century is open to question. Efforts to develop effective global structures for ecological security are likely to continue well into the twenty-first century, although the outcomes that can be expected are far from certain.

This chapter will first outline and evaluate some of the history, programmes, and emerging trends and challenges in UN environmental activities in the context of three time-periods: 1945–1965, environment as a marginal UN concern; 1966–1991, integrating environmental concerns into the UN system; and 1992–1997, Rio: the Earth Summit and beyond. We will then consider some possible futures, and suggest areas where peace research could make a significant contribution to, and benefit from, UN environmental efforts.

2. Environment as a marginal UN concern (1945–1965)

The United Nations' environmental activities during its first 20 years – few in number, limited in scope, and under the aegis of only a few specialized agencies – fell in two categories: (1) scientific research and exchange; and (2) the regulation of a few pollutants in certain environments. However, some of these activities provided the foundations for later UN environmental work.

The specialized agencies

The mandates of the World Meteorological Organization (WMO) and the International Maritime Organization (IMO) were more relevant to environmental concerns than most other UN-related bodies in this period. The WMO was established in 1950 to standardize and improve world meteorological activities and to encourage "an efficient exchange of meteorological information between countries in the aid of human activities."[1] Today, WMO provides authoritative scientific information on atmospheric-environment and climate-change issues and facilitates worldwide cooperation in geophysical observations. The IMO was established in 1958 to facilitate cooperation between governments on matters related to international shipping, including the preparation of conventions and agreements setting standards of maritime safety, navigational efficiency, and prevention of marine pollution.[2] Once operational, the IMO was given responsibility for implementing the previously adopted (1954) Convention for the Prevention of Pollution of the Sea by Oil. The IMO also became a vehicle for subsequent international treaties and policy development related to vessel-source pollution (UNDPI 1995).

Pollutants in the work environment and in food and consumer products were addressed by a few UN agencies in this period, including the International Labour Organization (ILO), the World Health Organization (WHO), the Food and Agriculture Organization (FAO), and the UN Human Rights Commission. Although the right to a healthy environment has not yet been made explicit in international human rights law (it was not included in the 1948 Universal Declaration of Human Rights, or in the other human rights agreements that followed), a healthy environment is a prerequisite for realizing many established human rights, including the right to health, the right to food, and the right to safe and healthy working conditions (UN Commission on Human Rights 1994). For example, the International Covenant on Economic, Social and Cultural Rights[3] urges governments to promote "the improvement of all aspects of environmental and industrial hygiene" (Art. 12(b)) as a step toward fulfilling the right to the "highest attainable standards of physical and mental health." Of course, the ILO, which was established in 1919 to promote social justice for working people everywhere, had been concerned about pollutants in the work environment before this.

WHO, which came into being in 1948,[4] approached the issue of pollutants from the viewpoint of consumer protection and human health. As early as 1953, through its World Health Assembly, WHO expressed concern about the use of various chemical substances in the food industry (Manley 1979). WHO and FAO jointly convened a conference on food additives in 1955, and in 1961 drafted principles governing consumer safety with regard to pesticide residue (Manley 1979). FAO, the largest agency within the UN system, was founded in 1945 to raise nutrition levels and end hunger by helping rural populations improve the production, processing, marketing, and distribution of food and agricultural products from farms, fisheries, and forests. In its early years FAO tended to promote higher agricultural yields by what would now be considered excessive use of pesticides and chemical fertilizers. However, the agency has since adjusted its standards to balance yield targets with long-range, environmental impact considerations. The FAO now promotes the conservation and sustainable management and use of soil, forest, and water resources, and the rational uses of fertilizers and pesticides (UNDPI 1992: 229–230).

UN development programmes and environmental harm

Environmental harm also resulted from other UN-related development programmes. In this formational period, numerous functional agencies and programmes were established to advance the UN Charter goal of "social progress and better standards of life." At the time, higher GNP scores and more favourable balances of trade and payments were the main measures of "economic progress." To achieve higher scores, countries were urged to exploit and export their natural resources. Forests were cut down at unprecedented rates, wildlife was diminished or disappeared, and agricultural production was stepped up, often through monocropping and overgrazing that depleted soils, caused desertification, and diminished or contaminated water, and ultimately led to economic decline. In some countries, huge hydroelectric dams were constructed to meet increased energy needs, displacing local peoples, destroying agricultural lands, and unbalancing whole ecosystems.

Governments did not internalize these environmental costs in their national accounts, so the true costs of development were not debited, and there was a distorted image of development gains and of the economic health of many nations. It would take several decades before the environmental harm became evident and UN agencies and programmes began to encourage environmental impact assessments for new development projects. However, the environmental costs of most development programmes are still not internalized in national accounting systems. A recent decade-long process undertaken by the International Monetary Fund (IMF) to have all countries harmonize their national accounting systems neither required nor encouraged inclusion of environmental costs. It may be many more years before the system is revised again to include the value of environmental capital (and conversely the cost of its loss) as part of the true picture of national and world economic health.

Nuclear issues and the environment

The environmental issue that caused most concern in this period was radioactive pollution from nuclear weapons testing. Between 1945 and 1991 some 1,900 nuclear bombs were exploded, 518 of them in the atmosphere, sending radioactive fallout around the earth (Bertell 1991; CDI 1989). The great majority, and most environmentally devastating, of these tests were done between 1952 and 1962. According to data from the UN Scientific Committee on the Effects of Atomic Radiation, by 1962 a total of 550 megatons of nuclear fission and fusion products had been released into the earth's biosphere (Bertell 1991). In the face of mounting public concern and outcries, a number of treaties were negotiated with measures aimed at controlling or prohibiting nuclear explosions in certain environments or global commons. Two in this period were especially important because of the precedent they set: the 1961 Antarctic Treaty, and the 1963 Treaty Banning Nuclear Weapons Tests in the Atmosphere, Outer Space, and Under Water. Unfortunately, the latter was only a partial test ban. It did not ban underground tests, which continued unabated. Moreover, although signed by the United States, the United Kingdom, and the Soviet Union, other countries continued to test in the atmosphere, including France and China. A comprehensive nuclear test ban remains an urgent need.

The Antarctic Treaty was more than an arms control treaty, having been inspired in part by scientists from different countries who wanted to conduct cooperative research in Antarctica unhindered by political and military obstacles. The treaty, which was initiated by US President Eisenhower in 1958, makes Antarctica the world's largest de facto nature reserve as well as a global commons. It prohibits any one nation from exploiting living Antarctic resources and bans activities that would cause deterioration of those resources. Unfortunately, the agreement did not include the surrounding oceans, where blue whales and other marine life were being decimated, or the air or ozone layer above it, where future threats to the Antarctic and global environment would emerge.

Although these two treaties were negotiated outside the United Nations, they provided a model for some later treaties that the United Nations facilitated, including the 1967 Outer Space Treaty, the 1967 Treaty Prohibiting Nuclear Weapons in Latin America, the 1970 Non-Proliferation Treaty (NPT),[5] and the 1972 Treaty Prohibiting the Emplacement of Nuclear Weapons and Other Weapons of Mass Destruction on the Seabed and Ocean Floor. Other, non-nuclear, disarmament agreements facilitated later by the United Nations also have environmental benefits, including the 1975 Biological Weapons Convention, the 1980 Convention Prohibiting Military or Other Hostile Use of Environmental Modification Techniques (the first disarmament agreement for which the UN Secretary-General is depository), and the United Nations' continuing efforts to secure a treaty banning chemical weapons.

The International Atomic Energy Agency (IAEA) was created in 1957 to help prevent the proliferation of nuclear weapons through the diversion of nuclear materials for military purposes and to "accelerate and enlarge the contribution of atomic energy to peace, health and prosperity throughout the world."[6] Its activities include promoting nuclear safety standards and providing technical assistance for dealing with nuclear materials. The IAEA's safeguards system is based primarily on nuclear material accountability verified by IAEA inspectors. Various types of safeguard agreements have been concluded with the IAEA since its founding. Those in connection with the Treaty on the Non-Proliferation of Nuclear Weapons (NPT), the Treaty Prohibiting Nuclear Weapons in Latin America, and the Treaty of Rarotonga all require non-nuclear weapons states to submit their entire nuclear-fuel cycles to IAEA safeguards. By 1991 there were 180 safeguard agreements in effect with 105 states (UNDPI 1992: 224–226; UNDPI 1986: 401–403).

Although these activities have implications for environmental protection and human health as well as worker safety and military security, the IAEA has often come under fire from environmentalists, health advocates, and arms control advocates for inadequacies in its measures and, more fundamentally, for its underlying assumptions – i.e. that the use of nuclear power should be promoted, and that the radioactive materials and waste from nuclear power can be made environmentally safe or effectively protected against military uses. From an environmental point of view, there is a built-in contradiction – i.e. being entrusted to *protect* the public from a technology it is mandated to *promote*.

3. Integrating environmental concerns into the UN system and agenda (1966–1991)

Beginning in the late 1960s and early 1970s, the UN system gradually developed more intentional, comprehensive, and coordinated responses to environmental threats, spurred by new scientific understandings of the earth as a total system and by increasing public awareness of global environmental threats. Legal instruments for addressing environmental issues multiplied both within and between countries. More than 100 multilateral environmental treaties were negotiated – many under UN auspices. NGOs and people's movements played a major role in these developments, increasingly pushing at the same time for democratization of the United Nations and a greater voice in global policy development.

The United Nations created some new structures and programmes to address environmental issues, but its main strategy was to infuse and integrate environmental concerns into existing structures and programmes. Thus the UN framework for addressing environmental concerns remained highly decentralized. The governing bodies of each UN agency or programme decided whether, when, and how to link environmental concerns to their particular mandates, priorities, and activities. Meanwhile, instead of coordinating environmental concerns throughout the UN system, as had been envisioned, UNEP's Governing Council was focused more on UNEP itself. By the late 1980s, it was apparent that the responses of the various UN agencies often overlapped, were sometimes repetitive or competitive, and occasionally, as in the earlier period, even contradicted or obstructed true environmental protection. Near the end of the period, efforts were intensified for greater coordination and efficiency in environmental efforts through the UN system.

The period was framed by preparations for and outcomes of two world conferences: the 1972 UN Conference on the Human Environment (Stockholm), and the 1992 UN Conference on Environment and Development (UNCED, or Earth Summit, in Rio de Janeiro). At the Stockholm Conference, participating governments defined the direction of UN environmental work for the next 20 years and proposed what came to be the United Nations Environment Programme (UNEP) under the General Assembly to catalyse and coordinate environmental activities within the UN system and to help develop a system-wide response to environmental concerns. The Rio Conference built upon Stockholm, mapped a plan of action into the twenty-first century (United Nations 1992), proposed the Commission on Sustainable Development (CSD) under ECOSOC to facilitate and monitor its implementation, and facilitated intergovernmental agreements on climate change, biodiversity, forest principles, and the Rio Declaration.

These developments were affected greatly by scientific, technological, and environmental ferment in the larger world. This was a rich period for scientific research that advanced more holistic views of the earth and of environmental issues, and more holistic paradigms and strategies for problem-solving. The following are some trends and events that helped catalyse and shape ecological thinking inside and outside the United Nations at the time.

The rise of environmental movements

At first, few political leaders saw or responded to these global environmental threats. With a vacuum in constituted leadership, non-constituted leaders came forward from the ranks of ordinary citizens. As early as the seventeenth century, some forest conservation measures had been introduced in England and France after increased demand for wood caused the disappearance of many forests. And, beginning in the nineteenth century, conservation and wilderness preservation movements began growing in the United States, Australia, South Africa, and some other countries, and succeeded in pushing governments to adopt conservation measures, establish national parks, and preserve wilderness areas. But such national conservation measures were not sufficient to redress the new, global environmental threats that were emerging.

In contrast to these earlier environmental movements, which had focused on the natural environment alone, the new environmentalism of the late twentieth century focused on interrelations between nature and human beings. The initial concern and target of many of the new movements was pollution. Rachel Carson was among the first to sound a wake-up call in her 1962 book, *Silent Spring*, alarming the public with her account of the devastating effects of chemical pesticides. Her diagnosis was global: she believed that growing pollution would ultimately lead to the pollution of the total environment of humankind. Her prescription was also global: the strict control, drastic reduction, and ultimate elimination of the use of chemical pesticides worldwide. Her work was translated into many languages and distributed worldwide, sparking environmental movements in many countries.

Some citizen movements were spurred by disasters that threatened their health and livelihood. Sulphur dioxide in the air had led to many deaths in London during the 1950s. Oil spills and ocean dumping destroyed beaches and contaminated fish. Nuclear-weapons testing had released radioactive pollutants into air, water, and soil, affecting the food chain and ultimately mothers' breast milk and children's bones and teeth. Chemical dumping in rivers and streams had killed fish and contaminated the food and drinking water of people downstream and across borders. In Japan, a powerful grass-roots environmental movement arose among the victims of mercury and cadmium poisoning and other industrially induced diseases. The government subsequently legislated some of the strongest anti-pollution requirements in the world, requiring industries not only to clean up their act, but also to compensate victims and pay into a national fund to cover the medical costs of any future victims. By the late 1960s, environmental movements in some other industrialized countries had also developed sufficient political force to get tougher anti-pollution and environmental protection standards enacted at the national level.

Response of the United Nations

In 1972, the Global Conference on the Human Environment was held in Stockholm, marking the beginning of concerted United Nations programmes for the environment. A number of UN steps prepared the way to Stockholm. In 1968, the General Assembly recommended to the UN Secretary-General the collection of data on the condition of the environment in all regions of the world and suggested protective measures (G.A. Res. No. 2398/XXII). The Secretary-General was mindful that the United Nations' twenty-fifth anniversary was only a year away and would turn a public spotlight on the successes and failures of the Organization, including the divisiveness between member states that often blocked effective UN action. He hoped that the threat of planetary pollution would unify member states in a way that a quarter-century of UN peace and economic efforts had not. In the introduction to his 1969 report, *Man and His Environment* (United Nations 1969), U Thant stressed that a common global foe confronted all humanity, requiring a new planetary politics and concerted global action.

In response to the U Thant report, the General Assembly requested that the United Nations Educational, Scientific, and Cultural Organization (UNESCO) organize regional symposia (held between 1969 and 1971 in Asia, Africa, Latin America, the Middle East, and Europe), and prepare a world conference on the environment (the 1972 Stockholm Conference). The Conference was preceded by a report, in 10 languages, written by more than 100 scholars, entitled "Only One World" (see Osmanczyk 1985).

The Stockholm Conference on the Human Environment

The UN Conference on the Human Environment was held 5–16 June 1972, with the purpose of encouraging governments and international organizations to take action on the protection of the environment.

Two heads of state, delegations from 113 countries, and representatives from 250 non-governmental organizations and UN specialized agencies attended the Conference in Stockholm. The Conference adopted by acclamation a Declaration with 7 proclamations and 26 principles of environmental protection, subject to observations and reservations by a number of governments. It also adopted a Plan of Action, with 109 recommendations for environmental action at the international level. And it set a framework for linking environment and development that would later be expanded and summed up in the phrase "sustainable development."

However, despite U Thant's hopes that environmental threats would unite countries, the Stockholm Conference stumbled on the same East/West and North/South fault lines that beset other UN deliberations. When the German Democratic Republic's right to participate was not recognized, the Warsaw Pact states boycotted the Conference in a show of solidarity. With the no show of the Warsaw Pact members, the greatest differences were between the wealthier, industrialized countries of the North and the poorer, developing countries of the South. These differences were to dominate UN approaches to environmental issues for the next two decades and beyond.

In Stockholm, many developing countries made it clear that they did not wish to adopt the same standards of environmental protection as some industrialized countries of the North. They argued for differential responsibilities, asserting that the causes of environmental problems differed according to levels of development, and so should the remedies. Accordingly, the Stockholm Declaration (1972) included a number of principles aimed at the special needs of developing countries, including calling for "the transfer of substantial quantities of financial and technological assistance ... to the developing countries" to overcome the "environmental deficiencies generated by the conditions of underdevelopment" (Principle 9), and to "preserve and improve the environment" and cover costs of "incorporating environmental safeguards into development planning" (Principle 12).

The Stockholm Declaration provided that, when in doubt, economic development took priority over environmental protection. Such allowances for developing countries, along with the reaffirmation of state sovereignty and the right of states to "exploit their own resources" (Principle 21), left ample rationale and loopholes for states to go their own way on environmental issues if they chose. At any rate, the Stockholm Declaration and Plan of Action were not legally binding agreements. Nevertheless, the Stockholm agreements set a framework for, and took first steps toward, the further development of international environmental law.

Although war and nuclear testing were forbidden subjects at the official conference (Knelman 1991: 438), the Stockholm Declaration urged states to "strive to reach prompt agreement ... on the elimination and complete destruction" of nuclear weapons and other means of mass destruction. A number of states made comments with specific regard to this principle, some wanting it to go further.[7] Ironically, the Stockholm Declaration, agreed to at the height of the Cold War and with the Viet Nam War still under way, went further in linking disarmament and environmental protection than the Rio Conference 20 years later, held when the Cold War was over and no major power was in a shooting war.

Citizen movements at Stockholm

A precedent-setting feature of the Stockholm Conference was the effort of NGOs and citizen movements to affect UN programme development. One of the most influential NGO initiatives was the Dai Dong Independent Conference on the Environment, convened by the International Fellowship of Reconciliation (IFRC) just before the UN Conference.[8] Concerned that the official conference would get derailed in conflicts, IFRC brought together 31 citizen representatives from 24 countries (half from the third world and one each from Poland and Czechoslovakia, which had boycotted the Stockholm meeting) to try to influence the direction of the negotiations. Together they developed the Dai Dong Declaration, which was presented in a plenary session of the UN Conference (Knelman 1991: 435–436).

Outcomes of Stockholm

Despite its limitations, Stockholm provided the most advanced inter-state understanding of environmental problems to date, along with a framework and recommendations for action. Many states established environmental ministries or environmental protection agencies. The number of such agencies grew from 10 in 1970 to 100 by 1982. Governments also developed national action plans (often modelled on the Stockholm Plan of Action); enacted national laws for environmental protection; and launched national campaigns for environmental clean-up, clean air, tree-planting, etc. In addition, NGO and citizen action groups in many countries were encouraged and energized by Stockholm and increased their efforts locally and nationally. Stockholm also provided new international contacts and opportunities for networking and information-sharing between scientific, educational, NGO, and citizen action groups.

Inter-state cooperation related to the environment also increased after Stockholm. Numerous bilateral, multilateral, and regional environmental programmes were developed. For example, the United States and the Soviet Union formed a joint mixed commission on environmental protection, which established 30 subjects for joint research. The European Economic Community (EEC) developed a joint programme for environmental protection for Western Europe, while the Conference on Security and Cooperation in Europe (CSCE) initiated a general European programme of environmental protection. Members of the Council for Mutual Economic Assistance (CMEA) also began joint work on environmental protection in 1972. And, despite their boycott of Stockholm, on 17 August 1972 the Warsaw Pact states submitted to the UN committee on the peaceful utilization of sea and ocean beds outside the jurisdiction of states a "Declaration on principles for the rational exploitation of the living resources of seas and oceans in the interest of all of the nations of the world" (Osmanczyk 1985: 236).

International environmental law began to mushroom after Stockholm. Virtually non-existent before 1921, it grew gradually in the five decades from 1921 to 1971, so that by the time of Stockholm some 50 multilateral treaties had been agreed to regionally or globally.[9] In the two decades following Stockholm – from 1972 through the 1992 Earth Summit in Rio – some 100 new multilateral treaties or agreements were transacted (Mische 1989b; UNEP 1992). UNEP played a catalytic and coordinating role in about one-third of these (UNEP 1992). Despite their limitations, these treaties signified a growing recognition by governments that the environment could not be safeguarded by national means alone.

The "ecologizing" of the UN system was another significant effect. Following Stockholm, some UN agencies initiated environmental projects or strengthened existing ones. UNESCO, for example, launched two international research programmes: "Man and the Environment," and "Man and the Biosphere," and cooperated with UNEP in launching the International Environmental Education Programme (IEEP) and in sponsoring a series of conferences, programmes, and publications to promote environmental education. The ILO drafted and accepted Convention No. 148 (1977) concerning the protection of workers against air pollution, noise, vibrations, and other environmental dangers in the work environment. WHO began producing documents on environmental health in the mid-1970s, and in 1980, together with the ILO and UNEP, launched an International Programme on Chemical Safety (IPCS) to assess the risks posed by toxic chemicals to health and the environment. Between 1979 and 1985, the FAO, the UNDP, UNEP, and the World Bank worked together to develop the Tropical Forest Action Plan (TFAP), and the FAO now coordinates its implementation. These are only a few of many examples of the upsurge in environmental work undertaken by the UN system.

The United Nations Environment Programme

Within the UN system the main outcome of Stockholm was the creation of the United Nations Environment Programme (UNEP). Believing that existing UN programmes and machinery were not adequate for new environmental demands, the Stockholm delegates proposed establishing permanent institutional and financial arrangements for protecting and enhancing the environment (UNEP 1992). Accordingly, the UN General Assembly established four new entities that, although not so named in the Resolution, became known as UNEP. These included: (1) a Governing Council composed of 58 countries elected by the GA for three-year terms, which serve as the United Nations' intergovernmental organ for the environment; (2) a secretariat, in Nairobi, to provide a focal point for coordination of environmental action within the UN system; (3) a voluntary Environment Fund, to help in the financing of environmental initiatives; and (4) an Environmental Coordination Board (ECB) to ensure coordination and cooperation among all UN bodies involved in environmental programmes.

Many people assume that UNEP has more power and resources than it actually has. UNEP is not a UN organ or agency, but a *programme*. Its function is "to catalyze, coordinate, and stimulate action within the UN system, not to execute or to finance it" (UNEP 1992: 7–8). It also has the power to convene conferences and meetings and to educate. UNEP pursues its goals with many different partners, primarily within the UN system, but also outside it, with intergovernmental organizations and also non-governmental organizations, the scientific community, and research institutes in many countries. Thus, although UNEP's powers and finances are limited, its catalytic, coordinating, and collaborative relationships allow it to do more than if it were the sole UN agency with responsibility for global environmental protection.

UNEP's early priorities included human settlements, habitat, health, and well-being; land, water, and desertification; oceans; the conservation of nature, wildlife, and genetic resources; and energy. For 1996/97 the Governing Council focused upon five areas, some previously underdeveloped: sustainable management and use of natural resources; sustainable production and consumption; linkages between environment and human health; globalization and the environment (including trade, environmental economics, and environmental law); and global and regional servicing and support (including environment assessment, support to regional and subregional cooperation, education and outreach, and a coordinated system for international information exchange).

UNEP also administers the implementation of a number of environmental treaties, including the Conventions on Biodiversity, International Trade in Endangered Species (CITES), Desertification, Ozone Protection, and Transboundary Movements of Hazardous Waste. To support and build environmental protection capacities, UNEP has sponsored public awareness programmes, environmental education and training, and a Clearing House to help countries formulate priority programmes and identify financial and other resources. UNEP is sometimes a broker, matching potential donors with identified projects, and linking developing countries with donors (UNEP 1992).

By its twentieth anniversary in 1992, UNEP's track record included a long list of environmental projects, multilateral agreements, publications, conferences, and research and educational programmes developed in collaboration with various UN agencies, national governments, intergovernmental organizations, and NGOs.[10] In addition, UNEP continuously promoted the integration of environmental protection in development planning. The need to link environment and development was increasingly stressed throughout the UN system and was eventually summed up under the catch phrase "sustainable development." Two 1987 reports elaborated on the relationships between environmental degradation and poverty, outlined goals for environmentally sustainable development, and proposed specific action to achieve them: *Our Common Future*, by the World Commission on

Environment and Development (chaired by Norway's Prime Minister, Gro Harlem Brundltand), and *Environmental Perspectives to the Year 2000 and Beyond* (UNEP 1988). These reports became major stepping stones to the 1992 UN Conference on Environment and Development in Rio.

Such UN efforts helped turn back some environmental threats and slow the growth of others. But, 20 years after Stockholm, some environmental problems appeared to be getting worse (see UNEP 1989b, 1993; and the annual Worldwatch Institute's *State of the World* Reports). Clearly, for some environmental threats the measures undertaken were too little, too late, too compromised, or too ignored.

4. Rio: The Earth Summit and beyond (1992–1997)

It was in this context that in June 1992, on the twentieth anniversary of Stockholm, the UN Conference on Environment and Development (UNCED) was convened in Rio de Janeiro. It was the first global conference after the end of the Cold War and it tested whether a new politics could be forged around a common global future. It was also the largest and most universally attended conference in UN history to that date, with 178 countries represented in the negotiations and 118 heads of state or government participating in the Earth Summit held in conjunction with the Conference. More than 7,000 delegates were accredited as members of governmental delegations, representatives of intergovernmental organizations, official observers, or advisers. The press and media turned out in the thousands. Thousands of NGOs were also accredited to the official conference, with a record number of them having members on, or advisers to, national delegations or intergovernmental organizations. In addition to the NGOs at the official intergovernmental meeting, tens of thousands more took part in the parallel Global Forum and other NGO programmes. Unlike at Stockholm, where most of the NGOs were from developed countries, in Rio record numbers came from the developing world.

The road to Rio had involved more than two years of intensive preparations, including treaty negotiations, preparatory conferences in every world region, many sectoral conferences, national reports, and expert contributions from many UN agencies and programmes and from NGOs. The results, however, were mixed, with some breakthroughs and some disappointments. An original goal to produce an Earth Charter to complement the UN Charter with a comprehensive framework of principles for global ecological security was defeated in the preparatory meetings. Instead, governments produced a watered-down, non-binding *Declaration on Environment and Development* (the Rio Declaration). Its 27 principles largely echo the Stockholm Declaration. A non-legally binding *Statement of Forest Principles* was agreed to at the last minute, when efforts for a legally binding agreement had failed and it seemed the Conference might end with nothing to show on one of the most urgent environmental issues of the day.

Agenda 21

Agenda 21, a programme of action for sustainable development into the twenty-first century, was a major outcome of UNCED. It includes 40 chapters with some 2,000 specific objectives and recommendations that countries are encouraged to implement as aspects of the transition to sustainable development. These are organized in four main categories: Social and Economic Dimensions, Conservation and Management of Resources for Development, Strengthening the Role of Major Groups, and Means of Implementation. As at Stockholm, the plan includes some joint but differentiated responsibilities. The biggest consumer countries are urged to curb their consumption levels, the most populated to slow their population growth, and the richest to increase their financial and technological assistance to the poorest in ways that facilitate their transition to environmentally sustainable development. The estimated cost of achieving the programme was US$660 billion. UNCED also recommended the creation of a Commission on Sustainable Development (CSD), subsequently approved by the General Assembly and now operational under ECOSOC, to facilitate and monitor the implementation of *Agenda 21*. Finally, two conventions were opened for signature in Rio: the Framework Convention on Climate Change, aimed at the stabilization of greenhouse gas concentrations, and the Convention on Biodiversity, aimed at the conservation of biological diversity, the sustainable use of genetic resources, and the equitable distribution of the benefits derived from them.

With the Cold War over, the old bloc voting patterns no longer held, and some new alignments emerged around perceived economic and environmental self-interest. For example, timber-exporting countries of the South, led by Malaysia, resisted efforts by the North to focus on the conservation of tropical rain forests alone. In addition to concerns about sovereignty over their resources, they argued that countries of the North that had already exploited and exhausted their own original forests were in no position to demand that countries of the South should not exploit theirs, especially in order to provide a carbon sink for the unchecked emission of greenhouse gases by the North. Furthermore, developing countries should be compensated for their economic loss and assisted in covering the costs of protecting the forests. For the Climate Convention, some of the oil-producing countries aligned with the United States against low-lying and island countries. The latter were concerned that a rise in ocean waters from global warming could devastate or totally wipe out their countries and wanted stricter regulation of greenhouse gas emissions. Oil-producing countries actively opposed measures that would lower consumption and demand for their principal export.

In June 1997, the 19th UN General Assembly Special Session – UNGASS – reviewed the implementation of *Agenda 21*, with the objective of accelerating its implementation in a comprehensive manner. With 53 heads of state participating, the Session produced a Statement of Commitment, of 6 paragraphs, and a programme for the further implementation of *Agenda 21*, of 15 paragraphs. UNGASS acknowledged positive results in components of sustainable development, such as lower fertility and population growth, and recognized progress in institutional development, international consensus, public participation, and private sector actions. But it was also noted that operationalization of sustainable development remains insufficient. And it was recognized that, in the five years since UNCED, consumption and production patterns remained unsustainably high, income inequalities had increased among and within states, and there had been continued deterioration in the state of the global environment.

UNGASS asserted that it is crucial that economic policies be integrated with environmental and social policies, and that peace and political stability are components of sustainable development. Also noted were that trade rules must be compatible with effective environmental policies and the need for corporate responsibility and monitoring of corporate activities. Among the main challenges to implementation of *Agenda 21* are the need for financial resources, the transfer of environmentally sound technologies to developing countries, and the setting of targets and timetables for greenhouse gas emissions reduction.

Five years after Rio, UNGASS stressed the need to change unsustainable and wasteful patterns of consumption and production, to implement environmental ethics, and to reduce overall poverty and inequalities. It recognized the need to move from words to deeds, owing to the trend of environmental deterioration and natural resource depletion, and stressed the key role of NGOs in this process. The next review of the process will take place in 2002, when priority issues are expected to include fresh water, energy, transport, forests, oceans, fishstock, atmosphere, and desertification.

The UN system

Within the UN system, the implementation of *Agenda 21* has been moving forward, despite UN restructuring and severe budget and staff cut-backs in many programmes and agencies. The concept of "sustainable development" is now accepted throughout the UN system as the unifying principle and guiding framework. Linkages between environment and development gave UNEP more partners in the UN system, and helped improve cooperation between some UN bodies that were not sure before how their mandates for development related to environmental work.

Inter-agency coordination for environment and development has been improving. Although there is still some overlap in the work of some of the UN programmes and agencies, progress has been made in delineating different tasks for the different UN bodies and improving coordination. The new Commission on Sustainable Development (CSD) has the responsibility to receive country reports and monitor progress on the implementation of *Agenda 21*. UNEP continues to have major technical, research, educational, and coordinating responsibilities along the lines mandated by Stockholm and its Governing Council (see above). The UNDP has a crucial role in the follow-up to UNCED, including use of its network of field offices for coordinating field activities related to sustainable development, and serving as the lead agency in capacity-building at local, national, and regional levels.

In addition, the specialized agencies and other UN-related organizations are implementing *Agenda 21* in their areas of competence. The FAO, which sees environmental and natural resource degradation as a constraint to achieving food security, now has a very large Sustainable Development department. Environmental considerations were widely reflected in the Action Plan produced at the 1996 World Food Summit in Rome. WHO has been linking health issues to sustainable development. The World Bank began integrating environmental concerns into a wide range of its activities before Rio, partly in response to public criticism of the negative environmental impact of some of the development projects it funded, and partly in response to mounting evidence that environmental degradation undermined the Bank's goal to reduce poverty. It also administers the Global Environment Facility (GEF), established in 1990 as a joint project with UNEP and UNDP to assist developing countries address four global environmental concerns: global warming, biodiversity, ozone depletion, and international waters.

Regional and subregional bodies related to the UN system – including regional commissions, regional development banks, and regional and technical cooperation organizations – are working in cooperation with UNEP and UNDP in the implementation of *Agenda 21*, particularly to strengthen national and regional capacities for sustainable development. The UNCED also became a building block for major UN conferences that followed, including Population and Development (Cairo, 1994), the Social Summit (Copenhagen, 1995), the Conference on Women (Beijing, 1995), and Habitat II (Istanbul, 1996). The concept of sustainable development at the core of the UNCED process and *Agenda 21* was given a central place in the programmes and action plans adopted at these conferences, showing a firm commitment to the concept within the UN system.

The states

Of course, the major responsibility for implementing the Rio Plan of Action lies with the governments of states. Here there is both good news and bad news. Three years after Rio, UNCED's Secretary General, Maurice Strong (1995), evaluated that Rio's fundamental purpose – to get major changes in economic life in a way that protected the life of the environment – had not been reached. At Rio, the developing countries had accepted the environmental challenge, but it was conditioned on industrial countries providing the means. In fact, aid to developing countries is subsiding, not increasing. The good news is that, despite this setback, many developing countries are not waiting for help from the rich countries, but are moving ahead on their own or getting help from the UNDP or the GEF. Apparently, Rio helped catalyse a greater sense of ownership in environmental concerns among developing countries.

An Earth Summit Watch report (ESW 1996) also gives mixed reviews. In the first year after Rio, 70 of the 178 participating states

333

designated a governmental institution to integrate sustainable development concepts into national law and policy. Within the next two years, there were another 33, bringing the total to 103. However, after that the momentum slowed; only four more governments identified national sustainable development institutions in 1995 and 1996. Of those that took these initial steps, it was not clear how many actually were implementing their plans. At the 1996 session of the CSD, 86 countries, most from the developing world, did not bother to report on their efforts to meet *Agenda 21* targets.

In assessing the reasons for this slow-down, ESW suggests that the problem is not primarily due to indifference, callousness, or bad motivations. The UNCED process succeeded in expanding awareness and commitment to the ideals and principles of sustainable development. But even where there is the best motivation, says ESW, "[t]he model of decision-making and policy generation set out in Agenda 21 is simply too expensive and complex to be achieved within ordinary societies. It is extremely difficult for the wealthier nations but virtually impossible for those with limited resources.... [T]he knowledge demanded is simultaneously too intricate and too vast. No one knows enough to make the projected system work" (1996: 3).

When governments rightly or wrongly feel forced to choose between the immediate economic needs of their population and protecting the environment, they usually choose economic growth. For example, criticism of Nicaragua for not adequately protecting its coastal resources against unsustainable agricultural practices drew this response from a Nicaraguan official: "we need the money. We would like to be able to have economic growth and protect the environment, but we can't afford it" (ESW 1996: 6).

Major groups

Among Rio's successes was the unprecedented participation and commitment to follow-up by other major groups. They came from every area of the world in the tens of thousands, including local authorities, indigenous peoples, women, children and youth, educators, health professionals, workers and trade unions, business and industry, farmers, the scientific and technological community, religious groups, artists and entertainers, and social movements. Many held parallel conferences of their own, setting environmental goals for their organizations, professions, or sectors. Such participation was unprecedented in UN history, in both sheer numbers and also the diversity of groups represented, many of which had never before taken much note of, much less taken part in, a UN-related event. The following are only a few examples.

Cities and local authorities

The potential of cities to be major global actors and partners in achieving UN objectives is growing rapidly, along with their demographic, economic, social, cultural, political, and environmental importance. The trend toward increasing urbanization is expected to continue as world population grows and increasing numbers of people flee landlessness, poverty, or strife in the rural areas and seek employment, education, and other opportunities in urban areas. Thus, many city and local authorities bear the burden and stand in the forefront of fighting many environmental problems. *Agenda 21* underscored this in a special chapter (28) devoted to recommendations for "Local Authorities." It proposed that "by 1996 most local authorities in each country should have undertaken a consultative process with their populations and achieved a consensus on a local agenda 21 for the community."

Many mayors and other local authorities were initially enthusiastic about their special role. A year before Rio, they began holding meetings to discuss the responsibility of local governments in protecting the environment and improving life conditions for ever-growing urban populations. The World Urban Forum, convened in Curitiba, Brazil, one week before UNCED, produced a document endorsed by mayors from all over the world. The *Curitiba Commitment* (World Urban Forum 1992) stated that many global environmental problems are generated within cities and, therefore, solutions should also be produced by cities. The mayors agreed to eliminate environmental degradation, reduce energy consumption and pollution, fight poverty, and give priority to children's needs (Ribeiro 1990). The mayors attending UNCED then formalized a proposal for more effective participation by local authorities within the United Nations system. These local authorities wanted more responsibility assigned to the municipal level, including the administration of funds. But the targets of investment set in *Agenda 21* were beneath their expectations and inadequate for the recommended tasks.

The implementation of *Agenda 21* at local levels is difficult to assess. According to one UN source, 1,800 local communities have developed, or are developing, their own Agenda 21s (Brown 1997).

This is indeed a major achievement. However, the precise nature and effectiveness of what is being done is hard to find. ESW (1996) reports that, of 42 governments responding to their 1995/96 survey, only six indicated progress by local governments in creating their own sustainable development plans. In Sweden, a majority of local governments have developed local plans of action to implement *Agenda 21*. Finland, Ghana, Pakistan, Thailand, and Zimbabwe also reported some progress, mostly in the form of pilot projects in a few cities or communities. The absence in other country reports may indicate a weakness in the reporting system and/or ineffective coordination between national and local implementation efforts. But it could also indicate some falling away of commitment by local authorities to *Agenda 21*.

Indigenous peoples

Indigenous peoples from around the world began gathering in Rio two weeks before UNCED. Staying together in tents near the conference site, they shared their experiences, concerns, visions, and hopes. They also prepared a consensus document and statements to present to UNCED delegates, NGOs, and the press, while developing networks and strategies for future collaboration and follow-up.

It was the first time indigenous peoples felt that the UN door was open to them and they came to Rio with high expectations. Once there, however, they met many obstacles from government delegates and the UN administration (Rojas 1994). Only at the very end did they succeed in getting governments to include some of their concerns in *Agenda 21*. Chapter 26 acknowledges the historic and holistic relationship indigenous peoples have had with their environments, and that their traditional values, knowledge, and resource management practices can contribute to sustainable development. It calls on governments and international organizations to strengthen their role in the formulation of national policies and programmes, as well as to commit financial and other resources for education and training to help indigenous peoples develop their capacities to advance sustainable development in their communities.

Among their unmet objectives was that of securing intellectual property rights for indigenous peoples in the Biodiversity Treaty, allowing them to have control of and benefit from their scientific knowledge of the healing and medicinal properties of various species in their environments. Their voice was ignored or lost in the battle between countries of the South that argued for state sovereignty over resources within state borders and those from the North, such as the United States, that pressed for the right to private patents by pharmaceutical and scientific interests that extracted, developed, and marketed them for international use.

In assessing the UNCED experience, Jose Dualok Rojas wrote: "For us the indigenous peoples, UNCED seemed to function like a commercial market.... Indigenous peoples perceive that the Northern and Southern countries are functioning under a common denominator of complete exploitation of the natural resources by the accumulation of riches in the hands of a few" (1994: 50). If this attitude is not changed, Rojas argues, "the earth will not be saved by having yearly earth summits" (1994: 51).

Women

Women were significant actors in the UNCED process and continue to be a major force in implementing *Agenda 21*. They had learned from the United Nations' Decade for Women conferences in Mexico (1975), Copenhagen (1980), and Nairobi (1985) that moving the women's agenda forward required continual vigilance, strategizing, lobbying, and collaboration by women. They were determined that women and their concerns should not be isolated in women's conferences, but be included in all aspects of global policy development.

When it was noticed that women and their concerns were not included in the early stages of the UNCED preparations, the Women's Environment and Development Organization (WEDO) launched the "Women for a Healthy Planet" campaign to inform, energize, and link women around the world. In November 1991, 1,500 women from 83 countries came together to develop *The Women's Action Agenda 21*. This consensus document, representing the views of women from North and South and across class, cultural, and colour lines, analysed the global environment/development crisis from women's perspectives and proposed steps to ensure that women would have an equal say in "Fate of the Earth" decisions. In Rio, a women's caucus met daily at the official UNCED site to strategize and divide lobbying tasks. Daily sessions at the parallel NGO conference (Global Forum), offered panels, speakers, and speak-out sessions, and an opportunity for women from different world regions to meet and plan together.

The women succeeded in getting a special chapter (Chapter 24) on "Global Action for Women in Environment and Development," and inclusion of their concerns in many other chapters of *Agenda 21*. Since Rio, WEDO and other women's networks have been monitoring the implementation of *Agenda 21* in countries around the world, ensuring that women are included in all aspects of UN work for environment and development, ranging from local to global. Building on their Rio experience, they have also been a powerful lobbying force at the world conferences that followed, on population, women, social development, and Habitat II.

NGOs and civil society

More than 100,000 people participated in the activities of the Global Forum, a parallel event organized by NGOs in Rio. NGOs and citizen groups also played an unprecedented role in the official UNCED process, beginning in regional preparatory conferences, through the Rio negotiations, and afterwards in monitoring and aiding the implementation of *Agenda 21*. As a result of their effective lobbying efforts, *Agenda 21* marked a growing change in UN attitudes toward NGOs. The document identifies NGOs – and their global and grass-roots networks – as important "partners" in the transition to sustainable development. It urges governments and international bodies to promote the participation of NGOs in formal procedures for the implementation of *Agenda 21*, and also calls on the UN system and all its related bodies to enhance mechanisms, or where they don't exist to create them, by which NGOs can "contribute to policy design, decision-making, implementation and evaluation." And it presses the UN system and governments to provide NGOs with accurate and timely access to data and information needed for their effective participation in sustainable development (Chapter 27, para. 9).

Many NGOs took these words seriously and are working earnestly on the implementation of *Agenda 21*. They have played an important role in operationalizing the CSD and in assisting its monitoring and implementation tasks.[11] In some other UN bodies, however, NGOs meet more obstacles. Nearly five years after Rio, the rhetoric of partnership is blooming everywhere in the UN system, but the mechanisms and procedures to enhance NGO participation in policy design and decision-making are lagging behind. Many governments and UN civil servants fear that increasing numbers of NGOs at their meetings could overwhelm UN decision-making processes, adding to the time, costs, and complexity of their work. The High Level Working Group on the Strengthening of the United Nations, which submitted its draft recommendations to the General Assembly in July 1996, did not allow NGOs to observe, much less give input, at their deliberations, not even those regarding the future role of NGOs and civil society. In a subsequent hearing, NGOs pressed for greater involvement and rejected the fear of governments that NGOs would overwhelm the UN system, pointing to their past history of disciplined and cooperative work with UN agencies.

Despite these contradictions and shortfalls, the UNCED process had positive benefits for NGOs and for their relationships with the United Nations. Many grew in confidence and commitment and are working collaboratively with each other and with UN agencies, not only to promote the Rio agreements but also on other global issues. They are freer to act across state boundaries for the global common good than are representatives of states. They have areas of expertise needed by the UN system, and are linked with grass-roots people whom governments and UN agencies do not reach. Given the United Nations' current financial and political constraints, it is only a matter of time before practical considerations, as well as the aspirations and demands of NGOs, necessitate new mechanisms that assure them a stronger voice and role.

Citizen treaties

Citizen treaties were among the most innovative initiatives by NGOs before and during UNCED. Unlike petitions in which citizens beg governments to do something for them, citizen treaties represent a new level of maturity in democratization in which citizens treat directly with each other across state boundaries and agree to accept mutual responsibility for their common future. States alone have not caused all the problems, and states alone cannot turn them around. Citizens also have major responsibility to alter their destructive habits and act for the global common good.

The idea for citizen treaties was first proposed in 1988 by W. H. Ferry to the Exploratory Project on the Conditions of Peace (ExPro), a think tank for peace research and action. Patricia Mische, a member of ExPro and co-founder of Global Education Associates (GEA), took the proposal to a 1988 meeting of Soviet and American citizens who were trying to build peace between their countries from the bottom up – by working together on common concerns. The group produced a Soviet–American Citizens' Treaty on Ecological Security (Mische 1989c). Then GEA expanded the project, initiating an international process in 100 countries for input into an *Earth Covenant: A Citizens' Treaty for Common Ecological Security*. The resulting treaty was translated into 20 languages and circulated worldwide for citizen ratification beginning in 1989. Used widely as an educational tool, a catalyst for reflection and action, and a guide for ethics, policy development, and strategies for sustainable development, by the time of Rio it had gathered more than 1 million signatures from people in more than 100 countries (Mische 1989c, 1992). By 1995 the number had grown to more than 2 million.

The Earth Covenant aimed to move the hearts and minds of people to live ecologically responsible lives – i.e. to build environmental law first in the hearts and minds of people. Only then can intergovernmental law be effective. A second goal was to get governments to agree to the same principles in a comprehensive framework for global ecological security, or Earth Charter, to complement the UN Charter. The Earth Covenant was endorsed by UNEP, whose North American regional director called it "the best available framework to use in drafting an Earth Charter."

By the time of Rio, interest in citizen treaties was growing rapidly. One of the Earth Covenant drafters, Maximo Kalaw Jr., an environmental leader from the Philippines, and others such as Peter Padbury, an NGO representative from Canada, resolved to involve Global Forum participants in developing more citizen treaties that would go beyond principles to agreements between citizens from the South and North to undertake common action. The Rio citizen treaties were preceded by the creation of Agenda Ya Wanantchi, a citizens' document emanating from an NGO conference in Paris in December 1991 that stressed issues treated later in the Rio citizen treaties. In all, 46 citizen treaties were drafted and opened for signature at the Global Forum, covering a broad range of issues (Pollard et al. 1992). Areas given significant treatment in the citizen treaties, but not in *Agenda 21*, included: alternative economic models, capital flight and corruption, ethical commitments, militarism, racism, and transnational corporations. Ethics and values were largely ignored in *Agenda 21*, but given great emphasis by NGOs and citizen groups. Virtually all the citizen treaties included ethical, social, and ecological principles, and an entire treaty was devoted to ethics.[12]

Militarism and its effects on environment and development were another area where NGOs and citizen groups ventured but governments feared to tread. As they had in Stockholm, governments in Rio blocked any discussion of the linkages between militarism and environmental degradation, claiming that military issues are a matter for the UN Security Council and thus not under the purview of UNCED. In contrast, the citizen-produced Treaty on Militarism, the Environment and Development identified strong links between militarism and the lack of environmentally sustainable development, and proposed concrete measures for addressing this question.[13] After Rio, Green Cross and other NGOs launched a campaign pushing governments to clean up and restore environments damaged by military toxins. Meanwhile, Greenpeace and other NGOs have continued their initiatives to end nuclear testing and other military activities that cause extensive environmental damage.

In their Treaty Against Racism, NGO and citizen groups pledged to fight "environmental racism, particularly the practice of disproportional dumping of hazardous and toxic waste on Third World nations and communities, and the imposition of this waste as a method of eliminating national debts." They also pledged to "fight developmental racism," including "the imposition of eurocentric models of development," and to "initiate and support sustainable development which empowers communities and is economically cooperative, humanly scaled, environmentally sound, culturally and spiritually sensitive" (Pollard et al. 1992: 149).

Although the idea for an inter-state Earth Charter was defeated in UNCED preparatory meetings, it did not go away. In his closing speech in Rio, UNCED's Secretary-General, Maurice Strong (1992), pledged to continue efforts for an Earth Charter and urged states and NGOs to include this in their follow-up. Subsequently the Earth Council, Green Cross International, Global Education Associates, and many other groups have held Earth Charter consultations around the world, gathering input from citizen groups. They hope to have states negotiate an Earth Charter by 2002, the thirtieth anniversary of Stockholm and tenth anniversary of the Rio Earth Summit. In the meantime, the International Union for the Conservation of Nature (IUCN), a leading environmental NGO, has completed many years of work on a draft charter, which is now being promoted in inter-state circles.

Critiques of the United Nations

Most of the citizen treaties affirmed and pledged to support the work of the United Nations and its specialized agencies in many fields. The major exceptions were in the areas of economy, trade, and finance.

The Bretton Woods institutions were a frequent focal point of criticism, especially for the way in which conditions imposed by the IMF, and the types of development programmes supported by the World Bank, were contradicting and undermining sustainable development approaches fostered by UNEP, UNDP, and other UN programmes. NGOs also criticized how funds for environmental programmes were being administered by the World Bank through the Global Environment Facility (GEF), and urged a more democratic decision-making process for GEF projects and fund allocations.

The most bitter criticism of the United Nations by NGOs was for its failure to adopt measures curbing environmental damage by transnational corporations (TNCs). Forum participants proposed creating international mechanisms to make transnational companies responsible for any noxious effects of their operational processes, including democratic regulation of TNC conduct and participation in audits by NGOs, consumer associations, trade unions, citizens' groups, district associations, and other grass-roots groups (Pollard et al. 1992: 74–75).

NGOs also criticized the United Nations for slowness, incoherence, difficulty in implementing integrated strategies, non-definition about what is to be centralized or decentralized, and an inability to have the results of its projects reach citizens. The Global Forum proposed creating new UN-related institutions and mechanisms for inter-state regulation, including an Environmental Court of Justice; mechanisms to monitor the implementation of *Agenda 21* and international environmental treaties; and an international agency to monitor, control, and bar the international trade of weapons.

5. Future directions and recommendations

What kinds of institutions will best assure global ecological security in the complex world that is dawning? With what kinds of powers, checks and balances, and participation by peoples and governments? With what mandate, capacities, and means? Based on what worldviews and paradigms? Do existing agencies or programmes come close? If so, how can they be modified, strengthened, or expanded to match future needs? If not, is it better to build new structures that are more relevant to present and future needs? Can these be built on the foundations of UNEP and other existing UN bodies and programmes? What obstacles or new problems would be encountered in modifying existing structures or building new ones, and how can these obstacles be overcome? How can the political imagination and will be moved to make ecological security an integral part of the matrix of global security for present and future generations?

These questions cannot be fully answered here, but they challenge us to explore three possible paths for the future role of the UN system in ecological security. Each has its own set of recommendations. Before exploring distinct features of these paths, some general assumptions and recommendations can be made that apply to all three.

General recommendations

Build on existing UN structures
There is currently no alternative to the UN system for redressing global-scale environmental threats. Even the third path below – a new, third-generation world organization – would need to build on some existing UN structures.

Undertake real UN reform: Overcome structural weaknesses, improve effectiveness
UN reform and restructuring measures must go beyond cutting the budget and improving efficiency as ends in themselves. The primary objective should be to make the United Nations more effective in its work for peace and security, human rights, economic development, and ecological sustainability. For ecological security the UN system must:
– overcome limitations and weaknesses in existing systems of governance, including UNEP's governing structure. Create a space for more players at the table, including environmental and scientific experts, NGOs and civil society, local authorities, business and industry, etc.;
– reconcile the gaps and contradictions between environmental and economic, monetary, and trade regimes;
– help member governments to overcome their preoccupation with immediate local and national issues and to recognize that national security is indivisible from global security and requires sustained commitment to long-term global ecological security;
– facilitate the further development and strengthening of international environmental law, closing gaps, eliminating loopholes, and improving measures for compliance;
– undertake more systematic analysis of, and holistic responses to,

the linkages between environmental, social, economic, institutional, and cultural sectors, and among different environmental issues, such as biodiversity, climate, land, water, etc.

Secure adequate levels of funding for environmental priorities
Long-range environmental priorities need to be established and scarce monies allocated where they will make the most important difference to global ecological security. Funding levels must be restored to at least 1992 levels as a bare minimum, but should go beyond that if essential goals are to be achieved. Funding levels must also be made more stable and predictable (Dowdeswell 1997). The current system of voluntary contributions should be replaced by a fair system of assessment. This should not rely too heavily on one or more states, that could then undermine the global common good by threatening to withhold their funds. Government contributions should not be earmarked for individual projects. If member-state contributions are insufficient to support ecological security, the United Nations should have the power to seek alternative sources of funding.

A working group of 80 NGO representatives, half from the North and half from the South, met in 1991 as part of the Rio preparations and, under co-chairs Richard Jordan of Global Education Associates and Lysinka Ulatowska of the World Citizens' Assembly, prepared a 40-page menu of alternative financial mechanisms that could be used to fund the implementation of *Agenda 21*. Alternative funding ideas have also been put forward by Harlan Cleveland, Hazel Henderson, and Inge Kaul (1995). Taxing or fining entities that engage in transboundary pollution or harm the global commons is a way to curb pollution while helping fund global environmental protection. It upholds the principle that "polluters should pay" rather than responsible citizens, who too often are made to subsidize polluters through added taxes for clean-up and heath care. Companies and individuals as well as governments should be held legally and financially accountable for the harm they do. Governments alone have not caused environmental degradation and should not bear all the costs.

Include ecological security in the UN matrix of peace and security
The ways environmental factors contribute to war or peace, conflict or cooperation, and ways of including ecological security in the UN matrix of peace and security, need to be taken into account. For example, environmental degradation and competition for scarce resources can cause civil unrest, conflict, and the breakdown of peace

and security. Thus, ecological security should be included in the UN *Agenda for Peace* initiatives such as peace-building, dispute settlement, preventive diplomacy, and peace-keeping. Cooperating to resolve common environmental problems is a way some conflicting groups and countries can transcend divisions, build trust, and move toward peace. When the environment is used, or threatened to be used, as an instrument of war, or is deliberately destroyed as an act of war, it needs to be included in deliberations by the Security Council. The International Peace Research Association (IPRA) and its Commission on Ecological Security could make a significant contribution to UN understandings and initiatives related to the linkages between ecology and peace and security.

With these general recommendations in mind, the following are three visions of how to strengthen the United Nations' work for ecological security. Each flows from different assumptions about the possibilities and constraints in the existing system. Each has particular recommendations for reforming or restructuring the UN system to improve its work for ecological security.

Three different paths: Specific recommendations

Path one. Modest reforms within the existing UN structure: Save and revitalize UNEP

The first path is the most modest. It is aimed at saving UNEP from elimination or further funding cuts and at holding the line against attempts to weaken UN environmental initiatives. It proposes reforms that would streamline but revitalize UNEP to address new environmental priorities that cannot be handled by other UN agencies. Advocates of this path include the current and past executive directors of UNEP (Dowdeswell 1997; Strong 1997; Tolba 1997). They would like to see UNEP revitalized as a strong, knowledge-based organization capable of mobilizing international environmental science and technology, and its related social, political, economic, and legal components. Advocates of this path seek more participation by NGOs, civil society, and the private sector, and believe this can be done without major changes in existing structures.

RECOMMENDATIONS, PROPOSALS, AND STRATEGIES
• Complete plans to improve UNEP's governance structure. Currently under way, the plan calls for a dual structure: (1) UNEP's existing Governing Council, with universal participation at biennial

meetings because of the universal nature of environmental problems; (2) a smaller intercessional body to give the secretariat timely and substantive policy guidance, and to present a powerful collective voice in environmental emergencies (Dowdeswell 1997: 4).

• Streamline UNEP's tasks to those that it does best and that cannot be done by other UN bodies. UNEP should undertake more practical and result-oriented action. It should focus on three main themes: gathering and synthesizing available science, deriving policy implications, and supporting international negotiations. These three have always been part of the UNEP mandate, but should now "comprise the entire program and be revitalized" (Dowdeswell 1997). Other activities that divert scarce resources from this focus should be jettisoned to other organizations.

• Restore UNEP's budget to 1992 levels. To this end, press the United States and other countries to restore their former levels of funding.

• Improve coordination between UNEP and other UN agencies and between UNEP and its regional offices.

• Tap the potential of other UN agencies, such as the World Bank, IMF, and UNDP. Increase the participation of local authorities, NGOs, civil society, and the private sector. Increase efforts to bring business to the table (UNEP was one of the first UN agencies to do this, beginning in 1992). Honour sustainable practices in business and ask the help of business in addressing global market forces. Explore ways to coordinate the complementary roles of the public and private sectors and to develop an environmentally effective balance between governmental regulation and self-regulation.

Path two. Moderate structural changes: Strengthen old structures and instruments and establish some new structures and instruments within the existing UN framework

The second path proposes some moderate structural changes within the framework of the existing UN system, including strengthening some existing UN agencies and programmes, and creating some new ones. Proponents of this path include some leading NGOs and environmental, scientific, legal, and professional organizations. Among the many who have publicly advocated some new or strengthened UN structures or instruments for ecological security are: the Earth Council, the Fundacion Futuro Latinoamericano, Global Education Associates, the International Council of Scientific Unions, the International Institute for Environment and Development, the Stockholm

Environment Institute, the Third World Academy of Science, the World Conservation Union, the World Federalist Movement, the World Resources Institute, and the World Wide Fund for Nature. During the Rio + 5 meeting held in Rio de Janeiro in March 1997, the International Union for the Conservation of Nature (IUCN) and other major NGO groups presented a resolution at the closing plenary endorsed by conference acclamation calling for a strong global environmental organization that would build on UNEP but have powers and support on a par with the Bretton Woods financial and economic institutions (*Environmental Reform at the Intergovernmental Level* 1997).

RECOMMENDATIONS, PROPOSALS, AND STRATEGIES

- Develop and adopt an Earth Charter to complement the UN Charter. It should provide a comprehensive framework of principles for global ecological security. Just as the Declaration of Human Rights provided a framework of principles that were subsequently elaborated in international human rights law, so the Earth Charter can start as soft law principles that are later elaborated in international environmental law. Among other principles, such a Charter could proclaim the right to a healthy and sustainable environment. (This has not yet been established in international law.)
- Transform the UN Trusteeship Council into an Ecological Security Council. The Trusteeship Council has now virtually fulfilled its original mandate. The concept of "Trusteeship" could be transferred to responsibility for the earth as a sacred trust for present and future generations. (Its functions could be those described below, under a strengthened UNEP.)
- Alternatively, upgrade UNEP to an authoritative rather than only a coordinating agency. It should be equal in power and capacities to the global economic institutions (*Environmental Reform at the Intergovernmental Level* 1997). This proposal, made by leading environmental organizations, was endorsed by more than 500 representatives of NGOs at the 1997 Rio + 5 Forum. Gross and Sheppard (1989) have proposed that a UN Environmental Protection Authority be empowered to initiate its own policies and independent funding, with accountability not only to governments but also to a wide range of people, including not only those with the latest technological development but also those engaged in subsistence farming or living in areas affected by toxic dumping. In addi-

tion to those in UNEP's existing mandate, this global environmental protection agency could have the following functions:

- to monitor environmental change with satellites provided by member states and promote more effective monitoring by national and private agencies;
- to promote and coordinate basic and applied scientific research on ecological systems;
- to train experts and help build capacity in developing countries for environmental security;
- to review environmental laws and regulations developed by legislative, judicial, and executive bodies at local, regional, national, and international levels;
- to promote conversion from environmentally destructive to environmentally responsible activities;
- to respond to environmental emergencies and plan for the prevention of, or quick coping with, possible future environmental disasters;
- to deal with grievance and compliance questions relevant to international environmental law;
- to research the links between environmental degradation and disruptive conflict and develop systems of early warning of environmental problems that might lead to social unrest and even violence;
- to deal with environmental aggression by states and the environmental effects of military activities;
- to work with the Secretary-General and Security Council to incorporate environmental initiatives and cooperation into the United Nations' war-prevention, conflict-resolution, peace-building, and peace-keeping activities;
- to work with the IMF, the World Bank, and other UN specialized agencies in relating environmental protection to programmes of public health, development, agriculture, disarmament, and education;
- to promote a major upgrading of environmental education at all levels, together with general education on human rights and responsibilities;
- to provide clearing-house functions, including an internationally available database, on all of the above.
• Strengthen the international legal regime to deal with international activities that undermine ecological security, including:
  - Strengthen international environmental law: define international

environmental crime and responsibility; remove loopholes, close gaps, and improve compliance measures in existing international laws; develop new, binding international legal instruments where necessary.
- Strengthen and use the International Court of Justice (ICJ) for cases of international environmental harm that cannot be handled nationally or regionally. Make it possible for cases of international environmental harm caused by individuals or corporate entities, as well as by governments, to be heard by the Court.
- Alternatively, create a World Court for the Environment with the capacity to hold individuals and corporate entities accountable for transnational environmental harm. (The ICJ currently lacks this capacity.) States are not the only or even the primary cause of environmental harm. Much of it emanates from the private sector.
• Restructure or reform the IAEA to eliminate contradictions inherent in having a mandate to both promote and protect people from a technology. An independent agency, not the IAEA, should be authorized to establish and monitor compliance with standards for protecting human and environmental health.
• Resolve contradictions in IMF and World Bank conditionalities that contribute to environmental degradation.
• Strengthen the participation and voice of civil society in the United Nations. Strengthen partnerships between UN agencies and NGOs for more effective action for ecological security.

Path three. Establish a third-generation world organization around an ecological vision
The third path to global ecological security is more radical. It includes a vision of local, decentralized approaches to ecological security, but also calls for replacing the United Nations with a third-generation world organization – one capable of addressing global-scale issues that cannot be handled locally. This new organization would build on scientific understandings of the earth as a total, living system. Its philosophy and structures would be informed by an ecological consciousness and vision of human beings and their diverse cultures and communities sharing in this larger life, with mutual responsibilities for one another and for the well-being of the life systems in which they dwell. This would be the foundation for true human security.

Just as the League of Nations was replaced by a second, stronger organization when it proved too weak to prevent World War II, so now a stronger world organization is needed to meet the new problems and opportunities of an emerging planetary civilization. Whereas the United Nations was informed and shaped by an expanded vision of peace and security that went beyond the League's and added human rights and economic development to the matrix of peace and security, so a third-generation organization would expand the vision still further to include ecological security in its matrix of peace and security.

The vision for this new world organization includes many features of paths one and two above, but its philosophical underpinnings go deeper than the humanitarian ideals and homocentric world-view of the Enlightenment that informed and shaped the existing United Nations. The new organization would not be less humanitarian; it would be humanitarian within a more ecological or bio-centric world-view.

Of course, not all who espouse a third-generation world organization do so with an ecological world-view. Some would build a new world organization on the same philosophical foundations of the existing United Nations, only making it stronger and more effective and democratic. But this would not address the problems inherent in homocentric and hierarchical assumptions that have produced many environmental disasters.

This vision does not assume that a third-generation organization will be state-centric. It calls for a United Nations that is more than a collection of states, each of which is pursuing its own national interests and only rarely focuses on the global common good. In this vision, states will continue to be actors, but civil society, cities and local communities, labour, business and industry, indigenous communities, and other actors would play a greater role than they now do. Some propose a bicameral world body, with a House of Nations, akin to the existing UN General Assembly, and a House of Peoples (or Peoples' Assembly.) This second house would provide a means for representatives of civil society (elected by local districts around the world) to deliberate and have a more direct role in global policy development. Other proposals for a second house have also been put forward, including that the second house be for parliamentarians (who would represent constituents in the United Nations as well as in their national parliaments or house of representatives); or that it be for religious or humanitarian leaders, who would give ethical advice on global problems and their solution.

350

RECOMMENDATIONS, PROPOSALS, AND STRATEGIES. Many of the recommendations in paths one and two above could be incorporated within the framework of a third-generation world organization. This organization would certainly include a strong Environmental Division, and an ecological vision would inform all other divisions as well. By incorporating and building on this vision from its inception, the new organization could avoid the contradictions between economic and ecological objectives that have plagued the UN system. In addition, the new world organization would include more democratic participation by civil society and local communities from its inception. Parallel to its development, local communities would undertake programmes to prepare their citizens for effective participation in the organization and for partnership and cooperation with it in implementing global policies at local and national levels.

To be achieved, all three of these paths must surmount serious obstacles of bureaucratic inertia and the need to develop greater public understanding of, and political, financial, and moral commitment to, the global common good. Although this is no small task, where the political and moral will are present it is possible to achieve even the most major changes in relatively short historical time.

6. Implications for peace research

Regardless of which path is pursued toward a more ecologically secure future, peace researchers can make a significant contribution. The most obvious area for this contribution is research exploring the links between ecological security and peace. For some years IPRA's Commission on Ecological Security has been exploring these linkages. So have other institutes, including the Stockholm International Peace Research Institute and the Environmental Conflict Project (ENCOP) of the Center for Security Studies and Conflict Research at the Swiss Federal Institute of Technology. The latter has published numerous case studies exploring various examples and facets of these linkages, and has also provided a definition of environmental conflicts and a framework for their analysis.

Relative to the United Nations and peace researchers, some fruitful areas for collaboration include research on:
- environmental degradation as a cause of disruptive conflict and the dynamics and role of ecological security in building a positive, sustainable system of peace;

- ways to incorporate environmental security in the UN *Agenda for Peace*, including the areas of conflict prevention, mediation, peace-building, peace-keeping, and regional cooperation;
- the effectiveness of existing peace-building activities that have included environmental components (e.g. cooperative water projects in the Middle East);
- the environmental effects of the production, stockpiling, testing, and trade of armaments, and proposed remedies;
- environmental warfare – its causes, effects, possible future threats, policy implications, and proposals for prevention;
- environmental implications of disarmament, including disposal of toxic materials from chemical, biological, and nuclear weapons that are or will soon be dismantled;
- ways that UNEP (or a new global environmental authority) could realize its potential as an instrument of peace;
- best practices and expert assistance in the prevention, mediation, and resolution of environmental disputes;
- best practices and ways to bring all the relevant actors to the table with meaningful results for cooperative approaches to advancing ecological security;
- best ways to strengthen structures and advance policies that will advance global ecological security;
- proposals for overcoming obstacles and inherent contradictions within the UN system that block progress toward ecological security.

In closing it needs to be stressed again that the United Nations has shown it is not a static, changeless structure, but a living organism that can adapt and change in the face of new needs and challenges. Peace research groups can make an important contribution to the United Nations in its current and future struggles to serve an emerging global community better.

Notes

1. The World Meteorological Convention, which created the WMO, was adopted in 1947 at the Twelfth Conference of Directors of the International Meteorological Organization (IMO). It entered into force in 1950, and in 1951 the WMO began operations as the successor to the IMO.
2. The IMO's Convention was prepared by the 1948 Geneva United Nations Maritime Conference, and went into effect in March 1958, after being ratified by 21 states, including 7 with at least 1 million gross tons of shipping each (UNDPI 1986: 423).
3. Drafted in this period under the aegis of the UN Commission on Human Rights and adopted by the General Assembly in 1966.

4. A World Health Organization had been proposed as early as the United Nations Conference in San Francisco in 1945, and its Constitution was adopted in July 1946.
5. Following the NPT Review Conference in 1995, 174 of the 185 member countries agreed to extend this treaty indefinitely.
6. The IAEA had its origins in a proposal by the President of the United States to the General Assembly in December 1953 that the United Nations establish a world organization dedicated to the peaceful uses of atomic energy. The GA endorsed the general lines of the proposal in December 1954, and the IAEA Statute was approved on 23 October 1956 at a conference at UN headquarters (UNDPI 1986: 401). The IAEA had been preceded by the Atomic Energy Commission, which had been established by the GA in January 1946 and consisted of the Security Council plus Canada, but which was later disbanded.
7. China maintained that the principle should have included the prohibition and destruction of chemical and biological, as well as nuclear, weapons. Peru, the Philippines, Sweden, and Tanzania wanted a stronger condemnation of the use of such weapons. Japan felt the principle should be interpreted to include nuclear-weapons testing. And the United States said that, although it supported the intent behind the proposal, the international agreements referred to must be adequately verifiable (Osmanczyk 1985: 781).
8. *Dai Dong* is derived from an ancient Chinese concept for a world in which one's family includes not only one's immediate family and children, but all the world, all families, and all children (Knelman 1991: 436).
9. In 1921 a convention concerning the use of lead in white paint was agreed to in Geneva. Not until 1933 was another multilateral environmental agreement registered – concerning the preservation of flora and fauna in their natural state. Three more were transacted in the 1940s, 16 in the 1950s, 26 in the 1960s, and more in the years 1970 and 1971. (See UNEP 1989a, 1991, or Mische 1989a for a full list of multilateral environmental treaties.)
10. In addition to some described above, the following are a few examples:
    • Binding multilateral conventions or agreements regarding protection of the ozone layer, the control of transboundary movements of hazardous wastes and their disposal, climate change, and biodiversity, as well as such non-binding legal agreements and declarations as the World Charter for Nature.
    • Water management and protection programmes, including the Regional Seas Programme and the Environmentally Sound Management of Inland Waters (EMINWA) programme.
    • Initiatives to help combat desertification, including sponsoring conferences, mapping degraded lands, formulating pilot projects, creating technical information databases, assisting in the development of national and regional plans of action, and adopting a World Soils Policy.
    • Programmes to combat deforestation, including the Tropical Forest Action Plan, a framework for the management and sustainable development of forests adopted by some 80 countries.
    • Initiatives to green industry, including those coordinated by UNEP's Industry and Environment Programme Activity Centre (IE/PAC), its Cleaner Production Programme, and, in co-sponsorship with the International Chamber of Commerce (ICC), the World Industry Conference on Environmental Management (WICEM), which in 1991 issued the *Business Charter on Sustainable Development*.
    • Energy programmes, including assessing the environmental impacts of different forms of energy production, promoting the use of renewable sources of energy, and assisting in the development of environmentally sound national energy plans.
    • Environmental guidelines for urban development, in collaboration with Habitat.
11. A senior staff member of the CSD affirmed the importance of NGOs in an interview with Patricia Mische. First, he said, without the NGOs there would be no Commission on Sustainable Development. NGOs got the CSD on the UNCED agenda and then in Rio pushed governments to agree to it. Secondly, since the CSD became operational, NGOs have participated in its meetings, ensuring greater transparency in the government reporting

process. Because of the NGO presence, however, governments have to be more honest. Thirdly, NGOs are monitoring and participating in the implementation of *Agenda 21* within countries. Because the CSD has no power to enforce, NGOs often play a critical role by prodding governments to implement their *Agenda 21* agreements.

12. Interestingly, after Rio some UNEP officials recognized that the lack of explicit attention to values and ethics was a serious omission in the UNCED process. In an effort to stimulate moral debate, UNEP published a volume that included essays by environmentalists, scientists, indigenous peoples, and religious and spiritual leaders (UNEP 1994).

13. These proposals included: the ratification of a comprehensive test ban treaty, military accountability for environmental damage, and the development of a permanent Environmental Crisis Response Centre to coordinate international responses to ecological disasters, including war (Pollard et al. 1992).

References

Bertell, Rosalie. 1991. *Testimony for the World Women's Congress for a Healthy Planet*. Preparatory Conference for the United Nations Conference on Environment and Development, Miami, 8–12 November 1991. International Institutes of Concern for Public Health.

Brown, Noel. 1997. *Jerry Mische Memorial Lecture*. New York City: New Global Education Associates.

Carson, Rachel. 1962. *Silent Spring*. New York: Fawcett.

CDI (Center for Defense Information). 1989. "Defending the Environment? The Record of the U.S. Military." *The Defense Monitor*, vol. XVIII, no. 6.

Cleveland, Harlan, Hazel Henderson, and Inge Kaul. 1995. *United Nations: Policy and Funding Alternatives*. Washington, D.C.: Global Commission to Fund the United Nations.

Dowdeswell, E. 1997. "The Promise of Stockholm." *Our Planet*, vol. 8, no. 5, pp. 3–4.

Environmental Reform at the Intergovernmental Level. 1997. Declaration by numerous environmental groups, endorsed at the 1997 Rio + 5 meeting, Rio de Janeiro.

ESW (Earth Summit Watch). 1996. *Agenda 21: Five Years After Rio*. An Assessment of National Actions to Implement Sustainable Development Strategies. Discussion draft. New York/Washington D.C., October.

Gross, Bertram, and Ceri Sheppard. 1989. "Some Suggestions for an UNEPA." In Patricia Mische, ed., *Ecological Security in an Interdependent World*. Special issue of *Breakthrough*, Summer/Fall. New York: Global Education Associates, pp. 28–29.

Knelman, F. H. 1991. "What Happened at Stockholm?" In Richard Falk, Samuel Kim, and Saul Mendlovitz, eds., *The United Nations and a Just World Order*. Boulder, Colo.: Westview Press, pp. 433–446.

Manley, Robert. 1979. "Forty-eight Global Level Issue Areas: A Survey of Policy Development, 1945–1977." *The Whole Earth Papers*, no. 12. New York: Global Education Associates, pp. 26–56.

Mische, Patricia, ed. 1989a. *Ecological Security in an Interdependent World*. Special issue of *Breakthrough*, Summer/Fall. New York: Global Education Associates.

——— ed. 1989b. "International Environmental Treaties." In Patricia Mische, ed., *Ecological Security in an Interdependent World*. Special issue of *Breakthrough*, Summer/Fall. New York: Global Education Associates, pp. 18–20.

———— 1989c. "Earth Covenant: The Evolution of a Citizens' Treaty for Common Ecological Security." In Patricia Mische, ed., *Ecological Security in an Interdependent World.* Special issue of *Breakthrough*, Summer/Fall. New York: Global Education Associates, pp. 31–33.

———— 1992. "Security Through Defending the Environment: Citizens Say Yes." In Elise Boulding, ed., *New Agendas for Peace Research: Conflict and Security Reexamined.* Boulder, Colo.: Lynne Rienner, pp. 103–125.

Osmanczyk, Edmund Jan. 1985. *Encyclopedia of the United Nations and International Agreements.* Philadelphia: Taylor & Francis.

Pollard, Robert, Ruth West, and Will Sutherland, eds. 1992. *Alternative Treaties: Synergistic Processes for Sustainable Communities and Global Responsibility.* Revised edition of the Alternative Treaties from the International NGO Forum in Rio de Janeiro, 1–14 June 1992. Millbrook, England: Ideas for Tomorrow Today, and International Synergy Institute.

Ribeiro, Mauricio Andres. 1990. "Ecological Security: Global and Local Administration Experience." Paper presented at the XIII Conference of the International Peace Research Association, Groningen, the Netherlands.

Rojas, Jose Dualok. 1994. "UNCED: Ethics and Development from the Indigenous Point of View." In UNEP, *Ethics and Agenda 21.* New York: UNEP, pp. 49–51.

Stockholm Declaration. 1972. Statement of the UN Conference on the Human Environment.

Strong, Maurice. 1992. Statement at Closing Press Conference at the United Nations Conference on Environment and Development, Rio de Janeiro, 12 June.

———— 1995. Speech sponsored by Foreign Policy Association – Youth. New York, 22 March.

———— 1997. "The Way Ahead." *Our Planet*, vol. 8, no. 5, pp. 6–8.

Tolba, Mostafa. 1997. "Redefining UNEP." *Our Planet*, vol. 8, no. 5.

UN Commission on Human Rights. 1994. *Human Rights and the Environment.* Report to ECOSOC, 46th session, by the Sub-Commission on Prevention of Discrimination and Protection of Minorities, E/CN.4Sub.2/1994/9, prepared by Mrs. Fatma Zohra Ksentini, Special Rapporteur.

UNDPI (United Nations Department of Information). 1986. *Everyone's United Nations.* New York: UNDPI.

———— 1992. *Basic Facts about the United Nations.* New York: UNDPI.

———— 1995. *A Guide to Information at the United Nations.* New York: UNDPI.

UNEP (United Nations Environment Programme). 1988. *Environmental Perspectives to the Year 2000 and Beyond.* General Assembly Resolution 42/186, December 1987.

———— 1989a. *Registry of International Environmental Treaties.* UNEP/GC.15/INF. 2, May.

———— 1989b. *United Nations Environment Programme Environmental Data Report*, 2nd edition, 1989/90. Prepared by the GEMS Monitoring and Assessment Research Centre, London. Oxford: Blackwell Publishers.

———— 1991. *Registry of International Environmental Treaties.* UNEP/GC.16/INF.4, May.

———— 1992. *UNEP: Two Decades of Achievement and Challenge.* New York: UNEP.

———— 1993. *United Nations Environment Programme Environmental Data Report, 1993–94.* Oxford: Blackwell Publishers.

———— 1994. *Ethics and Agenda 21: Moral Implications of a Global Consensus*. New York: UNEP.

United Nations. 1969. *Man and His Environment*. The U Thant Report. New York: United Nations, 26 May.

———— 1992. *Agenda 21: Programme of Action for Sustainable Development*. New York: UNDPI.

World Commission on Environment and Development. 1987. *Our Common Future*. New York/Oxford: Oxford University Press.

World Urban Forum. 1992. *Curitiba Commitment*. Report of the World Urban Forum, Curitiba, Brazil, May.

Worldwatch Institute. Annual. *State of the World: A Worldwatch Institute Report on Progress Toward a Sustainable Society*. New York: W. W. Norton.

11

Communications in the future UN system

Tapio Varis

1. Introduction

The rapid development in information and communications technology, especially in computer and telecommunication systems, is creating profound changes in the structure of world economic, political, and cultural institutions, as well as in the nature of diplomacy and the operations of the United Nations system. Two issues will dominate the future of communications for some time to come. First is the exponential increase in the quantity of information and communication in the emerging global information society. Escalating quantity is making concern for quality and direction of flow even more important. Second, knowledge is becoming the most important resource in a global information economy (Melody 1994). The key concepts are interconnectedness and network economy, but they imply growing importance of cultural issues. A recent study of the main areas of responsibility for the United Nations system and its future leadership included "strengthening understanding of the value of cultural diversity and efforts to conserve it" (Urquhart and Childers 1996: 14).

When discussing communications and the United Nations system, one must recognize the agencies that deal with communications and information issues. Since world communication creates a variety of

technical, juridical, and cultural problems, a number of UN agencies deal with these issues, including the following:
- International Court of Justice
- ITU (International Telecommunication Union)
- WIPO (World Intellectual Property Organization)
- UNESCO (United Nations Educational, Scientific, and Cultural Organization)
- UNU (United Nations University)

After the end of World War II, there were efforts to rationalize the international communications system by bringing various organizations (such as the ITU) under the aegis of the United Nations. The treaties and conventions were to be adjudicated by the International Court of Justice. However, the Court was given no official sanctions to impose its decisions on states. It had to rely on "world opinion" or "moral authority" to induce states to abide by its decisions. As a consequence, this philosophy has not really produced instruments to deal with the problems of world communications because they have often been felt to threaten the freedom of information.

The policy problems faced by the ITU have become significantly more complicated now than during the 1970s or even the 1980s (Soroos 1986: 346). For example, the filling up of the geosynchronous orbit was not an international issue until the launching of communication satellites became a frequent and routine phenomenon. Telecommunications may well become as highly politicized as other domains of global policy. Thus far, the conflicts have over-politicized the work of the ITU, but, for example, it will be very difficult to deal with the regulation of trans-border data flow, which could have major economic implications for both developed and developing countries.

Today, the issues of intellectual property rights and audio-visual and computer program pirate copying are becoming a major international problem in world trade. Consequently, WIPO and trade organizations have a new challenge to solve. UNESCO and the UNU deal with international intellectual cooperation and are highly dependent on world communications in their work. It is also their responsibility to facilitate world communications development. Consequently, they need to be analysed separately in more detail.

In the present world, all political, economic, and military operations, from preventive diplomacy to peace-keeping, must take into consideration the new media environment and world public opinion. World communication is a prerequisite for the work of the General Assembly and the Security Council. The media are seen to reflect the world's public opinion. It is important that the world media are as independent and free as possible to reflect people's views and opinions, as well as to maintain a critical reporting of governments. Issues that are reported by the press and discussed in daily public opinion will become important for the General Assembly too. The General Assembly cannot ignore violations of human rights if the mass media do not ignore them, but the opposite may well happen.

UN decisions and operations will increasingly take place under media scrutiny. This is especially true of UN peace-keeping operations. Growing telecommunications capabilities result in increasingly detailed, graphic, and timely information being available to audiences worldwide.

A recent research document by the United Nations Institute for Disarmament Research (UNIDIR) concludes that, in peace operations, national and international news media coverage plays a significant role in quickly framing public debate and shaping public opinion. Future peace-keeping operations will most likely be executed under the worst possible conditions, where preventive diplomacy has failed, impassioned calls for action submerge careful analysis in emotions and impatience, frustration supplants caution, and facts on the ground are judged primarily by media coverage. The report concludes that it is precisely for this type of environment that decision makers and peace-keeping operations should prepare themselves (Raevsky and Vorob'ev 1994).

The significance of these issues for the success of the United Nations became very clear in media coverage of UN operations in Somalia and the former Yugoslavia. The difficulties encountered by the United Nations are given wide publicity by the world's news media, which tend to stress action and war-related issues in a conflict more than diplomacy, which, after all, is the strength of the United Nations.

The great challenge to communications research, as well as to policy-making, is to find a new forward-looking approach that is based on past knowledge but remains free from Cold War conceptual frames. Information and communications technology represents continuity, which has a solid past because nations have always come together when technology has forced them to do so (postal traffic, radio waves, etc.). New technology challenges many previous assumptions such as sovereignty, but so did radio waves in the 1920s. Then some governments initially wanted to proclaim sovereignty over the "ether," the air space above their territories. Analysis of technological developments is useful in understanding the need for creating specialized agencies and efforts to introduce normative thinking in this field.

This chapter will focus on communications, structure, and power. First, it is important to look at the technological changes that have been decisive for many other changes. Currently, they are creating an entirely new learning environment for all international activities. Secondly, how academic thinking on communication and education has developed within the framework of the United Nations deserves study. Thirdly, it is important to understand that culture and communication skills are essential for the emerging global information society. Fourthly, a new challenge is given by the concept of global learning. A new, future-oriented vision of this concept as well as the future is needed for UN-related research, training, and educational institutions. Fifthly, a series of proposals are set out to guide thinking about future directions for communications issues in the UN system.

2. Technological developments

International communication has no precise origins but it has existed as long as there have been nations and states. As soon as groups establish their separateness, at least some members find the need to communicate with individuals in other groups. Of course, the media have changed from the earlier runners, drummers, pigeons, horses, and ships. With the advent of the telegraph, as early as 1837, a fundamental transformation began. Technological developments for telegraph, submarine cable, telephone, wireless, and radio led to the need for international control of the means of communication. The objective has been to facilitate the necessary international cooperation and avoid transnational interference in the operations of other countries.

The first international organization in this field was the International Telegraph Union (ITU), formed in 1865. Now a United Nations specialized agency, the International Telecommunication Union, is the oldest organization in the UN family. The ITU is an example of how the need for the international control of communications has emerged from the functional need to promote international communication.

The composition, purposes, and structure of the ITU are defined in the International Telecommunication Convention (Nairobi, 1982). The purposes of the Union are:

(a) to maintain and extend international cooperation between all Members of the Union for the improvement and rational use of telecommunications of all kinds, as well as to promote and to offer technical assistance to developing countries in the field of telecommunication;

(b) to promote the development of technical facilities and their most efficient operation with a view to improving the efficiency of telecommunication services, increasing their usefulness and making them, so far as possible, generally available to the public; and

(c) to harmonize the actions of nations in the attainment of those ends.

To this end, the Union shall in particular deal with allocation of the radio frequency spectrum and registration of radio frequency assignments in order to avoid harmful interference between radio stations in different countries, coordinate efforts to eliminate harmful interference between radio stations of different countries, foster international cooperation, coordinate efforts with a view to harmonizing the development of telecommunications facilities, foster collaboration with a view to the establishment of rates at levels as low as possible, promote the adoption of measures for ensuring the safety of life through the cooperation of telecommunication services, and undertake studies, make regulations, adopt resolutions, etc.

During the twentieth century, especially from 1933 to 1969, the field of international communications became a field of increasing politicization and propaganda (Fortner 1993). Although politicization never really ended during the period after 1970, a newly complex environment emerged, resulting from both the application of new communications technologies and the proliferation of new states with the breakup of Europe's colonial empires.

In recent years, fundamental changes have occurred in technology, political world order, and population growth that have had a profound impact on world economic, political, and human development. The rapid developments in telecommunications, microprocessors, and biotechnologies and the introduction of information super-highways are changing national and international economies and world order. National information infrastructures are planned to be connected to the worldwide efforts to create global electronic information super-highways, which are expected to revolutionize economic as well as education and learning environments.

It has been estimated that present decisions concerning telecommunications and electronic information highways will have socio-economic impacts similar to those experienced by the building of canals, railroads, and motor-highways. It is believed that information highways will be the key to economic growth for national and international economies. Already the information infrastructure is to the major economies of the 1990s what transport infrastructure was to the economies of the mid-twentieth century. These information super-highways have been compared to the building of interstate highways in earlier periods. Highways function only if all roads are connected to them. Similarly, in the field of information super-highways there are weak links that determine the outcome of the whole system.

Some critical researchers point out that, if future user requirements do not align with national information infrastructure provisioning capabilities, lengthy periods of wasteful and uneconomic network underutilization will result. For instance, the mid-1980s' unveiling of ISDN (Integrated Systems of Digital Network) has yet to overcome initial subscriber scepticism. In the interim, resources will not have been put to their best possible use.

From a global perspective, there is the threat that the information gap is increasing. Even in the technologically advanced countries, a great number of individual homes do not have computer connections and very few home computers have modems. In fact, the first utilizers of information super-highways will be those who have the necessary equipment. In the early stages of motor-highways the first users were those who had cars and could benefit from the new infrastructure. Highways changed the whole culture, including small business and shopping centres. The shops were no longer built at walking distance but near the highways. In the case of information super-highways, we do not yet know how much they will serve individual citizens and how much they will serve enterprises, organizations, and administration.

In the past ten years or so one has been able to observe the central role of information and communications technology for social and economic development. The traditional industrial societies have faced difficulties, and even collapsed, in cases where obsolete models of thinking have dominated management. Economies that have been able to utilize new communication and information resources have been increasing, for example in the Pacific region and also in North America. Small countries have also realized the importance of information highways to their development. Researchers and policy makers point out that companies, and even countries, that remain outside the global information networks may find themselves cut off from the whole global open economy.

The communications and information sector comprises approximately 20 per cent of world trade. Modern business and enterprises become all the more dependent on the availability of relevant information services and networks. Over half of a company's labour costs are estimated to be in this field. Information networks are needed not only within the business organization itself but also in the market connections to customers around the world.

Attitudes towards multimedia vary from enthusiasm to confusion. Combinations of texts, audio, graphics, animation, and video have been marketed since the mid-1980s as multimedia. In most cases the delivery system has been the CD-ROM type of discs. Nowadays, multimedia producers are already looking at cable systems as possible means of delivery. Soon it will be possible to store and update the multimedia. Advertising may be more interactive in the near future. Traditional advertising may have to give way to systems that combine advertising with simultaneous sales. In this development, enterprises that are active in both content and delivery will benefit the most.

The gigantic size of the companies reflects the importance of the information-based industries. We have to observe, however, that the era of giant corporations may also be ending because many of the giants are not flexible enough to respond to the new market needs and situations. Small and medium-size companies are very flexible and skilful in using the new information and communications technologies. They are able to build a virtual corporation through a network of companies.

This kind of organization can quickly connect talented people and know-how to where they are needed in a short period of time. When no longer needed, the system disappears. Old frontiers are overcome. Global telecommunications create possibilities for worldwide activity by small companies as well. With multimedia, telecommunications systems, media companies, and computer business will start to work together.

Those who first give substance to such cooperation will be winners in this development. In global operations, visual communication becomes important. It is no longer enough that a material product has a form; it has to communicate as well. Media, messages, and products all form a new audio-visual communication environment, a media landscape. We are creating a new visual vocabulary in the same way the motor-highways were once developed.

In light of the exponential growth in electronic communications, the role of telecommunications will grow quickly in world affairs.

Consequently, the ITU has to deal more and more with issues that are not just technical in nature. For example, the ITU has to define more clearly its role in relation to development. A significant move took place in 1984 when a Report of the Independent Commission for World-Wide Telecommunications Development, *The Missing Link*, was published. It concluded, among other things, that "all mankind could be brought within easy reach of a telephone by the early part of next century" (ITU 1984: 69).

In 1994, the ITU held the first World Telecommunications Development Conference in Buenos Aires, Argentina. A Declaration on Global Telecommunication Development for the 21st Century was approved. It recognizes that telecommunications are an essential component of political, economic, social, and cultural development. Importantly, the document refers to the principle of "the right of connection" between countries. The "telecommunications gap" between visions and reality persists, at technical and political levels, and hopes of closing it are modest. More than two-thirds of all households worldwide still have no telephone. Less than 2 per cent of World Bank lending goes to telecom projects.

3. Education and communications

The League of Nations

International governmental efforts in the fields of education and communication began as early as the League of Nations, but the role of international communication and the media was not perceived as central during the period of the League of Nations as it was after World War II. The League of Nations passed one resolution in September 1925 on the Collaboration of the Press in the Organisation of Peace. It spoke about "moral disarmament," which was understood to be a concomitant condition of material disarmament. In 1936, the League of Nations approved an International Convention Concerning the Use of Broadcasting in the Cause of Peace. This lengthy Convention came into existence after politicization and propaganda in radio and other forms of international communication in Europe. The Convention, which is still in force, speaks about the need to prohibit transmissions that are likely to harm international understanding. It probably had little impact, as reflected in deliberate interference in other countries' transmissions, which started in Austria in the early 1930s.

364

Of particular importance was the International Institute of Intellectual Cooperation of the League of Nations (even though a limited amount was accomplished) because it was the predecessor of UNESCO. It was a characteristic feature of the times that only 15 small and medium-sized states signed the Declaration Regarding the Teaching of History started in 1937. None of the bigger powers agreed to the Declaration, although for different reasons. The British government did not feel entitled to interfere in the field of local educational authority and the free expression of opinion. The United States refused to sign because the federal government had no control over education. France did not want to curb the independence of teachers and historians. The Nazi government of Germany opposed the aims of the Declaration totally (Mertineit 1979: 102).

UNESCO

The constitution of the United Nations Educational, Scientific and Cultural Organization (UNESCO) was approved in 1945. It says, among other things, that peace, if it is not to fail, must be founded upon the intellectual and moral solidarity of mankind. The means of communication between peoples should be developed and increased and these means should be employed "for the purposes of mutual understanding and a truer and more perfect knowledge of each other's lives."

The UNESCO constitution was drafted by an American poet, Archibald MacLeish, and a British politician, Clement Attlee. After the Axis governments had demonstrated the power of the communications media in controlling society, UNESCO's founders wrote into the organization's constitution a mandate to create a communication programme that would advance the "understanding of peoples."

The constitution of UNESCO reflects the spirit of the anti-Fascist struggle:

The great and terrible war which has now ended was a war made possible by the denial of the democratic principles of the dignity, equality and mutual respect of men, and by the propagation, in their place, through ignorance and prejudice, of the doctrine of the inequality of men and races ...

... Believing in full and equal opportunities for education for all, in the unrestricted pursuit of objective truth, and in the free exchange of ideas and knowledge, are agreed and determined to develop and to increase the means of communication between their peoples and to employ these means for the purposes of mutual understanding and a truer and more perfect knowledge of each other's lives." (UNESCO constitution, 1945)

In other words, UNESCO's mandate is to contribute to the preservation of peace and security by promoting cooperation between nations through education, science, culture, and communication. In the field of information and communications, the purpose is "to promote the free flow of ideas by word and images" (UNESCO constitution).

The doctrine of the "free flow of information" was assumed to be an obvious prerequisite for peace (Alger 1990: 36). The "free flow" doctrine was always problematic in light of the global economic structure and its impact on communications. Technological changes have made it even more problematic now.

The chairman of the Committee that drafted the Preamble, the American poet and librarian Archibald MacLeish, was once asked if we can educate for world peace. His answer was:

Of course we can educate for world peace. I'd be willing, for my own part, to say that there is no possible way of getting world peace except through education. Which means education of the peoples of the world. All you can do by arrangements between governments is to remove the causes of disagreement which may become, in time, causes of war. But peace, as we are all beginning to realize, is something a great deal more than the absence of war. Peace is positive and not negative. Peace is a way of living together which excludes war, rather than a period without war in which peoples try to live together. (*The Unesco Courier*, October 1985: 27)

Later history has shown us the difficulties of building truly international educational and communications systems. A lot of intellectual work has been carried out on the basic problems of peace. One clear finding is that the criterion of what is "peace" depends on the times and on who defines peace. For the earlier period, research on peace referred mostly to the causes and functions of war and the necessary and sufficient conditions for abolishing it. More recently, it includes a broad range of research that includes human rights and the quality of life. Communications and education are key issues. Now education is changing into a process of life-long learning in which communication skills are central.

In general, communications research can be seen as contributing to peace education in the broad sense. Whereas early peace research targeted decision makers and diplomats, it was later discovered that, in order to promote peaceful relations among nations, one had to increase the general level of consciousness. More recently, the rapid development of information and communications technology, especially telecommunications, has made the issue of media education and new forms of media literacy central everywhere. Furthermore, the potential of the information super-highways requires general communication skills for citizens as well as for organizations. Consequently, the relationship between peace education and media education will be increasingly relevant for the future.

Britain has been a pioneer in media education, which emerged out of its classical tradition of literary criticism. Teaching about the media contributes to the demystification of the media as well as to the positive use and enjoyment of them. In America, there have been projects on critical viewing skills education, or, more broadly, critical thinking. In the new communications and information technology there is an increasing need to have a communications competence in the new media environment.

In the past, communications research centred around three issues:

(1) The problem of news flow and the flow of information in general. News and other information were found to be biased and one-directional in their orientation from the North to the South.

(2) The transnational, monopolistic structure of the information and communications industry. In particular, the dominance of a few news agencies with their headquarters in the rich North was found to be a problem relevant to the United Nations, and especially to the world economy and related conferences and organizations.

(3) Communication policy. The inspiration came mainly from the movement of the non-aligned countries, which developed the idea of a new international order in the field of information. This debate was then moved to the UN agencies, especially UNESCO, where it became an overpoliticized issue of a New World Information and Communication Order (NWICO).

The efforts to establish a New International Economic Order (NIEO) since 1974 brought the demand for NWICO to UNESCO. The idea was to correct the imbalances and inequalities in present world communications, but major Western countries felt that it threatened the freedom of the press and information.

Even though it was unfortunate that information and communication issues became overpoliticized in UNESCO, it may have been necessary to have that debate somewhere in the UN system. It was an issue more for intellectuals and scholars, rather than governmental people. In principle, UNESCO would be an ideal place for cultural, scientific, and literary intellectuals to appear in a world forum. In the early years of UNESCO in the late 1940s, it was still perceived as an agency uniting qualified individuals from different civilizations, "representing the human mind" rather than representing governments.

Things turned out to be different, and foreign offices, rather than free scholars or representatives of cultural and educational institutions, came to dominate debate at UNESCO. It is worth observing that one of the high-level diplomats, Gabriel Warren, Director General of the Department of Communications in Canada, confessed at the 1st World Electronic Media Symposium organized by ITU in Geneva in 1989 that, although the new world information order was against Western views, the debate on it had a therapeutic influence: "there is now a better understanding on both sides and the will to decrease the gap and a recognition of the need for cooperation" (ITU 1989).

UNESCO started to reform its communications policy in the early 1970s. An important source for the new orientation was research carried out by communications scholars in many countries. The UNESCO philosophy is based on intellectual, normative, and operative documents. Since the late 1970s the intellectual basis was largely built on the report of the Independent Commission for the Study of Communication Problems (1980) led by the late Sean McBride (*Many Voices – One World*).

The normative debate centred around the 1978 Declaration on Fundamental Principles Concerning the Contribution of the Mass Media to Strengthening Peace and International Understanding, to the Promotion of Human Rights and to Countering of Racialism, Apartheid and Incitement to War. It was this document that caused the protests and criticism among the Western countries against UNESCO. Demands for a New World Information and Communication Order also caused much tension. The debate over these documents dominated world communication issues for years.

UNESCO took a pragmatic approach in the International Programme for the Development of Communication (IPDC), 1980. IPDC finances and promotes concrete communications projects in the developing countries. It has been based on voluntary and very limited funding from member countries and other sources such as foundations. It was believed that the gradual implementation of the IPDC recommendations would constitute an essential stage on the way to correcting the present inequalities and imbalances in world communications.

A UNESCO document in the field of information and communication noted in 1993 that the profound changes taking place in the political landscape of Europe and the world were changing UNESCO itself:

The end of ideological rivalries and divisions put to rest the bitter controversies of the past and made possible a new consensus on a strategy for the development of communication – a consensus of 161 Member States of UNESCO that accepted fully and without equivocation the fundamental principles of freedom of expression, freedom of the press and the free flow of information by word and image. (UNESCO 1993).

The new programme calls upon UNESCO to work for the development of free, independent, and pluralistic media in both the private and public sectors. A new critical look is needed to analyse whether or not the political and economic changes in the 1990s have confirmed the UNESCO ideals of free, independent, and pluralistic media.

Issues of quantity and quality

The scholarly views of communication when UNESCO was founded were reflected in a report entitled *Peoples Speaking to Peoples* by an unofficial organ, the Commission on Freedom of the Press, generally known as the Hutchins Commission (White and Leigh 1972). Communication was seen to link "all the habitable parts of the globe with abundant, cheap, significant, true information about the world from day to day, so that all men [*sic*] increasingly may have the opportunity to learn to know, and understand each other." The Commission set three objectives concerning international communication. The first task was to improve its physical facilities and operating mechanisms. The second objective was the progressive removal of political barriers and the lessening of economic restrictions. The third objective was the improvement of the accuracy, representative character, and quality of the words and images transmitted in international communications.

The report also noted that the "surest antidote for ignorance and deceit is the widest possible exchange of objectively realistic information – true information, not merely more information" (White and Leigh 1972). Many scholars have similarly questioned the success of

369

a mere quantitative increase in international information for understanding. Llewellyn White and Robert Leigh, for example, pointed out very early that there is evidence that a mere increase in the flow of words and images across national borders may replace ignorance with prejudice and distortion rather than with understanding (White and Leigh 1972).

As the representative of the University for Peace in Costa Rica, I was one of the university presidents from all regions and many cultures of the world who convened at Talloires, France, in September 1988. We believed that the universities of the world bear the profound moral responsibility for increasing understanding of the awful risks of the nuclear age and for reduceing those risks. In a world that is plagued by war, hunger, injustice, and suffering, we believed that universities nurture life through the creation and transmission of knowledge. There are 60 million university students and 2 million teachers engaged in higher education throughout the world who could join these endeavours.

One concrete proposal was a "global classroom." If universities design and implement an international information centre and communications consortium, these facilities would support the exchange of information, provide communications based on relatively low-cost technologies, offer access to computer networks, and afford one-way, and two-way, television linkages among university classrooms in various parts of the world. Since then there have been both global and regional projects – both multilateral and bilateral – implementing and promoting the idea. With the new communications technology and the information super-highways we may be closer to those ideals than we imagine. We may be close to the ideas of global learning that were developed in the early programmes of the UNU, where education and communication were seen as resources for the management of change.

Not only rapid changes in technology, but also fundamental social, political, and economic transformations, are challenging our traditional concepts of universities and communication. In 1985 the late Rector of the United Nations University, Soedjatmoko, observed that the problems educators face in the industrial world are vastly different from those faced in the developing areas (Soedjatmoko 1985). In the North, institutions of higher learning have not responded adequately to the new educational needs and opportunities of their rapidly changing economies and societies. As a result, many institutions and centres in the military and government other than universities have entered the field of education and research. We have to look for the new communications media as a partner in global university activities and in the dissemination of research findings.

Furthermore, rapid technical change has led to the need for specialization, which results in a process of fragmentation, growing alienation, and crisis in values. The fragmentation of the world is reflected and reinforced by the fragmentation of knowledge systems produced by the modern conception of science. Reality is broken up into bits and pieces according to the logic of technocrats rather than according to the logic of the reality itself. Because of the fragmented character of human knowledge it is becoming increasingly divorced from the reality it seeks to comprehend. In order to understand global development, we need new integrated and interdisciplinary approaches to study reality.

In the South, the basic issue is still both the quantity and quality of universities and communications systems. There are simply too few institutions to accommodate the relentless growth of the population. Very often the educational institutions in the South follow the European model in their curriculum even though it is no longer relevant in Europe.

As Soedjatmoko observed, we are witnessing a widening of the gap between those with ready access to information and those lacking such access. The North–South gap has become the information gap, demonstrating conclusively that information means power. One needs to look anew at the development process – which is essentially a learning process. Development succeeds when a society as a whole learns to make optimal use of its resources, through the application of science and technology, to improve the daily lives of its citizens in ways that are consonant with their basic values and aspirations.

4. Communications structure and power

There is an increasing understanding among scholars of international communication that the future basis for power will be analysed more in terms of culture and civilization. The transnational power structure of the production and dissemination of international information was broadly analysed by Latin American scholars such as Juan Somavia and Fernando Reyes-Matta in the 1970s (*Development Dialogue*, 1976, no. 2). Somavia was also a member of the McBride Commission. He analysed three different dimensions of the transnational power structure:

371

(1) the political–military–intelligence service dimension;
(2) the economic–industrial–trade dimension; and
(3) the communications–advertising–culture dimension (Somavia 1976: 15–28).

Somavia observed that the transnational communications system has developed with the support and at the service of the transnational power structure. It is an integral part of the system that affords control of that key instrument of contemporary society: information.

In the media field, we are only now learning what such new developments as real-time reporting and global journalism will mean. Discussion on the information super-highways, or Infobahn, and global information infrastructure is beginning. Technology has changed but many of the arguments are the same as before when new technologies were introduced. World communication encompasses cultural, economic, political, social, security, and military concerns. In fact, the rapid development of communications technology could make much of the political debates of the recent decades obsolete.

As confirmed by the wide range of research on the flow of information carried out in UNESCO and elsewhere, communications scholars have made significant contributions to the understanding of various aspects of the international flow of information. Special emphasis has been given to the mass media, trans-border data flow, satellites, and planetary resources of information flow. As noted in some of the conclusions of these studies, a close examination of these salient areas may assist us in analysing political, cultural, economic, technological, and professional practices affecting the international flow of information (see UNESCO 1974, 1985, 1994; Lewis 1993; also see Varis 1982).

However, critical academic literature has always pointed out that, in the analysis of communication between people, we deal with cultural differences. Most recently these views have been shared by more conservative researchers. Samuel P. Huntington, for example, claims that the fundamental source of conflict in the new world will not be primarily ideological or economic. Instead he claims that the great divisions among humankind, and the dominating source of conflict, will be cultural. For the relevant future, there will be no universal civilization, but instead a world of different civilizations, each of which will have to learn to coexist with the others (Huntington 1993: 22–49). A German novelist, Hans Magnus Enzensberger, observes that the post–Cold War world is entering a new civil war where cultural differences become emphasized. The mass media, especially television, contribute strongly to this moral corruption (Enzensberger 1993: 170–175; and 1994). Other scholars may disagree with this approach. Paul Kennedy, for example, stresses such factors as demographic explosion, the communications and financial revolution and the rise of the multinational corporation, and biotechnology in his approach to contemporary changes in the world structure (Kennedy 1993).

Critical international communications research is often ignored in scholarly debates because it has never produced any coherent theoretical frame of reference or paradigm to attract academic researchers. However, international communications research has often been socially relevant. Philip Elliott (1982), for example, in comparing the concepts and results of critical communications and peace research, found similar interests. Research on the production of the mass media has focused on such issues as concentration in the centres and transnational media oligopolies. The study of ideology has dealt with the content of communication, such as the nature of racism and materialism today. Studies of effects have explored the social impact of communication. They have demonstrated the increasing knowledge gap in the world. History and future studies dealing with media developments have analysed information and cultural industries. Such problems seem to be as relevant today as they were 20 years ago.

Carlos Gomez-Palacio and Ruben Jara (1989) point out that, in the Latin American context, critical scholars have emphasized mass media ownership, alternative communication, and democratization of mass media. Today, increasing attention is given to the role of alternative media in Latin America and elsewhere. A recent UNESCO publication, for example, described the present era as marked by the processes of concentration, commodification, and the slide towards a homogeneous world media system in which the commercial replaces the public and the citizen is redefined as a consumer (Lewis 1993). A counter-strategy would involve both the development of alternative, usually localized, media and critical monitoring, intervention in, and sometimes use of mainstream media. This kind of thinking is a logical continuation of research work from the 1970s.

Several efforts to bring about a structural change were started in the 1970s. Alternative news agencies, such as the third world news agency Inter Press Service (IPS), headquartered in Rome, were created. With the fall of the Berlin Wall a new process of realignment was activated in which the third world lost its strategic importance stemming from the East–West confrontation. In 1994, Inter Press Service concluded that it was obsolete, together with the concept of a third world. This has a very close correlation with the drop in financial aid for development, which has become widespread and in some cases dramatic, as in the cases of Italy, Finland, and Canada. The new thinking emphasizes the concept of global human security. In other words, current problems are always more global, to which no solutions can be found without the involvement of the South as well (IPS 1994). However, this is not yet recognized at all levels.

Marc Nerfin wrote in the *Dossier* of the International Foundation for Development Alternatives (IFDA) in 1991 that it was not possible to continue publication as before: first because today's world bears little resemblance to that of 1978, when IFDA started the *Dossier*, and second because of financial uncertainties (*IFDA Dossier*, April/June 1991). Nerfin wrote that the failures of the first real alternatives to world capitalism do not in any way exonerate capitalism from its negative record. Founded as it is on the bad side of human nature, greed, and selfishness, fostering competition and inequality, capitalism necessarily produces winners and losers, the latter's fate being determined by the winners' control of information.

Fundamental changes are also taking place in development research. Since the beginning of the 1990s, development research has entered into a process of reassessment in order to adapt paradigms and theories of its field to the new economic, political, and social realities that have emerged since the 1960s. Recent changes in population growth, world political order, and technology have brought down the geographical mental barriers of the development approach. Traditionally restricted to the problems of the South and North–South relations, development studies now have a tendency to extend their field to all regions of the world, because the nature of phenomena is now seen to be more similar everywhere. The philosophy of sustainable development has been introduced (Auroi 1993).

Current internationalization, however, provokes contradictory processes such as political and economic regionalism. Technology and communications media become international, but their use and content are regionally internalized and often modified. As globalization of consumption patterns grows, increased cultural reaction and resistance can also be noticed. Claude Auroi observes that cultural diversity has suddenly and violently (as in the former Yugoslavia) come to the forefront of development issues as a factor for explaining successes and failures:

Cultural arguments are not only challenging development as a process of modernisation, but also the centralising role of the State. This approach is also very close and reviews somehow alternative development theory while focusing on people-centered and people-oriented social and political movements. As processes of regional disintegration are going on and extending in Europe and Africa the importance of these approaches is magnified and will certainly be further strengthened in the future. (Auroi 1993)

The new orientation of UNESCO emphasizes the role of alternative media. Lewis (1993) stresses the importance of democratic participant media theory. This means, among other things, that individuals and minorities have rights of access to media and that the organization and content of the media should not be subject to centralized political or state bureaucratic control. Alternative media are being used in a contemporary social and theoretical context by old and new social movements.

5. Global learning

The World Summit for Social Development held in Copenhagen in March 1995 reflected the view that world economic development has to deal with issues such as the security of people. We are developing a new concept of security. Those who experienced the Cold War tended to view security in terms of the external and internal security of the state. With the ideological vision of the Cold War over, the sources of insecurity for people are increasingly seen to be unemployment, poverty, violence in the home and on the streets, political violence, discrimination, and drugs. In other words, the notion of security is increasingly coming to mean human security.

Unless we are prepared to deal with the great problems of human security, the transition to the twenty-first century will be far from peaceful. If the existing social tensions continue, we will likely have some sort of authoritarian response. Something like this could well happen in Latin America, which has a tradition of authoritarian responses and violent reactions in social situations. In the Islamic world it could mean more fundamentalism. In Eastern Europe there could be more ultra-nationalism and going backwards to the old. In the West it could mean growing xenophobia and an increasing feeling that democracies are not capable of dealing with the problems of people.

The global realities of technology, political order, population growth, and cultures require new planning for research on global development. The rise of regional groupings and the threat of protectionism create new options for economic development but also potential for conflict. Globalism can be hegemonic in nature and regionalism may lead to interregional conflicts. Spiritual values, which may take many forms from nationalism, fundamentalism, or ecumenicalism, are integral elements in the multicultural world.

The late Vice-Rector of the United Nations University, Edward Ploman, stressed that conventional systems of education can no longer absorb the range of knowledge now being generated or disseminate it in the usual educational time-span (Ploman 1985: 9–21). Conventional education cannot respond to demands for equitable, timely, and widespread access to knowledge and information or to learning needs caused by the rapid outdating of knowledge. His view was that new modes for learning and knowledge-sharing are required at all levels of society, using all available services and techniques. This, in essence, was the idea of global learning as a response to global change.

6. Future directions

The proposals that follow include initiatives that should be taken by scholars, grass-roots organizations, or specific UN organizations. The United Nations system rests on the principles of liberalism and humanism, the notion of economic and social progress, and the idea of development. The interpretation of these principles and the advent of modern communications technology have changed the ways governments and nations react to international events, thus increasing the importance of transparency (Bassin 1994). Decisions and their preparations become more available in the public media, too. Future UN staff must have competence in coping with the new media environment.

The creation of a new global vision for communications

Scholars are needed to define the role of communication in the future United Nations. In general, the main challenge is an intellectual one. In 1945, poets and intellectuals were used in drafting UNESCO's constitution. Leading independent scholars and other intellectuals should again be asked to contribute to the creation of a new global vision for communications. Since the future global information society will be a multicultural and multi-linguistic society with a diversity of minorities, the new approach must reflect a panoply of civilizations. Efforts to deepen the understanding of intercultural communication should be encouraged. These issues belong in UNESCO's field of interest.

Evaluation of the performance of the United Nations in the world media

Research by independent and qualified research institutions is needed in order to evaluate the performance of the United Nations in the world media. It is now widely recognized that media and communications issues are an increasingly important area for the United Nations. They are an essential element in efforts to develop an early-warning system, because the international media monitor real-time conflict developments all over the world. From time to time, the United Nations has carried out research on the press coverage of the United Nations. Research has shown that wars have always required propaganda for both their initiation and their conduct. Wars do not normally start without elaborate procedures of parliamentary or council discussions, with accompanying declarations, orders, and proclamations dealing with its means, ends, and justifications. However, destructive wars in the developing countries are not officially declared as wars. But a systematic monitoring of media coverage of potential crisis and conflict areas could be developed as a kind of early-warning journalism.

People's contributions

The UN General Assembly has recognized (United Nations 1994) that reliable statistics, monitoring a state's economic activity and tracking economic, social, and environmental change, are essential for informed decision-making and the formulation of acceptable and workable solutions. New ways of collecting and disseminating statistics and indicators are needed. In doing this, the contributions of grass-roots organizations and the independent research community, which understand the interrelatedness of economic, social, human, and sustainable development, are needed. One way of promoting this is to strengthen dialogue between the mass media and the research community.

Applications of the new technology

Specialized agencies, and other organizations in the UN system, require independent, critical contributions by communications scholars on several issues. Telecommunications philosophy is already searching for the relationship between development and telecommunications. They are asking questions such as: How do we guarantee a global, universal service in the planned global information infrastructures and information super-highways? How are users trained? Who pays? Is there any clever way of using existing old technology for delivering new services?

Threats of info-terrorism and cyber warfare

The new global network economy and the information society based on new information and communications technology also create new threats of "info-terrorism" and "cyber warfare" through which a few capable hackers could shut down major economies (Laquer 1996). The vulnerability of high-tech cultures is a new concern and must be dealt with as an aspect of terrorism. But the people's security is also threatened by the use of new communications for facilitating surveillance. These challenging new issues for UN agencies concerned with human security and human rights offer a demanding new agenda for international communications scholars.

Socio-economic aspects of the global information economy

The leaders of the G7 countries discussed in early 1995 the global information infrastructure. The key issues included networks and their inter-operability, the regulatory framework, and an assessment of the applications of the global information infrastructure and their social impact. This is of direct relevance to the ITU. The ITU has to define global priorities not only for the rich countries but for all countries. Furthermore, since global information infrastructures are changing the nature of work and introducing new concepts such as telework, the International Labour Organization (ILO) must have a higher profile in examining the social and employment impact of telecommunications.

Worldwide monitoring of piracy

Flow issues remain relevant because they have become a source of conflict even in world trade negotiations. Europe, in particular, wants to develop quota systems, whereas Americans favour a policy of free trade. Piracy and illegal copying of intellectual property in different parts of the world are becoming a major problem and a new research and monitoring area for the relevant specialized agencies. The role of WIPO is increasing because the definitions of authenticity, publicity, and intellectual property rights are affecting world trade. Action is needed to monitor and report on piracy worldwide. The demand for openness in the world telecommunications market must be combined with adequate monitoring of intellectual property rights.

Global training

Global learning is a challenge for the research and training efforts of the United Nations University system. There should be multicultural efforts to use modern communications and information technology effectively, especially satellites and computers. Closer cooperation with projects that already have experience in global electronic university experiments and affordable technology, such as the Global Systems Analysis and Simulation Association in the United States, would be useful.

Towards a virtual UN-related university

The United Nations could also make better use of inter-institutional communications and information-sharing, at least in training and research activities. Different research and training centres would form a virtual university linked by telecommunications.

Educating for the world information economy

The new global realities of information technology, political order, and cultures should be taken into account when planning research on global development. The United Nations University, for example, could take up new research issues such as the information and telecommunications technologies applied to education and training in the field of global economic development.

Communicative competence in world society

The implications of technological change for lifelong learning and human resource development in all parts of the world will be significant. The application of learning technologies in flexible and distance learning could reinforce and expand the role of the new technology in widening access to lifelong learning and in equipping the workforce with the skills and expertise required in modern global economic development. Critical research should be carried out on the regional implementation and global promotion of new learning and dissemination technologies. Issues should include the implementation of the principle of universal service, financing, and citizens' communication skills.

Other issues that should be addressed would include the pedagogical effectiveness of technology-based learning; its cost efficiency; identification of ways in which cultural and language barriers can most easily be overcome; the exploitability and re-usability of learning materials and their adaptation to divergent cultures; and the identification of appropriate management and organizational structures to support extensive, diversified, complex, and multifaceted infrastructure. More attention should be given to the new global satellite and other telecommunications systems, which are able to deliver almost as many services as the new fibre optic networks being built by many telephone companies, which can reach underdeveloped and rural areas typically cut off from advanced communications.

In summary, because the new information and communications technology, especially telecommunications, is central to the economic development of all countries, it will have a qualitatively more important role for all UN-related activities. The next communications era challenges many basic assumptions concerning the nature of learning, work, participation, and governance. The physical ecology of the planet may be affected by the introduction of telecommunications and related industries. The idea of a community of nations and people is modified when space and geography are added with the dimension of cyberspace – in which people are interconnected by technological means alone. In short, several issues that had a technical connotation in the past will become political and must be discussed in political terms in international forums.

An unstable and unpredictable world cannot favour harmonious world development. The preparatory work of the United Nations

Conference on World Social Development (1995) identified sources of insecurity emerging from unemployment, poverty, violence, discrimination, and drugs. These sources often have an economic base, but they are also communication issues because the media set the agenda, even for the United Nations, to deal with these issues.

The world is developing towards regional trade blocs whose impact on global development must be carefully evaluated. Technology is bringing the world together, but many cultural factors fundamentally divide people. The existing tension between the technologically strong and the weak is already creating political pressures in the world that are not conducive to a peaceful world order in the twenty-first century.

References

Alger, Chadwick F. 1990. "Telecommunications, Self-Determination, and World Peace." In Sven B. Lundstedt, ed., *Telecommunications, Values, and the Public Interest*. Norwood, N.J.: Ablex Publishing Corporation, pp. 36–51.

Auroi, Claude. 1993. "The State of the Art in Development Studies and Paradigmatic Prospects." UNU/WIDER Board Meeting, Helsinki, 28 June.

Bassin, Benjamin. 1994. "What Role for the United Nations in World Economic and Social Development?" UNU/WIDER seminar on The Politics and Economics of Global Employment, Helsinki, 17–18 June.

Development Dialogue. 1976. No. 2.

Elliott, Philip. 1982. *The Role of the Media in Creating or Reinforcing Perceptions of Security*. UNESCO SS-82/CONF.614/16. Paris: UNESCO.

Enzensberger, Hans Magnus. 1993. "Ausblicke auf den Burgerkrieg." *Der Spiegel*, no. 25.

———— 1994. *Civil War*. London: Granta Books.

Fortner, Robert S. 1993. *International Communication. History, Conflict, and Control of the Global Metropolis*. Belmont, Calif.: Wadsworth.

Gomez-Palacio, Carlos, and Ruben J. Jara. 1989. "The Growth of Communication Research in Latin America." Paper presented at the International Communication Association Annual Convention, May.

Huntington, Samuel P. 1993. "The Clash of Civilizations?" *Foreign Affairs*, vol. 72, no. 3.

Independent Commission for the Study of Communication Problems. 1980. *Many Voices – One World*. Paris: UNESCO.

IPS (Inter Press Service). 1994. Circular Letter, 24 May.

ITU (International Telecommunication Union). 1984. *The Missing Link. Report of the Independent Commission for World-wide Telecommunications Development*. Geneva: ITU.

———— 1989. "1st World Electronic Media Symposium." Geneva, 4–6 October.

Kennedy, Paul. 1993. *Preparing for the Twenty-first Century*. London: HarperCollins.

Laquer, Walter. 1996. "Postmodern Terrorism." *Foreign Affairs*, September/October, pp. 24–36.

Lewis, Peter, ed. 1993. *Alternative Media: Linking Global and Local.* UNESCO Reports and Papers on Mass Communication No. 107. Paris: UNESCO.

Melody, William H. 1994. "Communication and Information Studies: The Moulding of a New Social Science." Manuscript.

Mertineit, Walter. 1979. "Strategies, Concepts and Methods of International History Textbook Revision: A German Share in Education for International Understanding." *International Journal of Political Education*, no. 2, pp. 101–114.

Ploman, Edward W. 1985. "Communication, Education and the Management of Change." In *Coping with Change: The Democratic Way*. London: University of London, Department of Extra-Mural Studies.

Raevsky, A., and I. N. Vorob'ev. 1994. *Russian Approaches to Peacekeeping Operations*. UNIDIR Research Paper No. 28. Geneva: UNIDIR.

Soedjatmoko. 1985. *The International Dimension of Universities in an Interdependent World*. Eighth General Conference, International Association of Universities, University of California, Los Angeles.

Somavia, Juan. 1976. "The Transnational Power Structure and International Information." *Development Dialogue*, no. 2.

Soroos, Marvin. 1986. *Beyond Sovereignty: The Challenge of Global Policy*. Columbia: University of South Carolina Press.

UNESCO (UN Educational, Scientific, and Cultural Organization). 1974. *Television Traffic – A One-Way Street*? UNESCO Reports and Papers on Mass Communication No. 70. Paris: UNESCO.

——— 1985. *International Flow of Television Programmes*. UNESCO Reports and Papers on Mass Communication No. 100. Paris: UNESCO.

——— 1993. *UNESCO Activities in the Matter of Free Flow of Information and Freedom of Expression*. UNESCO Communication Division, 5 April.

——— 1994. *TV Transnationalization: Europe and Asia*. UNESCO Reports and Papers on Mass Communication No. 109. Paris: UNESCO.

United Nations. 1994. *Development and International Economic Cooperation*. General Assembly, A/48/935, 6 May. New York.

Urquhart, Brian, and Erskine Childers. 1996. *A World in Need of Leadership: Tomorrow's United Nations – A Fresh Appraisal*. Uppsala: Dag Hammarskjold Foundation.

Varis, Tapio. 1982. "Peace and Communication – An Approach by Flow Studies." *Journal of Peace Research*, no. 3.

White, Llewellyn, and Robert D. Leigh. 1972. *Peoples Speaking to Peoples. A Report on International Communication from the Commission on Freedom of the Press*. New York: Arno Press (reprinted edition).

Part IV
Developing the foundations:
Peace education

12

The United Nations' role in peace education

Sanàa Osseiran and Betty Reardon

1. Peace education: Vital to the mission of the United Nations

"We, the peoples of the United Nations" today comprise virtually all the peoples of the world. Indeed, this chapter argues that the United Nations should reaffirm the original ideals embodied in its Charter by acting as the promoter, and as the protector, of peace among the peoples of the world in whose name its existence is justified, and through which people's aspirations for justice and peace are legitimized. One of the significant ways to promote and protect peace is through education; thus, peace education has developed as an arena of concern for the United Nations and should be more prominent in its activities. Those who wrote UNESCO's constitution were indeed visionary when they proclaimed "that since war begins in the minds of men, it is in the minds of men [sic] that the defenses of peace must be constructed." Peace is a concept that derives from a vision of the world that transcends frontiers, ethnicities, nationalities, religions, and those human differences used to rationalize war and oppression. Peace education is an instrument for realizing this holistic vision. It comprises a complex, intertwined network of concepts, values, and approaches to learning that underlines the unity of being in all its diversity.

The United Nations, as the main diagnostician of the global ill-nesses of poverty, ecological destruction, human rights violation, and violent conflicts, is the main repository of knowledge about the prob-lems of justice and peace, which is the basis of much of peace educa-tion. Various commissions of inquiry convened by the United Nations have linked peace to disarmament, development, and security: the Olof Palme Report, the Brandt Report, and others. Indeed, Bengt Telin (1991) affirms that the conclusions of the Palme Report were nothing else than a reaffirmation of the principles of the United Nations Charter. And, as with most such reports, UN policy docu-ments, and campaigns, Telin implies that the derivation of cures requires learning, so education is seen as an essential therapy. Such education, however, should not be limited to students enrolled in formal institutions. It must include, of course, the non-formal educa-tion of the broad citizenry, and *all* of the social and political institu-tions that determine their lives. The holism of peace education involves not only a comprehensive view of the global issues and their interrelationships as subject matter, but also an integrated approach to communities, groups, organizations, and institutions. All such actors of civil society are both agents and subjects of learning.

It is this approach that informs the Teachers College Peace Educa-tion Program (TCEP) course entitled "The United Nations as Peace Educator." The emphasis of the course is on what is being learned about the needs and possibilities of peace-making by and through an organization created primarily and specifically to make peace and within the growing collaborative relationships between the United Nations and non-governmental organizations (NGOs). Indeed, the philosophy of the TCEP and the form of peace education it conveys assume that there is more to be learned than to be taught about peace, and that the most effective educators are primarily purposeful, effective learners (Reardon 1988).

The course participants, including the "instructor," have learned a good deal about institutional learning abilities and concluded that the United Nations, like the peace researchers whose work is intention-ally directed at producing the knowledge that will lead to peace, knows a good deal more about the causes of war and the conditions of violence and injustice than it does about how to achieve and maintain peace. Both the United Nations and peace research have produced valid diagnoses of the structures and circumstances that result in systemic violence and armed conflict, and both are equally lacking in clear conceptualizations of and strategies for achieving alternatives. This situation, we believe, derives from the state system that created and controls the United Nations, a system that legitimizes and makes frequent use of armed violence, and often poses obstacles to efforts to interrupt, overcome, and seek alternatives to the use of armed force in international conflict. The international organization itself is now making more of an effort to integrate capacities for non-violent conflict resolution into its repertoire of procedural possibilities. Indeed, this creature of the conflictual state system perceives a need for such capacity within the regular daily functioning of its administrative and programme personnel, and is seeking training opportunities for staff at headquarters and in the field. For instance, the International Center for Cooperation and Conflict Resolution at Teachers College, Columbia University, was engaged to offer such training beginning in 1996. However, criticisms of the Secretary-General's 1992 annual message, *An Agenda for Peace* (Boutros-Ghali 1992), which attempted to clarify and define UN operations in peace-keeping and peace-making, adding to the institutional repertoire a new and urgently needed UN operation – peace-building – noted the essentially military approach taken in the report.[1] In sum, it did not offer new non-violent alternatives for UN peace-keeping and conflict resolution. Peace-learning has revealed the urgent need for a range of possibilities for conducting the affairs of the human community under the presumption that violence is neither acceptable nor necessary.

A similar critique, we admit, can be made of peace studies and peace education, whose focus and emphasis have been problem rather than prescription oriented and focused more on preventing war than on building peace. There are, however, some significant differences between UN and peace education approaches to the problems. Whereas the fields of peace research and education recognize a need for systemic and structural change, including significant changes in the system of state sovereignty, the United Nations takes a somewhat contradictory view that systemic and structural changes, although needed, must be pursued within the continued context of the system of sovereign states, a position articulated even as it takes actions and makes recommendations that impose substantial limits on the power of states over their own citizens, the natural environment, and their relationships to each other.

State sovereignty is at once the organizing myth and the major obstacle to the success of the United Nations. One of the lessons resulting from this analysis is that it is in this contradiction that the failures of the United Nations as peace educator lie. It has not challenged the member states to consider alternatives to this system, nor has it been able to persuade them to educate their publics toward the construction of alternatives to a system that perpetuates and is perpetuated by war. It seems that the United Nations cannot acknowledge that peace-building requires peace-learning on the part of the member states themselves as well as those whose education they design and deliver. It is then a small miracle and a testament to the strength of globalism as an ethos and as a perspective on war and other world problems that the United Nations has been able to learn and to do what it has and continues to achieve in the field of peace education.

2. A goal-centred definition of peace education

What is peace education? The term has different meanings that vary with culture, political context, and socio-economic conditions. For us, the purpose of peace education is learning to become aware of and to act within the context of "the unity of being," by which we mean essentially the oneness of humanity and its symbiotic relation to our planet. Peace education, as figure 12.1 indicates, is a means of consciously participating in the unity of being. It is finding a common ground for comprehending unity in the diversity of humankind manifested in different cultural contexts. The illustration is constructed from a circle and an eight-pointed figure based on an Arabic mathematical form of eight circles or divisions multiplied into another eight circles or divisions forming the interdependent elements that can lead to local and global peace. It is but one approach, there being diverse ways in various cultures to conceptualize and illustrate the unity of being. This illustration derived from Arabic culture represents the "unity of being" in which humankind, other living creatures, and systems comprise the planetary whole. Peace is at the centre of the illustrative circle because it signifies the central and organizing principle of human purpose and evolution. However, for peace to exist requires at least 16 interdependent elements. None of these elements takes priority over others and each represents a part of the whole, essential to peace. So the presentation is circular rather than linear or vertical, a form that has both conceptual and normative significance.

At the core of peace education is, therefore, the consciousness and conscience of the human being. It seeks to develop persons with rational, ethical minds whose vision of the world and its inhabitants is

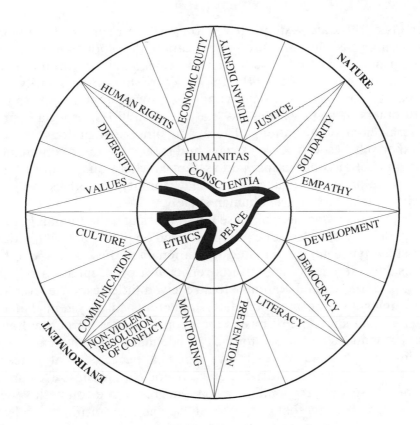

*" The freedom from want and the freedom from fear
which together with the freedom from ignorance to some
extent condition all other human freedoms. "*
(Federico Mayor Zaragossa, Director General of UNESCO)

Fig. 12.1 **Interdependence leads to peace and gives hope to humankind (Source:
designed by Sanàa Osseiran and Heysa Lakhder).**

that of a unity. The values that animate this unity can be expressed in
different cultural connotations according to varying modes of life, but
the unity does not imply that there is one conceptual vision of this
unity. Diversity and differences are a natural expression of this consciousness; however, peace remains the underlying value and the
instrument by which this unity is achieved through interdependence.
This unitary vision of the world is realized through the notion of
the right of the human being to dignity in living, receiving justice,
experiencing freedom, and all the rights that are recognized as essential to human dignity. The United Nations, within the limits and con-

389

straints of the state system, strives to assist the peoples of the world by raising consciousness through education, development assistance, and encouraging member states to redress inequalities. But it remains for the peoples of the world to work actively for solidarity and empathy with each other, and within their own environments to link with others through various associative possibilities, especially non-governmental organizations. These and other associations, as well as other vehicles, can serve as ways and means of better communication and better cooperation, and as venues where human norms and values are presented in such a way that morality and ethics can yield positive dividends for each human society.

To promote awareness of these possibilities and the humanity from which they arise, peace educators embarked on programmes to reduce the stereotyped images created by nationalism, Fascism, and other "isms." These educational efforts reflected a preoccupation of "the peoples of the United Nations" that received little response from the governments of the member states, adherents to a system that negates human unity and dismisses the people's hopes for peace; hopes that are tenuous and vague for lack of adequate peace education.

How many people are really aware of what peace is, what it means, and what it involves? Most societies, if not all, emphasize competitiveness in schools, responding in some degree to the competitiveness of a specific society, that of the Northern and Western industrialized states, which dominate the world economy and whose economic markets could not survive without this competitiveness. However, peace educators increasingly advocate that the route to peace-building lies in providing peace education based on culturally varied but common human values and ethics that valorize cooperation rather than competition, solidarity and empathy instead of indifference, interdependence in place of dependence and dominance.

Peace education regards the world, its peoples, and its problems in a holistic, interdependent framework where development, dignity, compassion, and sharing among the societies of the world should be highly present, and where women have an equal role with men in shaping the peaceful society. The United Nations has professed through its specialized agencies and affirms in *An Agenda for Peace* this interdependence and this need for solidarity, and reaffirms the principles of its Charter, upholding the notion that the dignity of humankind is not sustainable except in a democratic order that ensures justice, equitable development, and protection and restoration of the global environment, all dependent on both states and peoples learning new modes of relationships and problem-solving.

3. Operative concepts and purposes

From its very foundation, the United Nations has acknowledged the fundamental need for an educational dimension to achieve its mission to "avoid the scourge of war." Indeed, UNESCO was established as the agency to promote that dimension because the primary cause of the scourge lay in the human mind. Constructing the foundations of peace in the human mind was seen as essential to achieving its tasks. As the United Nations' major achievements have been in areas other than actual war–peace issues, so too the development of direct education about war and peace has not constituted the major UN accomplishment in the field of education. The day-to-day work of the UN system, conducted largely through the specialized agencies, has meant that its educational endeavours have been largely in the service of "national development." And national development, although clearly dependent on peace for its optimum realization, had not included any notable efforts in education for peace until recent years, when Lebanon did so in its 10-year plan for national post-conflict reconstruction and El Salvador became the site of some of UNESCO's primary efforts in the construction of a culture of peace. (This acknowledgement of the need for peace education was, in the case of Lebanon, the result of 17 years of civil war, and that of El Salvador 12 years.) None the less, the UN system has played a significant role in peace education, certainly inspiring and encouraging those minimal efforts forthcoming from educational ministries and the established instructional systems, and to an even greater degree in those private initiatives made outside the formal structure.

As a creature of the state system whose life and functions are determined by the perceptions and priorities of member states, the view the UN system has taken of education has been in general an instrumental one. Although more lofty and philosophical purposes have been espoused in such landmark reports as *Learning to Be* (Faure 1974) and, more recently, *Education for All* (UNESCO 1994), education has been conceived and implemented as a vehicle for other policy objectives, and those the United Nations system has been concerned with have been primarily economic. Although the work of UNESCO has in many respects been an exception, it, too, has devoted considerable effort to educational programmes directed toward the economic objectives embedded in "national development."

The educational efforts of the United Nations system, like those of ministries of education, have shown more concern for skill development and for proficiencies for contributing to processes of modernization, technical progress, and national development than for the development of the human mind or for introducing into it concepts and values conducive to peace. Indeed, modernist state-dominated education, many of us claim, is actually antithetical to peace and, as is now evident, to those values without which peace cannot be realized, or social justice and ecological responsibility achieved. Modernism, with its emphasis on specialization, its tendency toward fragmentation, and its encouragement of economic competition and the global market, reflecting a primarily Western world-view, has become a value system that many peace educators believe must be overcome if we are to overcome the war system. Some, especially those who pursue their efforts in the converging contexts of peace and ecology, see the two phenomena – contemporary war and modernism – as reciprocal and mutually reinforcing. Clearly, the homogenization of human society is antithetical to the political pluralism, multiculturalism, and economic diversity espoused by peace education.

State-centred, modernist views to a significant degree account for the disregard of many efforts undertaken by independent peace educators, especially the founders and early members of the Peace Education Commission (PEC) of the International Peace Research Association (IPRA), and their devaluation and, in some cases, denunciation, as much by the United Nations and its agencies as by the educational establishments of their respective states. PEC peace educators, in the tradition of the researchers whose work influenced the substance of the education they were developing, took a critical stance. Indeed, peace education, for the most part and in many countries, emphasized the development of the critical capacities it deemed essential to discerning the causes not only of war but of all forms of violence, including the cultural violence inherent in Western, modernist models of development, and now the economic violence that accompanies the globalization of free market capitalism.

Generally practised as a form of social education, peace education tended not to direct its pedagogy at socialization and transferring the knowledge and skills necessary for the maintenance or modernization of society as it exists, as do standard curricula and education. Rather, it aimed at eliciting the concerns and abilities likely to change society and eradicate the problems imposed by colonialism and modernism, so as to overcome structural and cultural violence and replace organized armed violence with non-violent alternatives for security and conflict resolution; in short, to transcend the lethal competition of the international system of sovereign states and the inequities of the global economy, toward the realization of the "unity of being."

PEC was founded and moulded in the early 1970s, years in which criticism of national policies on security, development, and human rights was integrated into new forms of education. There was a close alliance between peace educators and other educational reformers who stood in opposition to many of the traditional practices of the education establishment. Thus it was that the most critical and transformative approaches and materials being developed by peace educators were for decades marginalized, if not actually opposed, by the national and international institutional structures of education. So, too, "global" or "international" education, less critical than and not so intentionally transformative as peace education, was accepted into some formal schooling as a response to the implications of the mid-century international system and the lobbying of "global educators." These approaches focused primarily on discrete problems of the global order viewed from the perspective of the existing state system. This problem orientation led to a proliferation of forms of global and peace education. Whereas "interdependence" became a byword of international education, the interrelationships among and the systemic nature of the various global issues were not featured in the offerings slowly working their way into some schools of Western industrialized states. Indeed, it was not until the environmental education movement merged with other aspects of global and peace education that these systemic relationships were actually integrated into the development of curricula and methods. This led toward a holistic approach such as that advocated here and presaged in UNESCO's most recent statements and projects.

4. Instruments and objectives: UNESCO

Although various UN agencies and departments have acknowledged education as a significant contributing factor in meeting programme and policy objectives, and have undertaken educational activities that thus could be classified as peace education, it is UNESCO that is formally assigned the tasks of education. In undertaking to construct the foundations of peace in "the minds of men," UNESCO first took the route of international understanding, and under the constraints imposed by the demands of member states did not substantially, in fact, address the structural and political causes of war or alternative possibilities for peace as the subject of formal (or, indeed, non-formal) education.

This situation began to change with its landmark policy statement of 1974, "A Recommendation Concerning Education for International Understanding, Cooperation and Peace and Education Relating to Human Rights and Fundamental Freedoms" (adopted by the 18th General Conference, 19 November 1974). This policy statement, and widely accepted definition of what comprises peace and "global" education, was a monument to the essential role UNESCO played in keeping open a dialogue between East and West during the Cold War. The dialogue was neither sheltered from nor unaffected by the ideological and political tensions of those years, nor from the competitive state system in which they were played out. Indeed, all participants had to proceed with utmost prudence in order to achieve anything substantive, and a few were as ideologically oriented as their respective governments. None the less, most were sincerely committed to the purposes of peace education and convinced of its necessity, if not empowered to carry out the implementation of their recommendations. The 1974 Recommendation was carefully crafted by educators sensitive to the problems and adept at finding ways to get across essential points in terms acceptable to the full range of member states. Perhaps it is this commitment to purpose and need, complemented by the acumen of the drafters, that accounts for the long life and significant influence of the statement. For it remained the main policy instrument in the field for 20 years and provided the foundation for further steps.

Like most such "official" statements, its significance was not in its practical application to the educational policies and practices of member states. Indeed, as noted, national ministries have done very little and mostly nothing to advance the cause of peace education. The Recommendation, however, was a map of the terrain to be covered by the field and an argument for its necessity that could not be denied even if it was ignored. As such, it proved useful to those peace educators who were making the case that peace education should be undertaken by their respective institutions and communities.

The 1974 Recommendation, as is the usual procedure in the development of UN statements and declarations, was cited or used as

394

a precedent for subsequent statements relevant to peace education, most notably those emerging from the 1978 International Conference on Human Rights Teaching (Vienna, 12–16 September 1978, SS-78/Conf. 401), the 1980 World Congress on Disarmament Education (UNESCO, Paris, 9–13 June 1980, SS/MD/35), the 1993 Congress on Education for Human Rights and Democracy (UNESCO 1993), and, most recently, the Integrated Framework of Action on Education for Peace, Human Rights, and Democracy (Paris, 24 October 1994, Ed/BIE/Confid/44, 4), affirmed by ministers of education at the 1994 International Conference on Education, and adopted by the 1995 General Conference of UNESCO.

It is still too early to make any judgement on the effects of the latter two policy statements, but sufficient time has elapsed to conclude that the 1978 and 1980 documents did not appreciably influence the status of peace education. Certainly, the statements calling for and documenting the need for the Decade for Human Rights Education that the United Nations declared at the end of 1994, and the elaboration of a plan of action to carry it out, attest to the lack of impact of the statement on human rights teaching on the broader fields of education.

The Final Document of the World Congress on Disarmament Education fell victim to the Cold War and state interests. Even UNESCO seemed to "disown" it because member states, especially Western states and most particularly the United States in stating its reasons for withdrawal from UNESCO, cited disarmament education as evidence of the agency's "politicization." Indeed, the human rights document was seen by the East as the consequence of the machinations of the capitalist states, and the disarmament document was denounced as the result of communist peace propaganda. From the perspective of one of the authors who was involved in the planning stages of both policy meetings, there was from that vantage point little evidence of either claim. However, there were very evident attempts on the part of various interests to influence the discussions and the statements. As is the case in all events where any of the significant participants are representatives of government, the process is politicized with or without the intent of the organizers.

It is palpably clear that no agency of the United Nations could successfully pursue educational purposes that produced critical analysis of crucial issues related to peace as seen from the perspective of member states, i.e. military security and the maintenance of domestic social order. The West felt its security interests to be especially threatened by disarmament education, fearing that it could lead to questioning of the militarization of those societies, while the East perceived possibilities for undermining the authority of the state inherent in human rights education. There is little cause to doubt that the fundamental concern of both was criticism of authority and possible consequent change of the established power structures. Similar motives have caused authorities to avoid, and in some cases denounce as socially dangerous, education efforts that deal with other issues of social or economic justice, including racism and sexism. All, with the exception of sexism, designated in somewhat different wording of human equality and human rights, were taken to be integral to the objectives and purposes espoused in the 1974 Recommendation.

The phasing out of the Cold War, arising in part from the changing global economic and political trends that made its continued pursuit disadvantageous to the interests of both participants, helped to remove some of these barriers, but raised new and equally daunting challenges to UNESCO and all agencies of the United Nations concerned with peace education. UNESCO has responded not only with an emphasis on human rights and democracy, as reflected in its 1993 and 1994 documents, but with a move toward a more holistic approach, which should lend support to those peace educators who advocate holism. The most noteworthy manifestation is the Culture of Peace Programme. Although much of its early work has been in post-conflict situations, a culture of peace is conceived in a comprehensive fashion that embraces all of human culture.

World cultures today are still entrapped in the state system, where politics and economics comprise a global culture of war. This culture is maintained by military violence and mediated through the economically violent structures and processes of the global market, which oppress and deprive large portions of "the peoples of the United Nations."

UNESCO's efforts under the Culture of Peace Programme, its initiatives undertaken through the Year of Tolerance (1995), and its curricular contributions to the UN Decade for Human Rights Education (1995–2004) show promise of addressing these issues through learning programmes relevant to the needs and purposes of peace education.

5. Other United Nations agencies

Thus far, the work of the United Nations system that deals primarily with issues that peace research defines as structural violence is carried out by the specialized agencies and particular departments and programmes established within the Secretariat. Until recently, most of this work has been related to development (too often a thin veil for brutal processes of "modernization" and "globalization"). The best of these efforts have had significant effect on the quality of life of the poor, such as UNICEF's oral rehydration programme, which saves infants from dying of diarrhoea.

Although the initial design and purpose of the majority of these programmes have been mainly instrumental to economic objectives, such as the transfer of technology, the sorry history of development has brought forth a broader view of the role of education, encompassing social, cultural, and sometimes even political factors. These factors have proven to be especially important in the avowed UN aim of "integrating women into development." The original conception of women's potential role in development brought little significant change to the basic concept of development dictated by Western male economic and banking paradigms. However, the realities of the revolutionary and transformational potential of economic gender equity, and the needs of education for democracy, brought about an even greater change in the conditions in which all forms of social education are pursued than did even the demise of the Cold War.

It became obvious that one system change could not be undertaken without attention to many other, if not all, elements of the system concerned. A greater understanding of the fundamental interrelationship between global problems emerged among the agencies and peace educators. The gender issue also made evident the futility of trying to deal with economic and political factors as separate from social and cultural factors, an argument that was central to the evolving comprehensive and later holistic approach to peace education. Due in no small degree to the influence of the gender perspective, a clear trend toward the concept of peace education as learning to comprehend holism (as reflected in our illustration of the unity of being) has, indeed, emerged.

Most agencies involved in development mounted instrumental instructional and educational projects in the form of "technical training" to help carry out their objectives. Only UNICEF, however, evolved a form of development education that can be classified as peace education within the more widely espoused IPRA/PEC perspectives of comprehensiveness and holism and the integrated approaches of UNESCO's "Framework for Action."

Development education as initiated by UNICEF, and also by some

NGOs, was intended to provide not only students of the industrial countries but the general public as well with information about economic conditions in the "developing countries." Hence, the main focus of development education was on poverty as a problem and the economic and social consequences of global, structural violence, rather than on structural analysis and ethical consideration of the inequities of the global economic system. Consequently, there was a tendency to problematize and, indeed, to stigmatize the poor peoples and regions of the world. The educational results of these curricula were no more ethically acceptable than the concepts of "backwardness" that rationalized colonialism. Some members of PEC struggled against this approach in the private non-profit (some church-related) agencies in which they worked as educators. UNICEF, under the influence of the demands for a New Economic Order, and an awareness of the elements of neo-colonialism that ignored the ancient cultures, traditional values, and more appropriate technologies of the poor, agrarian peoples of the world, began to focus more on underlying issues and on the need for substantive education to replace exhortation.

Originally conceived as the information basis for "Trick or Treat for UNICEF" – the annual Halloween solicitation by American children for contributions to support UNICEF's efforts to improve the health and living conditions of children in the poor or warring countries – development education evolved into a sophisticated programme of materials development and teacher preparation for the education of children about the economic structures, systems, and conditions that cause ill health and poor living conditions. UNICEF's work in the field now focuses on interdependence, cultural integrity, and standards of justice. Its recent efforts such as *It's Only Right* (UNICEF 1993), a school curriculum on the rights of the child, place human rights in the holistic context we believe to be the most appropriate approach to peace education.

Like other agencies whose work is most relevant to peace education, UNICEF works in collaboration with NGOs as well as national committees for UNICEF and other relevant governmental and intergovernmental bodies. It is this intersectoral cooperation that has made possible the most positive developments in UN efforts at peace education. It is our assertion that this trend toward NGO–UN agency cooperation holds the greatest possibility for revitalizing the world organization, making it more relevant to the needs of "the peoples of the United Nations" and to its fundamental task of peace-making, a task doomed to failure so long as the dominant influence on UN efforts is the state system and not the voice and will of humanity, whose interests are better served by NGOs.

6. Collaboration with non-governmental organizations

Non-governmental organizations have been associated with the work of the United Nations from its inception. NGO–UN cooperation has grown over the decades to become a more integrated form of collaboration, including jointly planned and executed projects. NGOs have at times served the United Nations more faithfully than have member states in their devotion to the ideals and fundamental purposes of the United Nations. The 1991 UNESCO General Conference Report noted:

[S]tudies have shown that in Africa, Asia and particularly Latin America, it is the activities and actions taken by national and regional NGO's in education for Peace, Human Rights, Environment and Development which present the most satisfactory point of view in terms of immediate efficiency, flexibility and precision of their work, despite their modest financial and human resources. NGO's have proven to be pioneers and innovative in educational programs and are often well received by Government authorities after which they are incorporated into public education. (UNESCO 1991)

Collaboration between international NGOs, local NGOs, and the United Nations can also spread the good results of such cooperation. It reflects UN support for local initiatives and legitimizes participatory activities by the local population, empowering them to play a role in promoting a civil society and becoming the agents of their own decision-making. One example, and a case in point, is the joint effort between the International Peace Research Association (IPRA), UNESCO, United Nations Assistance for the Reconstruction and Development of the Lebanon (UNARDOL), and other UN agencies such as the United Nations Development Programme (UNDP) and UNICEF on peace-building in the Lebanon. The support of Pérez de Cuéllar, former Secretary-General of the United Nations, for IPRA's initiative, which was also supported by Boutros-Ghali, permitted the Under Secretary-General for Political Affairs, James Jonas, to travel twice to UNESCO Headquarters and participate actively in meetings on the Lebanon organized by IPRA, with the active participation of Lebanese NGOs and Lebanese educators. Jonas' interest did not end with the meetings, for he continuously followed IPRA's efforts through UNARDOL's office in the Lebanon. The importance of interest on the part of the United Nations in promoting local peace-building efforts cannot be overestimated. It gives encouragement, legitimacy, and empathy to what is being undertaken locally, in a relationship of global solidarity.

UN support was not only moral but also financial. This type of triangular relationship between local NGOs, international NGOs, and UN agencies should be strengthened. The Lebanese NGOs' Collective for Development tried to enlist UN agencies into their integrated development plan for one Lebanese region as a model to be applied to other Lebanese regions when total Lebanese sovereignty is achieved. They designed their development plans with the local population (Beka'a region), whether in villages or towns, invited members of the civil society to their meetings, and incorporated plans that concern not only economic development but also human development of the Lebanese citizen. Thus, peace education was on their developmental agenda. Unfortunately, the scheme was not supported by any donor agency within or outside the UN system. Donor agencies apparently had not come to understand that only an integrated, multi-sectoral, and holistic approach to development can yield adequate and appropriate results.

None the less, a continuous six-year effort that started even before the war ended was completed. It brought educators and Lebanese NGOs under the UNESCO umbrella to debate, recommend, and act on the best means to resolve the country's conflicts, the needs of a post-conflict society, and the ways and means by which peace-building could be consolidated. It produced a Lebanese handbook on peace education, conflict resolution, human rights, and democracy. This handbook was discussed in depth by the local population, who were very pleased to be consulted on the future of their educational system. Undertaking education for peace and appropriate changes in the curricula was one of the measures advocated by local participants. Recognition from within a given society of what needs to be changed and how it should be changed is tantamount to a rebirth of a people; a rebirth of a people manifested in a will to coexist and in searching together the horizons that can reinforce peace itself. This was a process of education for peace from the very bases of society, the people themselves.

The aspiration to coexist and search for common grounds for coexistence can be strengthened if more attention is given to local efforts. Such attention can be equivalent to an empowerment of local capacities of communities to envision their futures. It is an auto-determination expressed in a reaffirmation of their existence as a people through participation in the making of their society. It is made possible with adequate moral and financial resources providing an affirmation that they are dignified human beings, that their voices count and their ideas are worthwhile.

UN participation in these meetings reflected global interest in the fate of a country and a people. When interest faded throughout the war years, the UN separation from the people affected the attitude of the population and made them question whether the United Nations has a double standard in applying its resolutions. Nevertheless, the desire to have UN participation was articulated as an appeal to the United Nations not to abandon its role as promoter and protector of peace and as an expression of a continued belief in the United Nations' importance. Belief in the importance of the United Nations is strengthened more by direct collaboration with the "peoples of the United Nations" than by intergovernmental endeavours.

Another collaborative project integrates peace research, peace education, and United Nations work in the field of disarmament. A fairly recent effort, it also vividly demonstrates the constructive potential of cooperation between specialized agencies, departments of the Secretariat, and non-governmental organizations. The IAUP/UN Commission on Disarmament Education, an initiative of the International Association of University Presidents (IAUP), is a joint effort of the IAUP and the United Nations Centre for Disarmament Affairs. The Association and the Centre co-sponsor an effort bringing together academics and disarmament specialists to develop and introduce university curricula on a range of issues related to arms control and disarmament. The Commission is transnational and multidisciplinary, comprising lawyers, political scientists, physicians, educationists, and a range of other areas of research, education, and professional practice. The Centre's work in this project is a natural follow-up of the efforts it conducted to focus public attention on the arms race and its consequences in the UN World Disarmament Campaign of the 1980s. The IAUP, under the inspiration and leadership of Dr. Leland Miles, now President Emeritus, had been involved in transnational efforts in peace education for over a decade.

Meeting regularly at United Nations headquarters, the Commission formed a number of working committees to develop curricula for undergraduate, graduate, and professional school courses on arms control, disarmament, and some more comprehensive approaches to global security. It then took steps to introduce exemplar modules and courses into various institutions in several countries. The materials upon which the curricula are based are drawn from a wide range of sources in peace research and international relations scholarship, and most significantly from relevant United Nations documents. This latter source has been somewhat neglected by most peace studies courses. Indeed, disarmament *per se* has not been a featured topic in standard peace studies courses, for the field of peace education has not been as focused on disarmament education, or on other political issues, as believed by those who opposed both UNESCO's efforts and the entire field of disarmament education. Although the project was conceived to affect standard university curricula in various disciplines, rather than to expand the field of peace studies, it is having an effect on this field, largely as a consequence of having enlisted experienced peace studies practitioners to assist in the review and assessment of the curricula and setting them to work with UN disarmament experts.

One of the ways in which this NGO–UN collaboration has benefited from the assistance of peace studies practitioners is a series of seminars for training academics from Asia, Africa, and Latin America in the issues, literature, and teaching methodology of disarmament education. These seminars are built upon the substantive expertise of Disarmament Centre personnel and peace researchers and on the educational experience of professors of peace studies. Initially convened at Juniata College in Huntingdon, Pennsylvania, and hosted by the Baker Institute of Peace Studies, seminars such as these are now projected for other areas of the world. The intention of the project is to facilitate the introduction of disarmament education into universities all over the world.

To date, curricula have been developed for undergraduate and graduate political science courses and for medical schools. Currently in the process of development are materials for law schools and schools and departments of education. A global network of schools and departments of education involved in the work of the Commission is now being developed by two IPRA members, M. Haavelsrud and B. Reardon. The potential reach and effect of the project go far beyond what has thus far been the arena of action for peace studies. It is making its way into standard offerings for all students and is being facilitated by educators who are not, nor do they seek to be, part of the traditional peace studies community. Its association with the United Nations and professional associations concerned with international relations and peace issues has opened doors for the project that have long been bolted against peace studies *per se*.

This unique project has shown us that this kind of collaboration between the United Nations and concerned citizens can be as productive in formal education as the work in the Lebanon showed it to be in the non-formal sphere. It has also brought into peace studies the most crucial issue in the struggle to eliminate "the scourge of war" – the dependence of the world security system on armament. And it has been a vindication of UNESCO's pioneering efforts in disarmament education.

A programme similar in purpose and methods to the World Disarmament Campaign was the United Nations' Human Rights Information Campaign, which was intended to provide the public with information about human rights instruments and UN machinery for their implementation. It was the forerunner to the Decade for Human Rights Education declared in December 1994 (United Nations 1994). This Decade is also largely the result of private and NGO initiatives. The People's Decade for Human Rights Education, a transnational citizens' endeavour started in 1990 and pushed forward by educators and activists, lobbied the United Nations and member states and played an important facilitative role in the formulating and passing of the General Assembly Resolution. The People's Decade now initiates and facilitates many cooperative efforts between the United Nations and both NGOs and popular movements. It is an example of how the United Nations is seen by many citizens' groups as the arena in which to struggle for a democratic, global civil society.

7. Recommendations

Our recommendations for the future of the United Nations system are immediate, practical actions that derive from our review and criticism. Like the projects and principles we have described, these recommendations originate in our direct experience with the United Nations and its essential relationship with non-governmental organizations. It is in this relationship that the hope for a more democratic and peoples-centred international system is growing and giving voice to the aspirations of the human family, unfettered by the shackles of the state system. In this relationship, too, as we have recounted, are significant possibilities for advancing peace education. Our recommendations are intended to realize some of those possibilities.

Adequate teacher preparation

In spite of such developments and projects as those described here, peace education remains inaccessible as a subject in most schools of the world, and will remain so until there is adequate teacher preparation. Teachers need to be trained in the substance and methods of peace education to bring out concrete examples of peace-building and to be able to train their students to resolve conflicts. There is ample evidence that such training is effective.

A research project in urban schools in the United States is but one bit of that evidence demonstrating that teachers in urban schools using peace education practices can have a positive impact upon levels of conflict in their classes. Professor Ian M. Harris, initiator of this work, wrote that "students in classes where teachers use a peaceful pedagogy and teach peaceful subject matter exhibit higher levels of conflict resolution skills. Students exposed to peaceful adult role models learn from the non-violent responses to conflict" (Harris 1995). Collaboration between UNESCO and NGOs helping ministries of education to provide teacher training for peace education could aid greatly in bringing about similar results in most schools. Perhaps UNESCO–NGO collaboration could even have political impact if they monitored the impact of global trends on different countries toward the end of preventing violent conflict, rather than reacting afterwards with humanitarian assistance, whose financial and human costs are so much higher. Such monitoring might provide cycles of peace learning, instead of cycles of violence that people experience and remember for centuries.

Conflict-resolution training

The trend today is towards using conflict-resolution techniques as a means to provide actors in a post-conflict society with conflict-resolution techniques so as to advance the peace-building process. This trend could either have a limited impact or open avenues in a post-conflict society towards an in-depth behavioural change. The limitations to the achievement of in-depth change are of two kinds. The first is linked with the simplistic view that internal conflicts are caused by internal conditions, without connecting the internal factors to global ones, such as outside economic and political pressures in a given conflict, the type of rule and the legitimacy the international community gives to dictatorships, and other factors taken into account in the holistic framework of peace education. The second limitation is the behaviours of some professional conflict-resolution trainers. A great number of them do not interest themselves in learning about the whole human context of conflicts (the people and the roots of the conflict), but confine themselves only to transmitting conflict-resolution techniques. One cannot overestimate the need for conflict-resolution trainers to have a comprehensive understanding and the capacity to show empathy and to go beyond the role of a teacher giving a lecture to students. Teachers have to learn in advance about the conflict itself so as to make their skills serve the people and provide them with a methodology. Certain skills used by conflict-resolution trainers may be inappropriate to a given culture. Therefore, those trainers who fly around the world with a fixed package of skills can actually do harm in a post-conflict society rather than achieve what their mission was meant to do. Nevertheless, the United Nations can and should learn from all such experiences.

Collaboration between INGOs and UN staff

International NGOs versed in various approaches to peace education could teach UN staff how their work has contributed concrete solutions to specific problems. On the one hand, this can clarify theory for those who write about peace and conflicts as they listen to the practical problems of the UN staff. On the other hand, the positive experiences of NGOs in the field can provide UN staff with ideas about alternative approaches to a particular issue.

In-service education for UN staff

The United Nations should undertake programmes of in-service education to ensure that all the staff see their tasks in a broad global perspective, rather than the narrow national views some still bring to their responsibilities. Competitive national visions and rigid hierarchical behaviours, so reminiscent of the colonial past the United Nations is committed to transcend, are not conducive to the achievement of the goals of the Organization. Individual commitment to the spirit of the Charter is as important as experience and efficiency in UN personnel and consultants, some of whom are as élitist as the governments that dispatch their bureaucrats and delegates to the Organization. Whereas bureaucrats and delegates often forget that the UN mandate is to serve the peoples of the world, the staff have often been models of global citizenship. All UN personnel should be enlisted from those committed to such service.

The creation of a peace education fund

We also envision the creation of a peace education fund by the United Nations to which UN employees, private individuals, and NGOs contribute monthly a small sum. The money raised may be used for peace education projects, especially those promoting peace activity in conflict or post-conflict situations, such as educating former militias in ways of integrating into the society peacefully and actively. The fund could also be used for providing peace education to United Nations staff, as advocated in the foregoing proposals.

The United Nations as peace educator

Our final two recommendations are intended to emphasize the notion of the United Nations as a peace educator, instructing the world's peoples in the problems of and possibilities for peace. For example, the United Nations could call attention to national legislation that contradicts the spirit and principles of the Charter. Although the United Nations does not have the mandate or the power to take action to rectify the contradictions, it can serve the international community as an impartial teacher of universal norms and values, and so affect the behaviour of a country in contradiction with those norms and values. These contradictions are also issues on which peace researchers, peace educators, and NGOs can work together in developing programmes of public education and in raising issues about the legal and system changes that are required for the achievement of peace.

Similarly, the United Nations and NGOs could make known those states that have not ratified UN conventions and treaties or adhered to Declarations, and could cooperate in developing mechanisms to promote the accountability of states. In so doing, local NGOs and INGOs can contribute to raising awareness among the international community about these standards, which should be the basis of education for world citizenship. It has to be underlined here that the United Nations should attract the media more, especially television networks, so as to bring attention to its past achievements and the obstacles it needs to overcome, and to present itself to the public as capable of anticipating and responding to crises and challenges in all parts of the world.

8. Conclusions

The Yamoussoukro Declaration on Peace in the Minds of Men (UNESCO 1989) affirmed that "[h]uman beings cannot work for a future they cannot imagine." In effect, the United Nations needs to set out a vision of the future for the peoples of the world that could inspire them with hope, invigorate them with energy and pride in their respective cultures, and make them aware of the common humanity they share with others. This is a task that requires conscious learning and the involvement of practising peace educators.

The future of the United Nations depends upon its unequivocal commitment to the welfare of the peoples it is called to serve. To do this, it must be an intentional peace learner and peace educator. It must undertake to recognize and transcend the limits of the state system and to lead enquiry into a redefinition of the central features of the world political system, especially its most delicate and problematic features – sovereignty and war. It must work to educate the peoples of the world to participate in this enquiry and to become proactive in movements for change.

Indeed, if "we, the peoples of the United Nations" want to play a role in peace-building, peace-making, and non-violent resolution of conflict in a democratic framework, we must insist on our right to participate in the Organization, and we must take the responsibility that goes with the right. All of us who conceive of ourselves as world citizens should play some part in the transformative changes that can be made in the United Nations, so that the United Nations may function as an instrument of transformation in the world. Transformation is primarily the consequence of learning. "We, the peoples" and the world organization that represents us must undertake to be intentional learners as we endeavour to confront the global problems that affect us all, demonstrating that we are all part of one planetary system.

Beginning with active involvement in the growing collaboration between the UN system and NGOs in a range of efforts to make and build peace, we can all be transformative learners – as we attempt to eradicate the roots of violent conflict, as we monitor potential conflicts, and as we interrupt and prevent violence. Even as we try to teach peace, as self-reflective learners we can distil from our efforts the learning that may prepare the United Nations to educate for peace in the spirit of the Charter, which calls for an acknowledgment of the unity of being. It is this concept that illuminates the meaning of peace and makes it the essential goal of all humankind.

407

Acknowledgements

The authors are IPRA representatives to the United Nations: Osseiran in Paris, Reardon in New York. This essay is the product of participatory research, both authors having been involved in the major programmes described.

Note

1. The critique closest to a perspective that might be taken by peace educators is one drafted from a feminist perspective that calls for a more direct approach to the central concern of all peace efforts – violence (UN Experts Group Meeting on Gender and the Agenda for Peace, New York, United Nations Division for the Advancement of Women, December 1994).

References

Boutros-Ghali, Boutros. 1992. *An Agenda for Peace*. New York: United Nations.

Faure, Edgar, ed. 1972. *Learning to Be*. Paris: UNESCO.

Harris, Ian M. 1995. "Teachers' Response to Conflict in Selected Milwaukee Schools." In Horst Lofgren, ed., *Peace Education and Human Development*. Malmo, Sweden: School of Education, pp. 197–219.

Reardon, Betty A. 1988. *Comprehensive Peace Education*. New York: Teachers College Press.

Telin, Bengt. 1991. *Learning to Live in Security*. Paris: UNESCO.

UNESCO. 1974. "A Recommendation Concerning Education for International Understanding, Cooperation and Peace, and Education Relating to Human Rights and Fundamental Freedoms." Adopted by the 18th Session of the General Conference. Paris: UNESCO.

———— 1989. *Yamoussoukro Declaration on Peace in the Minds of Men*. Paris: UNESCO.

———— 1991. *UNESCO General Conference Report*. 26 C/32. Paris: UNESCO, October.

———— 1993. *Report by the Director General on the Work of the International Congress on Education for Human Rights and Democracy and Follow-up in Member States to the World Plan of Action on Education for Human Rights and Democracy, Montreal, March 1993*. Paris: UNESCO.

———— 1994. *World Declaration on Education for All and Framework for Action to Meet Basic Learning Needs Adopted by the World Conference on Education for All, Jomtien, Thailand, 5–9 March 1990*. Paris: UNESCO, 3rd printing.

———— 1995. "Integrated Framework of Action on Education for Peace, Human Rights and Democracy." Adopted by the 28th Session of the General Conference. Paris: UNESCO, November.

UNICEF. 1993. *It's Only Right: A Practical Guide to Learning about the Convention on the Rights of the Child*. New York: UNICEF.

United Nations. 1994. "Decade for Human Rights Education (1995–2004)." General Assembly Resolution 49/184, 23 December.

Conclusion
The potential of the
United Nations system

Chadwick F. Alger

The contributors to the 12 chapters of this volume have recommended the establishment of over 60 new UN institutions and programmes. These are presented in the Appendix, which should be particularly useful for readers concerned with specific UN issues. It is the purpose of this concluding chapter first to place these recommendations in the context of other recent proposals for the future of the UN system. I shall then attempt to draw some general conclusions from these proposals by emphasizing themes that have emerged in several chapters.

1. Recent proposals for the future of the UN system

Celebration of the fiftieth anniversary of the United Nations Charter was enriched by the appearance of a diversity of volumes focused on the future of the United Nations system. They include a creative volume by Erskine Childers and Brian Urquhart, former members of the Secretariat. Their broad programme for "non-constitutional improvements" includes: (1) a Common Seat of the United Nations system, carrying through with the intention of the first General Assembly that the headquarters of specialized agencies should be located at the seat of the United Nations itself, (2) a United Nations

System Consultative Board comprising representatives of bureaus of ECOSOC, governing bodies of major specialized agencies, and representatives of bureaus of other agencies, (3) a UN Parliamentary Assembly, eventually to be directly elected, and (4) revitalization of the Trusteeship Council as a UN Council on Diversity, Representation and Governance, so as to peaceably accommodate cultural and ethnic aspirations (Childers and Urquhart 1994).

There also have been reports by groups of distinguished leaders, as in the case of the Commission on Global Governance, with members from 26 countries, chaired by Ingvar Carlsson of Sweden and Shridath Ramphal of Guyana. Their report, *Our Global Neighborhood* (1995a), as in the case of the Childers and Urquhart volume, is broad in scope. Particularly notable is a basic premise of their report: "The emergence of a global civil society, with many movements reinforcing a sense of human solidarity, reflects a large increase in the capacity and will of people to take control of their own lives" (1995b: 9). Based on this proposition, they would create a new "'Right of Petition' for non-state actors to bring situations massively endangering the security of people within states to the attention of the Security Council" (1995c: 11). At the same time they see a need for a vision for UN reform that rivals that which existed at the time of its founding. Here they see that special responsibility devolves on "We the Peoples ... to a far greater extent than fifty years ago. We call on international civil society, NGOs, the business sector, academia, the professions, and especially young people to join in a drive for change in the international system" (1995c: 19).

Also contributing have been scholarly works, although these tend to be much more restrained in their proposals for the future. An example of this genre is J. Martin Rochester, *Waiting for the Millennium: The United Nations and the Future of World Order* (1993). As the foundation for his thinking about the future of the United Nations system Rochester asserts:

If a global security-community comes to pass, it will not be planned but will also emerge as a product of historical forces which likewise can be nudged along in small ways if we have the knowledge and the will to do so. (1993: 246)

First in his three basic operating principles for the future is "an enhanced capacity of the international system as a whole to respond to problems confronting humanity, without foreclosing or limiting local and regional efforts." With few exceptions, as in the case of the United Nations Environment Programme (UNEP), he sees a tendency to view global and sub-global approaches as separate rather than interrelated and reinforcing. He urges that the United Nations build sub-global components into its programmes, serve as a clearing house for information on sub-global collaborative undertakings, and facilitate "bandwagoning where subglobal cooperation has the potential to be enlarged to the global level" (Rochester 1993: 201, 202).

2. The major conclusions and proposals of this volume

I have drawn attention to these examples of broad overview works on the future of the UN system in order to illuminate the nature of this volume more clearly. Contributing scholars share a strong orientation toward the future, and each has a personal vision of a future peaceful world. They aspire to contribute to the fulfilment of this vision through their research. But the chapters on 12 UN issue areas were written by scholars who have not collaborated with authors of other chapters. They have made no effort to ensure consistency, nor have they attempted to pull their proposals for the future into an integrated strategy. Thus we have a volume that is complementary to more holistic approaches. Authors have focused on single-issue areas, illuminating what has been achieved, identifying key problems to be confronted, and offering proposals for the future. Or, we might say, readers have been informed about what has been learned by peace researchers working in 12 different UN "laboratories."

In this concluding chapter I shall attempt to pull together the major conclusions and proposals that have emerged out of the dozen issue "laboratories," with an emphasis on those contributed by several authors. But before doing this it is necessary to underline one theme that emerges from all chapters: *the interdependence of issues*. It is of fundamental significance that it has been impossible for Johansen (chap. 3) to discuss peace-keeping without bringing in preventive diplomacy, peace-building, early warning, and education aimed at reconciliation among groups. McSpadden and Chol (chap. 9) could not propose solutions to refugee problems without including development, human rights, and diplomacy. Rupesinghe (chap. 5), in approaching internal violence, found it necessary to propose a light weapons register, an Office for Preventive Diplomacy, and human rights. Brauch, Mesjasz, and Möller (chap. 1) link disarmament to preventive diplomacy, peace-keeping, and post-conflict peace-building; ask peace educators to address images that legitimize the use of force against minorities; and see economic adjustment strategies as important for disarmament. Mische and Ribeiro (chap. 10) identify pieces of the environmental puzzle in WMO, IMO, ILO, WHO, FAO, IAEA, UNDP, the World Bank, and other agencies. Obviously this justifies my assertion in the Introduction that it is necessary to take a UN system view. At the same time it is consistent with Childers and Urquhart's conclusion:

Earlier assumed divisions between work on peace, security and political affairs, and economic-social and humanitarian problems are increasingly exposed as unreal and even counter-productive. (1994: 189)

I shall now proceed to identify 15 significant conclusions by our authors that cut across the 12 interdependent issue areas. Based on my reading of the chapters, I have identified 12 key items and classified them under five headings: (a) strengthen UN response capacity, (b) broaden the participating community, (c) strengthen institutional competence, (d) enhance knowledge, and (e) promote UN outreach. Obviously, these are the arbitrary selections of one reader. Nevertheless, I do believe that they illuminate the fact that those working on any UN issue are dependent upon the quality of political, social, and administrative processes that transcend single issues. Again the significance of a UN system perspective is affirmed. Not only are the issues themselves interdependent. But there is a shared need across issues for strengthening response capacity, broadening participation, strengthening institutions, enhancing knowledge, and broadening outreach. Before discussing the 15 conclusions, it may be helpful for the reader to have the complete list:

(a) Strengthen UN response capacity
    1. Long-range planning
    2. Early warning
    3. Rapid reaction
    4. Extension of non-military options
(b) Broaden the participating community
    5. Wider participation of non-governmental organizations
    6. Wider participation of local governments and organizations
(c) Strengthen institutional competence
    7. Strengthen UN institutional infrastructure
    8. Enhance institutional memory
    9. New financing sources
(d) Enhance knowledge

10. Research
11. Education and training
(e) Promote UN outreach
12. Extend UN information collection and dissemination
13. Extend publicity about UN activities and achievements
14. Offer rewards for the fulfilment of UN standards
15. Visions of the future

Strengthen UN response capacity

Perhaps no reader has been surprised by the fact that almost all chapters assert that the United Nations has not had advanced plans for coping with specific contingencies, has not had adequate warning of emerging crises, and has not responded rapidly enough to these crises.

1. Long-range planning

Pervasive in this volume are explicit and implied appeals for planning that would cope with underlying causes of endemic violence, the squalor of refugee camps, violations of human rights standards, and ecological disasters. McSpadden and Chol see a need for planning that would respond to the root causes of refugee flight by working within countries, protecting human rights, peace-building, and diplomacy. Rupesinghe would create a global coalition for war prevention, involving a cross-section of those directly concerned with the elimination of war. Brauch, Mesjasz, and Möller would take a comprehensive, long-range approach to conversion that would include economic strategies, concepts, and tools, as well as financial assistance for the conversion of military, manpower, and bases. It would involve not only the UN Disarmament Department, but also the IMF, the World Bank, UNCTAD, UNIDO, and other agencies. Osseiran and Reardon would have UNESCO collaborate with NGOs in helping national ministries of education to provide teacher training for peace education.

2. Early warning

An array of proposals would significantly extend the capacity of the United Nations to monitor world events, through both technological devices and human eyes and ears. Johansen would have roving ambassadors who would meet with those involved in festering conflicts.

Their work would be supported by an International Monitoring Agency employing satellites and high-altitude aircraft. Rupesinghe proposes the mobilization of peace constituencies within countries for designing early preventive action, including forums of eminent persons and roundtable seminars involving NGOs, international organizations, and states. At the same time he would broaden the involvement of the Security Council by having it look at all potential conflicts, not just those "threatening international peace and security."

3. Rapid reaction

Enhanced long-range planning and early warning would enable reaction to extend into preventive modes. Mische and Ribeiro propose a UN Environmental Protection Authority with the capacity to prevent and quickly cope with environmental disasters. Johansen advocates the creation of conflict-resolution committees in each major world region and the preventive deployment of peace-keeping forces. Both would be supported by a UN Institute for Mediation and Dispute Resolution, which would provide seasoned mediators. These efforts could be complemented by Rupesinghe's multifaceted rapid response force, including military, police, civilian, and technical personnel. Boulding and Oberg would dispatch NGO Rapid Response Teams, which would work with local groups in efforts to dampen escalating conflicts.

4. Extension of non-military options

Civilians have tended to play increasing roles in UN peace-keeping operations, as observers, as unarmed police, and as deliverers of humanitarian services. This volume includes suggestions for extending and making some of these developments more formal. Rupesinghe would have a corps of White Helmets to investigate gross human rights violations. Boulding and Oberg would utilize unarmed NGO peace teams for conflict monitoring. At the same time they would advocate an explicit three-legged peace-keeping organization consisting of armed Blue Helmets, unarmed peace teams, and humanitarian NGOs.

Broaden the participating community

5. Widen participation of non-governmental organizations

It is significant that all of the authors in this volume advocate extension of the participation of actors other than states as they search for solutions to global issues. They do not advance comprehensive proposals for new linkages between civil society and the United Nations system, as does *Our Global Neighborhood*. Nevertheless, actual, and potential, roles for non-governmental organizations are encountered throughout the volume. I will not repeat the tasks for NGOs already introduced under early warning, rapid reaction, and extension of non-military options. Other examples are the suggestion by Boulding and Oberg that humanitarian NGOs provide emergency aid that would evolve into reconstruction activities. Jeong would involve NGOs in economic policy-making and implementation. Osseiran and Reardon would have NGOs work with UNESCO in assisting ministries of education to provide teacher training for peace education. Later I will note recommendations for using NGOs for the collection and dissemination of information in the implementation of human rights standards.

6. *Widen participation of local governments and organizations*
Similarly, scholars working on specific issue areas are responsive to Rochester's appeal for collaboration between global and sub-global efforts to cope with world problems. Mische and Ribeiro emphasize roles for cities and other local authorities in efforts to cope with global ecological problems. McSpadden and Chol emphasize the need for local leadership and for education and advocacy programmes in local communities if the root causes of refugee flights are to be addressed. Pietilä and Vickers underline the need for national and local efforts by women if UN standards for women are to be implemented.

Strengthen institutional competence

7. *Strengthen United Nations institutional infrastructure*
Contributors articulate ways in which the United Nations institutional infrastructure could be strengthened. At this point I will choose only examples not yet mentioned in this summary. Brauch et al. advance a number of proposals that would strengthen disarmament, arms control, and conversion. They advocate new machinery for a coordinated system to address major disarmament problems promptly, an effective global conventional arms transfer regime, and a UN Conversion Projects Register. Rupesinghe would restructure the Trusteeship system and thereby strengthen the capacity for response to demands of aggrieved minorities. This would include the possibility of establishing new UN Trust Territories. Väyrynen and

Johansen would strengthen the Security Council by broadening its membership, making it more reflective of present political realities and also more democratic. Johansen also calls for a permanent UN peace-keeping force, with obvious implications for facilitating rapid response. Apodaca, Stohl, and Lopez would have the UNHCHR direct and coordinate UN human rights machinery and regional components. They would give compulsory jurisdiction of global and regional courts over breaches of human rights, and ask for regional conventions to establish human rights courts and fact-finding commissions.

8. Enhance institutional memory

Only Pietilä and Vickers explicitly emphasize the importance of institutional memory, but they do it very convincingly and succinctly:

Because neither UN officials nor the new generations of diplomats are benefiting from the lessons of the past in relation to development and economic issues, there is inevitably a great deal of "reinventing the wheel" within UN bodies.... [T]he lack of an "institutional memory" within the UN system is catastrophic. Because of it, UN bodies are doomed to learn the same lessons over and over again. It is urgently necessary for a full, analytical view of UN activities since its inception in 1944 to be undertaken, even beginning with the first attempts at international action under the League of Nations.

9. New financing sources

Authors in this volume tend not to dwell on the financial implications of their many recommendations for strengthening the United Nations system, although Johansen does advocate a UN tax on the US$900 billion international currency exchanges each day, Mische and Ribeiro would tax or fine individuals, corporations, and governments who engage in transboundary pollution, and Väyrynen asserts that a workable system of collective security would require more adequate funding. At the same time, it is obvious that any serious attention to the many recommendations of our authors would require substantial increases in funds available to the UN system.

Childers and Urquhart are helpful in placing UN financing in context. In 1992, the UN system's total expenditures were US$10.5 billion. This was only 0.0005 per cent of the world's GDP, and only 0.0007 per cent of the GDP of 24 industrial countries. It represented an expenditure of US$1.90 per human being alive. Meanwhile, the world spent US$150 per human being on military expenditures in 1992. And citizens of the United Kingdom alone spent on alcoholic beverages in 1992 three and a half times the expenditure of the entire

UN system. Yet "members making the larger contributions have long demanded that the rate of growth of the UN's budget must be held as close to zero as possible in line with their own claimed domestic policies" (Childers and Urquhart 1994: 142–143). Childers and Urquhart offer a penetrating commentary on the bizarre financial performance of the wealthy states by pointing out that 39 per cent of total UN budgets in 1992 (US$4.09 billion) was spent on emergency work in peace-keeping and humanitarian assistance. "This underscores the failure to use the UN system to tackle the root causes of what usually become extremely costly problems" (Childers and Urquhart 1994: 144).

In contrast, it is encouraging that the involvement of NGOs in UN activities has been growing, and that our authors are proposing even more important roles for them in implementing strategies focused on root causes. Obviously the extensive self-financed activities of NGOs enhance the size of financial resources available for achieving UN goals. If states maintain their unwillingness to take advantage of exceedingly painless ways for giving the UN system an adequate financial base – minuscule taxes on arms sales, transnational movement of currencies, international trade, international travel, etc. – NGOs may themselves have to assume wider responsibility for financing global governance. Might such action offer such a glaring indicator of the potential irrelevance of states that it could prod wealthy states into becoming more creative supporters of solutions to UN financial problems?

Enhance knowledge

10. Research
It should not be surprising that peace researchers and educators have offered a plethora of suggestions for research, education, and training. In approaching the communications issue, Varis takes a broad view of the significance of communications for the UN system. He includes the need for communication between the system and the people of the world, the need for the people of the world to understand their personal linkages to the world, and the significance of these linkages for global governance. Thus he sees need for research on press coverage of the United Nations; the communications dimensions of global problems such as unemployment, poverty, violence, discrimination, and drugs; contradictions raised by the globalization of finance, the economy, and the media, in contrast to individual

quests for local identity and culture, and group pursuit of self-determination; and the implications of technological change for lifelong learning in all parts of the world. Obviously Varis has drawn our attention to the fact that all global problems are to some degree shaped by increasingly extensive and intrusive global communications. We have need for knowledge that would enable us to take them into account.

McSpadden and Chol ask that peace research address root causes of refugee flight and identify conditions that could lead to a sustainable, just peace. Pietilä and Vickers ask for research that demonstrates the impact of the empowerment of women and illuminates the relationship between women's equal rights and the achievement of a just and peaceful world. Mische and Ribeiro would like to have research on the links between environmental degradation and conflict.

11. Education and training

The need for enhanced education and training is underlined in a number of issue areas. Illuminating is the diversity of approaches – ranging from global broadcasting to training for specific tasks; and from education of UN secretariats to teacher training.

Johansen takes the broadest approach, advocating that the United Nations establish its own worldwide electronic information and education programmes aimed at reconciliation. This effort would be aimed at supplanting a culture of combat with a culture of compliance.

Osseiran and Reardon see a need to educate UN staffs in order to liberate them from the structure of competitive national visions to an international, global one. They are concerned that the spirit of the United Nations is not infused in the hearts and minds of all its staff, believing that some of them are as élitist as the governments that dispatch their officials to the United Nations. They assert that the United Nations must be an intentional peace learner and peace educator, working to educate the peoples of the world to participate in this enquiry and become proactive in movements for change. They urge reciprocal learning between NGOs and UN secretariats, believing that NGOs versed in various approaches to peace education could share with UN staff how they have devised concrete resolutions to a particular problem. At the same time, UN personnel could deepen the insight of NGOs on practical problems that they continually confront. They also have concern that professional conflict-resolution trainers learn about the whole human context of conflicts (the people and the roots of conflict), and not confine themselves just to transmitting conflict-resolution techniques.

A wide range of suggestions for research and training that would be led by NGOs and educational institutions have emerged. Boulding and Oberg urge the peace research community to train practitioners in mediation, negotiation, and conflict resolution, both military and civilian. Osseiran and Reardon urge that peace researchers, peace educators, and NGOs work together on programmes of public education, raising questions about the legal and system changes that are required for the achievement of peace.

Brauch et al. advocate research and training on conversion. Pietilä and Vickers desire that educational programmes on the economic and social activities of the United Nations be available in national universities, in diplomatic and civil service training, in the development research community, and in women's studies. Osseiran and Reardon advocate that peace education be included in training for pre-collegiate teachers. Mische and Ribeiro would promote a major upgrading of environmental education at all levels in conjunction with education on human rights and responsibilities.

Brauch et al. are unique in their recommendation that one kind of research should be curbed – research that would lead toward the development of new offensive-oriented conventional arms.

Promote UN outreach

Education and training, already discussed, include aspects of outreach, as in the case of more roving ambassadors, regional conflict-resolution committees, NGO Rapid Response Teams, etc. But the collection and dissemination of information have always been key functions of the UN system. Usually this information reaches only very specialized audiences. In addition, efforts are made to disseminate information on UN activities and achievements to wider publics. But member states have been exceedingly miserly in funding UN public information activities. At the same time, offering rewards for the fulfilment of UN standards and disseminating visions of the future are two particularly creative kinds of outreach that merit special attention.

12. Extend UN information collection and dissemination

Obviously most of the proposals discussed under long-range planning and early warning involve information collection. In addition, Brauch et al. see a particular need for gathering and disseminating information that would provide a knowledge base for strengthening conversion efforts. They ask for a Conversion Projects Register that would (1) collect information provided by governments, corporations, and NGOs about conversion projects, (2) collect information on experts in conversion, (3) collect data on possible sources of assistance and investment for conversion, and (4) perform research and training on conversion.

Apodaca et al. ask for the creation of human rights field offices. And they ask for a more explicit partnership between NGOs and the United Nations, in the belief that "NGOs enjoy the trust and respect of the common citizen needed to gather and document cases of human rights abuses."

Osseiran and Reardon advocate that the United Nations and NGOs cooperate in disseminating information on states that have not ratified or have not adhered to treaties and Declarations. They also would have the United Nations and NGOs collaborate in developing mechanisms for engendering wider adherence to these standards.

13. Extend publicity about UN activities and achievements

Most readers were probably surprised to read this conclusion by two women, Pietilä and Vickers:

> The record of the advancement of women during the 50 years since the United Nations was established – and particularly during the past 25 years – is astonishing ... In all of this, the UN system has taken the lead. On average it represents significantly more advanced norms and practices concerning women than those of its member states.... But the normative impact of the United Nations in the advancement of women could be vastly more efficient if its information and education programmes were better.

Pietilä and Vickers assert that it is indispensable that women be informed about the "programmes, provisions, and conventions of the UN system, adopted by governments on their behalf, in order to be able to monitor implementation in each country." Of course, these insights and recommendations would also apply for a broad array of economic, social, and cultural rights.

Osseiran and Reardon take an even more strident approach:

> [T]he United Nations could call attention to national legislation that contradicts the spirit and principles of the Charter. Although the United Nations does not have the mandate or the power to take action to rectify the contradictions, it can serve the international community as an impartial teacher

of universal norms and values, and so affect the behaviour of a country in contradiction with those norms and values.... It has to be underlined here that the United Nations should attract the media more, especially television networks, so as to bring attention to its past achievements and the obstacles it needs to overcome, and to present itself to the public as capable of anticipating and responding to crises and challenges in all parts of the world.

Of course, these authors are well aware that the United Nations would have great difficulty in carrying out these recommendations. It is not only that financial resources are not now available. But UN agencies that offered significant information about their programmes within these countries, or dared to criticize member states, would likely jeopardize support by these members for their programmes and budgets. Perhaps this is yet another function that will, at least over the short run, have to be assumed by non-governmental organizations.

14. Offer rewards for the fulfilment of UN standards
Perhaps rewards for adherence to Charter goals and for implementation of UN standards for economic well-being, ecological balance, social justice, and non-violence could be a more effective strategy than those that would be perceived as punishment by member states. Here Johansen is relevant in his proposal that economic benefits be offered to those states that reduce military expenditures and demilitarize their societies. At the same time, Brauch et al. consider the possibility that the IMF and World Bank might provide assistance for conversion.

15. Visions of the future
Every chapter of this book has offered a vision of a preferred future in the context of specific UN issue areas. Because these visions have emerged out of in-depth research and thought focusing on specific aspects of UN activities, we believe that these visions are realistic and plausible. On the other hand, dialogue is necessary between these partial visions and holistic preferred visions of the future. It is important that Osseiran and Reardon draw our attention to the need for holistic visions of the future by quoting from the Yamoussoukro Declaration on Peace in the Minds of Men: "Human beings cannot work for a future they cannot imagine." They ask the United Nations "to set out a vision of the future for the peoples of the world that could inspire them with hope, invigorate them with energy and pride in their respective cultures, and make them aware of the common humanity they share with others."

3. Conclusion

Some readers may be disappointed with the conclusions that have emerged from the efforts of the 22 scholars who have contributed to this volume. Perhaps they would have preferred a more cohesive set of institutional reforms, possibly involving UN Charter revision. Some might have been expecting concrete proposals for coordination of the UN system, and perhaps even proposals for centralized direction of this system. In contrast, I find the product to be very encouraging for three fundamental reasons.

First, the 12 chapters have revealed how much the United Nations has achieved in only 50 years. It has widened its agenda to include new issues, as in the case of environment. It has invented new tools such as peace-keeping. It has extended its mission to include violent conflicts within states. It has broadened peace-keeping to include an array of supportive humanitarian operations. It has drafted a broad array of human rights conventions covering economic, social, cultural, civil, and political dimensions, as well as special conventions for women, children, refugees, and other groups. It has outstripped member states in the pursuit of rights of women. It has shown remarkable creativity in extending its capacities by collaborating with NGOs in virtually all of its programmes. Of course, by extending its mission, the UN system has taken on new challenges, and endured many failures as well as successes.

Secondly, scholars focusing on 12 "laboratories" perceive a wide array of feasible opportunities for strengthening the capabilities of the UN system. Of course, many of these proposals cannot be achieved without struggle. But the message is that there are many opportunities scattered throughout the system in issues significant for global governance that rarely command headlines. It would be a mistake for those working for strengthening the UN system to be totally consumed by one or two issues, such as reform of one of the Councils, the General Assembly, or UN financing. For example, our authors have proposed a number of modest institutions, summarized in the Appendix, that could greatly strengthen long-range planning, early warning, and rapid reaction. These could significantly strengthen the mission performance of the Security Council and the General Assembly, whether or not their Charter provisions are changed.

Thirdly, and perhaps most importantly, our authors have creatively revealed that the strengthening of global governance can involve "tasks for everybody," a phrase used by Johan Galtung (1980) in his proposals for "individual activation" in the pursuit of preferred worlds. What is needed are people of vision, in a wide array of institutions around the world, devoted to employing multilateral processes in solving global problems. Of fundamental importance is creative involvement not only of representatives of states and members of international secretariats but also of people in NGOs directly linked to the UN system, as well as a multitude of other NGOs, citizens' groups, and provincial, urban, and rural governments. Global problems reach from towns and cities – in their smoke stacks, economic depravity, torture, and death squads – across state borders, to regional organizations, and eventually to the field offices, headquarters, councils, and assemblies of the UN system. Effective global governance must link local people who know the UN system with UN people who are in touch with their local roots. I believe that the recommendations of the contributors to this volume would move the future UN system in this direction.

References

Commission on Global Governance. 1995a. *Our Global Neighborhood*. Oxford: Oxford University Press.

———— 1995b. *Our Global Neighborhood: The Basic Vision*. Geneva.

———— 1995c. "A Call to Action: Summary of Our Global Neighborhood." Geneva.

Childers, Erskine, and Brian Urquhart. 1994. *Renewing the United Nations System*. Uppsala: Dag Hammarskjold Foundation.

Galtung, Johan. 1980. *The True Worlds: A Transnational Perspective*. New York: Free Press.

Rochester, J. Martin. 1993. *Waiting for the Millennium: The United Nations and the Future of World Order*. Columbia, S.C.: University of South Carolina Press.

Appendix
Recommended new UN institutions and programmes

1. Controlling weapons

- New coordination machinery creating the ability to address major disarmament problems promptly
- An effective global conventional arms transfer regime
- A UN Conversion Projects Register
- Effective economic strategies, concepts, tools, and financial assistance for the manifold conversion of military production, manpower, and bases
- A peace research agenda: link disarmament with preventive diplomacy, peace-making, and post-conflict peace-building.

2. Enforcement and humanitarian intervention

- Rules defining the goals, means, and limits of admissible humanitarian interventions. Using military forces for "mini-enforcement," if necessary, such actions would draw on Chapter VII, but the Secretariat would have a stronger role than in collective security
- Realistic mandates for humanitarian interventions in which objectives, resources, and rules of engagement match
- An autonomous voluntary force, available at all times, that could

be promptly dispatched to conflict spots before the local situation has deteriorated beyond repair
* A strengthening of the division of labour between the Security Council and the Secretary-General, with the Security Council in charge of enforcement operations and the Secretary-General responsible for diplomatic mediation under Chapter VI and implementation of the non-enforcement provisions of Chapter VII

3. Peace-keeping

* An International Monitoring Agency (satellites and high-altitude aircraft)
* A conflict-resolution committee in each major world region
* A UN Institute for Mediation and Dispute Resolution (early warning and seasoned mediators)
* UN information and education programmes, broadcast around the world, aimed at reconciliation
* UN peace-building programmes that provide economic benefits for those that lower military expenditures and demilitarize their societies
* A permanent UN force
* New peace-keeping finance sources (e.g. a tax on international currency exchanges)

4. UN peace-keeping and NGO peace-building

* A three-legged peace-keeping organization (Blue Helmets, unarmed peace teams, humanitarian NGOs)
* Conflict monitoring carried out by NGOs
* NGO Rapid Response Teams (work with local groups in dampening escalating conflicts)
* Peace researchers who train both civilian and military practitioners in mediation, negotiation, and conflict resolution

5. Coping with internal conflicts

* Reform of United Nations decision-making processes by developing mechanisms that would specifically address conflicts in a preventive manner
* Commission on Human Rights to dispatch White Helmets to investigate gross violations of human rights

- A Trusteeship Council (aggrieved minorities could request UN trusteeship status)
- Effective NGO coalitions that focus on the non-military aspects of pre-conflict peace-building, early warning, and prevention
- Integration of the conflict-preventive action undertaken by the NGO community with preventive diplomacy of states
- Mobilization of peace constituencies within countries for designing early preventive action, including forums of eminent persons and roundtable seminars involving NGOs, international organizations, and states
- A global coalition for war prevention, including the United Nations, regional organizations, states, and popular movements, with NGOs as catalysts

6. Human rights

- Office of the UNHCHR to direct and coordinate UN human rights machinery and regional components
- Human rights field offices
- A more explicit UN–NGO partnership
- Compulsory jurisdiction of global and regional courts over breaches of human rights
- Regional conventions to establish human rights courts and fact-finding commissions
- The opening of regional human rights commissions and courts to individual petition

7. Wider participation in forming global economic policies

- Closer relationships between NGOs and various UN technical agencies
- Bringing UN agencies together in support of coherent commitment to the human dimension of economic development
- Redefinition of the relationship between the international financial institutions, UN technical agencies, and grass-roots development groups
- Conversion of operational structures into regional development agencies
- A North–South debate to explore, jointly, their differences in perception and to find common ground

8. Advancement of women

- The creation by each state of procedures for monitoring its implementation of obligations assumed in the United Nations. Each state to develop a coordinated capacity to act consistently on women's issues throughout the UN system
- An International Equality Unit in each country (in the Prime Minister's office or other relevant ministry) to implement the Forward-looking Strategies for the Advancement of Women
- Strengthening the "institutional memory" of the UN system, including refresher courses for UN staff on women and development issues
- Each state to ensure that courses on organizations in the UN system are available in universities and diplomatic and civil service training colleges

9. Protecting the rights of refugees

- Coordination of the work of UNDP with that of UNHCR, so long-term development goes hand in hand with the return of refugees, including adequate funding
- Coordination of the work of the UN Centre for Human Rights with the UNHCR, in order to cope with the root causes of refugee flight, including adequate funding
- Education and advocacy programmes in local communities
- Day-to-day field cooperation between the UNHCR and NGOs

10. Ecological security

- An Earth Charter providing a comprehensive framework of principles for global ecological security
- Upgrading of UNEP into a UN Environmental Protection Authority, empowered to initiate its own policies and with independent funding
- A World Court for the Environment with the capacity to hold individuals and corporate entities responsible for transnational environmental harm, or a strengthening of the ability of the International Court of Justice to hear environmental cases
- Elimination of the contradiction whereby the IAEA both promotes nuclear power and protects people from its environmental and health effects. An independent agency should monitor standards for protecting human and environmental health

- Incorporation of environmental issues into the United Nations' war-prevention, conflict-resolution, peace-building, and peace-keeping activities
- Provision for environmental protection in the work of the IMF, the World Bank, and other UN specialized agencies with respect to programmes in public health, development, agriculture, disarmament, and education

11. Communications

- The creation by scholars of a new global vision for communications and a definition of the role of communications in the future United Nations
- Evaluation of the performance of the United Nations in the world media by independent research institutions
- United Nations University project on the application of telecommunications technologies to education and training for economic development
- Better inter-institutional communication and information-sharing in the UN system, at least in training and research
- Definition by the International Telecommunication Union of priorities for the global information infrastructure, which includes all countries
- Intensification by the International Labour Organization of efforts to examine the social and employment impact of telecommunications
- A strengthening by the World Industrial Property Organization of efforts to monitor and report on piracy of intellectual property rights

12. Peace education

- Collaboration between UNESCO and NGOs in helping national ministries of education to provide teacher training for peace education
- NGOs versed in various approaches to peace education to teach UN staff how their work has contributed to the resolution of specific problems
- Education of UN staff so as to liberate them from competitive national visions
- A peace education fund, to which individuals and NGOs contribute

monthly, which would be used for peace education in areas of conflict or for education of UN staff
- Mechanisms for state accountability, such as: calling attention to national legislation that contradicts the spirit and principles of the Charter, and making known those states that have not ratified conventions and treaties or have not adhered to those they have ratified

Contributors

Chadwick F. Alger
Secretary-General, International Peace Research Association, 1983–1987; Mershon Professor of Political Science and Public Policy Emeritus, The Ohio State University; President, International Studies Association, 1978–1979; co-editor (with Gene Lyons and John Trent) of *The United Nations and the Policies of Member States*. Has published widely on the UN system, transnational people's movements, and the world relations of people in local communities.

Clair Apodaca
Visiting Assistant Professor of Political Science at the University of Memphis, Tennessee. She has published her work in the *Journal of Refugee Studies* and *Human Rights Quarterly*. Her research interests include human rights, the rights of women, and the status of refugees.

Elise Boulding
One of the founders of IPRA in the early 1960s, with her husband, Kenneth Boulding. IPRA Newsletter editor in the 1960s and again in the early 1980s, and Secretary-General from 1988 to 1991. Norwegian-born and US-reared, has published extensively on women, peace learning, the international civic order (NGOs), and the future.

Hans Gunter Brauch
Founder and first chair of IPRA Study Group on Weapons Technology and Disarmament (1986–1991), member of IPRA Council (1992–1996). Guest professor for international politics and regional studies, Ernst-Moritz-Arndt University, Greifswald, Germany. Chair of Peace Research and European Security Studies (AFES-Press). Has authored, co-authored, and edited more than 25 books in English and German on weapons technology, disarmament, climate, and energy policy.

Anthony Ayok Chol
Chair of IPRA Commission on Refugees, Member of IPRA Council,

430

African Refugees and Immigration Services (ARIS), Toronto.

Ho-Won Jeong
Former Chair of IPRA Commission on Global Political Economy. Editor of *International Journal of Peace Studies*. Institute for Conflict Analysis, George Mason University, Fairfax, Virginia. Born in Korea. Current research focuses on peace and economic development issues. Has published articles on economic development, international organizations, and political economy.

Robert C. Johansen
Director of Graduate Studies at the Joan B. Kroc Institute for International Peace Studies and Professor of Government at the University of Notre Dame. Author of *The National Interest and the Human Interest: An Analysis of U.S. Foreign Policy* and co-editor of *The Constitutional Foundations of World Peace*. Directs a project on enhancing UN peace-keeping and enforcement supported by the US Institute of Peace.

George Lopez
Faculty Fellow, Joan B. Kroc Institute for International Peace Studies, and Professor of Government and International Studies, University of Notre Dame. Research interests focus on the problems of state violence and coercion, especially economic sanctions, and gross violations of human rights. Has served in an advisory capacity to numerous foundations and organizations involved in human rights, international affairs education, and peace research.

Czeslaw Mesjasz
Convenor of IPRA Security and Disarmament Commission, 1992–1996. Adjunct Professor in Economics, Cracow University of Economics. Major research areas: systems analysis, quantitative decision theory, conflict resolution and negotiations, application of systems

analysis in peace and security studies, and military economics. Recipient of a NATO Democratic Institutions Fellowship in 1991 for his project "Economic Negotiations: A Survey of Methods and Procedures."

Lucia Ann McSpadden
Research Director, Life and Peace Institute, Uppsala, Sweden, an international, ecumenical peace research institute. Dr. McSpadden, a cultural anthropologist and fellow of the American Anthropology Association, has recently published a book on conflicts between UNHCR and the Eritrean government over the repatriation of Eritrean refugees. She has researched and published on a number of refugee issues, including resettlement, gender, repatriation, and human rights.

Patricia M. Mische
Co-founder of Global Education Associates, a network of men and women in 90 countries who collaborate on research, publishing, and educational programmes on global issues. Has taught courses on environment and peace and on the United Nations at Columbia and Fordham universities, and has written extensively on peace and environmental issues. As a MacArthur grant recipient, she did research on environmental conflict and cooperation in the East Asia Region.

Björn Möller
Secretary-General of IPRA; Senior Research Fellow at the Copenhagen Peace Research Institute; editor of the international research newsletter *NOD and Conversion*; founder and director of the global Non-Offensive Defence Network; a member of the UNIDIR Expert Group on Confidence-Building in the Middle East; part-time lecturer at the University of Copenhagen. Author of books on non-offensive defence and

alternative defence, including *Dictionary of Alternative Defence* (1995).

Jan Oberg
Born in Denmark; co-founder and director of the Transnational Foundation for Peace and Future Research, TFF, Lund, Sweden; served as Secretary-General of the Danish Peace Foundation; member of the Danish government's Commission on Security and Disarmament Affairs, 1981–1992; chief of the TFF Conflict-Mitigation team in former Yugoslavia (since 1991) and in Georgia (since 1994). Awarded the Buddhist Soka University Award of Highest Honor in 1992.

Sanàa W. Osseiran
Former IPRA Vice President and IPRA representative to UNESCO. A Lebanese national. Has studied in Beirut (B.A.) and London (M.A.) and at the Sorbonne University (DEA). Directed two IPRA projects in collaboration with UNESCO: Peacebuilding and Conflict Resolution in the Lebanon and Cultural Symbiosis in al-Andalus. She has developed a handbook for teacher training in public schools, and published five books, at different educational levels, linking culture to peace.

Hilkka Pietilä
A long-time member of IPRA and its Women and Peace Commission. Secretary-General of the Finnish UN Association, 1963–1990. In charge of the INSTRAW Focal Point in Finland since 1960. Honorary President of the World Federation of UN Associations. Participated in the UN World Conferences on Women in Mexico City 1975, Copenhagen 1980, Nairobi 1985, and Beijing 1995. Co-author with Jeanne Vickers of *Making Women Matter: The Role of the United Nations*.

Betty A. Reardon
Former member of IPRA Council, and a member of IPRA's Peace Education Commission since its founding. IPRA representative to the United Nations in New York City. Teaches graduate courses at Teachers College, Columbia University. Has published widely on peace education.

Mauricio Andres Ribeiro
Co-chair of the IPRA Commission on Ecological Security, and member of IPRA Council. President of the State Foundation for Environment in Minas Gerais State, Brazil. Former Vice President of the City of Peace Foundation, Brasilia. Author of books (*Uma Cidade se Forma* and *Migracoes de um arquiteto*) and many articles in Brazilian newspapers and journals on world federalism, peace and environment, and culture and environment.

Kumar Rupesinghe
Secretary-General of International Alert, London. Formerly chairperson and now on the advisory council of the Human Rights Information and Documentation Systems; adviser to the Programme on Governance and Conflict Resolution at the United Nations University, Tokyo; member of the International Negotiation Network in Atlanta. Has published and edited many articles and books in the field of conflict resolution.

Michael Stohl
Former chair of IPRA Commission on International Human Rights. Dean of International Programs and Professor of Political Science, Purdue University. His research publications have focused on the state's use of violence against its own and other citizens, and the development of effective means by which to monitor, measure, and confront human rights abuses.

Tapio Varis
Former chair of IPRA Commission on Communications and former member of IPRA Council. Professor and Chair of Media Culture and Communication Education at the University of Tampere, Finland. Former Rector of the University for Peace in Costa Rica, Director of Tampere Peace Research Institute in Finland, and Professor of Media Studies and Communication at the University of Lapland.

Raimo Väyrynen
Former Secretary-General of IPRA. Professor of Government and the Regan Director, Joan B. Kroc Institute for International Peace Studies, University of Notre Dame. Citizen of Finland. He has special research interests in international security and cooperation, conflict theory, and humanitarian issues. He has written and edited 16 books, and has published in numerous scholarly journals in more than eight languages.

Jeanne Vickers
Born in the United Kingdom, she has been associated with UN work for refugees and children since 1946. With UNICEF from 1973 to 1984, setting up its development education programme in collaboration with NGOs, educators, government aid agencies, and other UN agencies. Established a UN/NGO programme group on women and development in 1980. In 1984 initiated the Women and World Development series by Zed Books, London, with *Women and the World Economic Crisis*. Author of *Women and War* and co-author with Hilkka Pietilä of *Making Women Matter*.

Index